Contributors

Robert D. Arbuckle, History, New Kensington; Robert C. Baldwin, Forest Resources; Michael Barton, Social Science, Capitol; Samuel P. Bayard, English and Folklore; George H. Beatty, Entomology; Robert S. Beese, Agriculture; Helen E. Bell, Home Management; Barry L. Borland, Behavioral Science, Hershey Medical Center; Dorothy L. Bordner, Mathematics; Leo Bressler, English; Ira V. Brown, History; John D.C. Buck, English; Robert L. Butler, Biology; Rae D. Chambers, Agriculture; Allen Cohen, Library; Donald M. Crider, Rural Sociology; Harold E. Dickson, Art History; Mark H. Dorfman, American Studies, Capitol; Charles Douts, Jr., Student; John Paul Driscoll, Museum of Art; Robert B. Eckhardt, Anthropology; Irwin Feller, Economics; Ronald Filippelli, Library; Roland Fleischer, Art History; Carole Franklin, Library, Music; John B. Frantz, History; George W. Franz, History, Delaware County; Stuart H. Frost, Art; Robert J. Graham, American Studies, Capitol; Cyril E. Griffith, History and Black Studies; Dale B. Harris, Psychology; John M. Harrison, Journalism and American Studies; Luther H. Harshbarger, Religious Studies; James W. Hatch, Anthropology; Heinz K. Henisch, Physics; William Hull, Museum of Art; Harry K. Hutton, Education; J. Thomas Jable, Physical Education, McKeesport; Philip S. Klein, History; Lawrence A. Krezo, Publications; Peirce F. Lewis, Geography; Robert Lima, Spanish and Comparative Literature; Walton J. Lord, Art History; William J. Mahar, Music, Capitol; Charles W. Mann, Library, Rare Books; Willard Martin, German; Hugo A. Meier, History; Harrison T. Meserole, English; E. Willard Miller, Geography and Mineral Science; Yvonne Milspaw, American Studies and Folklore, Capitol; Lemuel Molovinsky, American Studies and History, Capitol; Charles J. Nolan, Jr., English; Michael A. Ondik, Wildlife Research; Michael Paquet, English, Mont Alto; John S. Patterson, American Studies and History, Capitol; John M. Pickering, Press; J. Lorell Price, History, Berks; Fred Prouser, Student, Capitol; Irwin Richman, American Studies and History, Capitol; M. Susan Richman, Mathematics, Capitol; Leonard R. Riforgiato, History, Shenango Valley; Cyril D. Robinson, Law; Bruce A. Rosenberg, English and Folklore; Glenn Ruby, Press; John E. Searles, Education; Marie Secor, English; Robert Secor, English; David Shetlar, Entomology; Eugene R. Slaski, History, Allentown; Philip E. Stebbins, History; Jacob L. Susskind, Social Science and Education, Capitol; Kenneth A. Thigpen, English; Nancy M. Tischler, English, Capitol; Daniel Walden, American Studies; Rodelle Weintraub, English; Peter White, English; Ruth Ann Wilson, Clothing; George D. Wolf, American Studies and History, Capitol; Philip Young, English; Wilbur Zelinsky, Geography

Pennsylvania 1776

Robert Secor *General Editor*

John M. Pickering *Associate Editor*

Irwin Richman *Picture Editor*

Glenn Ruby *Designer*

Editorial Board

Irwin Feller, John B. Frantz,
Philip S. Klein, Hugo A. Meier,
Irwin Richman, Bruce A. Rosenberg

The Pennsylvania State University Press

University Park and London

Second Printing, 1976

Contents

The Land and the People

How They Lived

Politics and War

Preface

Pennsylvania 1776 has been an all-university book from the beginning. The idea of an illustrated sampler of life in William Penn's "Peaceable Kingdom," focusing on events surrounding the Declaration of Independence, was first advanced in 1972 by Stanley Weintraub, Director of the Institute for the Arts and Humanistic Studies and Research Professor of English. Chris W. Kentera, Director of The Pennsylvania State University Press, consulted the Press Committee and other faculty members to develop the book's present plan: a broad and deep reconstruction of life in the Keystone State at the time of the American Revolution, showing how the people of Pennsylvania reflected the colonial experience in general and also how they were unique.

Recognizing that special funding would be needed for such an ambitious book, in order to keep the price within reach of a wide audience, Mr. Kentera presented the project to his fellow members of the University's Bicentennial Commission appointed by President John W. Oswald. The Commission quickly granted *Pennsylvania 1776* its full support including a substantial subsidy. The book thus became an activity sanctioned by the national American Revolution Bicentennial Commission and by the Bicentennial Commission of Pennsylvania.

The Director of the Press, in consultation with the Press Committee, designated Robert A. Secor of the University's American Studies program as general editor, in association with John M. Pickering of the Press. Together they selected an editorial board of six specialists in Pennsylvania history and culture, naming Irwin Richman of the Capitol Campus American Studies program as picture editor. After issuing a call for volunteers, the editorial group recruited eighty-one faculty members from thirty-seven of the University's departments to write or illustrate portions of the book. Fitting the parts into a well-joined whole has been the pleasant task of the editorial group, assisted by Glenn A. Ruby, Carole Schwager, Janet L. Dietz, and Robert F. Paradine of the Press.

Pennsylvania 1776 contains five main parts and twenty subsections, together with a prologue and an epilogue on Pennsylvanians before and after the Revolution. The book is written to be read either straight through or in parts according to a reader's interests. Throughout the book are sixty-eight vignettes of significant persons, groups, places, things, and processes. Closely coordinated with vignettes and text are 512 pictures (forty-two in color)—mostly from colonial or Revolutionary sources—as well as ten maps and diagrams. Following the text is a chart showing the Development of Pennsylvania Counties from colonial times to the present. The Suggestions for Further Reading were prepared by Allen Cohen, associate librarian of the University, and his more complete bibliographical essay on the subject is available from the Office of the Dean, Pattee Library, University Park 16802.

Although the chief authors of portions of the book are identified on the table of contents, the editors have been unable to indicate the source of every textual and pictorial idea. Contributors from the Penn State faculty and staff are listed alphabetically opposite the title page. A project of this size could succeed only with the cooperation of the University's entire administration, staff, and faculty. Notable support has been given by Richard G. Cunningham, Vice President for Research and Graduate Studies; by Stanley F. Paulson, Dean, and Arthur O. Lewis, Associate Dean, of the College of the Liberal Arts; by the American Studies programs at the University Park and Capitol (Middletown) Campuses; and by the members of the Bicentennial Commission and Press Committee, whose names are listed on the copyright page.

Special thanks are due to many persons outside the University for help in locating information and illustrations. Invaluable assistance has been given by the staff of the Pennsylvania Historical and Museum Commission, especially at the William Penn Memorial Museum and Archives in Harrisburg, the Pennsylvania Farm Museum at Landis Valley, and the Ephrata Cloister. The Bicentennial Committee of Chester County has shared its resources with the editors, as have the Historical Societies of Berks, Bucks, Chester, Lancaster, and York Counties. Philadelphia's historical treasures have been made available by its Library Company, Free Library, and Museum of Art; by the Historical Society of Pennsylvania, American Philosophical Society, Pennsylvania Academy of Fine Arts, Pennsylvania Hospital, and Insurance Company of North America; and by our fellow educators of Drexel University, Haverford College, the University of Pennsylvania, Villanova University, and William Penn Charter School. Other Pennsylvania sources of help have been the Western Pennsylvania Conservancy, the Fort Pitt Museum, the Moravian Museum of Bethlehem, the Hans Herr House Association, and State College's The Tavern and *Centre Daily Times*. On the national level, full support has been extended by the Library of Congress, National Gallery of Art, National Park Service, and Smithsonian Institution. Good neighborly cooperation has come from Delaware's Henry Francis du Pont Winterthur Museum; New York's Historical Society and Metropolitan Museum of Art; Virginia's Abby Aldrich Rockefeller Folk Art Collection, Colonial Williamsburg Foundation, and Institute of Early American History and Culture; Harvard and Yale Universities; the Chicago Historical Society; and the St. Louis Art Museum.

The editors are grateful to all the individuals and institutions listed in the Sources of Illustrations at the back of the book. Among the many off-campus friends who gave guidance in the search for pictures were Eric de Jonge, George H. Ebner, Carroll J. Hopf, John L. Kraft, James E. Mooney, Stefanie A. Munsing, Harry L. Rinker, and Harry E. Whipkey.

Prologue

When Paul Revere came riding into Philadelphia in the spring of 1774, he entered a city very different from his native Boston, indeed almost another world. Not only was Philadelphia larger and more cosmopolitan than Boston, but Pennsylvania was still "the peaceable kingdom" compared with Massachusetts. Despite growing opposition to British policy among some merchants and farmers, most Pennsylvanians remained skeptical about cutting ties with London not merely in 1774 but right down to the adoption of the Declaration of Independence. No shots were exchanged between colonists and redcoats in "Penn's Woods" until late 1776, seven years after the "Boston Massacre." When Bostonians staged their famous "Tea Party" in 1773, Philadelphians held a mass rally and turned back a tea ship by means of resolutions. Even after the Minute Men at Lexington and Concord "fired the shots heard 'round the world," in April of 1775, Pennsylvanians—while organizing fifty-seven militia battalions just in case of need—still elected to their Assembly a Moderate majority who rejected "Separation from our Mother Country."

Although Pennsylvania colonists felt the same indulgence toward King and Parliament that most foster children feel toward their parents, Massachusetts colonists—the original New Englanders—experienced the passions that burn hottest among blood relatives. Almost all New Englanders were of English ancestry, were in fact descended from those very Puritans who had ruled England a century earlier, under the Commonwealth. Having failed to "purify" England, they sought to create a *New* England and were enraged by corrupt stay-at-home cousins who seemed intent on thwarting their efforts. (Fellow colonists who actually remained loyal to the homeland were beneath contempt.) Pennsylvania, by contrast, grew out of William Penn's "Holy Experiment"—an effort to create a "nation of nations" based on the active tolerance of the Society of Friends (the Quakers). Thus about a half of colonial Pennsylvania's population was non-English—chiefly German or Scotch-Irish but with scatterings of many other nationalities—and a large portion of the English were guided more by Quaker "inner light" than by

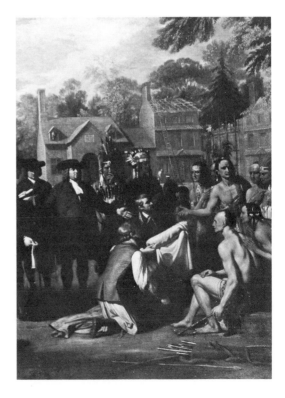

traditional "rights of Englishmen." For the non-English, British rule at its worst was less oppressive than what they had known before; for the Friends, it was not galling enough to overcome their pacifistic persuasions.

Pennsylvania's already legendary prosperity helped to muffle discontent. "Fat Pennsylvania" held a wide patch of rich farmland immediately adjacent to the sheltered port of Philadelphia, together with large and accessible supplies of water, timber, game, iron, fireclay, and building stone. The New Englander—unless he was a merchant, lawyer, or preacher—was forced to choose between hardscrabble farming in rockstrewn fields and dangerous fishing off rockribbed coasts. No wonder all visitors saw Pennsylvania as a cornucopia with Philadelphia at its mouth.

Yet, even in Pennsylvania, as 1776 approached, many colonists were feeling an economic pinch. Ever since the French and Indian War (1752–1763) prices seemed to keep rising—in spite of frequent depressions—wiping out hard-won wage increases among the growing class of urban artisans. Many small tradesmen were bankrupted by alternating periods of tight money and inflation; some even landed in debtors' prisons, although insolvency laws were gradually liberalized. On the Appalachian slopes of the frontier, farmers found the going rougher than in the fertile limestone valleys of the eastern counties. Radical political factions, while still in the minority, gained converts among such discontented classes. Among every class, moreover, there was an increasing tendency to blame all economic ills on British mercantilism: the doctrine that colonies exist for the benefit of the mother country. By the summer of 1776, therefore, a fair number of Pennsylvanians welcomed the separatist firebrands from Massachusetts and Virginia.

Nevertheless, before the shots fired at Lexington and Concord were heard west of Philadelphia, most Pennsylvanians had other things on their minds. For the most part they were farmers, many of them Germans unfamiliar with the English language and unaware of the issues involved in the revolutionary movement in its early stages. On the farm, joys were simple and problems—drought, frost, caterpillars—more immediate than political grievances against England. While Sam Adams was agitating his fellow Bostonians to recognize the usurpation of their rights by Parliament, St. John de Crèvecoeur was expressing the thoughts of the Pennsylvania farmer:

> Often when I plough my low ground, I place my little boy on a chair which screws to the beam of the plough—its motion and that of the horses please him [and] he is perfectly happy and begins to chat. As I lean over the handle, various are the thoughts which crowd into my mind. I am doing for him, I say, what my father did for me, may God enable him to live that he may perform the same operations for the same purposes when I am worn out and old!

Crèvecoeur

When the Revolution reached the farm, Crèvecoeur was confused and troubled: "If I attach myself to the Mother Country, which is 3000 miles from me, I become what is called an enemy to my own region; if I follow the rest of my countrymen, I become opposed to our ancient masters." Crèvecoeur could see no solution to his dilemma: "What can an insignificant man do in the midst of these jarring and contradictory parties . . . ? And after all who will be the really guilty? Those most certainly who fail of success."

The men and women we associate with the political and military role of Pennsylvania during the Revolution were of course more aware of events as they unfolded than the farmers removed from the metropolis of Philadelphia. These budding leaders too, however, had other concerns and ambitions in the years before the war, and they above all would find their lives most seriously disrupted and altered by the events of 1776. Some were prosperous merchants, like Thomas Mifflin and Charles Thomson. The fruits of the peaceable kingdom seemed Mifflin's to enjoy in his luxuriously furnished home at the falls of the Schuylkill, but his talents as a speaker drew him into politics. There he became one of the youngest and—on the issue of independence—most radical members of the First Continental Congress, while his talents as a soldier made him a general and earned him a reputation for personal courage. John Adams thought Mifflin the "animating soul" of the American Revolution.

Mifflin

Before entering the mercantile trade Thomson was a Master of Latin School in what became the William Penn Charter School. He did not know then that his political activity in the years of the Revolution would cause the conservative Joseph Galloway to call him "one of the most violent of the Sons of Liberty (so-called) in America." Prevented by Galloway from being chosen delegate to the Continental Congress, Thomson nevertheless served for fifteen years as its secretary. From his seat, it has been said, "the great drama of the American Revolution as enacted on the stage of the Continental Congress he beheld from beginning to its consummation as did no other man."

A third leader of the Radical party was Timothy Matlack. (When Benedict Arnold ordered Matlack's son to serve as his valet, the Radicals were so incensed they sought Arnold's court-martial and drew up charges against him for misusing public funds. Arnold was convicted and let off with a reprimand, the incident contributing to Arnold's later treason.) In the years before the Revolution, however, Matlack seems to have had more trouble with his business and the Society of Friends than with Parliament. In 1765, at the time of the Stamp Act crisis, Matlack was disowned by the Quakers for "frequenting company in such manner as to neglect business whereby he contracted debts, failed and was unable to satisfy the claims of his creditors." Before the news from Lexington in 1775, Matlack had no experience in public affairs.

Matlack

Paine

Peter Muhlenberg

Dickinson

There were others, like Tom Paine and Peter Muhlenberg, who in the years before the Revolution did not seem destined to be remembered for their roles as patriots. Not long before the Revolution, Paine was an Englishman with a not very promising future. The son of a corsetmaker (a trade to which he had been apprenticed), Paine had by 1774 gone through two brief, unsuccessful marriages, various towns, and several abortive careers, including schoolmaster, teacher, tobacconist, and tax collector. On Franklin's recommendation, however, he came to Philadelphia in 1774, became editor of the *Pennsylvania Magazine*, and with the publication of *Common Sense* in 1776 became known as the leading spokesman for the Revolution.

Peter Muhlenberg, on the other hand, seemed to have found himself by 1772, when after a rocky Pennsylvania adolescence he had settled in Woodstock, Virginia, as a minister in a German parish. When the drums of war began to beat, however, he startled his congregation by throwing off his robes to reveal his martial uniform—according to legend, announcing that "there is a time to pray and a time to fight." Several hundred of the congregation are said to have enlisted that day, and General Muhlenberg is now known as the "Fighting Parson."

If Muhlenberg had to change his profession to contribute to the Patriot cause, others brought their talents with them. Benjamin Rush, considered the "most influential American medical scientist of his day," became a member of the Continental Congress, signed the Declaration of Independence, and served during the war as a surgeon-general in the Continental Army. Robert Morris, banker and leading importer of colonial Philadelphia, became the Superintendent of Finance for the Continental Congress, using his abilities and resources to supply money and munitions to the Revolutionary cause. John Dickinson was an eminent Philadelphia lawyer, whose carefully reasoned *Letters from a Farmer in Pennsylvania* (1767–1768) were so pursuasive he became known as the "Penman of the Revolution," even though he had argued for conciliation as a member of both Continental Congresses and had refused to sign the Declaration of Independence.

The major figures of the time did not all come from Philadelphia, however. Robert Whitehill, for example, was born in the Pequea settlement of Lancaster County, while Anthony Wayne was a prosperous farmer and tanner in Chester County. Whitehill in the pre-Revolutionary period was a spokesman for the democratic instincts of frontier Pennsylvania. In the hope that separation from London would lessen the influence of the eastern counties in provincial politics, Whitehill was an outspoken advocate for independence as early as the spring of 1776. Wayne, who had taken over the profitable tannery of his father when the latter died in 1774, gave up the comforts of his 560-acre estate to share a winter with Washington at

Valley Forge. "Mad Anthony," as he came to be known, was made brigadier general in 1777.

The fortunes of other leading Pennsylvanians, like Joseph Galloway and Justice William Allen, declined as the movement toward revolution progressed. Galloway was a leading Philadelphia lawyer, vice-president of the American Philosophical Society (1769–1774), Speaker of the Pennsylvania Assembly, and member of the 1774 Continental Congress. When his compromise Plan of Union was first accepted, then defeated by one vote, Galloway castigated the Congress, withdrew to his country home, and in 1778 emigrated to England. The story of William Allen, Chief Justice from 1750 to 1774, is similar. For several decades before the Revolution, Justice Allen was probably the most influential figure in Pennsylvania politics, but he wanted no part of rebellion, and like Galloway when his own plan for reconciliation failed, he ended his fifty years of active service to Pennsylvania, resigning his judicial position, and left for England.

Franklin

By the 1770s the most famous Pennsylvanian of them all had already played his role as Philadelphia's leading citizen. Long ago he saw to it that the streets were paved and cleaned and lit. He had been a young man when he helped establish a fire company and police department, a circulating library, and the American Philosophical Society. It was twenty years since Ben Franklin had experimented with electricity, and even longer since he had written his *Account of the New Innovative Pennsylvania Fireplace*. His famous *Almanack* had published its last issue in 1758, and it was half a century since he had been apprenticed to his brother James and had begun his career in printing. Now—in fact since 1757—he was in England representing the colonies. It was a good time for Franklin. He had become an intimate of the leading English thinkers, Hume and Burke and Chatham and Adam Smith. Three British universities had awarded him degrees, and he was continuing to pursue his scientific studies, issuing a pamphlet which would anticipate the population theories of Malthus. The events of 1776, however, were to focus Franklin's energies. From his forum in England, and before the House of Commons, he protested the punitive acts of the Tory ministry. When he returned to Philadelphia (before going to France) he played such a vital part in the political events of the Revolution, we are likely to forget that when he signed the Declaration of Independence he was seventy years old.

There were many other Pennsylvanians of 1776 who we remember for their roles in the political and military events of that time. Their nationalities and religions differed—they could be Scotch-Irish like James Wilson or Swedish like John Morton or Jewish like Haym Salomon. They could be women, like Molly Pitcher and Lydia Darragh, as well as men. But behind them stand the many nameless farmers and tanners, merchants and ministers, lawyers and

Molly Pitcher

Piedmont

Allegheny Front

Appalachian Plateau

Ridge-and-Valley

The variety of Pennsylvania's natural landscapes

Simply to survive, a tiny colony on the margin of a hostile continent had to secure certain environmental advantages. To begin with, it needed dependable connections with its mother country and other potential trading partners, both in North America and elsewhere. Clearly it was important that ocean-going ships could approach the coast safely, and could load and unload easily. That meant a sheltered anchorage, adjacent to well-drained land, with an open passage to the sea, free of hidden rocks and sandbars. Then the settlers needed decent farmland once they had landed: reasonably level terrain with adequate drainage and soil which was not only initially fertile but would stay so under cultivation. Finally, if the colony were to thrive, it had to be capable of territorial expansion: adjacent to large chunks of potentially productive farmland, with no great barren areas or topographic obstacles to bar the way inland.

None of these requirements was hard to fulfill if taken individually. There were plenty of good anchorages along the North American coast, for example, and reasonably good soil was not hard to find. But it was not so easy to find these advantages combined in a single place, and it was Penn's good luck that the west bank of the upper Delaware—from about Wilmington to the neighborhood of Trenton, New Jersey—met most of these colonial needs and met them well. By contrast, most of the rest of the North American coast fell grossly short of meeting them, and, given the technology of the times, the geographic deficiencies were almost impossible to correct, except at a cost which nobody was willing or able to pay. To the north, from New York City on into New England and the Canadian Maritimes, the mainland consisted of an ancient platform of crystalline rocks, from which recent glaciation had scrubbed most of the productive soils and then had strewn the surface with gravel, sand, and boulders as the ice withdrew. Thus, while New Englanders had no trouble finding safe and sheltered anchorages, agriculture was a backbreaking, unrewarding way to make a living. It is not surprising that hordes of impoverished New England farmers fled westward for the Genesee Country of upstate New York as soon as the Indians had been driven from those lands during and after the Revolution. Southward from Pennsylvania, from Chesapeake Bay to the Savannah River and beyond, inland soils were reasonably good—although these proved later to have little staying power, degenerating rapidly as cotton and tobacco were planted repeatedly over the years.

The main trouble in the South, however, especially in the early days, was in getting ashore. From Long Island south through New Jersey, Delaware, Maryland, the Virginia capes, and on into the Carolinas, a wide sandy coastal plain confronted the ocean with wave-pounded beaches, shoals, and sandbars—pleasant enough for twentieth-century bathing, but the traditional graveyards of uncounted colonial sailing ships. (Cape Hatteras developed the most

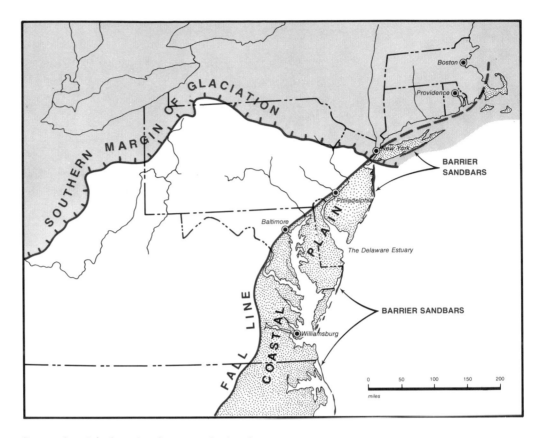

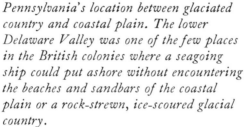

Pennsylvania's location between glaciated country and coastal plain. The lower Delaware Valley was one of the few places in the British colonies where a seagoing ship could put ashore without encountering the beaches and sandbars of the coastal plain or a rock-strewn, ice-scoured glacial country.

infamous reputation, but it was merely the worst part of a bad coast.) Nor was the immediate inland much more hospitable. Behind the barrier beaches, shallow water alternated with brackish, indecisive river channels and malarial swamps; and in those rare places where solid landing could be found, coastal soils were often so sandy and sterile that they defied the best efforts of newly landed farmers.

In contrast with these horrors, Penn's new colony was sheer delight. Here, well south of the boundary of glaciation, the broad estuary of the Delaware permitted ships to sail completely *through* the coastal plain, and, at the sheltered anchorage of Philadelphia, to land almost directly on the unglaciated Piedmont, a well-drained rolling plain of uncommon fertility. Furthermore, the Piedmont extended inland for nearly a hundred miles before a traveler encountered the Appalachians; even there, the mountains were unusual, offering several wide-open avenues to the west, avenues which were denied to New Englanders and Southerners alike.

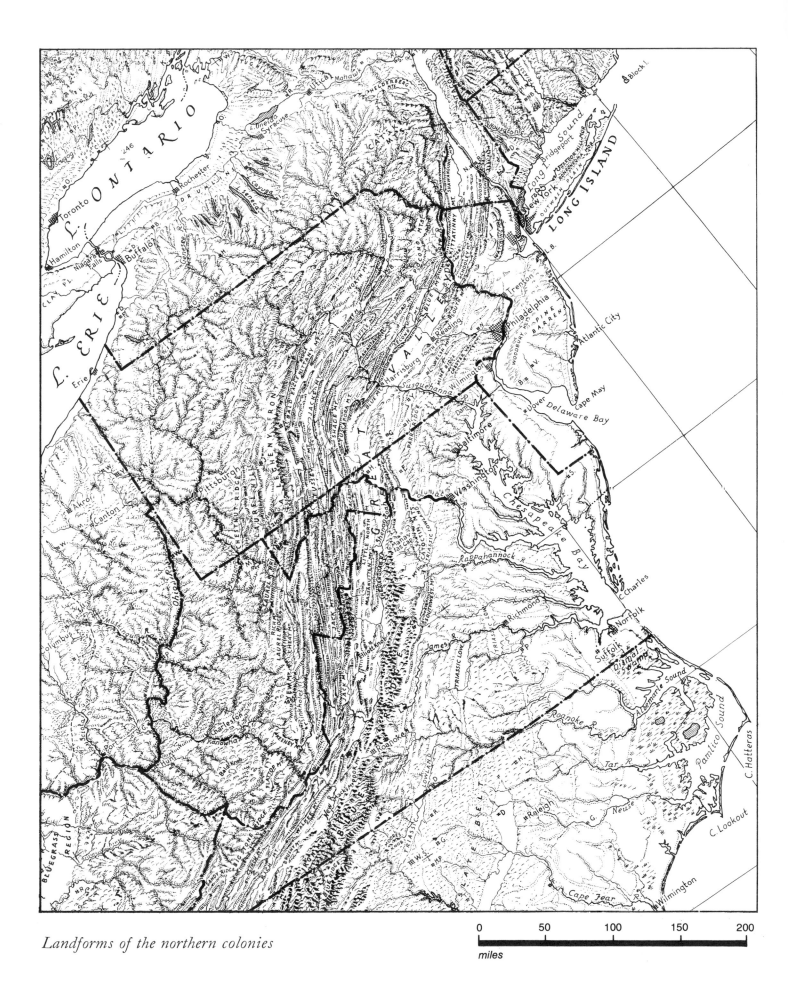

Landforms of the northern colonies

The Appalachian Mountains and the Geology of Pennsylvania

To the pre-Revolutionary settlers of Pennsylvania, the Piedmont was seen simply as a large productive patch of land between Delaware Bay and the first ridges of the Appalachians. To the geographers and geologists who came later to study Pennsylvania's remarkable landscape, the Piedmont is best understood as part of the Appalachians themselves; in fact, it is the geologic core of the Appalachians, as it was the geographic core of early settlement in the state. Indeed, nearly all of Pennsylvania (except a bit of coastal plain along the Delaware River, and an equally small bit of lake plain at Erie) can be viewed as the eroded remnants of the Appalachian chain itself, a mountain system that was once perhaps as formidable as the Alps but now remains only as a skeleton of its former self. This idea is vital to the understanding of Pennsylvania's present physical environment—first, because the state sprawls across nearly the full width of the ancient Appalachian system and thus contains samples of all its internal variety; second, because different kinds of rocks determine that landforms and soils also will be different from place to place. Thus, to understand the layout of bedrock geology is to understand the gross patterns of physical geography, a geography which has shaped the forms of human settlement in Pennsylvania from the day that Penn first set foot on the shores of the Delaware.

Like most large mountain systems, the Appalachians are formed in a highly regular fashion: a long and narrow chain with internal divisions stretched out in belts parallel to the main axis of the range. As we travel parallel to that axis, we encounter similar landforms and soils for huge distances, all the way from New England to Alabama. In contrast, as we cross the range transversely, we encounter belt after belt, with systematic changes in landscape occurring one after another in rapid succession. It was thus with the early Pennsylvanians, who moved west from Philadephia to lay out a commonwealth that would cut squarely across the grain of the Appalachians and thereby sample the whole gamut of Appalachian landforms. Indeed, of the thirteen original colonies only Virginia comes close to matching Pennsylvania in topographic variety.

In gross outline, the state cuts across three major geologic belts, and each belt produces its own topography and soil composition. If we travel inland, crossing those geologic-topographic belts in the same order that Pennsylvanians settled them, we find that the rocks grow progressively less complex.

To understand the layout of these belts, it is helpful to remember that the entire Appalachian chain originated some 600 million years ago as a trough which gradually sank below the sea while simultaneously collecting immensely thick accumulations of sedimentary materials, eventually compressed into sedimentary rocks. Gradually

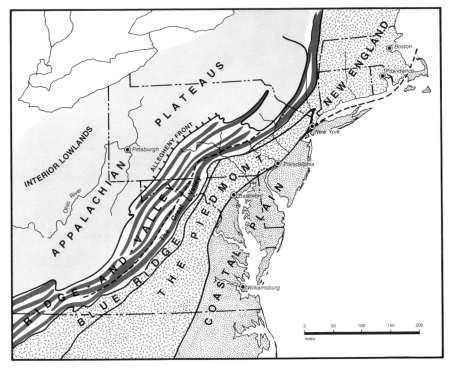

Key

Bedrock Geology

 Weak young Coastal Plain rocks, nearly flat-lying. Often sandy.

 Crystalline igneous and metamorphic rocks along the main axis of the ancient Appalachians.*

 Sedimentary rocks, of varying resistance, crumpled and folded along the western flanks of the ancient Appalachians.

Nearly flat-lying sedimentary rocks, slightly warped, but otherwise untouched by Appalachian mountain-building.

*Includes small but important sections of sedimentary rock, interbedded with igneous rock.

Landform Regions
Note that boundaries (heavy black lines) conform almost exactly to geologic boundaries.

COASTAL PLAIN: Very low relief, often poorly-drained, soils often sandy and quite infertile; glaciated from New York City northeastward.

PIEDMONT: Rolling, well-drained surface, soils range usually between good and excellent.

BLUE RIDGE: Low but rugged mountains; steep slopes; rocky, infertile soils.

RIDGE-AND-VALLEY REGION: Extremely long, linear ridges, aligned with linear valleys. Ridges commonly about 1,000 feet from foot to crest, rocky and infertile. Valley soils range from poor to excellent.

APPALACHIAN PLATEAU: Table-land, deeply dissected by streams, especially along eastern margin. Soils variable, but often sandy and infertile. Slopes often steep. Western margins grade imperceptibly into Interior Lowlands.

this trough was uplifted and further compressed. Along the main axis of compression, near the center, sedimentary rocks were deformed into metamorphic rocks—slates, marbles, and quartzites—and the entire contorted mass was injected with igneous rocks: basaltic lavas near the surface, granite and similar rocks deeper down. This ancient contorted core of the Appalachians was repeatedly eroded and now forms the two easternmost regions of the mountain chain, the Piedmont and the Blue Ridge. The Piedmont is largely underlain by easily eroded metamorphic rocks, so much so that the mountains are now almost entirely gone, yielding to the gentle rolling plain inland from Philadelphia that the early Pennsylvanians found so hospitable and travelers came to call "fat Pennsylvania." Occasionally, more resistant rocks produce low ridges, mainly left to forests, and occasionally these complex rocks contain metallic minerals, mainly iron, which formed the basis of Pennsylvania's early iron industries. But the most important resources of these complicated Piedmont rocks were its soils, seldom really bad, often very good, and in a broad belt of marbleized limestone around Lancaster, truly superb. These were certainly the best soils in the original colonies, and are still among the most productive in the entire United States.

The inland margin of the metamorphic belt contains much more resistant rocks, slower to erode and poor in the soluble minerals that make for fertile soils. Along most of the Appalachians, this marginal belt of resistant rocks produces the Blue Ridge, the highest and most formidable country in the eastern United States. Its lofty elevations and wretched soils made these mountains the most serious barrier to east-west transportation in colonial America. The Smokies of the Carolina-Tennessee borderland are part of this complex, as are the White Mountains of New Hampshire, the two highest elevations in the Appalachian chain.

If the Appalachians had been laid out that way in Pennsylvania, the early settlers would have run into a major mountain barrier just west of Lancaster, and the history of the eastern United States would surely have been different. But, again, Penn's geographic luck held. Here, one hundred miles inland from Penn's original landing place, faulting has reduced Pennsylvania's Blue Ridge to a pitiful remnant of its former grandeur: two stubby prongs of low wooded hills, one projecting from New Jersey to the vicinity of Reading, and the other from Maryland to around Carlisle. Between these two mountain remnants (geographers call them respectively the Reading Prong and the Carlisle Prong), the Blue Ridge is completely gone, and in its place lies a gap so wide that it was never given a name and most people are unaware of its existence, but through this gap colonial Pennsylvanians poured westward past the Blue Ridge in numbers matched in no other English colony in North America. Thus, by the time of the Revolution, geology had played an important part in making Pennsylvania one of England's most important colonies, with the Piedmont as a foundation for extraordinary agricultural wealth and the gap in the Blue Ridge as a funnel through which Pennsylvanian ideas spilled inland to dominate much of interior North America.

West of the Blue Ridge gap the Appalachians continue, but in distinctly different forms. As one travels inland, the metamorphosed crystalline rocks of the Piedmont and Blue Ridge give way to sedimentary rocks: limestones, shales, and sandstones, and occasionally coal. In an eighty-mile belt which slashes southwest-northeast across central Pennsylvania, the sedimentary rocks are tightly folded, reflecting their proximity to the main axis of Appalachian deformation. In this belt, which geographers call "the folded Appalachians," the rocks are crumpled, very much like a thick rug which has slid

The Pennsylvania Prairie

Although almost all of Pennsylvania's land was forested when the colonists arrived, there were also a few treeless areas which the first settlers called "glades," "drylands," "plains," or "prairies." Some authorities today are cautious about using the word "prairies" to describe these areas, but others are certain that they were indeed outliers of the midwestern tall grass prairie. Botanists now assume that many of them developed during the hot dry period following the Pleistocene glaciation. Undoubtedly the plains areas of Pennsylvania were maintained in this condition through fires started by the Indians, or by lightning, through grazing by deer, elk, and bison, and through specialized conditions of local climate.

*We now know that there were nine such grass communities. In the far eastern part of the colony several thousand acres of grassland sprawled in the area around Easton. Another such area at Clearfield was the site of the Indian village Chincleclamosse. South of Clearfield is an area of shallow soil with underlying stratigraphy containing an abundance of iron. Since this region did not support a forest, it was also known as a prairie. Near Allensville just east of Frankstown the "glades" were bare of timber and covered with shrubs, ground oaks, and hazels. This type of growth supported whatever bison grazed here throughout the eighteenth century. The Conococheague valley, near the present town of Chambersburg, was at that time luxuriant grass-*land. *To the northwest two other grassy areas developed on the outwash plain of the former glacier, around the present towns of Mercer and Meadville. These areas became known as blazing star prairies, since it was here that a wild flower, the blazing star, was found in great abundance. This plant, which covered the western prairies of Pennsylvania, was from two to five feet tall, and during August and September was topped with rose purple spikes between five and fifteen inches long. The blazing star grew in profusion amid the various species of tall prairie grass found elsewhere in the state, particularly the tall Indian grass and the big and little bluestem which the bison herds favored.*

All of these areas were recognized by the Pennsylvania settlers as prime farming lands and so were the first to be settled beyond the Piedmont. Captain James Potter came to Penns Valley in 1764 to take up ownership of a 3,000-acre tract called at that time the "Great Plain." Stationed at Fort Augusta (now Sunbury), he took a leave of absence in the summer of 1764 and went up the west branch of the Susquehanna to the mouth of Bald Eagle Creek near Lock Haven, then up Bald Eagle Creek to where Spring Creek empties into it at Milesburg. From the top of Nittany Mountain, Potter viewed the Great Plain, and, upon seeing the prairies and the noble forest beneath him, he cried out to his attendant: "By Heaven, Thompson, I've discovered an empire."

The "Jennings Blazing Star Prairie," a nature preserve near Butler, is Pennsylvania's last surviving prairie.

across a slippery floor. When these folded rocks are eroded, as they have been for over 200 million years, only the roots of the folds are exposed at the surface. The topographic results are remarkable—long linear ridges, rising like waves of an endless sea, separated by equally long linear valleys often very remote from the outside world. On a map of Appalachian landforms this country looks as if some cosmic rake had been dragged the length of the Appalachians. The most remarkable of these valleys lies immediately inland from the Blue Ridge. It is a zone of weak limestones and shales, a belt of lowland less than twenty miles wide but extending from northern New York to central Alabama. This valley has many names—the Great Valley; or in southern Pennsylvania, the Cumberland Valley; or in Virginia, the Shenandoah Valley. It was this valley that most of the settlers used after they poured west through the Blue Ridge gap, for the Great Valley leads almost uninterrupted through western Virginia toward Cumberland Gap and the headwaters of the Tennessee.

For a traveler heading west toward Fort Pitt and the Forks of the Ohio, however, it was quite another story. One wavelike ridge after another, each about one thousand feet from foot to summit, extended in what must have seemed an interminable array, a range which early frontiersmen quite naturally dubbed "The Endless Mountains."

This ridge-and-valley region only seemed endless, of course. At about the present line of U.S. Highway 220, between Williamsport and Hagerstown, Maryland, the geologic environment changes abruptly, as does the topography. At this distance from the main axis of the Appalachian geologic deformation, the sedimentary rocks are no longer folded but are warped into a broad elongated saucer. Over the entire region, rocks are nearly flat-lying, and rivers have eroded deeply into them, to form the dissected tableland which we know today as the Appalachian Plateau. The eastern edge of this saucer is a frowning escarpment some fifteen hundred feet high, called the Allegheny Front. The front was then (and has continued to be) the single most formidable barrier to east-west transportation in Pennsylvania, but beyond the front to the west, things were not much better. There, on the Appalachian Plateau, an intricate network of twisting streams has cut deeply into the high surface, carving it into the most forbidding mountain country in all of Pennsylvania. Indeed, when early Pennsylvanians spoke of the Appalachians, they were really talking about this much-eroded eastern fringe of the plateau, country so steep and desolate that nobody traveling west would find it worth settling. In extreme western Pennsylvania, where some of the original tableland remains uneroded, farms were laid out on the uplands, but even today much of Pennsylvania's Appalachian Plateau remains in forest, a country beloved of fishermen and hunters but generally bereft of agricultural promise. To a native of the fat Piedmont of southeastern Pennsylvania, this plateau country was best left to Indians and wild animals. Ironically, there lies below the surface of the plateau some of the continent's most valuable deposits of bituminous coal, not to mention oil and gas. But Pennsylvanians of 1776 could not know of this wealth, for the technology of the times simply offered no means of using these materials.

Rivers of Pennsylvania

It was a nasty shock for the Pennsylvanians to discover that the fertile Piedmont, so rich in agricultural promise, was crossed by streams that were uniformly shallow, rocky, and unnavigable. Indeed, the Delaware itself, actually an arm of the ocean, is the only navigable stream of consequence in southeastern Pennsylvania. Along the eastern margin of the Piedmont lies the so-called fall line, the place where rivers drop abruptly in rapids and waterfalls to reach tidewater. A line of towns grew up along the fall line, where waterpower provided energy for early industry, and the extension of Philadelphia itself upstream along the Schuylkill was a repetition of the same kind of urban growth that produced Wilmington, Baltimore, Georgetown, Fredericksburg, Richmond, Columbia, Augusta, and Macon—all fall line towns in exactly the same kind of location.

Inland, however, streams which flowed to the Atlantic—and that means the entire Delaware, Schuylkill, Lehigh, and Susquehanna systems—were navigable only at high water and by small boats, and even then at considerable risk. Thus, in the very heart of pre-Revolutionary Pennsylvania, where booming agriculture was demanding dependable transportation, there were only two choices if one wished to avoid complete isolation in a trackless interior: build roads or improve the rivers by building canals. Pennsylvanians did both with enthusiasm, at a time when most of the populated world was still roadless and the building of canals almost a black art. Looking backward, we can see this combination of rich land and unnavigable streams as a kind of blessing in disguise, for the circumstances forced early Pennsylvanians to learn the arts of road-building and canal-building many years before other American colonists had begun to think about them.

The rivers of western Pennsylvania differ from those of the east, just as eastern and western Pennsylvania differ in many other ways. The headwaters of the Ohio, the Allegheny, the Monongahela, the Conemaugh, the Beaver, and the Youghiogheny are admirably navigable for long distances, and nineteenth- and twentieth-century Pennsylvanians would find them cheap and handy avenues for exploitation of mineral and lumber resources. For Pennsylvanians in 1776, however, they were mainly irrelevant, since their watersheds were still trackless wilderness. Within a few years they would

Susquehanna River near Millersburg

serve as major arteries of transportation, but it is ironic that those very rivers, the most easily navigated in the entire state, were mainly used by Pennsylvanians to get out of Pennsylvania into Ohio, Kentucky, and the new Northwest. Even in 1776 the future was already clear: east of the Allegheny Front, Pennsylvanians would face toward the Susquehanna system, toward Philadelphia, and toward the Atlantic. To the west, the Ohio and its tributaries would lead Pennsylvanians toward Pittsburgh, the Ohio Valley, and the great lowlands of the North American interior. Nature had laid the groundwork for two quite different Pennsylvanias: one old, maritime, and facing toward Europe; the other young, continental, and facing toward new lands. Even now, two hundred years later, this dual orientation persists.

Forests and Animal Life In Colonial Pennsylvania

Pennsylvanians well know the literal meaning of their state's name, "Penn's Woods." At the time William Penn purchased the first eastern sections of Pennsylvania from the Indians in 1681, ninety-eight percent of that area was covered with forests. A century later John David Schoepf, former surgeon with King George's German mercenaries, described the Pennsylvania forests as "so thick that the tree trunks almost touch, by their height and their matted branches making a dimness, cold and fearful, even at noon on the clearest day. All beneath is grown up in green and impenetrable bush. Everywhere lie fallen trees or those half fallen, despite of their weight not reaching the ground. Thousands of rotten and rotting trunks cover the ground making every step uncertain; and between lies a fat bed of the richest mold that sucks up like a sponge all the moisture." Even today about fifty percent of the state is still sheltered by many timber species of the past.

Vast stretches of maple, beech, and hemlock forests carpeted the northern part of the colony. In the uplands of the Appalachian Plateau rose the large five-needled white pine, an important wood to the colonial craftsmen of Pennsylvania. In the southern part of the state, particularly in the Piedmont, could be found the oak-chestnut forests. Here also in the river bottom lands grew large black walnuts, along with huge buttonwoods and tall straight tuliptrees. Visitors to colonial Pennsylvania were amazed by the abundance of chestnuts.

Penn's Woods experienced great seasonal variation in the late eighteenth century. There was the wide sweep of green in the summertime, a continuous canopy of shade that maintained cool conditions throughout the summer. Pennsylvanians know the brilliance of the colors of autumn in their present forests, but it is difficult to imagine the display when most of southeastern Pennsylvania was in deciduous forest. The winter must have been stark, with naked trees etched against the whiteness of the winter landscape. The only occasional accent upon this starkness would have been the evergreen of mountain laurel, rhododendron, white pine, and hemlock, the state tree.

There have of course been changes in the forest. The American chestnut, destroyed by blight, has passed from the scene. White pine and black walnut trees are smaller, because the large older trees were cut so recklessly by lumbermen. The tanning industries, established in the mid-nineteenth century, decimated the virgin stands of Pennsylvania hemlocks for their bark, which was used in the tanning process. Yet, in spite of this devastation, the state tree flourishes today in the ravines of all mountain areas. In fact, although the Pennsylvanian today does not find the same expanse of forest covering his commonwealth as did the eighteenth-century colonist, he comes upon a greater diversity of plants and so enjoys in autumn a more varied display of color.

In colonial Pennsylvania's sylvan setting, extensions or outliers of prairie, together with cuts made by the river systems, provided much "edge effect." Elk, deer, and some buffalo roamed through the forest and could be seen frequently along these edges. Bison and elk were tracked by their natural predators: the mountain lion and the timber wolf. Black bear fed on the fruits of the forest and occasional small animals and insects. The state mammal, the white-tailed deer—so avidly sought today by hunters—had more reason to fear carnivorous beasts than humans, outside the settled areas.

Mosquitoes, blackflies, and deerflies plagued the Indian and troubled the white man in his early attempts to live on the land. Other insects not harmful to man abounded, such as the present state insect, the firefly, which relieved the darkness of the forest night. When the shad moved up the streams to spawn, mayflies hatched in great abundance. And at the same time the shad-bush bloomed, an early flower on the Pennsylvania hillsides.

In the spring jack-in-the-pulpit, trillium, and mayapple sprawled on the forest floor. Partridge berry in dense carpets, as well as wintergreen and the trailing arbutus, huddled as today under the hemlocks. Mountain laurel, the state flower, bloomed in great profusion, occasionally beside the fragrant mountain azalea. The witch hazel's small but abundant yellow flowers bloomed as the last tree flower of the season. In the skies Canada geese flew south down the major waterways. Flocks of passenger pigeons would darken the sky, or they might join the wild turkeys who were fattening on the mast of oaks and chestnuts. Eagles and ospreys had fledged their young and with the hawks headed down the ridges on their southerly migration. Brook trout, recently chosen as the state fish, spawned in Pennsylvania mountain streams during October and November of 1776.

Farms now cover the Piedmont, where the first settlers cleared the land of some of the country's finest hardwood timber so that they might work the soil. Many of the mammals are gone: the elk, the bison, the wolf, and the mountain lion. Only a few bears remain in the northern part of the state. Ridge upon ridge of deciduous hardwood is nature's main legacy to today's Penn's Woods.

Flora and Fauna

Even though the shape of its mountains and rivers remains about the same, the face of Pennsylvania today differs greatly from its aspect of 1776. Well into the eighteenth century Pennsylvania was almost entirely covered with ancient forests—dense stands of mature trees interrupted only by streams, lakes, and small, scattered treeless areas. An estimated ninety-seven percent of Pennsylvania was forested when European settlement began, compared with much less than half of that today. Even after thousands of acres had been cleared during the first century of intensive settlement, the almost continuous forest loomed menacingly, a formidable obstacle to cultivation, travel, and safety.

These tall, dense forests supported extensive populations of wildlife, including such large animals as the wolf, panther, bear, deer, and elk. In more open areas buffalo probably roamed, and innumerable smaller mammals, including such plentiful fur-bearers as beaver, marten, and otter, were everywhere. The Indians—wise conservationists—lived in harmony with the wildlife, killing animals almost apologetically, and only when they were really needed. Thus the stocks remained at a high level until the depradations of the colonists began. Though they survived elsewhere, the wolf, panther, elk, and marten were gradually exterminated by hunters, and the population of wildlife declined alarmingly. Formerly abundant birds, the turkey, heath hen, passenger pigeon, and Carolina paroquet, were finally seen no more, and though the turkey has reestablished itself, others have vanished from the earth. The devastation of Pennsylvania's flora and fauna, relatively stable under the care of the Indians, began soon after the first European settlement. By 1776, a sylvan paradise had been changed into a scene where animals were killed in wholesale numbers for their skins alone and uncounted marvelous trees were cut down and burned in piles to speed the clearing of land.

Other changes resulted from less reprehensible causes. Deforestation was a natural consequence of settlement, and the lumber industry grew steadily until it consumed more trees than were lost to reckless land-clearing. The once abundant chestnut trees were totally wiped out by disease that man was helpless to control. By

Carolina paroquet

Passenger pigeon

planting foreign trees—apple, peach, pear, horse chestnut, weeping willow—colonists changed the landscape, and by unintentionally spreading European weed-seeds they gave roadsides and town lots a different look that persists to this day.

These sweeping changes in the aspect of Pennsylvania's flora and fauna did not involve large numbers of species. Although several kinds of birds and large mammals have been lost, the total number of species has changed little. Except for the deer, groundhog, and opossum (which have benefited from influences of man), most mammals are now fewer in number, and many species are, for this reason, rarely seen. To be sure, when there were more animals, the forest hid them. Of birds, only a few species have been lost, and it is probable that more birds, of more different kinds, can be seen today than were present in the eighteenth century, when ubiquitous forests gave open-land species little opportunity. The largest change in the face of Pennsylvania has come from the cutting of trees. No *species* except chestnut has been entirely lost, but almost all of the enormous trees of 1776 are gone, and two-thirds of the area that was then covered by them is now totally treeless or supports only meager growth. Loss of forest cover has brought other changes besides increasing many bird populations. Pennsylvania now has over 175 species of grasses, many of which could not have existed in an area ninety-seven percent forested. Agriculture has brought foreign weeds and insect pests, and so total numbers of species are greater in those categories, too. In spite of a few conspicuous losses, an increase in kinds of flora and fauna is undoubtedly one consequence of the settlers' changing the face of Pennsylvania by cutting down most of "Penn's Woods."

Most of our comprehension of the flora and fauna of Pennsylvania in 1776 comes from interpretation of eighteenth-century accounts in the light of more recent information. Many plants and animals mentioned in these early writings were not formally described and named until later. Although the great Linnaeus (1707–1778) introduced modern biological classification before the Revolutionary War, it was not quickly adopted, even by conscientious scientists, let alone by non-scientists. Thus there are constant problems in determining what the early writers were talking about. Their wake-robin may be our jack-in-the-pulpit; William Bartram's fieldfare is our robin; John Bartram's spruce is our hemlock.

In eighteenth-century Europe, appetites for news about the New World were insatiable, and this demand encouraged numerous travelers and opportunists to grind out books about America. Most of these writers fell short of being objective reporters of what their own eyes saw, and, as was the custom, they freely "borrowed" published and unpublished information. The worst of them were plagiarists, thieves, and liars. One writer, describing Pennsylvania, lifted a description of Florida from another's book, and the illustrious

Porcupine	Opossum	Raccoon
Deer	Fox	Turkey
Elk	Weasel	Chipmunk
Bear	Squirrel	Ruffed grouse

Hispid buttercup

Dutchman's breeches

Bloodroot

Cardinal flower   Indian pipe

Jack-in-the-pulpit

Pink lady's-slipper

Dogwood

     Blue lobelia

Rhododendron

Mountain laurel

Columbine

Chateaubriand wrote that the moose relieves his epilepsy by drawing blood from his left ear with his left hind foot, recommending this hoof of a moose as sovereign remedy for human epilepsy. Under provocation of such tall tales, Benjamin Franklin, with a straight face, told English listeners about whales jumping over Niagara Falls. Not only was there much sensationalistic writing, but some respected European savants concocted the "doctrine of degeneracy," a notion that everything in America was weaker, smaller, and generally inferior because America was a "new world." When Jefferson succeeded Franklin as Minister to France in 1784, he was so incensed by this idea that he told the Count de Buffon, France's "High-Priest of Nature," that he was grievously wrong in asserting in his forty-four volume *Natural History* that the American moose was inferior to its European counterpart. From Paris, Jefferson sent home for a moose. When it arrived the great Buffon is said to have declared, "I should have consulted you before publishing my *Natural History;* then I should have been sure of my facts."

Moose

John Bartram, Colonial Botanist

John Bartram (1699–1777) has been called America's first native naturalist. So much has been written picturing John Bartram as an unschooled Quaker farmer—almost a bumpkin (who made good)—that it is too easy to overlook his eminence in his own time. Born near Philadelphia, he developed an early passion for plant study, exploration, and innovative investigations, which led him to immortality as a colonial scientist.

A shrewd farmer who grew record crops of wheat, flax, oats, and maize on his farm of several hundred acres on the outskirts of Philadelphia, Bartram established there in 1729 the first North American botanic garden to survive the eighteenth century and the oldest surviving today. With enthusiastic encouragement from Peter Collinson, a wealthy, influential English Quaker plant fancier, Bartram developed on his farm one of the most famous horticultural establishments in the world, and the best collection of native plants in America. A distinguished visitor and colleague from South Carolina, Dr. Alexander Garden, called Bartram's unsophisticated garden "a perfect portraiture of himself."

Bartram shipped plants and seeds to at least fifty-seven European gardens, and was responsible for the first introduction of nearly two hundred species of American trees, shrubs, and herbs to cultivation in England and on the continent. But this was only one facet of a singularly versatile career. John Bartram was an explorer. Both to find new plants for his garden and for science, and to reveal new information about a little-known country, he traveled over nearly all of the United States then known, from Lake Ontario to Florida. Not content merely to botanize, he examined nature in all her aspects. He explored rugged mountains and almost impenetrable swamps, and from every journey brought home journals, data, specimens, plants, and seeds to his cherished garden. Though writing was not his favorite occupation, Bartram's output was surprisingly large. The published journal of his 1743 travels to Onondago has been called "one of the most appealing in the history of scientific exploration." He contributed an essay on growing timber as a crop to Poor Richard Improved *(1749) and voluminous notes to a book on medicinal plants (1751)—both printed by Benjamin Franklin. Through Collinson he contributed scientific observations to the* Philosophical Transactions *of the Royal Society of London on insects, rattlesnakes, mollusks, and the aurora borealis.*

The importance of Collinson to Bartram must not be overlooked because Collinson's influence, encouragement, and material efforts in enlisting customers for American plants were the making of Bartram as a historic figure in the chronicles of Pennsylvania and of botany. In England it was smilingly said that the famous John Bartram was the creation of Peter Collinson—which, in a measure, he was.

But extensive farming, copious international horticultural activity, exploratory travels far and wide, and scientific writing and publication could not exhaust Bartram's energies. Head of a large family, who sat at the table with his food in one hand and a book in the other, he still found time to plan the first geological survey and work as a pioneer experimental plant breeder. He was also one of the first ecologists, studying habitats, soil, drainage, weather, and reproduction in conjunction with his plant collections and propagation. He called all Pennsylvania his garden and had experimental plantings in many places. With typical Quaker shrewdness John Bartram made botany profitable. Almost every ship out of Philadelphia carried his plants, roots, seeds, and specimens from the New World to the Old. He carried on a lively correspondence with dozens of the greatest naturalists and horticulturists in the world. Next to Franklin, he was undoubtedly the preeminent scientist of colonial Pennsylvania—ingenious, versatile, philosophical. Lewis Evans (1700–1756) wrote in 1753, "scarce any thing of the kind [botanical] . . . has escaped his scrutiny; he has great skill in Botany and is the most diligent man living." Peter Kalm said, of one of his books, that he had not told one thousandth of what he knew. Carl Linnaeus, founder of modern systematic natural history, called Bartram "the greatest natural botanist in the world."

Spotted turtle

Morning glory

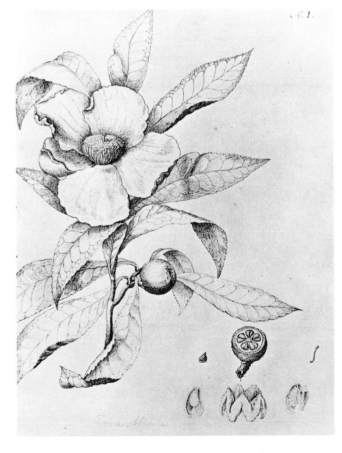

Franklinia (*Franklin Tree*), *John Bartram's best known plant discovery. Drawn by William Bartram.*

John Bartram's bookplate

William Bartram, Extraordinary Traveler

In 1794 the only American in Meyer's list of "all living zoologists" was John Bartram's remarkable son William (1739–1823). He was so famous in Europe that he eclipsed numerous contemporaries now better remembered. His five-year trip of exploration and observation in the Carolinas, Georgia, and Florida (1772–1777) resulted in a book unique in literature. "Bartram's Travels," *first published in Philadelphia in 1791, was the earliest native production of its kind, so eloquent and arresting, with idyllic or earthy Indians, iridescent landscapes, and vividly menacing alligators, that it burst like a bomb on the literary circles of England, Ireland, Germany, Austria, France, and Holland, with pirated editions rapidly issued in all those countries.*

The author of this phenomenal book was a gentle, quiet, unassuming Quaker who never married. In his travels he lived with the Indians, who respected him and called him Puc-Puggy. A resourceful man, he was adept at swimming, fishing, shooting, horsemanship, and cooking. Like his father he was an ingenious mechanic, and could turn his hand to microscopic dissection as well as drawing and painting. Also like his father, he was a pioneer ecologist, weaving environmental information into his Travels. *Though appearing to comply with the notorious eighteenth-century custom of spinning fabulous yarns, William Bartram's* Travels *has been shown by modern scholarship to be accurate, even in its most astonishing parts, even while exaltedly poetic. William Bartram was noted for his veracity and his almost Indian simplicity—which led him to receive, in his bare feet, members of Congress visiting his garden. Puc-Puggy, the flower hunter.*

By many he was considered a bit daft because of his simplicity, unaffectedness, and candor. Actually a balanced, practical person who was said to have had "that rarest of combinations, the mind of a scientist with the soul of a poet," William Bartram's influence on American science was surprisingly profound. Though often dismissed as a talented artist and moderately successful author of one highly venerable book ("biblical," Carlyle called it), he was the pioneer American ornithologist, publishing in 1791 the first scientific list of eastern birds, and the first Pennsylvania bird list (divided into year-round residents, summer residents, and winter residents). Called the "Pillar of American Ornithology"

he was Alexander Wilson's ornithology teacher and he and his niece Ann Bartram taught Wilson drawing and painting. He was also the guiding influence on his great-nephew, Thomas Say (1787–1834), who has been commemorated as the "Father of American Entomology." William Bartram's work on insects remains unpublished, but its influence on Say's work must have been considerable.

William Bartram's significance extends into other notable lives. Like Wilson (who called the garden "a little paradise"), Thomas Nuttall (1786–1859) and F.A. Michaux (1770–1855) lived with him in his house, studying with him while they prepared their seminal botanical publications. And he helped Benjamin Smith Barton (nephew of David Rittenhouse and an eminent academic botanist) perhaps more than he should have—Barton's Materia Medica *(1798) is actually Bartram's work.*

Preceptor of illustrious followers, skilled botanist, accomplished artist—the only worthy native-born natural history illustrator of the colonial period— author of a transcendental book unique in literature, William Bartram in later times has received even less acclaim than his quiet father. But both had such extensive knowledge and experience, and so much versatility and bold originality, that they would have been remarkable wherever and whenever they had lived.

William Bartram after a portrait by C.W. Peale

"The Alligator of St. Johns, Florida" by William Bartram

"Witch Hazel"

"The Great Black Bream"

"The Great Mallard"

Botanic Gardens and Plant Collecting

In eighteenth-century England a gardening craze swept over the country. Rare plants were so coveted that garden robberies were frequent, causing Parliament to intervene with an act punishing plant thieves by transporting them to America. It was then also the "Age of Linnaeus"—the great Swedish naturalist who originated and popularized the modern classification of plants and animals. These influences brought about a "botany boom" that made the New World the focus of many European eyes, and naturalists and collectors came to America to discover new species. Residents of the colonies also were excited by the unlimited new plants of their land, and an unprecedented interest in American botany, centered in Philadelphia, grew apace.

In 1699 when Philadelphia was a green country town, Irish-born James Logan (1674–1751) came over as William Penn's secretary. An educated, cultivated gentleman, he rose to become one of the most outstanding and respected leaders in the colony. Mayor, governor, chief justice; revered by the Indians, he was possessor of a botanic garden of medicinal plants and a library of over two thousand choice books on science, medicine, philosophy, geography, history, and ethics—the finest in the colonies. He himself performed and published the results of pioneer experiments demonstrating the function of sexual structures in the fertilization of maize.

Although a medicinal botanic garden was planted at Philadelphia before 1700 by Kelpius (1673–1708), and another by about 1718 by Christopher Witt (1675–1765)—last of the early Rosicrucian mystics—neither these gardens nor Logan's survived for more than a few years. The growth of Philadelphia was phenomenal, and the building boom may have swallowed them up. Logan was John Bartram's preceptor, providing him with books, instruments, and advice on study and experiments. John Bartram's garden, begun under Logan's influence, was a mecca for all with botanical interests, and numerous eighteenth-century contributors to botanical and natural history literature were frequenters of the place, which had grown old before the end of the century. Presided over, in later years, by the serene and amiable William Bartram, it was renowned as the finest collection of native plants. It is to be expected that Philadelphia naturalists sought out the garden and were often seen there, but this unpretentious retreat also attracted Washington, Jefferson, Madison, Hamilton, Humboldt, William Dunlap ("The American Vasari"), Charles Brockden Brown, and many others among the famous and illustrious, who came seeking solitude and to pay homage to William Bartram and the memory of his father.

John Bartram's cousin Humphry Marshall (1722–1801) started his own botanic garden and nursery not far from Philadelphia in 1773. This led to his composition of *The American Grove* (1785), the

Contemporary drawing of John Bartram's garden

first completely indigenous American botanical book—written by an American, on an American subject (trees and shrubs), and published in America (Philadelphia). (William Young [1742–1785], an upstart rival nurseryman and neighbor of the Bartrams, had published a faintly similar book in Paris in 1783.)

Although botanic gardening and plant collecting (especially for export) had their enthusiastic practitioners in the Philadelphia of 1776, academic botany was still in its infancy. In 1762 Adam Kuhn (1741–1817) made the hard journey from Philadelphia to Sweden to study under Linnaeus, of whom he was called a favorite pupil. He was the only Linnaean disciple, except Kalm—a visitor—to be locally involved in eighteenth-century Pennsylvania natural history. Returning home, after graduating in medicine at Edinburgh, he was appointed, in 1768, the first professor of botany in North America, a post he held for ten or twelve years. He then went on to become a highly respected professor of medicine, but he left no botanical contributions that have come down to this day. His successor, Professor Benjamin Smith Barton (1766–1815), often took his University of Pennsylvania botany classes on field trips to Bartram's Garden. Barton was an aggressive, prolific scholar, but in his many publications he used other people's material too often, depending heavily on information obtained from William Bartram.

Peter Kalm (1715–1779) was the best qualified foreign naturalist to visit the American colonies (from 1748 to 1751), and this Swedish professor's book remains the best scientific account of eighteenth-century Pennsylvania. As a disciple of the great Linnaeus, he collected dozens of Pennsylvania plants for his famous teacher to describe and name, including *Kalmia*, the mountain laurel.

J.D. Schoepf (1752–1800), a German officer attached to mercenary troops hired by the British in the Revolution, later explored the flora and fauna of Pennsylvania and wrote an important book. Observations by Schoepf and Kalm give us some of the best information on the trees, plants, mammals, birds, and other animals of the Pennsylvania of 1776.

Penn's Woods

Eighteenth-century immigrants into Pennsylvania, struggling to meet their material needs, were pleased to find native plants and animals which they had known in the Old Country, such as oak trees, grapes, rabbits, and ducks, although they were curious about the plants and animals that they found strange, grotesque, or dangerous, such as the rattlesnake, skunk, opossum, hummingbird, persimmon, paw paw, and poison ivy. Pioneers who followed were often more resourceful and experimental and gave close attention to the food habits, hunting and fishing practices, agriculture, and medicinal

The famous cypress tree in Bartram's garden, grown from a shoot originally cut by John Bartram as a buggy-whip. Circumference at the base is 27 feet, 6 inches.

The years have come and gone—
The summer's heat, the winter's frost—
Men have passed and stones grown old
And hoary moss has crept
Over all thou lovedst;
And yet, O Bartram! in these mighty trees
Thou livest still!

Liberty Hyde Bailey,
"In Bartram's Garden"

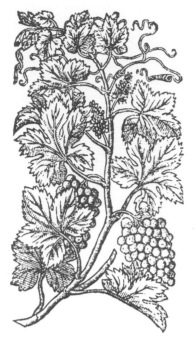

Grapevine

plants of the Indians. Almost all of our earliest information about native Pennsylvania food plants, as well as those used for medicine, fiber, and dye, was learned from the Indians who lived in Pennsylvania when the white man came or who moved through the colony in what were, for Indians, tragic times.

Perhaps only in the realm of timber trees and their wood did the white colonists themselves accumulate a fund of useful information not obtainable from the natives. Lacking saws and steel axes, the Indians enjoyed simple lives that did not lead to detailed knowledge of properties of different kinds of wood, in contrast to the experience of the white man who sawed up many kinds of trees felled in clearing the land, and thus gained useful information analogous to what he already knew from generations of experience with similar timber trees and woods in Europe. However, the Indians did know their trees well as sources of food, medicine, fiber, dye, tanning, shelter, and canoes (they made colossal dugouts as well as classic birch-barks).

Except for total loss of chestnut, and enormous reduction of such towering forest giants as white pine, hemlock, tuliptree, and black cherry, the tree species of Pennsylvania were about the same in 1776 as now. The longevity of most major Pennsylvania species is in excess of two hundred years, so quite a few individual trees of 1976 surely were living in 1776. (This is true of at least 37 of Pennsylvania's approximately 120 tree species.) What has changed drastically is the *aspect* of the forests—indeed, the aspect of the whole land. In 1776 the Pennsylvania scene was dominated by trees. Schoepf, who complained of seeing mainly trees every day, vividly recounts forest journeys, illuminated by foxfire: "There was now thick darkness among the high, close-standing trees, obscuring the friendly light of the moon which shone clear but not for us, and it would have been neck-breaking work to keep on horseback. We could find our way only by knocking from time to time into the trees and stumps on both sides, and thus being put back into the narrow path. The dull light from the many rotting trunks was pleasant to be sure but of no use."

Pennsylvania was originally completely forested except for scattered Indian fields of 20 to 200 acres, many areas deliberately burned by settlers or regularly burned over by Indians, and some considerable areas swept clear of trees by wildfires. Scrub-oak barrens, such as those near Nazareth, were burned over every year by the settlers to encourage grass for cattle, but without killing the oak trees—which were only three to four feet high. There were also scattered beaver meadows, elk and deer (and perhaps buffalo) licks, and here and there open areas that probably never have been forested—some of them possibly eastern outposts of the great mid-American prairies. Including water areas, only about three percent of the total area of Pennsylvania was treeless when the white man came. Everywhere else the province was so covered by forests of

large trees that Peter Kalm found cattle pasturing in the woods because there were no fields.

These dense, mature forests were of the oak-chestnut type (now oak-hickory) except across the northern portion of the colony and along the higher mountain ridges, where pine and hemlock predominated. Along with oak and chestnut were ash, hickory, tuliptree, maple, and walnut, with "coves" of white pine, pitch pine, and scattered hemlock. The prevalence of chestnut and the size and density of the other trees were the predominant features of the colonial landscape. (Of the original 28,000,000 acres of forest, less than half now support any woody growth, and, of this, 5,000,000 acres, though technically wooded, are barren and unproductive.)

The Trees of 1776

When the carefully planned town of Philadelphia was laid out in 1682, William Penn named most of the streets for trees: Chestnut, Walnut, Locust, Spruce, Pine, Filbert, Cherry, Vine, Poplar, Apple, Quince, Peach, Plum, Orange, and Lemon still exist where he drew them on his plan; others—Mulberry, Sassafras, Cedar, Oak, Elm, Larch, Laurel—were later renamed. Penn's choice of trees for street names was catholic—many were familiar kinds in Europe and England, but others, including chestnut, locust, poplar, mulberry, and sassafras, were more distinctively American. Just as eighteenth-century travelers were struck by seeing mainly trees every day, so were the burghers of old Philadelphia accosted by tree names from Penn's Woods wherever they went along his carefully laid-out streets.

Peter Kalm records that within a few days of his arrival at Philadelphia in 1748 he had recognized forty species of trees and eighteen of shrubs and ranked them according to abundance. He sent specimens of most of these to Linnaeus in Sweden, who, by 1763, had scientifically described and classified sixty of the hundred and twenty-odd tree species that occur in Pennsylvania. Most of our best-known trees—white pine, hemlock, red cedar, black walnut, sweet birch, red, white, and chestnut oaks, elm, mulberry, cucumber-tree, tuliptree, buttonwood, black locust, silver and red maples, basswood, persimmon, and white ash—were thus formally named by Linnaeus, chiefly from Kalm's material.

At the same time that native Pennsylvania trees were being recognized, described, and named, Old World trees were being imported and planted in Pennsylvania, and many of these soon escaped from cultivation and joined the spontaneous flora of Pennsylvania. Planted early were varieties of apple, peach, pear, plum, and cherry, as well as Norway spruce and weeping willow. Some of these were established so early that certain eighteenth-century observers thought them native. William Penn didn't know whether the peach was native, and Kalm, in 1748, thought the apple so. Man's tendency to carry desirable (and undesirable) plants wherever he settles makes it much more difficult to define native floras later. The horse chestnut appears to have been introduced by John Bartram in 1746, and it became naturalized nearby, though not widely dispersed. William Hamilton (1745–1813), whose Woodlands estate in Philadelphia was a great showplace of the post-revolutionary period, introduced ginkgo, Lombardy poplar, ailanthus, and Norway maple in 1784, and spontaneous offspring of these soon became part of Pennsylvania's tree flora. Thus the number of tree species increased at the same time that the native tree flora was becoming known and its species described by eighteenth-century botanists.

White Pine. Before the white man came, Pennsylvania Indians occasionally used the inner bark as food, but they certainly had no idea of the timber value of the white pine, since lumbering was unknown to them. The Pine Tree Flag, first flag of the Revolution, is a reminder of oppressive British measures to insure a supply of pine masts for their navy. Few if any masts for British ships were cut in Pennsylvania, but the straight, towering (up to 180 feet) trees dominated the northern part of the state and were soon being felled in land-clearing operations. Everything from covered bridges and large dimension timbers in churches, to shingles, clapboards, carvings, and ornamental woodwork, called for this versatile, attractive, easily worked material. A half million white pine houses were reported to have been built in the colonies by 1805, according to F.A. Michaux (1770–1855), who, with his father, Andre, was a pioneer botanical explorer, and wrote the first treatise on American trees.

White pine

Starting in 1772 vast white pine lands in northwestern Pennsylvania were purchased from the Indians, and the slaughter began. Spectacular log drives on the Susquehanna led to Williamsport—later known as the Sawdust City, built on a sawdust pile three miles long. As long as it was abundant, white pine was the most frequently used timber, and so greedy were the old Pennsylvania lumber barons that they cut down hundreds of titanic pines, too big to move, and left them rotting in the ravished forests.

Hemlock. Pennsylvania's "state tree" was widely used by the Indians: the bark for tanning and dyeing, and twigs and leaves to make a medicinal tea—also popular with the settlers—that was held to be anti-scorbutic and effective against venereal diseases. Healing poultices were made from the inner bark, and root beer was brewed from hemlock roots by the Indians. Settlers who tried to use the wood were disappointed because the weak, decay-prone, twisted-grain wood compared so unfavorably with white pine. But as Michaux predicted in 1807, when white pine became scarcer more and more hemlock would be used in house-building—later making Pennsylvania a leading hemlock-cutting state. A much smaller tree than white pine (seldom over eighty feet in its maturity), hemlock often occupied the same forests and was left behind when the pines were removed. Later the devastation became complete when the hemlocks were clear-cut for tanbark. Though not the best for tanning (Michaux called it inferior to oak, but together they are better than either bark separately), hemlock was in copious supply, and so the "peelers" went into the forests, cut and stripped the felled trunks, and left them rotting on the ground. Abundant in Pennsylvania only in the Alleghanies, the hemlock was introduced to cultivation in England by seeds sent by John Bartram to Peter Collinson.

Hemlock

Black walnut

Hickory

Paper birch

Black birch

Black Walnut. Recognized at once as the source of highly valuable wood for cabinetmaking, black walnut was cut and used recklessly because there was so much of it. West of Pittsburgh houses were built of it, even to the shingles. Fence posts and rails were made of walnut in other areas, and it was wasted as fuel by "peasants" reproachfully referred to by Kalm. Indians, of course, always used the nuts as food, and the husks for dye, and settlers followed these Indian uses even while valuing the wood as the finest cabinet wood of North America. That it was appreciated from the first is shown by records of shiploads of black walnut sawlogs exported to Europe in 1610. Demand for this wood has always far exceeded the available supply, leading to eradication of large trees, though small ones are still abundant.

Hickory. Pennsylvania has at least five species of hickory trees, but the shagbark (or shellbark) leads in size, abundance, and usefulness. Indians valued hickory nuts highly, and regularly made from them and walnuts a hickory milk concoction that was important in Indian cookery. Sometimes a tree yielded several bushels of nuts, which were considered so good that they were even exported to Europe. Indians used the bark for dye and tapped the sap to make sugar just as maple sugar was made. Hickory wood was recognized early for its great value for timber and fuel. The wood was very important because it was needed for barrel hoops (almost everything was shipped in barrels), mill wheels, chairbacks, whip handles, ramrods, rake teeth, flails, ox yokes, bookbinders' presses, mast rings on sails, and handspikes. It made the strongest hammer and axe handles then, and is still so used today. Perhaps most important, hickory has the highest fuel value of any North American wood except locust, one cord being equivalent to one ton of anthracite. It wastefully fed the roaring hearth-fires of the pioneers, though the Indians viewed with disgust the destruction of so many fine nut trees.

Paper Birch. Inseparably associated with Indians and the north country, paper birch was not common in colonial Pennsylvania, appearing only in the northern parts. It is notable that, as the old forests were destroyed, paper birch increased. Although Indian uses of the beautiful bark are familiar, it is less well known that Indians tapped the sap to make sugar, as they also did with hickory and the abundant sugar maple.

Black Birch (Sweet Birch). A valuable timber tree sometimes growing eighty feet tall, and the best fuel next to hickory and locust, this is a common Pennsylvania tree that had other delightful uses in colonial times. Its sap was tapped to make birch beer (a single tree could yield two tons of sap), and saplings and twigs were distilled for oil of wintergreen, for which there was much demand. Michaux called it a very desirable tree that should be guarded and preserved, and said that the wood was next in esteem to black cherry among cabinetmakers.

Chestnut. Foresters estimate that chestnut was once the most common tree of Pennsylvania, and now it is a memory—totally wiped out, but not vanished. Penn's Woods are full of sucker saplings springing from roots of giant chestnuts that were destroyed by the blight beginning in 1906, but these in turn will fall victim to the lingering fungus, and it is probable that the great chestnut trees, up to a hundred feet tall, which were so useful in the eighteenth century, will never again be duplicated. Chestnut was Pennsylvania's leading wood for fence rails and posts—necessities in pioneer days—because it split readily and withstood the elements. For the same reason, it was, in 1776, highly esteemed for shingles, superior to any oak, and the bark was one of the best for tanning. Though not preferred for fuel, chestnut was cultivated around ironworks in the mountains of Pennsylvania as copses cut on a ten-year rotation to provide a steady supply of charcoal. The nuts of the chestnut were, as mast (food for animals), much more dependable than beech or oak because chestnut trees didn't flower until all danger of frost was past. As they did with walnuts and hickories, the Indians cooked up chestnuts into a liquid that was used regularly with other food. Mapmaker Lewis Evans (1700–1756) thought American chestnuts much better tasting than the famous European species.

Chestnut

White Oak. The rolling hills of southwestern Pennsylvania, now in the counties of Somerset, Fayette, Greene, Washington, and Westmoreland, were covered in 1776 by a mature forest nine-tenths of which was white oak—trees that might grow ninety feet tall. Whole towns were built entirely of this wood, and millions of feet of the timber were converted into barrels. For liquid contents—tight cooperage—white oak barrels were (and still are) the best, but colonists accustomed to the wonderful European oak for shipbuilding thought of our white oak chiefly for that use, in which it does not really excel. As long as the United States had a wooden navy, white oak built our ships, resulting in a constant battle with rot that had direr consequences than many a naval battle. Though white oak is said to be good for nearly any wood use, supplies were swallowed up by the shipbuilding boom of the eighteenth century and by 1807 had become scarce and expensive. William Penn foresaw this in 1682 when he proposed that one acre of trees be preserved for every five acres felled, "especially to preserve oak for shipping and mulberry for silk." White oak acorns were widely used as food by Pennsylvania Indians, who dried, ground, and percolated them to prepare sweet meal for breadmaking, though botanist Humphry Marshall thought of them as food for swine.

White oak

Chestnut Oak. Always a dominant component of Pennsylvania forests, chestnut oak had many uses in 1776. Fuel, fence rails, shipbuilding, tanbark, all were important. As food the Indians considered the mast second only to chestnut, and they used the bark for dyeing. On some Pennsylvania mountain ridges ninety percent of the trees were chestnut oak, which thrives on stony soil. As fuel in the eigh-

Chestnut oak

Elm

Red mulberry

Cucumbertree

Tuliptree

teenth century it ranked next to hickory in importance, if not in heat value.

Elm. "The most magnificent vegetable of the Temperate Zone"— this is what F.A. Michaux called the American elm. Trees of great size and age were everywhere in Pennsylvania. Perhaps he was thinking of the wonderful old Penn Treaty Elm at Shackamaxon, under which William Penn and the Indians signed what has been called "the only absolutely upright treaty and the only one scrupulously honored by both sides for 50 years." The elm was the major tree symbol of Iroquois mythology and art, and Pennsylvania Indians of the colonial period had many uses for it: utensils from the bark, rope from bark fibers, and a sort of cloth which they wove without a loom. Settlers wove the tough, flexible bark into chair seats, but they had little use for the wood. Relatively few elms were cut in Pennsylvania, but disease in the twentieth century has vanquished the majority and threatens to overtake the rest.

Red Mulberry. Peter Kalm was sent to America in 1748 by the Swedish Academy of Sciences to study trees with environmental requirements similar to those in Sweden, especially mulberry trees for silk culture. He made repeated observations of the red mulberry, but silkworms proved to be reluctant to eat its leaves. The Indians, however, liked the fruit enough to plant mulberry trees and thus extend the distribution of the species which, although found in Pennsylvania in 1776, was really a more southern tree. Farther south the Indians made a kind of cloth from the bark, beating it to separate the fibers and then weaving cloth in a manner that required no loom. Mulberry trees could be sizable—up to seventy feet tall— and produced timber valuable in shipbuilding. Eighteenth-century shipbuilders would have used more mulberry timber had it been available.

Cucumbertree. The only large magnolia in colonial Pennsylvania forests, the cucumbertree was uncommon but conspicuous, and only occasionally cut. John Bartram gave it careful attention on his travels and several other early Pennsylvania travelers found the green fruit being steeped in whiskey by pioneers to make malaria medicine. Anything bitter was tried as a substitute for the scarce and costly quinine-containing true "Peruvian Bark," and so the pleasantly bitter fruit, bark, and twigs of cucumbertree were used, made even more pleasant with whiskey. Cucumbertree wood was similar to that of tuliptree, and both were occasionally used by the Indians for making large dugout canoes holding up to twenty persons.

Tuliptree. Closely related to cucumbertree, this member of the magnolia family was one of the largest and most valuable timber trees of colonial Pennsylvania and had similar light, soft, eminently workable wood. Kalm found the cloister doors at Ephrata made of single boards of tuliptree. Ravished early because it occupied the best land, the tree was made into Indian and pioneer dugout canoes, and it later figured in great sawlog drives on the rivers of Appalachia. The bark, including root bark, was used for malaria medicine because of its bitter taste, and Kalm reported the leaves as a headache cure.

Sassafras. The first cargoes from the New World to the Old in the sixteenth century were of sassafras logs, and throughout the colonial period the European demand for sassafras was insatiable. Used by all Indians in and around Pennsylvania as a tonic and blood purifier —more as a charm to ward off evil than as a therapeutic agent—the earliest whites took it up as a real medicinal cure-all, said to be effective for malaria, lameness, eye troubles, dropsy, and ailments of the liver, stomach, breast, and head. It was also considered a repellant for bedbugs. Large trees were cut down just to get the flowers, tea from which was said to purify the blood. Fabulous tales of the healing powers of sassafras sent fleets of ships to the New World to bring back sassafras. Virginia exported the roots in quantities equal to tobacco, and still the demand increased. In England the fashionable drinking of sassafras tea took a tumble when word got around that it was a cure for venereal disease, and after that the craze diminished. While it lasted, however, the sassafras craze was a model for the twentieth-century excitement over sulfa drugs.

Sassafras

Buttonwood. Colossal hollow buttonwoods on Pennsylvania riverbanks served as homes for chimney swifts long before the settlers built chimneys; and after the settlers' honeybees went wild, buttonwood housed the colonies. The largest Indian canoes—some sixty-five feet long and carrying 9,000 pounds—were made of hollow buttonwood trunks. (Buttonwood is also known as sycamore.)

Buttonwood

Black Locust. Of all the wood in North America, black locust is the strongest, stiffest, and most decay-resistant; it has the highest fuel value, shrinks the least, and takes a high polish. But in Pennsylvania, in the last twenty years of the eighteenth century, a wood-boring beetle appeared that has nearly wiped out this valuable tree as a commercial commodity. Before that, it had been a favorite material of shipbuilders. Almost all wooden ships were fastened with locust pegs—"treenails." Later it was used chiefly for fenceposts unequaled in durability. Corner posts of early settlers' houses (not log cabins) were often of locust, and remained standing long after the rest of the house had disappeared completely.

Black locust

Black Cherry. Like those of tuliptree, towering stands of black cherry in colonial Pennsylvania were raped because they stood on the best ground for agriculture. Mature black cherries, like cucumbertree and tuliptree, were often over a hundred feet tall and their wood rivaled mahogany in beauty and usefulness. Next to black walnut in value, the knot-free, clean, broad planks from those mature trees were coveted by cabinetmakers who knew that the beauty of cherry furniture improves with age and use, while walnut does not.

Black cherry

Sugar maple

Red maple

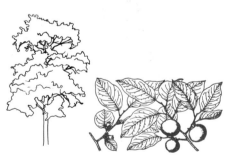

Persimmon

Indians and white men alike have enjoyed the ripe fruit, which the black bear also loves so much that he violently resents being disturbed while getting and digesting it. "Beware of Cherry Bears" was an old frontier admonition in Pennsylvania.

Sugar Maple. Next to the lamented chestnut, sugar maple was once probably the most abundant tree in Pennsylvania. As a source of sugar it was an everyday resource that the Indians appreciated and conserved, because (along with occasional tapping of birch and hickory) maples were their only source of sweetening before the Europeans came with bees, and later molasses. It is to this day remembered among the Iroquois with an annual festival of thanksgiving. Sugar maple timber was found by Pennsylvania pioneers to be so valuable that its use as a sugar source became secondary. Up to 120 feet tall, it produced straight, knot-free sawlogs almost unrivaled among our hardwoods. Farmers often did not hesitate to sell such trees to log buyers for twenty or thirty times as much as they could receive for one tree's annual production (averaging three pounds) of refined sugar. Dr. Benjamin Rush, who believed it had medicinal value, instigated a great promotion of native maple sugar cultivation in the hope that the United States could become independent of West Indian sugar.

Red Maple. An abundant tree in the hardwood forests of Pennsylvania, red maple was also more valued in colonial times for its timber than for its sugar, which is about half as plentiful as that of sugar maple. Curly maple lumber was in great demand and came only from old trees. Bird's-eye maple stock from the sugar maple was even scarcer and more expensive, but there was an eager market for all that could be found. Other important colonial products of red maple were tinder (a fungus on dead trees), ink, and dyes.

Persimmon. Early settlers in Pennsylvania took an interest in persimmon trees out of all proportion to their real importance. Coming from the Old World, where fruit trees were everywhere, the new arrivals looked in vain for the same trees in their new homeland. There were no apples, peaches, pears, or large plums. The only fleshy tree-fruits other than small plums, cherries, and crabapples were paw paws, mulberries, and persimmons, and these were new to the settlers. (Underripe persimmons that have not experienced frost are a gustatory catastrophe, although when ripened they are indeed excellent.) Larger persimmon trees, which could be a hundred feet tall, were never numerous, but they could yield several bushels of delicious fruit. There was enough of the fruit around in 1768 that Isaac Bartram, John Bartram's eldest son, published a technical discussion of the making of persimmon brandy. Quite a few other persimmon products were made—one like apple-butter and another a medicinal bread for treating dysentery. Persimmon wood was valued for making shuttles for weaving. Only dogwood and persimmon, among normally available materials, had the requisite hardness, smoothness, and fine grain.

Pennsylvania Plant Life

Although Pennsylvania trees made the strongest impressions on eighteenth-century settlers and visitors, numerous smaller woody plants and vines are frequently mentioned in literature of the period. Grapes, familiar to Europeans and valued highly, received much attention. William Penn sought to establish cultivation of native grapes, and Kalm describes several different species in detail. Kalm's name was immortalized in *Kalmia*, Pennsylvania's mountain laurel, by Linnaeus, who also named the rhododendron of shady mountain valleys. Both of these broad-leaf evergreen shrubs do much to give Pennsylvania forests their essential character, and the blossom of the mountain laurel has been designated the state flower. Among Pennsylvania fruits well-known and important to the Indians are many that do not grow on trees: blackberries, raspberries, blueberries, cranberries, and elderberries are bush fruits valued by Indian and pioneer alike. Pennsylvania was a natural orchard, with dozens of kinds of tree, bush, vine, and small fruits in common Indian use before colonization, as well as thirty-odd kinds of nuts and acorns. Among the shrubs used by the Indians were spicebush, witch hazel, and various viburnums.

Plants Used in Tanning. Leather was a most important material in eighteenth-century Pennsylvania. Besides hemlock, oak, and chestnut, colonial Pennsylvania tanners used the bark of beech, yellow birch, sumac, and bearberry in preparing different kinds of leather. Local availability often determined the tannage, and until the later days of the infamous hemlock "peelers," trees were seldom felled just for tanbark; it was a case of using all of the pig but the squeal.

Dye Sources. In literature of the period a wider range of plants was mentioned for dyes than for tanning, since this process, along with weaving, went on in almost every colonial home. The pink middle bark of the hemlock and the barks of willow, red maple, and hickory trees made popular dyes, as did black walnut shells, pokeweed, New Jersey tea, and bearberry. Goldthread, wild indigo, and touch-me-not were herbaceous plants frequently used in dyeing.

Fiber Plants. Pennsylvania Indians in the eighteenth century continued to use many of the fiber plants of their ancestors, even though flax was extensively grown by the settlers and linen and woolen cloth were used as items of barter between white and red men. Indian hemp was extensively used, and probably cultivated, for nets and cordage, and elm and mulberry barks were pounded to separate the fibers, which were then twisted and woven in various ways. Basswood bark was made into food bags and rope, and several eighteenth-century observers describe uses of leatherwood, a small tree that yields material for bags, baskets, straps, and cords.

Introduced Plants. The first white men to arrive in America brought Old World plants deliberately and accidentally, and by

Mountain laurel

Rhododendron

Tanner

53

Plantain

Dandelion

Jerusalem artichoke

mid-eighteenth century there was much uncertainty about what was native and what was not. The common European plantain was called by the Indians "White Man's Foot" because wherever he trod, this plant sprang up. Many of these plant-invaders were quickly adopted by the Indians for their own uses and seemed to work for them just as well as their native standbys. Dock, mallow, wild carrot, peppermint, elecampane, yarrow, tansy, burdock, and dandelion were quickly taken up by the Iroquois, and without instruction from Europeans the Indians managed to find the same uses for them as had been traditional in Europe for centuries. It has been estimated that over a thousand species of Old World plants have become naturalized in America since the white man's arrival.

Plants Introduced into Europe by Bartram. Among the nearly two hundred plant species sent to Collinson and other Europeans by John Bartram were some of Pennsylvania's most outstanding trees and shrubs: hemlock, river birch, cucumbertree, sugar maple, witch hazel, rhododendron, pinxterflower, mountain laurel, meadowsweet, and buttonbush. These were first brought into cultivation through the joint efforts of Bartram and Collinson—who often sent specimens along to Linnaeus for scientific description. It remains a nagging mystery why Linnaeus, who honored everybody he knew by naming plants for them, conspicuously failed to do so for Bartram, whom he esteemed preeminent in his field.

John Bartram's herbaceous introductions to Europe include horsemint, which Linnaeus named *Collinsonia* after Peter Collinson. Others were skunk cabbage, mayflower, shooting star, ginseng, and lady's-slippers (which Collinson told Bartram he would rather receive than anything else except possibly turtles). Collinson of course was interested in living material; many dried specimens from Pennsylvania were sent on to Linnaeus for formal botanical description, and so it happens that so many North American plants described by Linnaeus have Pennsylvania as their type locality.

Forests so dominated the scene in eighteenth-century Pennsylvania, and trees and their wood were so important to the colonists, that colonial observers wrote chiefly about trees. But Kalm, in his *Travels*, has observations on bloodroot, mayflower (trailing arbutus), Indian hemp, cattails, garlic, sorrel, lamb's quarters, and pokeweed—the last three cooked for food. He also observed the absence of green pastures in Pennsylvania in 1749, when cattle had to eat the tops of young trees. Though colonial writers usually found more to say about trees than herbs, medicinal plants were an exception. Such an herb as horsemint, with reputed anti-snakebite properties, was discussed by numerous writers.

Native Food Plants. Indians had such an abundance of game that their incentive to agriculture was limited, but they had become thoroughly adept at cultivating corn, beans, pumpkins, and squashes. They also grew Jerusalem artichokes, brought from west of the

Mississippi, to use as we use potatoes, which they probably didn't have, and they certainly cultivated tobacco, which was a sacred plant used in ritual, not for pleasure. Pennsylvania Indians were also highly competent foragers, and contemporary accounts list dozens of wild plants used as food. Roots of the arum family were especially popular: sweet flag, jack-in-the-pulpit, skunk cabbage, wild calla; and starchy roots of various lilies, solomon's seal, spatter-dock, and arrowhead (wapatoo) could be stored for winter or made into bread. Ground-nuts and cat-tails were further starch sources. Some Indians had much practical botanical information and knew hundreds of plants.

Although he appreciated and utilized the "natural orchard" of the native Pennsylvania flora, the red man was quick to adopt white man's fruits, and Indians were cultivating peaches (derived from trees Spaniards planted in Florida) around Philadelphia by the time of William Penn's arrival. They also cultivated apples in Pennsylvania, but they preferred peaches. Indians later adopted other crops from the colonists, especially cucumbers, melons, and peas.

Medicinal Plants. Perhaps the commonest reaction of colonial settlers and travelers alike, when encountering a new plant, was "what is it good for?" Illnesses, injuries, and indispositions were frequent then—more so than now because protective measures now taken for granted did not then exist—and almost every plant was looked upon as a known or possible source of medicine. A rich medicinal plant lore of Old World origin and long tradition was brought by immigrants who were no sooner in their new homes than they commenced looking around for the same or equivalent plants. They also planted and grew many traditional medicinal plants of which they brought over the seeds. That the Indians of colonial Pennsylvania had their own long-standing science of medicinal plants was soon discovered, and more inquisitive settlers who were untrammeled by prejudice studied and adopted Indian medicines and combined this indigenous knowledge with traditional European pharmacology. The Indians, in turn, adopted many of the medicinal plants brought from Europe, and after a few generations neither white nor red man knew which plants were native and which were imported.

Some plants such as sarsaparilla, horsemint, and boneset were, like sassafras, considered effective for almost any ailment; the common elder was a "whole Iroquois pharmacy." Such plants were kept on hand and used pretty freely, more so in cases of doubt. Others had specific applications: blue lobelia for venereal diseases, maidenhair fern for chest complaints, prickly ash for toothache, bloodroot for jaundice, and robin's plantain for tumors; these were used either as "simples" (plants used alone) or in complicated concoctions.

The dominant medicinal plant of eighteenth-century America was ginseng. Colonial travelers and observers wrote about ginseng as much as they did on the rattlesnake—not because it was so effective

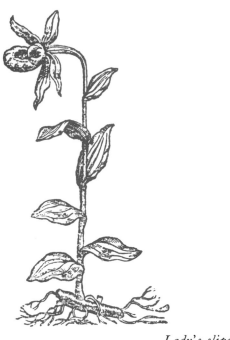

Lady's-slipper

Corn

Tobacco

Ginseng

medicinally but because it was worth so much money. Known to the Chinese as the most precious of medicinal plants, especially effective for sexual problems, ginseng was found in 1716 to have an American counterpart, a standard Iroquois remedy. The native Chinese plant was in short supply, and trade with China in American ginseng was soon flourishing. Wholesale collecting during the ensuing ginseng boom all but wiped out the more accessible American supplies. Boom led to bust when the Chinese trade was broken off in 1754 because too much and too inferior material was sent, causing the price to collapse. Later, after the Revolution, there was a revival of the trade, which lasted many years. Ginseng was not esteemed as a medicinal plant in America, but in France it was used for asthma, as a stomachic, and to promote fertility. The French bought it wholesale and shipped, very profitably, to China what they did not use themselves. In spite of glowing tales of its abundance, excessive collecting made ginseng so scarce that in 1786, forty man-days of labor were required to get one hundred pounds of roots.

Mammals in Eighteenth-Century Pennsylvania

Pennsylvania mammals were instantly of interest to immigrants and pioneers of the eighteenth century because some—rabbit, hare, squirrel, bear, elk, deer (now the state mammal)—represented good food sources to augment inadequate supplies of domesticated meat. Others—especially the wolf and panther—represented sources of danger to man and his livestock. Mammals as sources of fur and skin included rabbit, beaver, gray and red foxes, bear, marten, fisher, mink, otter, elk, and deer. Many mammals provided both meat and skins or furs, and they were valued accordingly. But curious eighteenth-century Pennsylvanians were far more intrigued by the dramatic or bizarre aspects of abundant, unfamiliar mammals without common counterparts in England and Europe; the opossum, raccoon, porcupine, skunk, beaver, groundhog, and flying squirrel.

Opossum family

The surrealistic landscape of Australia—populated by kangaroos, koalas, and platypuses—was yet undiscovered, so early observers were fascinated by the opossum, our Pennsylvania marsupial, and the mysteries of its reproduction. The opossum's pouch was recognized as one of the most captivating curiosities of the animal kingdom, and his death-feigning antics deemed equally marvelous. The raccoon, with masked face, wonderful tail, and curious feeding habits, likewise fascinated Pennsylvanians who, early on, learned to value his rather coarse yet attractive fur, which gave the frontiersman his highly prized coonskin cap. Another curiosity was the porcupine, but despite the number of valuable hounds incapacitated by a face full of quills, this quiet animal was not closely observed.

Beaver

Porcupine

Everyone who wrote about him in early days insisted that he could throw his quills, often for stated long distances—a misconception which still persists. Misconceptions also existed about the skunk, and Chateaubriand claimed that this little animal's pungent liquid scent was the "prime remedy for headache." Lewis Evans thought the skunk "might be esteemed by those who have no smelling as a very beautiful animal." The intricate social life and the hydraulic engineering of the amphibious beaver were reported with admiration, but only by observers who had the dedication and patience to watch this shy beast with utmost finesse. Less observable were the groundhogs: "As I have never seen them," wrote Evans, "I cannot describe them." As agriculture converted much of Pennsylvania into cultivated fields, however, this portly cousin of the squirrel became more common and, out in the open, more conspicuous. Flying squirrels, shy, exquisite forest creatures which, said Evans, "wafted themselves from tree to tree," were adversely affected by the same agricultural progress so beneficial to groundhogs.

Dangerous Animals: Wolves and Panthers. So prevalent were wolves in colonial Pennsylvania that William Penn declared a bounty on them. Penn favored conservation of fur-bearers as well as trees, but in 1699 wolves were "howling at the gates of Philadelphia" and something had to be done. As large game animals—deer and elk—became scarce during the 1700s, wolves turned to domestic animals for subsistence, and during the Revolutionary War, while the men were away, they decimated the livestock. They were often blamed for the work of two-legged cattle thieves as well, and ill-will toward wolves ran high. For over a hundred and fifty years bounties were paid on wolves in Pennsylvania until they were completely exterminated. Though once an established element in predator-prey relationships, the wolf proved incompatible with the settlers' ways.

Wolf

Panther, or mountain lion

The panther, or mountain lion, was also in colonial days a formidable reality, even close to Philadelphia. John Bartram, writing to Peter Collinson in 1738, observed, "they have not yet siezed any of our people, but many have been sadly frightened with them. They have pursued many men both on horseback and on foot. Many have shot them down, and others have escaped by running away. But I believe, as a panther does not much fear a single man, so he hath no great desire to sieze him, for, if he had, running from him would be but a poor means to escape from such a nimble, strong creature, which will leap above twenty feet at a leap." The panther suffered a sequence of misfortune similar to that of the wolf. His natural food, young deer and elk, dwindling from overhunting by white and red man alike, he turned to domestic cattle in order to live; but owners of the cattle, fanatical over their property rights, had a price put on his head and he was wiped out as a resident of Pennsylvania by bounty hunters.

Wild Animal Food Sources. Settlers in colonial Pennsylvania were rather taken aback to discover the Indians using almost any available mammal for food, except, probably, bats and mice. Opossum, porcupine, raccoon, groundhog, beaver, muskrat, wildcat—all were recognized as food. The Indians tended to use natural resources in proportion to availability, and to kill nothing not actually needed. Animal populations therefore remained quite sizable and stable, setting the stage for the slaughter that was to come. "The Great Circular Hunt" of 1760, allegedly held in central Pennsylvania, appears so frequently in serious natural history literature that it remains an interesting picture, though it seems a fictitious synthesis of several such events. As the story goes, 200 hunters formed a 30-mile diameter circle which they proceeded to close by converging on Pomfret Castle, an old fort that still exists in Snyder County. Although many animals escaped, when the ring was closed the following were said to have been killed: 41 panthers, 109 wolves, 112 foxes, 114 mountain cats, 17 black bears, 1 white bear, 2 elk, 198 deer, 111 buffaloes, 3 fishers, 1 otter, 12 gluttons, 3 beavers, and 500 "smaller animals." The choicest hides were taken, together with the buffalo tongues, and a heap of carcasses as high as the tallest trees was burned. The mound of bones, it was said, could be seen there for many years. The Indians were so disgusted by this wasteful, indiscriminate, bloodthirsty slaughter that they soon after murdered the organizer-leader of the hunt.

Groundhog

Rabbit, hare, squirrel, bear, elk, and deer were the game animals routinely hunted by Pennsylvania pioneers. By 1750 numbers were drastically reduced, while the colonial population and demand for meat had greatly increased. Elk had inhabited the whole state, almost to the outskirts of Philadelphia, in William Penn's time, but overkilling during the next sixty years reduced this stately animal to a remnant of the original population that had been so judiciously conserved by the Indians. Deer and bear suffered the same fate, and when John Bartram traveled from Philadelphia to Pittsburgh (a frontier fort just taken from the French) in 1761, he had to report to Collinson that on the whole trip he saw no large animals except two or three deer and a tame bear—not a single wolf or fox. Kalm quoted Bartram as stating that bears kill cows by biting a hole in their skin and blowing them up. Like his friend Franklin, Bartram sometimes engaged in leg-pulling to test the credulity of listeners. Schoepf, traveling in western Pennsylvania, was impressed by the excessive abundance of squirrels—219 killed by three lads in three days—and the presence of squirrel on the tavern table at every meal. He inferred that these great numbers of squirrels were migrating westward to escape a food shortage. Schoepf goes on to comment on the increasing scarcity of game. He refers familiarly to the buffalo as if it was certainly encountered in western Pennsylvania, but not in the large numbers suggested by the apocryphal tale of "The Great Circular Hunt" of 1760, or as anything more than stragglers from the great herds, passing through Pennsylvania in their wander-

White-tail deer

Elk

Squirrel

Otter

Black bear

Raccoon

ings. Fabulous tales of huge buffalo herds in other parts of Pennsylvania are almost certainly just that: fables. Habitat requirements of the buffalo were for territory quite different from anything commonly found in Pennsylvania and although his incidental presence in Pennsylvania can scarcely be dismissed, all literature accounts referring to large herds or established residency east of the westernmost parts of the state have been copied and recopied and might be traced back to fictitious hunters' tales.

Fur Animals. Colonial Pennsylvania possessed a staggering array of fur-bearing mammals; the major ones were beaver, gray and red foxes, black bear, raccoon, marten, fisher, mink, and otter. Deer and elk provided skins, in heavy demand for the practical clothing of frontiersmen and Indians alike. Indians had little fondness for furs as articles of luxurious attire, so these were a by-product of meat-getting. To kill an animal just for his fur was contrary to Indian religion, which saw all animals as sharers with the Indian of a common heritage of nature. Nevertheless, the white man induced the Indians to kill fur-bearers far beyond their own needs, to exchange for firewater, steel axes, iron pots, and cheap cloth, and rapid decimation of mammal populations followed. Beaver, in heavy demand for raw material to feed the early eighteenth-century beaver hat craze, was one of the first to be extirpated, and fur trapping drastically reduced the numbers of marten, fisher, and otter. Beaver and otter populations have since experienced great ups and downs, and still make Pennsylvania their home, but the marten and fisher are no longer found in the state, having gone the way of the wolf, panther, lynx, and elk.

Raccoon and foxes managed to survive. Gray foxes were widespread in Pennsylvania when the first Europeans arrived, but red foxes appeared only later, when settlement of the state had progressed considerably. Because they looked like the familiar red fox of Europe, they were originally thought to have somehow immigrated or been introduced. Recent scientific investigations, however, have shown that the red fox of Pennsylvania is distinct from that of Europe, having moved in from the north as man-made changes made Pennsylvania more to his liking.

Early literature, from William Penn's time, refers to whales, porpoises, and seals in the Delaware River at Philadelphia. Beginning in Penn's time, stocks of almost all game and fur animals went downhill, so that in 1890 observers found "game in Pennsylvania was practically gone—deer almost extinct." Rapacious lumbering had reduced the state to a shambles, irrational bounties and uncontrolled hunting and trapping had wiped out the animals, and conservation was a controversial, untested idea. Invoked, it brought regrowth of the forests, rebuilding of some animal stocks, and everywhere unbalanced regeneration of some of what had been lost. Many decimated species have been restored, but new relationships thus created are unstable, and the future is obscure and perilous.

Birds in Colonial Pennsylvania

Except in extreme cases where attention was directed to an animal because it was strange, dangerous, or hard to understand, eighteenth-century Pennsylvania commentators usually responded to animals in proportion to their practical significance. Among birds, those most frequently mentioned in early journals and travel accounts were species of high value for food: ducks, geese, quail, grouse (now the official state bird), heath hen, turkey, and passenger pigeon. Ducks, geese, quail (then called "partridge"), and ruffed grouse (usually called "pheasant"—long before the ring-neck pheasant was imported as a game bird) were terribly reduced by overhunting, but they managed to escape statewide extermination.

The wild turkey, abundant enough so that the "Flying Hills" near Reading were named for the large numbers of turkeys that flew down from them, was hunted to extermination in Pennsylvania, probably more than once. Only the turkey's ability to recolonize lost territory fully accounts for his widespread presence in Pennsylvania today. The native turkey, frequently seen near Philadelphia in 1748, was, Kalm said, almost a dooryard bird, interbreeding with domestic turkeys (turkeys originally domesticated in Mexico, then introduced to the Old World, acquiring further breeding and refinement there, and finally returned by later colonists, quite different from their native counterparts).

The heath hen (or heath cock) was a different matter. Not widespread, even in early colonial times, the eastern population of the prairie chicken was later confined to a few northeastern counties, where it was heavily hunted for market and soon wiped out. Surviving longer in New England, another subspecies, the true heath hen, was totally extinct by about 1930.

The passenger pigeon, certainly once one of Pennsylvania's most conspicuous birds, was a wonderful example of a species inherently destined for extinction. How there ever came to be so many, no one knows. The estimate of 17 million bushels of mast per day as food for one flock of maybe 2 billion birds may be exaggerated, but the food volume would still run into the millions. Mast is notoriously unreliable; some years there is practically none over large areas, when late frosts keep oak and beech from bearing fruit. A combination of large areas of oak-beech-chestnut cut down for clearing and for timber, plus a few bad "mast years," plus inordinately heavy market hunting was, given the gregariousness of the birds, a sure formula for extinction. The prodigal market hunting alone could never have wiped out these countless billions of birds; they were slaughtered in such incredible numbers only because there were so many of them. Colonial Pennsylvania skies were sometimes darkened by flights of pigeons, though their chief territory was farther west.

Also extinct now is the Carolina paroquet. Although William

Bald eagle

Killdeer

Flicker

Cardinal

Turkey

Osprey

Canada goose

Pileated woodpecker

Quail (bobwhite)

Robin

Mockingbird

Belted kingfisher

Wood thrush

Woodduck

Ruffed grouse

Bartram, writing before 1790, did not cite it as a Pennsylvania bird, B.S. Barton, in 1799, did, and he got most of his information from Bartram. That this, the only native parrot of the eastern United States, once occurred in Pennsylvania is pretty certain, especially since there are records from farther north as well. These gregarious, gaudy yellow, green, and red parrots were conspicuous, and not readily confused with any other bird. Portraits of Indian princesses often show them with the paroquet perched on their shoulder.

William Bartram incorporated in his *Travels* (1791) an extensive list of Pennsylvania birds, some 175 in number, including many of the birds familiar to Pennsylvanians today: bald eagle, great horned owl, screech owl, whippoorwill, ruby-throated hummingbird, pileated woodpecker, kingbird, barn swallow, purple martin, raven, crow, mockingbird, robin, and cardinal to name a few.

The ruby-throated hummingbird was, by all odds, the bird that excited the most admiration and wonder on the part of eighteenth-century Pennsylvania observers. Crèvecoeur was captivated by them: "nature has lavished her most splendid colors; the most perfect azure, the most beautiful gold, the most dazzling red . . . on this insect bird." Kalm describes the nest in detail, and also rhapsodizes on this jewel of bird life, which he calls "the most admirable of all the rare birds of North America," adding that the Swedes near Philadelphia call it the King's Bird. The genuine kingbird, a flycatcher, also comes in for its share of attention, and Crèvecoeur marvels at its fierceness and audacity toward hawks and crows, and its ravenous appetite for honeybees. He shot one that had been raiding his apiary, and upon opening its stomach found that 41 of

Pintail

Nighthawk

Broad-winged hawk

Eastern kingbird

Purple martin

Ruby-throated hummingbird

Sparrow hawk

Woodcock

Mallard

Great horned owl

the 171 bees it contained revived and flew back to the hive. Kalm found the purple martin equally audacious in repelling hawks and crows, and B.S. Barton, with William Bartram's concurrence, asserts that they are migratory birds, in contradiction of the then strongly held belief of numerous naturalists that they hibernate, buried in the mud. It has been reported that this bird, now always associated with dwellings man-made for his special use—from gourds to elaborate apartment houses on poles—was loved and honored by the Indians, who were the first to provide housing accommodations for him.

The mockingbird was a delight to eighteenth-century observers. Crèvecoeur rhapsodically describes the song and behavior of this talented vocalist, and Kalm, having encountered a caged mockingbird, relates the process of domesticating them, and goes on to state that "several people are . . . of the opinion that they are the best singing birds in the world." Alexander Wilson (1766–1813), finding mockingbirds peddled by a street vendor in Philadelphia ("good singers, $50–100; average, $7–15"), was inspired to write the famous mockingbird essay in his *American Ornithology*. The robin also pleased early Pennsylvanians with its friendliness and melodic song. The "red thrushes" praised by Crèvecoeur were none other than our easy-going robin. Equally popular was the cardinal. Under the name of "Baltimore Bird" he is said to have been the favorite pet of colonial bird fanciers—trapped and sent to market in hampers. Kalm relates dismal tales of trapping and sending them in cages to England where, like mockingbirds so treated, they either sang or died.

Fanciful European impression
of American rattlesnake

Black snake

Reptiles, Amphibians, Fishes, and Invertebrates

Snakes. No other member of the flora and fauna of eighteenth-century Pennsylvania had quite as much impact on the mind, imagination, and emotions of travelers and settlers as did the rattlesnake. Men were beguiled by the reputed curative powers of sassafras, the opossum's pouch, and the ferocity of the panther; they were lost in admiration of lady's-slipper orchids and gemlike hummingbirds. But when all these marvels had lost their novelty, their power to grip the thoughts and feelings of the beholder—when medicinal plants appealed to misplaced confidence no longer and the panther's threat was rationally overcome—then *his* power stood undiminished and unchallenged: the rattlesnake still remains the symbol and the reality of the ultimate powers of nature.

More of our eighteenth-century Pennsylvania travelers and observers had something vivid to record about the rattlesnake than about any other animal. John Bartram, in journals of all of his trips, seldom failed to mention seeing a rattlesnake. He sent a communication to the *Philosophical Transactions* of the Royal Society (1742) on rattlesnake teeth, and published in *Gentleman's Magazine* (1765) a discussion of the rattlesnake's "power of fascination." B.S. Barton published an extensive scholarly examination of this question (Do rattlesnakes hypnotize, or paralyze, intended victims just by staring at them? Barton decided that they do not.) and later a carefully organized discussion of treatments for snakebite. Carver, Chateaubriand, Crèvecoeur, Kalm, and Schoepf all published detailed observations on the rattlesnake, ranging from Chateaubriand's amusing fabrication about the forest being filled with the rattling lovesong of male rattlesnakes wooing their females (to which he added the well-worn yarn about baby snakes taking refuge in their mother's mouth), to Crèvecoeur's vivid description of a fierce battle between a rattlesnake and a blacksnake that reads like an actual observation, not fiction. But his credibility might be questioned when he claimed that the copperhead served as a pilot for the rattlesnake, or told of a pet rattlesnake, or offered a tall story about a rattlesnake fang, imbedded in a boot, that kept on killing victims for a long time. Kalm and Schoepf discussed bird-eating by rattlesnakes and blacksnakes and make the sober assertion that a dog bitten by a rattlesnake consequently develops a large worm in its liver. Lewis Evans declared mistakenly that the Pennsylvania blacksnake digests its food almost instantly. (He was accurate, however, in observing that rattlesnakes become scarcer going northward from Pennsylvania.) Schoepf gave an enormous list of reputed snakebite remedies, most of which he dismissed as worthless while retaining others that are equally irrational, and he soberly recorded an eighteen-foot rattlesnake in western Pennsylvania. Opportunity to tell snake stories made liars out of observers otherwise quite respectable.

Turtles. So great was Peter Collinson's passion for turtles that John Bartram was constantly trying to cope with the problem of getting them to him alive and healthy. After receiving a large, live snapping turtle, Collinson wrote, "Don't send any more. One is enough." Schoepf, an authority on turtles who published a major scholarly work on the subject, described the soft-shell and snapping turtles with care, and commented on their use as food.

Amphibians. Frogs, turtles, and rattlesnakes were eaten by the Indians, and Kalm guardedly referred to the legs of bullfrogs as good food. Numerous accounts by colonial travelers are embellished by fictitious tales of enormous frogs.

Fishes. William Penn, writing in 1685, reported sturgeon in the Delaware River and a shad fishery at the Schuylkill River, where 600 large shad were taken in one haul of the net. Lewis Evans, in 1753, stated that there were scarcely any trout in Pennsylvania, except in remote streams, and that salmon and trout were everywhere scarce when he traveled to Onondago with John Bartram in 1743. He did record sturgeon in Pennsylvania rivers, and such useful fish as perch, chub, sunfish, suckers, and catfish, "taken with the angle." John Bartram, with whom Evans traveled, described trout-spearing by Indians in central Pennsylvania. Schoepf observed that

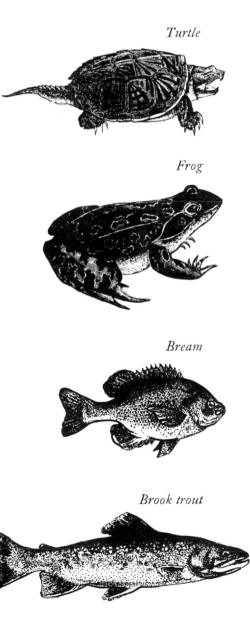

Turtle

Frog

Bream

Brook trout

Mussel

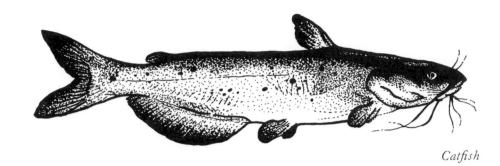

Catfish

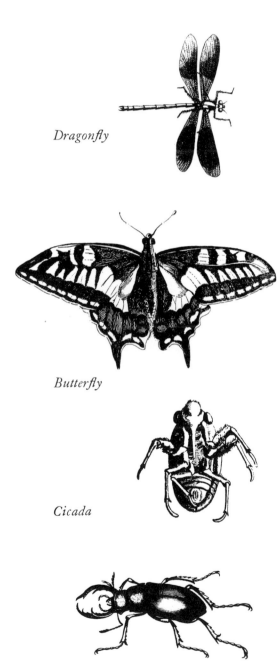

Dragonfly

Butterfly

Cicada

Stag beetle.

the fish fauna of western Pennsylvania is different from that to the east, and so it is. He wryly exposed fish stories claiming weights of eighty to a hundred pounds for catfish that weigh only thirty to fifty pounds.

Shellfish. In 1745 John Bartram published an account of fresh-water mussels, but he thought some species to be vegetable-like. Kalm reported eating the "finest oysters" near Philadelphia, an indulgence probably learned from the Indians. Schoepf was interested in the pearl mussels in the Lehigh River, containing "pretty large and clear pearls," and he told an amusing tale of muskrats eating these mussels and spitting out the pearls, which could be found in the sand at their feasting place.

Insects and Other Arthropods. More than in any other part of the flora and fauna of eighteenth-century Pennsylvania, observations of insects in 1776 were confined to practical matters. If there were collectors of butterflies or beetles, they lay low, for it was not until after 1800 that a relevant publication appeared: Melsheimer's pioneer beetle catalogue of 1806. Before 1800 there was some interest in insect pests, but it appears that crops of the early inhabitants had few pests. Foreign pests had not yet been introduced in any quantity, and few native insects changed over to cultivated crops from their native hosts. During the Revolution and shortly after, five new insect pests appeared: the Gage bug (named for a hated British general), the Hessian fly (similarly named), coddling moth, angoumois grain moth, and chinch bug.

In 1753 Lewis Evans, in describing Pennsylvania, briefly cited mosquitoes and midges, bugs (bedbugs) he believed were from the East Indies, ticks from Spanish cattle (not from Dutch or English cattle), and honeybees (from Europe); and he described the seventeen-year cicada in detail. Cicadas, eaten as a delicacy by the Indians, were of great interest to early Pennsylvanians because of their dramatic massive outbreaks and strange appearance. The firefly, now Pennsylvania's official state insect, charmed the colonists. Kalm recorded their appearance in Pennsylvania on April 26—a remarkably early date for these insects, even at low elevations in southern Pennsylvania. Other insects native to Pennsylvania also

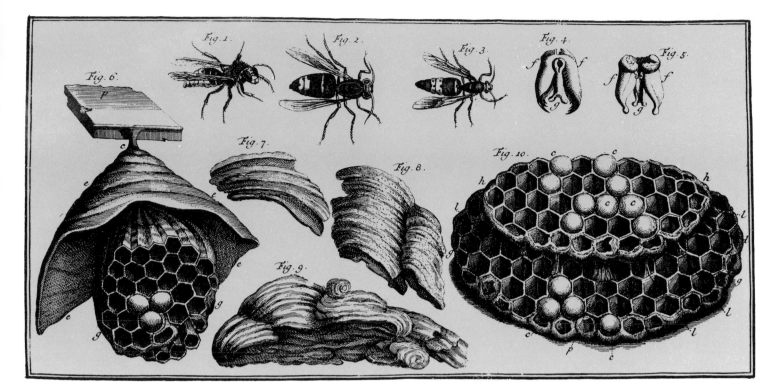

interested both colonists and Europeans. John Bartram published five papers in England, through Collinson's efforts, accurately treating dragonflies, mayflies, and wasps while Crèvecoeur wrote inaccurate rhapsodies on fireflies and mayflies.

Honeybees. Honeybees were brought by some of the earliest colonists and soon went wild and became established near the settlements. Indians called the bees the "white man's fly," asserting that they appeared in advance of settlement. Both white men and Indians began to use the wild honey as soon as the first wild colonies were found. Hollow buttonwood trees were favorite locations. Crèvecoeur gives a thoroughly practical description of how to locate a bee tree. One of B.S. Barton's contributions is a thorough investigation concluding that the honeybee is not native to North America. William Bartram kept bees and was once badly stung. Alexander Wilson commiserated: "had they known you, my dear friend, as well as I do, they would have distilled their honey into your lips, instead of poison."

Wasp nest

Flea

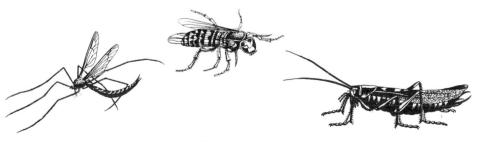

Crane fly   *Hornet*   *Grasshopper*

Beehive

Buffalo in Pennsylvania

Buffalo in Pennsylvania? That seems unlikely to most people. After all, buffalo, like Indians, were creatures of the western frontier. But in 1776 Pennsylvania was still part of that frontier.

The romantic link between the American Indian and the buffalo preserves, like many myths, more than a little truth. It is not possible to fix precisely the time that either entered this continent, but all evidence indicates that both came during the geological epoch known as the Pleistocene, or ice age. This lasted from about three million to ten thousand years ago. Within this timespan there were alternating climatic phases. During colder periods enormous amounts of water which evaporated from the oceans fell as snow. Sea levels dropped as glacial ice sheets expanded from mountain tops and the poles. In the north the shallow Bering Sea became a land bridge, which ancestors of the Indians crossed sometime within the last forty thousand years. Like other Americans they had evolved in the Old World, acquiring there all important details of their present appearance before spreading through North and South America.

Buffalo arrived here somewhat earlier. The term buffalo is incorrectly applied to these massive herd-living horned animals of North America; really they are bison. *But as the confusion of names suggests, bison are closely related to the true buffaloes of southern Asia and Africa, as well as to the domestic cattle descended from them. Bison continued to evolve as they spread across this continent from Atlantic to Pacific and from Florida to Canada. In the plains region they reached gigantic size, some having a horn spread of about ten feet. But in Pennsylvania bison were smaller, probably very similar to the woodland bison that still survive in Canada, and not too different from the European wisent that live in isolated forest areas of eastern Europe.*

Evidence for the presence of bison in Pennsylvania a century ago is provided chiefly by historical data. Historian Gail Gibson has noted several references to buffalo in Pennsylvania during the eighteenth century. Arriving at "Lick Creek" (now Lick Run, southeast of Uniontown), an officer in Braddock's army recorded in his diary in 1755 what he had been told was the meaning of the name: "This Creek takes its Name from a lick being there, where Deer, Buffaloes & Bears come to lick the Salt out of the

Swamp." A British army engineer seems to verify this explanation in his journal. Describing his experiences in this same area, he notes that game "is exceeding Plenty of all Kinds hereabouts, consisting of Buffaloes, Elchs, Deer—Bear, and innumerable Quantity of wild Turkeys—of which last, we were so satiated that the Hunters would kill no more." A third reference to buffalo in the same general area is made in a letter from Fort Cumberland, alleging that a group of men attacked some Indians who "were barbecuing a Buffaloe, not thinking of danger." In addition to such references, place names provide circumstantial evidence for the existence of buffalo in Pennsylvania. When these occur sporadically they prove little about the distribution of the creatures to which they refer. For example, Wayne County has a town called Angels although no documented sightings of celestial beings. But there are many buffalo place names on present maps, and even more spread through older maps, journals, and histories. Howells' A Map of the State of Pennsylvania *(1792) includes Buffalo Creeks in what are now Washington, Armstrong, and Perry counties; Buffalo Runs in Bedford and Centre counties; Buffalo Lick Creek in Somerset County; and Buffalo Hill in Perry County.*

Those who question the assumption that buffalo once roamed Pennsylvania point out that there is no documented evidence that skeletal remains of the animal have ever been identified in the state. However, this is not really surprising. Bison would never have been as numerous in woodland areas as on the open plains. And the bones of animals that die in a forest do not usually last very long. Rats, squirrels, and porcupines gnaw bones for the mineral salts they contain. The more abundant moisture and acid soils typical of forests hasten the decomposition of what fragments the rodents leave. And of the few bones that might survive these ravages, most would be similar enough to comparable parts of large oxen to pass unnoticed.

Pennsylvania's bison are gone now. Like the Indians some died quietly, others were killed, and the rest moved west with the advancing frontier.

The Indians

"I am very sensible of the unkindness and injustice that hath been too much exercised toward you by the people of these parts of the world, who have sought themselves and to make great advantage by you rather than be examples of Justice and goodness unto you, which I hear hath been a matter of trouble to you and caused great grudgings and animosities, sometimes to the shedding of blood. . . . But I am not such a man." That was William Penn's promise to the Indians when he wrote to them from England in 1682. His desire to "settle a free, just and industrious Coloney" extended to a concern for peaceable relations with the Indians. He sent word to the Delawares from England that "the King of the country where I live hath given unto me a great province in "your parts of the world," and that he hoped "to enjoy it with your love and consent, that we may always live together as neighbors and friends." The Indians responded with warmth to Penn, or "Onas" as they called him: "We will live in love with Onas and his children as long as the creeks and rivers run and while the sun, moon, and stars endure." Benjamin West's painting of Penn's treaty with the Indians under the elm tree at Shackamaxon symbolized the best hopes and intentions of both peoples.

Hopes and intentions, however, could not stand up against the natural distrust and conflicting interests between the settlers and the Indians. Their ranks decimated by warfare among themselves and with the white man, the Indians sold their land piece by piece, or were displaced from it, and gradually moved west. The 1790 census showed only 1,300 Indians left in Pennsylvania.

Archeological evidence and early historical records indicate that the territory now occupied by the Commonwealth of Pennsylvania had been the home of numerous successive tribes for thousands of years. Little is known of the Monongahela Indians, who disappeared quite early. Their fate probably was like that of the Erie Indians in the northwest, who were driven out or absorbed by an alliance of Delawares and Iroquois. The Delawares (the name given by the English to the Lenni Lenape Indians) occupied the Delaware River valley east of the Allegheny Mountains. The Iroquois Indians were

Susquehannock Indian burial in Washington Boro, Lancaster County

a confederation of five culturally and linguistically related tribes—Mohawks, Oneidas, Onondagas, Cayugas, and Senecas—who had settled from the Mohawk Valley west to Lake Erie. These tribes had banded together in a powerful league with a mission pursued with the zeal of crusaders: to unite all Indians in a harmonious confederacy. Hence the Iroquois nations went to war with neighboring tribes in an attempt to convert them. Holding sway along the shores of the Chesapeake Bay and in the Susquehanna River valley were the Susquehannocks (or Conestogas), enemies of the Iroquois nation, but by 1700—ravaged by disease and war with the Iroquois—they had dispersed. In the early 1700s the Tuscaroras, migrating north from the Carolinas up the Susquehanna valley, became the sixth Iroquois nation.

Mico chlucco
King of the Muscogulgee or Cricks
call'd the Long Warior

Although the Iroquois brought other displaced tribes into the area—the Conoys and Nanticokes from the Chesapeake Bay and the Eastern Shore, the Siouan-speaking Tutelos from Virginia and North Carolina, the Algonquian Shawnees from the Carolinas—the attrition of various wars, particularly the French and Indian War, greatly reduced the Indians' strength. By 1774 the Shawnees and Delawares had been displaced to Ohio, while the other tribes not absorbed by the Iroquois had already been dispersed or destroyed by marauding whites. In the western part of Pennsylvania, only the Seneca and a few Delaware Indians remained. The Revolutionary War then played a major part in breaking up the League of the Iroquois.

The Indians of Pennsylvania in 1776 were no stone age savages. A people of considerable political sophistication, they were primarily farmers. In fact, according to the reports of white observers, they were extremely skillful and inventive, and had introduced the Europeans to the cultivation of corn, beans, potatoes, squash, tomatoes, and tobacco. The Indian chiefs governed by consensus, the whole tribe meeting in council. As William Penn remarked, "how powerful the Kings are, yet how they move by the breath of their people." It is said that Thomas Jefferson studied the political organization of the eastern Indians when considering the design of the Constitution of the United States.

Establishing a complex system of allegiances and alliances, the Iroquois and Delaware peoples resorted to force as a last resort when political persuasion failed, and frequently acted with great political subtlety. In the Wyoming Valley in 1748, for instance, recognizing how important it was for his people to hold the land against possible incursions of whites from the north, Teedyuscung of the Delawares obtained guarantees of protection from the Six Nations and occupied the valley with a skeleton force of fewer than seventy Indian settlers. At the same time, he secured the support of Pennsylvanians who feared that the valley would be settled by New Englanders. Talleyrand could hardly have been more adroit.

The Indian Fort SASQUESAHANOK

An inaccurate and highly romanticized view of an Indian village (with palm trees!), but it does suggest that the Indians often lived in substantial dwellings.

Life among the Delaware Indians

Like the white man, the Delawares (or Lenni Lenape) had only one god: the Great Spirit who created all things. To him all Indians prayed, though they knew no rigid orthodoxy and each individual's faith was, in its details, a personal matter. To these native Americans of eastern Pennsylvania all things in nature—the rocks, the stones, the trees—had souls and were worthy of reverence. The most important religious holiday of the year was the Big House Ceremony, in which the great bear (seen in the night sky as Ursa Major, or the Big Dipper) was overtaken in a cosmic hunt and killed. Winter would then come on, but spring would not be far behind.

The men could hunt for game when the grass shot up. The hunters often traveled in groups, surrounding their quarry as it lay in the meadows. Braves set the grass on fire in a circle around the entrapped game, the flames were driven inward, and the men followed the march of the fire, howling and shrieking. When the smoking circle had tightened, the meat-giving animals were killed: rabbit, buffalo, and deer. The women planted corn, beans, and pumpkin squash in plowed fields and picked apples and

berries from the wild. All knew how to catch fish, usually in baskets. Forest trees were made to yield sugar and syrup, a delicacy which delighted the first French explorers. In jars which they molded and baked themselves, or whittled from the bark of hardwoods, Indian women had mastered a variety of cooking skills: they roasted meat on spits, knew how to boil anything, could even charcoal-broil. Corn—known to the white settlers as Indian corn, or maize—was their basic food. To avoid the monotony of only one cereal, they learned to prepare it in a dozen ways—with chopped meat, with fish, with chopped nuts, with maple sugar, boiled, roasted, ground.

Corn, however, rapidly depletes the soil, a sad fact for the Indians in Pennsylvania. Instead of rotating crops, they changed the locations of their villages every few years. This was no simple matter, for they did not live in portable tepees. The Delawares, like the Iroquois, lived in log "long houses," semi-permanent structures which might shelter several families, partitioned off from each other. In the long house the wife tended her children (who were literally hers, should the family divide), made household uten-

72

Scene of Indian life from an early map

Pipe and pipe bowl

sils, prepared the game which the man had killed, and made the family's clothing. She was, in the cold terms of the blood money by which she could be precisely valued, worth twice as much as a man.

In the fall the earth no longer yielded corn, and the game was harder to follow in the snow. To thank the Great Spirit for the fruitful season past, and to beg his mercy during the winter to come, the tribe went again to the Big House. Oriented from east to west, it symbolized the world: its floor was the earth; its ceiling was the sky; the great pole in its center was the world tree, the earth's connection with the creator above. Up there, beyond the sky, if the Delaware had shown himself worthy, he would one day go—to a land without pain, abounding with deer and buffalo, brightened with a light clearer than that of the sun itself.

Pots

Axe head   *Arrowheads*

Relations between the whites of North America and the natives were not peaceable in the years preceding the Revolution. The same Teedyuscung who had worked so hard to secure a homeland for his fellow Delawares was burned to death in his cabin fifteen years later, in a fire of mysterious origin. Within a month of his death families from Connecticut began to establish themselves in the Wyoming Valley. But their settlements were short-lived. In the fall of the next year (1763) a son of Teedyuscung, Captain Bull, led a Delaware war party in a sweep through the Wyoming country that left no white survivors. A number of captives were tortured; about a score were left alive to serve as Delaware slaves. But, in a pattern which would be repeated a century later on the western plains, avenging frontiersmen behaved with as little restraint. Benjamin Franklin once lamented that the "frontier people are yet greater Barbarians than the Indians" because the settlers' murderous treatment of the red men continued through times of peace.

There were many stories of Indian atrocities, both real and imagined. This is a frontispiece from Affecting History of the Dreadful Distresses of Frederic Manheim's Family . . ., *1794*

The Indians Choose Sides

When the colonists formally declared war against England, both sides at first urged the Indians to remain neutral, but this attitude quickly changed. The British were particularly effective in recruiting the Indians to their side, as several agents from Detroit traveled among the natives' villages fomenting hostility against the Americans. The colonists tried to buy Indian support by promises—needless to say, never fulfilled—of a fourteenth, an Indian state. But any chance the Continental Congress may have had of securing Indian neutrality was severely compromised by the February 1778 "Squaw Campaign." American militia, frustrated and angry over the failure of their mission to sack the British base at Cuyahoga, released their fury on several friendly Delaware encampments in what is now western Pennsylvania and eastern Ohio. Several women, a boy, and—much more important politically—the mother of Delaware Chief Captain Pipe were casualties. This senseless act eventually lost Delaware support to the new nation. The Iroquois resisted commitment for two years; when they did choose sides, each of the Six Nations had to choose for itself. Most chose the British.

The Continental Congress lacked an Indian agent of the caliber of Conrad Weiser, who had been largely responsible for keeping the Iroquois Confederation on the side of the British colonies during the French and Indian War. Born in the Mohawk country of the province of New York, Weiser lived with the Mohawks—learning their language and ways—after his father moved to the Tulpehocken valley near Reading. Weiser also won the confidence of the Mohawks and, through them, of all the Iroquois. After rejoining his father, Conrad Weiser became the official Indian agent and interpreter for the province of Pennsylvania. In addition to negotiating treaties with the Iroquois at Lancaster and Easton, Weiser persuaded some of the tribes outside the Iroquois Confederation to renounce violence against the settlers in return for fair payment in land transactions. After failing to win all the Indians to the British side, Weiser raised a battalion for defense against the Indian allies of the French, and was commissioned a colonel in the Pennsylvania militia. He also was an active Lutheran layman and spent several months as a participant-observer in the Ephrata Cloister.

The Indians generally fought bravely and well during the American Revolution, whatever their allegiance. A company of Oneidas, posted as the rear guard of Lafayette's army as it crossed the Schuylkill to observe Philadelphia, fought valiantly and effectively to hold off the attacking British while the colonists made good their escape. The Indians on the British side raided frontier settlements at will through the summer of 1778, satisfying British expectations by drawing the colonists' attention away from the main theaters of operation in the east. One series of raids destroyed farms of Penns, Bald Eagle, and Kishacoquillas valleys; another struck the West

Carved figure

Turtle carving

In 1735, Gustavus Hesselius was commissioned by the Penn family to paint portraits of the Indian chiefs of the Lenni Lenape (Delaware) tribe during negotiations for Indian land in the path of colonial expansion. Agreeing to sell all the land that could be circumscribed by a day's walk, the Indians then watched their adversaries hire trained runners who sped through secretly beaten trails in order to double the area the Indians thought they had agreed to give up. In his portrait of Lapowinsa, one of the two chiefs who participated in the so-called Walking Purchase, Hesselius captured the troubled and puzzled dignity of a doomed race. The sober and realistic portrayals of Hesselius' Indians are an early artistic reflection of the scientific realism which characterized the intellectual life of Pennsylvania in the eighteenth century.

Branch of the Susquehanna, from Muncy and Williamsport to Northumberland. In the latter raids, the Delaware Chief, Bald Eagle, killed young James Brady, brother of Ranger Captain Samuel Brady, an event which led Captain Brady to vow he would spend the remainder of his life destroying Indians. The raids along the West Branch and the Juniata sent settlers flying east in "the Great Runaway," reminiscent of the months after Braddock's defeat in 1755. Most of the Delawares had joined in the Tory cause and raided with impunity. In June of 1782 they attacked Upper Sandusky (Ohio), where a portion of revenge was theirs: they captured Colonel William Crawford, who had participated in the "Squaw Campaign," and burned him at the stake. So far as the frontiersmen could see, their new government provided less protection for them than even the despised Quakers had afforded.

The Wyoming Massacre

Frontier warfare came to its bloodiest and most shocking climax at Wyoming (Wilkes-Barre) on July 3, 1778. British Colonel John Butler with some 400 Tory Rangers and about 700 Seneca Indians planned to destroy the Wyoming settlements, against which the

Indians held a particular grudge. The leaders at Wyoming decided to meet Butler's advancing force with about 300 men, mostly too old or young for the regular army. Under the command of Colonel Zebulon Butler (no kin to his British namesake), this small detachment marched out to attack the British, but induced into a fatal trap by the Senecas, who feigned a retreat, the American garrison found itself outflanked. The Indians scalped, tortured, and massacred all the soldiers they could capture; Indian Queen Esther Montour, in a wild war dance, was said to have tomahawked prisoners forced to their knees in a circle around a huge flat rock. The British commander destroyed the Wyoming settlements and ordered the inhabitants to leave, but prevented any Indian assault upon the civilians.

Bad as it was, the "Wyoming Massacre" became more horrible with each retelling, until it became the major atrocity story of the Revolutionary War and served a significant propaganda function at home and abroad. Represented in the American press as the wanton murder and torture of helpless women and children by Indians under the direction of British officers, the affair strengthened the American will to fight and raised a storm in the British Parliament. The Wyoming Massacre completely destroyed the prospects of a British peace mission. Every war seems to acquire some battle-cry, like "Remember the Maine" or "Remember Pearl Harbor," associated with a particularly dramatic atrocity and uniting the injured side in a deep emotional commitment. In the American Revolution the cry was "Remember Wyoming."

The Indians Defeated

The Ohio country had so little protection that when Washington left Valley Forge in the spring of 1778, he sent the Eighth Pennsylvania regiment under Colonel Daniel Brodhead back to Fort Pitt. At Carlisle they were joined by a force under Captain Samuel Brady, who had just learned of his brother's death at the hand of Chief Bald Eagle. Brady conducted many minor forays against the Indians from Fort Pitt, avenging his brother's death by killing Chief Bald Eagle in an ambush near Kittanning, but the Mingoes, Delawares, Senecas, and Wyandots continued to terrorize the western counties. Having persuaded General Washington to authorize a major invasion of the Seneca country southeast of Lake Erie, Brodhead sortied from Fort Pitt in August with 600 troops to harass the western Senecas—in the expedition which burned Chief Cornplanter's town. Proceeding up the Allegheny, Brodhead destroyed Seneca towns and grain fields in what is now Warren County, returning to Fort Pitt by mid-September without losing a man. These raids did not secure any major strategic point, few prisoners

Cornplanter, Indian Statesman

If his name had been more exotic, like Red Cloud or Cochise, or more fierce, like Crazy Horse or Sitting Bull, Cornplanter (born John Abeel) might also be a household name. But Cornplanter was not destined for the fame of those later illustrious warriors of the plains; although he fought effectively in the service of the English during the Revolution, his great contribution to his people was less dramatically on behalf of peace.

His father had been a New York Dutch trader, his mother a Seneca of chiefly lineage. When he was still a boy (he was born some time after 1740) he was sent to see his father, but the Albany Dutchman showed little interest in his son, who returned to his mother to make his own way in the world. Since the Senecas measure lineage through the mother, John would probably have assumed an Indian name in any event, but his father's casual attitude toward him settled the matter. Though not a hereditary chieftain, he became his tribe's leader during the war, and was among the most effective of the Indian allies of the British. A raid by American Colonel Daniel Brodhead from Fort Pitt in the summer of 1779 ravaged much of the Seneca country, and burned Cornplanter's town, Jenuchshadego; but for the most part victory belonged to the western Senecas. They had, for over two years, kept the American garrison penned up in their strongpoint, and had raided what is now western Pennsylvania and eastern Ohio at will. When the war came to an end, and Cornplanter's continually harassed enemies demanded his surrender, the Senecas were astounded.

Cornplanter committed the destiny of his people with that of the new nation, and during the next ten years, when Indian warfare proliferated, the neutrality of his warriors helped the Americans preserve their republic. From warrior-hero he had become statesman-hero, traveling on behalf of the new nation as far west as Detroit. He met frequently with Congress, and had audiences with President Washington. Cornplanter became, in those postwar years, white America's expert on Indian affairs.

*Ki-on-Twog-ky (Cornplanter).
Painting by F. Bartoli, 1796.*

For his role as conciliator Pennsylvania gave his people three tracts of land in the state; the last one to survive, now under the waters of the Kinzua Dam, was on the northern border of the state near New York. Toward the end of his life Cornplanter went back to the ways of his people entirely. He burned the gifts which the famous and powerful whites—including George Washington and Thomas Jefferson—had given him, cast out the Christian preachers who had come to proselytize his people, and took a new, Seneca, name. He died a deeply bitter man; yet in 1866, when a monument honored him, his white American adversaries accurately and sincerely depicted him as "one distinguished for talents, courage, eloquence, sobriety, and love of his tribe and race." Not Sitting Bull, not Red Cloud, not even Crazy Horse deserved it more.

were taken, and the Iroquois were not seriously crippled, but its psychological effects were great: the Americans had shown that the seemingly invincible enemy was in fact vulnerable.

In May 1782, however, a group of frontiersmen made a strategic mistake. To retaliate for some murders in their vicinity by roving Senecas, they seized the Moravian Indians at Gnaddenhutten, Ohio. Though only the flimsiest evidence connected these Christian Indians with any Seneca raids, the frontiersmen marched forty men, twenty women, and thirty-four children into a slaughterhouse, where a work force killed them with mallets and hatchets. This cold-blooded mass murder aroused all the Indians and sparked a general assault on white settlements west of the mountains. The Indians dealt their hardest blow to Hannastown (near Greensburg), which they completely destroyed in July 1782.

In the northeast, after the 1778 Wyoming Massacre, the Indians continued their rampage. Determined to stop their forays, General Washington launched a major expedition into Iroquois country to destroy the heart of the Six Nations. He gave the command of 5,000 troops to General John Sullivan, who mobilized his force at Easton and marched through Wyoming and Tioga into New York. On August 29, 1779, at Newtown, he defeated Colonel John Butler's Rangers and 1,500 Indians and systematically destroyed forty Iroquois towns and all the orchards, fields, and crops around them. Sullivan so denuded the countryside that he could not live by forage when his own supplies failed. His position might have become serious except for Brodhead's march, which distracted the western Senecas at the very moment they might have moved against Sullivan. The ensuing winter of 1779–1780 brought four feet of snow to central Pennsylvania and New York. The Iroquois, deprived of their food stores, starved by the hundreds. The combination of Sullivan's raid and the "winter of deep snow" so weakened the eastern tribes that they never seriously threatened the Pennsylvania frontier again, though sporadic raids continued throughout the war.

The Early Settlers

By the last quarter of the eighteenth century, Pennsylvania had established a reputation throughout the North Atlantic world as an unusual and important place. Although it was a relatively young colony (less than one hundred years had elapsed since Penn had stepped ashore on the banks of the Delaware), it was already second only to Virginia in total population. In 1776, there were perhaps a third of a million persons in the colony, a fact doubly remarkable when one recalls that the scattering of Netherlanders and Swedes before Penn's arrival probably did not number more than a few hundred. The capital city of Philadelphia had close to 40,000 people; in the whole British Empire only London was clearly larger. Pennsylvania of 1776 was no mere huddled mass of displaced Europeans, clinging by their fingernails to a hostile shore; it was a large and firmly established commonwealth of prospering people.

It was not mere size that made Pennsylvania remarkable. Penn's Holy Experiment had been based on one of the most successful jobs of real estate promotion in all of North America, and the advertisements to take up the good land of the Delaware Valley had been widely distributed throughout northwest Europe. Unlike so many American colonies, however, whose glowing advertisements chronically overstated their virtues while naturally understating or ignoring their deficiencies, the promotion of Pennsylvania was based on fact. Penn's colony really was a superior place for pioneer farmers. A fine rolling land with fertile soils, it was immensely preferable to the hardscrabble hills of Massachusetts or the malarial swamplands of the Chesapeake tidewater. The news spread, by letters and by word of mouth, and it was not long before advertising became unnecessary. Migrants wrote glowing reports back to the old country, and the trickle of immigrants became a quickening flood. Quite unlike the earlier colonies, whose very existence remained for some years in doubt, Pennsylvania was almost instantly successful, well-known throughout Western Europe, and widely admired.

Then, too, Penn's approach to the act of colonization had produced a population radically different from those typical of most

A Map for Revolutionaries

Drawn almost at the moment when the opening guns of the Revolution were being fired, the map of Pennsylvania inscribed to the provincial governors was well-known during the war, and was doubtless used by both sides in military campaigns.

The map is interesting not only for the information it displays but also for its cartographic style. With its finely etched detail and its hachured mountain ranges, the map's design stems from a Renaissance tradition of mapmaking that had reached its pinnacle in Holland during the sixteenth and seventeenth centuries. By contrast with those old Dutch maps, however, this eighteenth-century English map is very restrained. It lacks completely the Baroque embellishment of floral embroidery that commonly ornamented the older maps, where hippogriffs, rampant unicorns, bare-bosomed savage maidens, and Aeolian horn-blowers frolicked around the borders and conveniently invaded unexplored regions to cover embarrassing gaps in geographic knowledge. Dutch cartographers would have thought this Pennsylvania map crude, but it probably pleased the Quakers with its straightforward no-nonsense design. It is obviously a map to be used.

Maps like this served to entice explorers and settlers into previously unknown regions, and gross inaccuracies were simply intolerable. As in any map, some inaccuracies were inevitable, for the mapmaker had no easy way to judge the reliability of his sources: travelers' accounts, explorers' rough sketches, and earlier published maps, which often contained substantial errors. But inaccuracies could be deadly, in the literal sense of the word. Many of the sixteenth-century Dutch maps had contained deliberate fantasies, and nobody can count the expeditions that had disappeared in agonies of hunger and thirst, vainly looking for islands and rivers that existed only in the imagination of some cartographic entrepreneur in Amsterdam, who sought to sell his maps more briskly because they contained more "information" than his competitor's down the street.

As one might expect, the best known part of Pennsylvania was the well-settled southeast. Between the Delaware River and the "Blue Mountains" the map is filled with names, mainly of waterways, and shows many towns. These names abruptly become sparser as one's eye moves toward the northwest—beyond Blue Mountain to the interior. Toward the west and

north locations are less certain, outlines more vague and generalized. Big important things are omitted or misshapen or mislocated. The Allegheny Front, for example—the highest and most formidable of all the Appalachian ridges—is shown simply as one of several big ridges, and it appears about forty miles west of where it belongs. Some features (like the large puddle-shaped "Buffalo Swamp" just west of the inscription) must be regarded as sheer invention, or were merely meant to suggest that some of northwestern Pennsylvania is swampy.

But these are minor matters; the important point is how much the mapmaker got right. The river system is quite accurate, and that is not surprising. Those rivers were major routes of travel, and their shapes were well-known. The important distinction between the rolling Piedmont of southeastern Pennsylvania and the formidable linear ridges of the Ridge-and-Valley country of central Pennsylvania is clearly shown. Indeed, in the populated southeast, the map is so accurate that it might serve a traveler today, if only the modern highway network were drawn in.

But there are some major differences, and they help us understand the kind of place Pennsylvania was in the 1770s. In the west, gigantic Cumberland County sprawls willy-nilly across country that was mostly unsurveyed and empty. (It would soon be overrun with people.) Pittsburgh was still tiny "Fort Pitt," little different from "Sewicklys Old Town," a few miles upstream on the "Allegeny." In the east, northern Delaware is shown simply as "Part of New Castle County," one of several eastern Pennsylvania counties. Berks County is enormous in size and peculiar in shape, its parallel boundaries marching inexorably northwestward. (Those lines had been drawn at right-angles from the lower Delaware River, Pennsylvania's main avenue to the outside world. It was the river that was important, not the county boundary lines.) But already the lower southeastern end of Berks is carved into smaller counties—Chester, Bucks, and Philadelphia (then much larger than now)—portending the time when the rest of Berks and other big counties would be chopped into smaller and smaller bits as people moved inland and demanded that the old giant counties be reduced to manageable human size.

Not surprisingly, towns are located correctly, but

1770 map of Pennsylvania based on the map of W. Scull

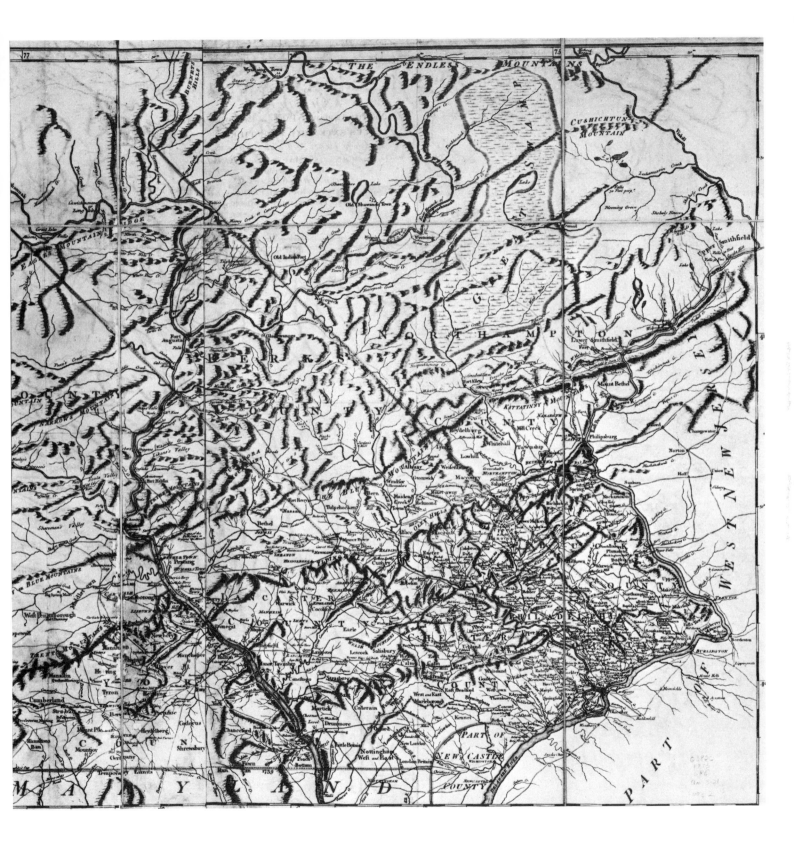

they are so small as to be almost invisible—which they really were in a colony that was almost entirely rural. One must look hard for Lancaster and York, for example, and both cities are best spotted if one looks for the spiderweb of roads, then as now fanning outward from each place. The Great Valley towns of Carlisle, Shippensburg, and "Chambers Town" (Chambersburg) are shown as large as Bethlehem and Reading—which they were, approximately, since none of them amounted to very much in 1776. And Harrisburg, to become the state capital by 1812, is still merely "Harris Ferry," noted in letters so small that they are next to illegible.

What the map omits is just as interesting as what it shows. Whole chunks of northwestern Pennsylvania are blank, or nearly so, depicting only a sketchy outline of the Allegheny River and its tributaries. The inscription itself conveniently blankets a sizable area of ignorance, covering much of what is today Cameron, Elk, and McKean counties. The main omission is in the far north, where the map simply quits, well short of the New York boundary. That land was still unsurveyed, a fact that would help provoke a feud with Connecticut in years to come, when a good deal of American blood would be spilled to decide who held title to that wild country. For this cartographer, however, northeastern Pennsylvania seemed worthless territory—"Great Swamp," "The Endless Mountains," or, more ignominiously, a zone of nameless squiggles, presumably mountains.

For all its deficiencies, however, the map is really an extraordinary achievement, and it tells us two important things about Pennsylvania on the eve of the Revolution. It tells us what Pennsylvanians knew about their own country—and that was a good deal. But it also says something about those Pennsylvanians and what they had done. In less than a century, a handful of northwest Europeans had converted ten thousand square miles, more or less, from wilderness to a settled land, and they had laid out a framework of roads and fields and towns and names that has withstood two centuries of social upheaval.

But, above all, this map is a statement of intention. Those long straight surveyors' lines—the Berks County boundaries; the "Temporary Limits" with Maryland, later to be remembered as the Mason-Dixon Line—are thrust into the vitals of the interior, ignoring barriers, brushing aside whole mountain systems. They seem to say in cartographic shorthand: "This land is ours. Never mind if details in the west and north are fuzzy or incomplete. We'll fill those in, and it won't take us long."

Those early Pennsylvanians were right in their optimistic view. By 1800 a new map would have to be drawn to reflect the explosive growth of towns in the east, mass migration to the west, and a whole mosaic of new counties across the Commonwealth. This map, then, shows the beginnings: the half-finished design for a state of imperial scale and imperial ambitions.

One of the original stones marking the Mason-Dixon Line

English possessions. Massachusetts and Virginia promoters had recruited settlers almost entirely from the British Isles, and overwhelmingly from England. When they talked of creating "*New* England," they used the words in a literal sense: old England renewed and purified in the New World. Penn's Holy Experiment had no such intent. Pennsylvania was to be a place where all men of peace and good will could find haven. Nationality was unimportant, as long as a settler worked hard and behaved himself. And, providing that one was a Protestant and believed in some sort of God, Pennsylvanians were not particular about an immigrant's religion, either.

The mixture of people who became Pennsylvanians made this state a revolutionary place, although in politics the settlers remained fairly moderate. The mixing of peoples made Pennsylvania the least English of all England's colonies and a portent of the America that was to come—not yet a "melting pot," but more accurately "a nation of nations." Tolerance of the kind practiced by Pennsylvania Quakers in 1682 was a rare and precious commodity in late seventeenth- and early eighteenth-century Europe—a Europe still in the final throes of a three-century religious war that had strewn the Continent with corpses and provoked uncounted acts of atrocious cruelty. Small wonder that tolerant Pennsylvania seemed a wonderful place. It was one of the few parts of the entire Western world where citizens could hold unconventional opinions without being terrorized by governors, priests, or soldiers. Small wonder that when the persecuted people of war-wracked western Europe heard of Penn's Holy Experiment, thousands upon thousands of them abandoned their ancient homes and moved to this new hospitable place.

National Origins of Pennsylvanians

From the beginning, then, Pennsylvania had a more international flavor than any of the other of Britain's North American colonies, and this naturally excited a good deal of comment by interested and sometimes astonished visitors. Actually, the internationalism was fairly limited. After all, despite the publicity, most of eighteenth-century Europe had never heard of Pennsylvania. Most European peasants could not afford to pay the passage across the ocean or to buy land; nor was transportation available from most of interior Europe to a seaport where a ship to Philadelphia could be found. And in much of Europe, trans-Atlantic emigration was unthinkable; after all, nobody had done it before! As a result, only a few parts of Europe contributed many migrants to Pennsylvania. Yet estimates of the non-English population of colonial Pennsylvania run as high as fifty-three percent.

The first reliable data on Pennsylvania nationalities come from an estimate in the 1790 Census, based on the surname of the head of the

National origins of white population in early America. Pennsylvania compared with the United States, 1790. Persons of English ancestry formed the overwhelming majority of population in the country at large, but a bare majority in Pennsylvania. There were more Germans and Scotch-Irish in Pennsylvania than in any other colony—and Pennsylvania was seen as the most "foreign" (non-English) of all the thirteen colonies. Although these data come from the 1790 census, they can be applied with reasonable accuracy to 1776 as well; there was relatively little European migration to America during the Revolution, and post-war migration was continually disrupted by European warfare.

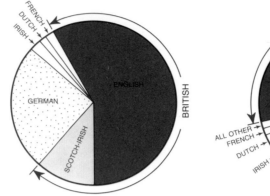

PENNSYLVANIA

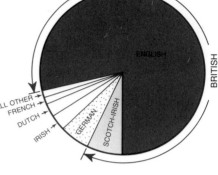

THE UNITED STATES AS A WHOLE
(The Thirteen Original States)

family. According to this count, the majority of Pennsylvania names, about sixty percent, were English. (Of course a large number of non-English colonists had Anglicized their names—Müller becoming Miller, Schmidt becoming Smith, and the like.) Another twelve percent of the names were Scotch; two percent, Irish; and a scattering, Dutch and French. Twenty-six percent of the population was estimated to be German (and Swiss), mostly Protestants from the Rhine Valley, who became the ancestors of today's "Pennsylvania Dutch," more correctly, Pennsylvania *Deutsch*. These Germans considered Pennsylvania an especially blessed place, a new permanent home, not merely a way station en route inland. Thus Pennsylvania became the destination for an overwhelming majority of North America's early German population; of all the Germans who came to the British colonies before 1790, approximately seventy percent of the total ended up in Pennsylvania.

The religious piety of the Pennsylvania *Deutsch* set them apart from other newcomers. A considerable proportion of them were "plain people," among whom the Amish and Mennonites are best known. Whether "plain" or not, they clung to traditional rural ways in steadfast defiance of the more wordly settlers who made up the colony's majority. Moreover, the Germans behaved like most other migrants to foreign lands and settled as close to one another

as they could. Certain parts of the Pennsylvania Piedmont thus became overwhelmingly German: Berks County alone was seventy-five percent German; Northampton, forty-seven percent; York, forty-two percent. In many areas, the concentration of Germans was so great that an English-speaking person needed an interpreter to make himself understood. If Pennsylvania seemed less British and more "foreign" than other colonies, it was the Pennsylvania Germans who gave it this flavor, and their accumulated impact over the years has been far greater than their rather small absolute numbers.

The Scotch names in the 1790 Census were mostly what we call today Scotch-Irish: Protestant Scots who had been moved into Northern Ireland (Ulster) during the British attempt to smash Catholic power in Ireland. Most of those Scots remained in north Ireland, but many had found north Ireland no great improvement over the Scotland they had departed, and when the green pastures of Pennsylvania's Piedmont opened, they left their foggy island in droves. By 1790, Pennsylvania had one-fifth of all the Irish in the United States, and about a quarter of all the Scots.

Since the Germans and Scotch-Irish seemed exotic to other settlers, and because they tended to keep to themselves (the English

Romanticized nineteenth-century illustration, but the foreground is typical of the colonial Pennsylvania frontier.

settlers found them "clannish," and often criticized them for their hostility to outsiders), a considerable mythology has grown up around both groups. According to these stories, the Germans sought out "good limestone land" and settled down to become prosperous farmers, with well-manicured farms and well-scrubbed children. The Scotch-Irish, according to the same story, were a rather rough lot who despised civilization and headed straight for the frontier. Daniel Boone's cry for more "elbow-room" is a classic tale of the Scotch-Irishman who began to feel himself crowded when he could see the smoke from his neighbor's chimney.

Today, we have learned to be properly skeptical of such ethnic generalizations, but there is at least a germ of truth in some of them. Many Germans did settle on fertile limestone lands north and west of Philadelphia, and many Scotch-Irish did settle farther inland. But the legends obscure several important facts about the population of Pennsylvania in 1776. First, most Germans got good land largely because they got there first, not because they had a special nose for limestone, and the Scotch-Irish leapfrogged over them simply because the best land was taken. Then too, many Germans *were* clannish, and the Scotch-Irish were not keen on settling in territory where they had to learn to speak Deutsch. On the other hand, many Scotch-Irish did not go to the frontier but settled down happily next door to Germans, and promptly began to intermarry with them. And there were famous German frontiersmen, like Conrad Weiser, "Pennsylvania's ambassador to the Indians."

There were other minorities, to be sure: a few Welsh, a few French Huguenots, a scattering of Swedes and Dutch from pre-English settlement, a few Jews, a handful of Negroes. These other minorities received a good deal of attention at the time, as well as in latter-day history books, partly because the Penns publicized the ethnic variety as a badge of their own tolerance and partly because some of the minorities were conspicuous.

The Afro-American population is an obvious example. Blacks were very noticeable in a nearly all-white population, but they numbered less than ten thousand in all of Pennsylvania, not even three percent of the colony's people, a very small number compared to the total of about twenty percent in the thirteen colonies as a whole. Most of colonial Pennsylvania's black people lived in cities and towns, and, by 1776, Philadelphia had already become a haven for freed slaves.

Other minorities, like the Welsh in the so-called Welsh Tract around Lansdale northwest of Philadelphia, advertised their presence with place-names like Bryn Mawr and Radnor. But mythology tends to exaggerate the number of these Welsh, just as romantic tales of rugged Scotch-Irish frontiersmen tend to make us forget that Germans settled on the frontier also, and that those of English ancestry probably outnumbered all the rest.

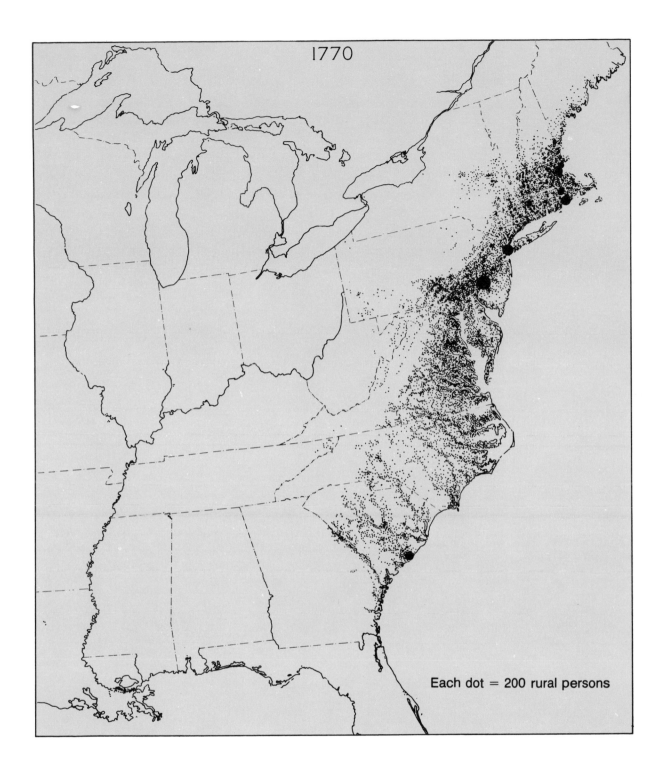

1770

Each dot = 200 rural persons

Distribution of the American population on the eve of the Revolution. Although most of the good land east of the mountains had been settled, people had begun to spill through the mountains only in two places: via the Mohawk Valley of upstate New York, and across central Pennsylvania, where people had already begun to move down the Shenandoah Valley into western Virginia and westward toward the upper Ohio at Pittsburgh.

Port of Philadelphia, the major passageway for immigrants to the New World

Advance of the European frontier in Pennsylvania, 1690–1780. Pre-Revolutionary migrants into Pennsylvania entered the colony almost exclusively through Philadelphia. Note the slow rate of spread for the first fifty years after Penn landed, but by 1740 nearly all the land had been settled between the Delaware River and Blue Mountain—which briefly marked a sharp western boundary of settlement. The explosive growth of population into the mountains and upper Ohio Valley, which began just before the Revolution, continued during and after the war.

Rolling Back the Frontier

By 1776, Pennsylvania's population was growing rapidly, and between 1700 and 1800 it roughly doubled every twenty-five years. (If it had continued at that rate, Pennsylvania would now contain about 75 million people, instead of its present 12 million!) As the numbers increased, of course, the population was spreading over new territory, so that a map of Pennsylvania's 1776 population must be regarded as a single frame from a motion-picture film—useful to illustrate a fast-changing process, but incomprehensible unless one knows what came before and what happened afterward.

The rapid growth of Pennsylvania's population was not unique in British North America; the numbers were increasing rapidly almost everywhere in the colonies. But the geographic distribution of population in Pennsylvania differed from other areas in several major respects.

First, most of the immigrants were arriving in one place, through the port of Philadelphia. Penn's capital was the colony's only significant seaport, and by far its largest city; it dominated Pennsylvania both economically and psychologically. By contrast, the coastlines of New England and the South were dotted with coastal settlements, some big and important like Boston, some no larger than a plantation landing on the shore of the Chesapeake Bay. But Pennsylvania was uniquely oriented toward the *land*, and once the immigrants had gotten ashore, they wasted no time in moving inland. A series of population maps placed atop one another reveals that the population spread northwest into the interior like the blot from a spilled inkbottle spreading over a flat tablecloth. The growth at first was slow, simply because the absolute number of original settlers was small. In all, it took half a century to push the frontier fifty miles outside the city limits of Philadelphia, a rate of about one mile per year. By approximately 1730, however, the population had begun to explode, and by 1740, most of the Piedmont had been occupied. By 1776, Pennsylvanians were striking out in new directions and at an astonishing rate.

In effect, then, the 1776 map of settled land in Pennsylvania is deceptive, for it is like taking a picture of a bottle of ink in the process of being spilled. In 1750, settlement was still confined mainly to the Piedmont. Twenty years later, Pennsylvanians had occupied most of the valleys in the central ridge-and-valley country and had converted the upper Ohio Valley around Pittsburgh from howling wilderness into settled land. In sum, Pennsylvania in 1776 was in the early stages of a population explosion which, before the century was out, would spread the new American conquests from the Atlantic to the shores of the Great Lakes.

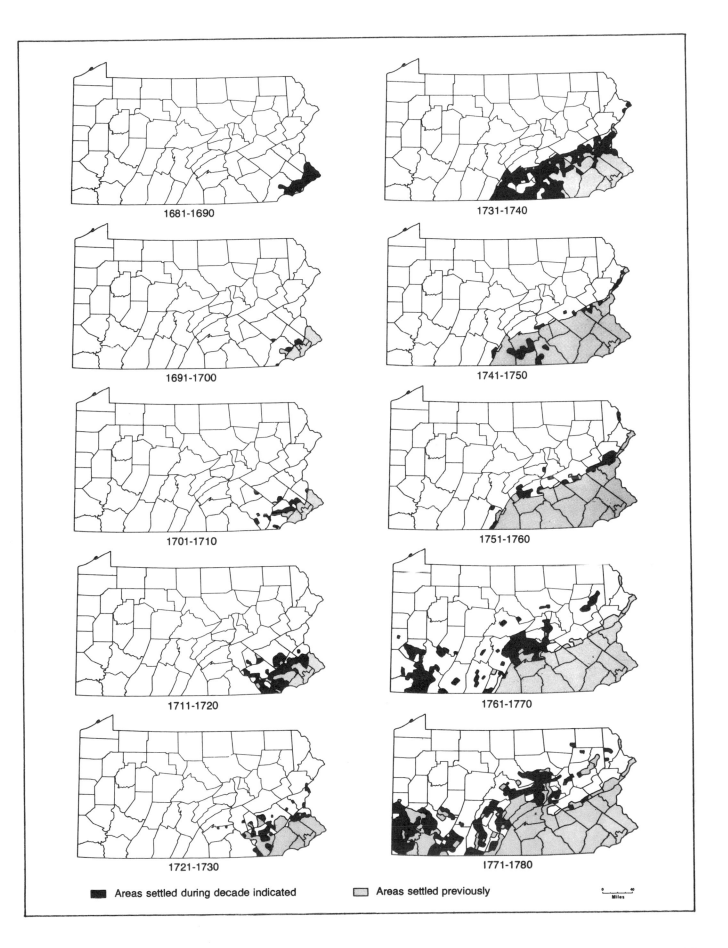

1681-1690

1691-1700

1701-1710

1711-1720

1721-1730

1731-1740

1741-1750

1751-1760

1761-1770

1771-1780

■ Areas settled during decade indicated   ▢ Areas settled previously

0   40
Miles

The "Fair Play" Settlers of the West Branch Valley

Between 1769 and 1784 more than a hundred families settled in an area some twenty-five miles long and about two miles wide located on the north side of the West Branch of the Susquehanna River, extending from the mouth of Lycoming Creek (now the location of Williamsport) to the Great Island (just east of the present site of Lock Haven). They established a community and a political organization called the Fair Play system. The political system of these predominantly Scotch-Irish squatters demonstrates vividly the impact of the frontier on the development of democratic institutions. Occupying lands beyond the reach of the provincial legislature, and comprising some forty families of mixed national origin by 1773, these frontier "outlaws" had to devise a solution to the question of authority in their territory. Their solution was the creation of a de facto rule which a contemporary legal scholar described in these words: ". . . in violation of all law, a set of hardy adventurers had from time to time seated themselves on this doubtful territory. They made improvements, and formed a very considerable population. It is true, so far as regarded the rights of real property, they were not under the protection of the laws of the country; and were we to adopt the visionary theories of some philosophers, who have drawn their arguments from a supposed state of nature, we might be led to believe that the state of these people would have been a state of continual warfare; and that in contests for property the weakest must give way to the strongest. To prevent the consequences, real or supposed, of this state of things, they formed a mutual compact among themselves. They annually elected a tribunal, in rotation, of three of their settlers, whom they called fair-play-men, who were to decide all controversies, and settle disputed boundaries. From their decision there was no appeal. There could be no resistance. The decree was enforced by the whole body, who started up in/mass, at the mandate of the court, and execution and conviction was as sudden and irresistible as the judgment. Every newcomer was obliged to apply to this powerful tribunal, and upon his solemn engagement to submit in all respects to the law of the land, he was permitted to take possession of some vacant spot. Their decrees were, however, just; and when their settlements were recognized by law, and fair play had ceased, their deci-

sions were received in evidence, and confirmed by judgments of courts."

These hardy frontiersmen were aware of the debates over independence in Philadelphia. Undoubtedly the noblest political action of the Fair Play settlers was their own declaration of independence on July 4, 1776, which was made under the great "Tiadaghton Elm" on the west bank of Pine Creek. In her widow's pension application, Anna Jackson Hamilton said, many years after the event, "I remember well the day independence was declared on the plains of Pine Creek, seeing such numbers flocking there, and Independence being all the talk, I had a knolege of what was doing." Unfortunately, no record of the resolutions has been preserved—if they were actually written down.

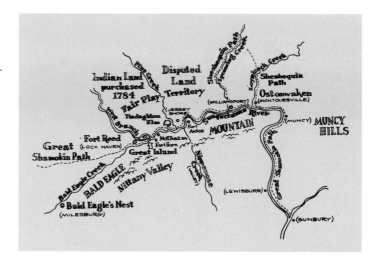

Fair Play territory

Roads, Villages, and Towns

This expansion would not have been possible without a good system of roads. Since Pennsylvania's Piedmont rivers—the Susquehanna, the Schuylkill, the Lehigh, the upper Delaware—were uniformly difficult to navigate, Pennsylvanians quickly realized that good roads were not a luxury but essential if farmers were to maintain connection with the outside world. Early American farmers certainly wanted to be independent, but very few of them wanted to be isolated. Most wanted to buy manufactured goods from Philadelphia or abroad, and since they needed money to make such purchases, they had to sell surplus commodities: grain, cattle, or their own handmade goods.

The road system, designed to serve a growing population, quickly became as much a cause of population distribution as it was an effect, dictating the location of hamlets, villages, towns, and eventually cities. There were very few intersections without a tavern of some kind, and major intersections promptly became places for considerable trade and social intercourse. Most of those towns in 1776 were tiny by present-day standards: Lancaster had fewer than four thousand people; Reading and York boasted populations of two to three thousand; Bethlehem, Lebanon, and Harrisburg each had less than one thousand inhabitants; Chambersburg, Carlisle, Wilkes-Barre, Allentown, Easton, Gettysburg, Huntingdon, Shippensburg, Bedford, Uniontown, and Brownsville were rural villages. Pittsburgh was a frontier settlement where three hundred or so persons made their homes around the fort in the now famous Golden Triangle.

Nevertheless, these road-based villages had already become the cores of towns which, in combination, would eventually make Pennsylvania one of the most urbanized states in America. The settlers were moving inland, and Lancaster would soon become the first big American town whose location was not dependent on navigable water. It may not be an exaggeration to suggest that America's passionate romance with roads and highways did not begin in Detroit, but was in fact born on the Pennsylvania Piedmont in the six decades before the Revolution.

Home of the Indian agent Conrad Weiser, one of the planners of the village of Reading

The Unsettled Areas

At the same time, some areas of Pennsylvania which later would become important centers of population were still almost empty in 1776. In the northeast, the Scranton-Hazleton-Allentown area was largely unsettled, even by farmers; it was not until the opening of the great anthracite fields between Scranton and Shamokin in the mid-nineteenth century that the population approached its present density. In the west, farmers had just begun to take up land in the upper Ohio Valley along the boundary with upland Virginia (now

Reading, a Revolutionary Crossroads

Reading, Pennsylvania, was founded by William Penn's son Thomas in 1748. The site of the original village was at a ford on the Schuylkill River where a number of Indian trails converged and near where the Tulpehocken Creek flows into the Schuylkill. Tradition has it that Daniel Boone, who was born in the area, shot panthers in the nearby valleys. The village was named for Reading, the seat of Berkshire, England. It was laid out in gridiron fashion, with streets named after English royalty and Penn family friends and relatives. Four years after its founding, Reading became the seat of the new county of Berks. Before 1752 all lands east of the Schuylkill were administered from Philadelphia and those west of the river from Lancaster.

Although its settlers included, in addition to the English, Swedes, Welsh, French Huguenots, Scotch-Irish, Jews, and a few Negro slaves, Reading was one of the most thoroughly German towns in the New World. By the Revolutionary period probably nine-tenths of her nearly two thousand people were German. The German farmers and artisans had a reputation for superior craftsmanship, hard work, and orderliness. The town was known for hatmaking, weaving, cooperage, and brickmaking. During the French and Indian War, Reading furnished General Braddock with wagons.

Reading's central square was dominated by the courthouse, which held the "Liberty Bell" of Berks County, rung on July 8, 1776, to call the citizens together for the reading of the Declaration of Independence. The main streets were lined with the houses of prominent residents, shops, and taverns (thirty-one were listed in 1762). By 1764 the town had a library, and in 1773 the Rainbow Company of volunteer firemen was formed. The Lutheran, German Reformed, and Friends' were the most prominent churches. The Schuylkill was navigable for flat-bottomed boats and was used for carrying grain, whiskey, and other provisions from Reading to Philadelphia. Commerce was carried on through barter, or with English currency, Spanish and French coin, and Pennsylvania currency, which usually circulated at half its face value.

No person is more closely identified with the early history of Reading than the famous Indian agent Conrad Weiser of nearby Womelsdorf. One of the planners of the village of Reading, Weiser frequently represented the town's interests in Philadelphia and with the proprietary family. Edward Shippen, brother-in-law of Benedict Arnold, served in Reading as prosecutor for the Crown. The district's representative in the Pennsylvania Assembly was Edward Biddle, who was that body's last speaker. Biddle was a delegate to the First and Second Continental Congresses, although inexplicably he did not sign the Declaration of Independence.

The people of Reading threw their support to the rebel cause in 1774, when a town meeting adopted a resolution of support for Boston in the wake of the Tea Party and British reprisals. In January 1775, before the hostilities at Lexington, a Reading committee of defense was established to supervise the raising of militia and the gathering of munitions. In July, a company of Reading riflemen joined General Washington near Boston and saw action the following month. Another Berks County company participated in Arnold's ill-fated Canadian campaign. In all, more than nine thousand men from Reading and Berks County served in Revolutionary forces. During the war several Reading churches were used for military hospitals. British and Hessian prisoners were interned in the town. For a short time Continental currency was printed there. Dr. Bodo Otto, chief surgeon of Washington's Valley Forge encampment, is buried at Reading's Holy Trinity Lutheran Church. On September 21, 1777, Reading entertained the fugitive Continental Congress on its way to York.

Model of market shed in Penn Square, Reading

West Virginia), but the dense network of cities now found in the Monongahela and Allegheny valleys would be the creation of heavy industry, based on bituminous coal mining—and that too was almost a century away. In the northwest, the Lake Erie shoreline was still inhabited only by a thin scattering of Indians. And the whole of northern Pennsylvania (the "northern tier" along the New York state line) was still empty, awaiting the tide of Yankees who would flood westward into that territory through the Mohawk Valley as part of the great surge of migrants from New England after the building of the Erie Canal.

Migration to the West

Nevertheless, portentous things had begun to happen. Although the state was only half-settled in 1776, and although people were still coming in by the thousands, Pennsylvania, even before the Revolution, had begun to serve as an exporter of people. Most of this population movement involved people who had begun to fan out westward to take up land beyond the mountains. The British government had tried to stop that migration, lest the Indians become inflamed against European incursions, but the flood was not to be

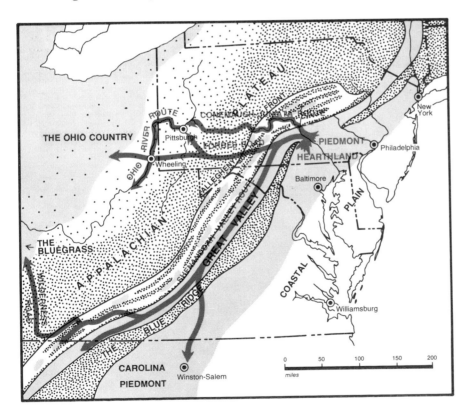

The main routes out of Pennsylvania, 1776. Even though Pennsylvania was only about half settled by 1776, it had already begun to export population westward and southwestward. By the beginning of the nineteenth century, Pennsylvanians would have spread themselves in a great fan-shaped swath across the interior of the United States from the southern Appalachians to the lower Great Lakes. The total area of Pennsylvania influence in the American interior far exceeded that of any other eastern state.

The great productive lowlands

Mountain barriers

Main migration routes outward from Pennsylvania

Old Lancaster Town

Lancaster County was carved from Chester County in 1729, and the following year James Hamilton, later governor of Pennsylvania, laid out the plan for a town on the bank of Conestoga Creek. Here George Gibson operated the Hickory Tree tavern, at the place then called Hickorytown from the large tree which had formed the center of an earlier Indian settlement. James Wright named the new settlement of fifteen people after his English home. Incorporated as a borough in 1742, Lancaster soon became the largest inland town of the American colonies. The new county seat became the marketplace for what was to become the richest agricultural county of the new nation. From its location due west of Philadelphia, it also became the first American city to bear the title "Gateway to the West."

By 1733 the Old Conestoga Road had been completed, linking Lancaster with Philadelphia. Pennsylvania German wheelwrights and blacksmiths began to build the huge Conestoga wagons at this time, until, by 1750, 7,000 were in use, drawn by the rugged local breed of Conestoga horses.

As the commercial and political center of a rapidly growing community of Scotch-Irish and German farmers, many of the latter being "Plain folk," Lancaster soon acquired skilled craftsmen and a coterie of distinguished citizens. The town itself reflected memories of old England—a center square from which radiated King and Queen streets, with nearby thoroughfares called Prince and Duke. Along these streets lived such colonial worthies as the fur-trader Joseph Simon; Justice Jasper Yeates; botanist Gotthilf Henry Ernst Muhlenberg; Timothy Matlack, who penned the official draft of the Declaration of Independence; General and later Governor Thomas Mifflin; Dr. Thomas Bond, co-founder with Benjamin Franklin of The Pennsylvania Hospital; and ironmasters Peter Grubb and Henry William Stiegel.

The town hosted the conference between the Iroquois Confederacy and the provinces of Maryland, Virginia, and Pennsylvania, culminating in the "Grand Treaty" of Lancaster in 1744. In 1763 it was the unhappy site of the massacre of Conestoga Indians, who were in the Lancaster jail for protection, by the irate Paxton Boys. Many of the famed Pennsylvania rifles (later called Kentucky rifles because frontiersmen carried them there) were made by Lancaster gunsmiths, especially William Henry. Henry was a resourceful craftsman who successfully propelled a boat by steam power on the Conestoga in the 1760s, but left to Robert Fulton the task of perfecting this invention. The young painter Benjamin West lived in Henry's house during his Lancaster stay, as did Thomas Paine, who wrote part of "The Crisis" under Henry's roof while the British occupied Philadelphia. Lancaster became the federal capital briefly in September 1777, as the fleeing Continental Congress met there on its way to York. The town provided one of the major military prisons for captured English and Hessian troops during the war. The courthouse in Lancaster's Center Square welcomed many of the most distinguished Revolutionary figures—among them George Washington, John Hancock, George Ross, the Marquis de Lafayette, Baron Steuben, and Benjamin Franklin.

Courthouse

stopped. Even before the Declaration of Independence was signed, these emigrant Pennsylvanians had begun to drift out of the settled southeastern part of the province to seek pastures elsewhere. (If these pastures were less green, at least they were less densely settled.) In the western Piedmont, migrants had run up against the Blue Mountains, the first of the Appalachian ridges, and had been deflected southwestward down the Cumberland-Shenandoah Valley. Some of these displaced Pennsylvanians moved out onto the Piedmont of North Carolina, while others settled in the mountains of eastern Tennessee. The Tennessee group formed a Yankee stronghold which, during the Civil War, would earn the wrath of Jefferson Davis, who called the southern Appalachians "the rotten heart of the Confederacy." Some of these migrants followed Boone's Wilderness Road through the Cumberland Gap and ended in the Kentucky Bluegrass, where Pennsylvania long rifles and Pennsylvania whiskey became the "Kentucky rifles" and "Kentucky bourbon" of contemporary folklore. But the most important stream of emigrants, both in numbers and in long-run national influence, followed two overland roads to the upper Ohio Valley. One was Forbes Road, which led west via Bedford to the Forks of the Ohio. (It became the approximate route of U.S. 30, the Lincoln Highway, and is roughly parallel to the Pennsylvania Turnpike.) An easier, though more circuitous route followed the Juniata River to its headwaters near Altoona, climbed the Allegheny Front, and descended through the Conemaugh and Allegheny rivers, ending in Pittsburgh. (This Juniata route would eventually become the route of the Pennsylvania Canal, the Pennsylvania Railroad, and U.S. 22. Until the building of interstate highways, it was the most important trans-Appalachian route in Pennsylvania.)

The latter routes both terminated at or near Pittsburgh and helped turn Braddock's Fort at the Forks of the Ohio into one of America's great urban centers. But the growth of Pittsburgh, like the migration of Pennsylvanians to Tennessee, obscures a larger point. Both the Shenandoah Valley and the Ohio River served as ways out of the colonial eighteenth-century East into the independent nineteenth-century West, shortly to become the heartland of the United States. Standing at the apex of a widening band of diverging routes, Pennsylvania, initially confined to a narrower portion of Atlantic seacoast than any of the other original colonies, eventually spread its migratory influence over a larger interior territory than any other eastern state.

The year 1776, then, is really an anniversary of not one but two events. It marks a war of independence, fought to break the political hold of England over thirteen impatient Atlantic colonies, and it marks also the time when Americans had begun to turn their faces west across the Appalachians toward the continental interior. It is small wonder that these imperial-minded Pennsylvanians were im-

Nineteenth-century engraving of Washington at Fort Duquesne

Fort Pitt, Western Bastion of the New Nation

The shot that was heard "round the world" is reputed to have been fired at Lexington in 1775, but many believe that the musket was primed in 1753 when the Marquis Duquesne, Governor of New France, ordered a string of forts to be built along the Ohio River and its tributaries to solidify France's claim to the upper Ohio Valley. After the forts had been constructed at Presque Isle (Erie), Le Boeuf (Waterford), and Venango (French Creek) on the Allegheny, Governor Robert Dinwiddie of Virginia was ordered to warn the French to withdraw from "the limits of his Majestie's Dominions." George Washington, aged twenty-one, was sent by the governor to deliver the English ultimatum.

Arriving at the Forks of the Ohio, Washington recorded in his journal that the site was "extremely well situated for a fort, as it has the absolute Command of both Rivers." The French thought so too, and both sides then made a rush to build the fort at the strategic Forks—a contest culminating in the skirmish that launched the "Great War for Empire," or the French and Indian War.

On February 17, 1754, William Trent, acting on Dinwiddie's orders, began to construct the fort which he dubbed Prince Henry George (Second), but a large French force drove the British from the place, finished building the fort, and named it after the Marquis Duquesne. Fort Duquesne served as a base for French trade in the Ohio Valley and as a base for Indian raids against English settlements in Pennsylvania, Virginia, Maryland, and the Carolinas.

The French abandoned and burned the fort on November 24, 1756, rather than fight a superior force led by General John Forbes, Colonel Henry Bouquet, and Colonel George Washington. Forbes began to rebuild the fort, renaming it after William Pitt, head of the English Ministry. Colonel Bouquet became commander of Fort Pitt in October 1760 and supervised its completion in the winter of 1761. The fort covered eighteen acres and was in the form of an irregular pentagon, surrounded by a moat. Fort Pitt was one of the few frontier forts not destroyed by Indian forces. When the Revolutionary War started, the Continental Congress used it as a barrier between the British at Detroit and the colonial settlements to the east.

After the surrender of Lord Cornwallis, Fort Pitt was relinquished by the central government and turned over to Pennsylvania. It fell into ruins and, with renewed Indian hostilities, a new fort, called Fort Fayette, was built a short distance away and then also abandoned. By the beginning of the nineteenth century, Fort Pitt was in ruins; its moat had become a ditch and its rampart a crumbling wall. The passing years turned the land at the Forks of the Ohio into a maze of railroad tracks, ugly warehouses, and dilapidated dwellings. Buried in this quagmire was the old blockhouse. In 1945, however, the outlines of the original fort's redoubts were surveyed, and Point State Park was planned. Today the park is complete, with the Fort Pitt Museum, Blockhouse, and Fountain as ever-present reminders of the nation's "gateway to the west."

Washington's map

Model of Fort Duquesne

patient of British imperial control. It is no coincidence that Americans fought their war for independence exactly at the same time that settlers were pouring west to transform the geography of Pennsylvania—and the history of a whole continent.

Fort Pitt blockhouse

Earning a Living

Shopkeeper

The first drudgery of settling new colonies, which confines the attention of people to mere necessaries, is now pretty well over; and there are many in every province in circumstances which set them at ease." So Benjamin Franklin assessed the changing conditions in the colonies in the 1740s. By the early 1770s, the standard of living in Pennsylvania, as in most of the other colonies, was high. Gauged in terms of the quantity and variety of goods available for consumption—food, shelter, clothing, household possessions—the standard of living enjoyed by the average colonist compared favorably with that of most West European countries from which immigration to America was occurring, and by 1776 probably even ranked very close to that of Great Britain.

Population and Prosperity

A major reason for the colonists' rising prosperity was the growth of the population, which rose in the colonies from 250,000 in 1700 to 2.1 million in 1770. Pennsylvania over the same period rose from 18,000 to 240,000, which made it the second most populated colony after Virginia. The natural rate of population growth (birth rates minus death rates) alone approached thirty percent per decade. This high rate of natural increase appears to have been possible in part because cultivation of newly settled lands gave rise to a prosperous and healthy population, so that high birth rates were not checked by high rates of infant mortality, and in part because additional children were welcomed in an economy where families depended largely upon their own members for the labor to cultivate their farms.

Cabinetmaker

A Varied Economy

With the good fortune of its geography, its climate, and the political and legal basis on which it was settled and land was distributed,

Pennsylvania had become by 1776 one of the most economically diversified of the colonies. Unlike New England, the Pennsylvania economy was devoted primarily to agricultural rather than maritime activities such as shipbuilding and shipping, although in Philadelphia these too became an important part of the economy. In its focus on agriculture, Pennsylvania resembled the southern colonies, but unlike them its chief agricultural products were grains and livestock, not tobacco, rice, and indigo. Moreover, Pennsylvania's agriculture was based on the family farm, comprised of a farmer, his family, and the labor of a small number of indentured servants, whereas in the southern colonies agriculture was to a large extent carried out on plantations, which initially made use of indentured servants but increasingly during the eighteenth century came to rely on slave labor.

Pennsylvania also was the center for much of the commercial and manufacturing activity of the colonies. Philadelphia was the largest city in the colonies, well ahead of its closest rivals, New York, Boston, Charles Town, and Newport, and in the entire British empire, only London was significantly larger, only London and Liverpool were busier ports. No wonder then that Pennsylvania's manufacturing sector was among the largest and most diverse in all the colonies. Over sixty different types of goods were produced in Philadelphia immediately before the Revolution. The rich agricultural hinterland

High Street Market, Philadelphia

Colonial Money, A Chronic Problem

Colonial America faced two chronic money problems. One was maintaining an adequate supply of money to finance a growing economy. The other was developing a uniform currency for trade among the colonies. Specie—gold and silver—was the accepted monetary standard, but not much of either was discovered in the original colonies. The colonies did gain specie through their favorable trade balances with the West Indies and other countries, but most soon was exported to pay for the usually more expensive goods that the colonies purchased from England. The colonies' position worsened when the British prohibited coin from being exported to the colonies and refused to permit the colonies to mint foreign bullion into coin.

Short of coin, the early colonies often substituted "commodity money." Specified products were made acceptable means of payment to the government for taxes and other public debts, and by the government for its purchases. When a commodity could be used to pay taxes, individuals accepted it in payment for private transactions. At various times between 1683 and 1700 Pennsylvania laws gave the status of money to hemp, flax, wheat, rye, oats, barley, Indian corn, tobacco, beef, pork, and hides. Colonial laws usually specified values for designated commodities—for instance, a barrel of pork as the equivalent of 50 shillings. The system had several weaknesses. The commodities were often perishable; maintaining stable ratios among them was difficult; often the worst quality of a crop was used as money; trade among the colonies was handicapped because, from one province to another, different crops might serve as monies or have different values.

The colonies next resorted to forms of paper money, including personal promissory notes, tobacco-warehouse receipts, and bills of exchange. The two major sources of paper money, however, were the "currency finance" policies of colonial assemblies and the land banks. When they needed money, particularly as the result of a war, colonial assemblies issued official promissory notes as currency. They promised to redeem these notes through subsequent taxation, payable in the paper currency. Land banks represented an effort to "melt down" real property into credit. The paper money issued by these banks comprised certificates of indebtedness backed by land holdings. It was accepted for public purposes and occasionally also for private transactions. As

the landholders repaid their "loans," the currency was withdrawn from circulation. Land banks were set up with initial maximum limits, but new ones could always be created.

Pennsylvania's experience with paper money was among the most successful of all the colonies. Indeed, Pennsylvania merchants were among the most vocal opponents of British policies which sought to restrict the use of paper currency.

Paper currency

This worked (embroidered) purse, forerunner of the wallet, was made for sea captain John Vicary. Folded size is 7½ by 4½ inches.

Port of Philadelphia

provided the basis for a thriving processing industry, which converted the raw materials (wheat, livestock) received from the farms into flour, dressed meat, and leather goods for export. Widely available timber and mineral resources in the region provided the basis for a variety of industries, including shipbuilding, wagonmaking, furniture-making, and the manufacture of agricultural implements and household wares.

Merchants

Tanner

Pennsylvania Agriculture

"Her husbandry (though not perfect) is much better and her crops proportionately greater" than those of the other colonies—this was George Washington's assessment of Pennsylvania agriculture in the eighteenth century. The earliest farmers in Pennsylvania were the Indians, who cultivated corn (maize) and grew crops of beans and melons to supplement their primary sources of food: fish, game, wild fruits, and nuts. Thereafter, farming had some place in the lives of each of the major immigrant groups, at least in the early period of their settlement. The Dutch, for example, who were primarily fur traders, developed in 1659 a farming community near Stroudsburg. They later moved south into Bucks County, where they began to specialize in dairy farming. Immigrants from Sweden settled in the Chester area in the 1640s, where they sought to produce a variety of grains and livestock, as well as tobacco, grapes, and silk. By the end of the seventeenth century, they had developed a prosperous, agriculturally based community. The English, who settled in largest numbers in Philadelphia, Bucks, and Chester counties, also had success as farmers, although by the late eighteenth century much of their economic activity had shifted toward trade and commerce. The Scotch-Irish farmers were limited by the land they had settled, for they bypassed the best farmlands, which the Germans had settled, and migrated instead into the Cumberland Valley region, and from there northward into central Pennsylvania (or southward into other colonies). They have been accused of not paying enough attention to the conservation of soil, apparently preferring to move on to new lands (and regions) rather than maintain the soil's fertility on the lands they originally settled.

The Pennsylvania German Farmers

Washington singled out the Germans as superior farmers; he was particularly impressed by the appearance of farms in Lancaster and York counties. The Pennsylvania Germans made up more than a quarter of the population of the colony in 1775, and most of them were farmers. Their tendency to settle together for religious reasons reinforced their inclinations of stability, sobriety, and devotion to work as a necessary part of man's lot. Because they regarded their farms as legacies to be passed on from generation to generation, they were more likely to work for the improvement of their holdings and to employ a husbandry of conservation than were those farmers who regarded their land merely as a steppingstone to greener pastures.

With their peasant background in Germany, they were experienced at cultivating small holdings which would yield a livelihood only through intensive farming and careful management. Prepared to work hard for a bare subsistence and to limit their needs to the

Rye grass beehive, or kip

few essentials that their simple tastes required, most Pennsylvania Germans preferred to do the work that some others relegated to slaves. In 1790, in the German county of Berks, there was only one slave for every 465 whites, while in Cumberland County, originally settled by Scotch-Irish, the ratio was one slave to every forty-four whites. Although the Germans employed indentured servants extensively, most of their work was done by their large families. Children went to work in the fields at an early age, and wives and daughters worked side by side with husbands and fathers. Certainly this cooperative enterprise contributed markedly to the prosperity of their farms.

It was not just their willingness to work, however, that made the Pennsylvania Germans successful farmers. By such practices as rotating their crops and irrigating their fields, using fertilizer intelligently, and caring for farm animals properly, the Pennsylvania Germans made their farms outstandingly productive. The German newspapers, *Die Germantauner Zeitung* and *Neue Unpartheyische Lancaster Zeitung*, contained articles on agriculture so frequently that they may be regarded as the forerunners of present-day agricultural journals. Some of these articles indicate an advanced knowledge of agricultural practices. Especially noteworthy are detailed accounts of the process of fruit farming and discussions of the value of animal fertilizers.

Amish farming techniques have changed little since the eighteenth century.

This nineteenth-century Berks County
German farm could just as well have been
in operation in 1776. It retains the
Germanic two-doored farmhouse, the
geometric vegetable garden, the bank barn,
and the cider press.

German gardens often had raised beds
edged with boards.

Letters from an American Farmer

Michel-Guillaume Jean de Crèvecoeur lived and traveled in Pennsylvania in the decade preceding the Revolution before taking the Anglicized name of John Hector St. John and settling on a farm in Orange County, New York. A Norman-French gentleman, who had served as a mapmaker under Montcalm in Canada before entering the English colonies in 1759 or 1760, Crèvecoeur prided himself on his knowledge of Pennsylvania and its people. In a note on Shippensburg, he says: "I knew this village in its infancy; I saw the neighboring forests become fertile fields, and the swamps, beautiful prairies. Never have my thoughts returned to this place without arousing in me the most vivid memories." Throughout his writings he sings his praises for "Happy Pennsylvania! Thou Queen of Provinces."

The twelve essays which comprise Crèvecoeur's Letters from an American Farmer *(1782), all but one written before the war, give a first-hand account of life in the Middle Colonies. William Hazlitt, the English essayist, praised Crèvecoeur for rendering "not only the objects, but the feelings of a new country." In these essays, Crèvecoeur puts on the mask of an unlettered Pennsylvania farmer named James.*

Franklin's humanitarian efforts to improve man by improving his conditions in the city have their counterpart in Crèvecoeur's insistence that life on the farm in the American climate turns poor immigrants into productive citizens. "Men are like plants," Crèvecoeur writes, "the goodness and flavor of the fruit proceeds from the particular soil and exposition in which they grow. We are nothing but what we derive from the air we breathe, the climate we inhabit, the government we obey, the system of religion we profess, and the mode of our employment." At the same time, Crèvecoeur was wary of the influence of the dark forest frontier on the American character. When immigrants find their lives "regulated by the wildness of the neighborhood," he writes, they become "ferocious, gloomy, and unsocial . . . no better than carnivorous animals of a superior rank, living on the flesh of wild animals." When war comes, however, Crèvecoeur's James finds himself in danger of Indian attack, worried about the safety of his family, and confused by his conflicting loyalties to his neighbors and to his homeland; and so in his last letter he reluctantly decides to move westward to join a peaceful Indian village "in the great forest of nature."

Crèvecoeur has been accused of being too idealistic and sentimental. D.H. Lawrence felt that Crèvecoeur was the emotional counterpart of Franklin, the prototype of the practical American. Others have defended Crèvecoeur's romantic vision. As one recent critic has put it: "His portrait of America . . . is idealized and sentimentalized, but it is nonetheless a perceptive, sympathetic articulation of the feeling that underlay the myths of America as Paradise and America as Hope, as they appeared in the first generation's version of the American dream."

Crèvecoeur

Loading grain on a wagon. The sheaves would later be deposited on the barn's threshing floor.

Felling axe for clearing land

The Limestone Land

Attracted by topography similar to that of their homeland, or selecting land by their knowledge of soil fertility, the German farmers preempted practically all the limestone regions of Pennsylvania. As the historian Frederick Jackson Turner said, "the limestone areas in a geological map of Pennsylvania would serve as a map of German settlements." Benjamin Rush tells us that the Germans distinguished themselves from the English by their methods of clearing land. Instead of girdling the trees and letting them die, the Germans cut them down and burned them. Next they grubbed out the underbrush, so that they had the advantage of the immediate use of the land and could plow, harrow, and reap with greater ease. Their farms were apparently somewhere between 150 and 200 acres, although advertisements of farms for sale in German newspapers seem to indicate that most farmers cultivated fewer than 100 acres. Without today's efficient tools, rapid transportation, and more certain markets, they often found it uneconomical to farm their entire acreage.

German Farm Buildings

The barns erected by the Pennsylvania Germans were unusually commodious and substantial. "As large as palaces," Lewis Evans, a contemporary observer and mapmaker, called them. The barns were from 60 to 120 feet long and 50 to 60 feet wide. The upper story was made to project 8 to 10 feet over the lower story in front; sometimes a forebay was attached to shelter the entries to the stable and passageways. The size, utility, and sound construction of these buildings, known as Swisser barns, were an important contribution to the agricultural economy of Pennsylvania.

The magnificence of the barns was not matched by the dwellings of the German farmers. The log huts common early in the century were frequently replaced by stone structures, occasionally fairly large, with four rooms on each floor and a cellar under the entire house. The furnishings, in keeping with the frugality and simple wants of these farmers, were limited and austere in even the large stone houses of wealthy farmers in Berks, Dauphin, and Lancaster counties. A contemporary traveler in America, John David Schoepf, described a typical interior: "A great four-cornered stove, a table in the corner, with benches fastened to the wall, everything daubed with red, and above, a shelf with the universal German farmer's Almanack and Song-book and a small 'Garden of Paradise,' Habermann, and the Bible." These farmers practiced the domestic frugality customary in Germany; they had no desire to imitate the more gracious living of their English neighbors.

A necessary adjunct to the house was a springhouse: a building, usually of stone, constructed over a cold spring. Here such perishables as milk and butter were refrigerated. In the caves various herbs and roots were stored. Sometimes the farmer's house was built over a spring so that the cellar served as a springhouse.

Front views of barns showing weather protection of forebay

Rear view of bank barn showing banked entrance to upper level

Farm Implements

The implements which the Pennsylvania Germans used to work their fields differed little from those used by other groups. For the most part, they were the tools that had been used for centuries: wooden-toothed harrows and rakes, old-fashioned spades, pitchforks, hoes, and mattocks. Threshing was done with the ancient flail or by using horses to trample the wheat on the barn floor. For most of the eighteenth century wheat was cut with the primitive sickle. The grain cradle, which replaced it in the last decades of the century, was one of the few improved tools used by the Germans. (It was not known in New England until after 1800.) It consisted of a broad scythe to which was attached a light frame composed of four wooden fingers almost the length and shape of the blade. By swinging it properly and giving it a dexterous turn, the operator could cut the grain, gather it, and put down a swath ready to be bound into sheaves. Unfortunately, no such improvement was available for plowing. The plow was a heavy affair, with a moldboard generally made of wood but sometimes of wood and iron. The moldboard frequently became clogged with grass and manure, so that a boy had to run alongside and keep it free of debris. Plowing was a back-breaking job; plowing deeply was almost impossible.

The only noteworthy farm machinery used by at least some German farmers was a grain fan, or cleaning mill. Several manufacturers of these mills advertised in German newspapers as well as in *The Pennsylvania Gazette*. As early as 1756 one Adam Acker advertised a "Dutch Fan" that would clean wheat, rye, and other grains, stating that it would clean two hundred bushels a day. Since others were also manufacturing the fan, its use must have been fairly wide. Although it was heavy, requiring the efforts of a strong man to turn it, the Dutch Fan was no doubt a great improvement over the common method of cleaning grain by throwing it into the air with a shovel and letting the air blow out the chaff. This machine was still in use at the turn of the present century.

Caring for Livestock—The Conestoga Horse

A visitor from Maryland, J.B. Bordley, noted the poor care given cattle south of the Pennsylvania German country. He said they were kept "meanly, in winter on cornhusks and straw, without roots or 'drank' or any aperient or diluent material that could correct the costive effects of dry food unless mayhap a nibble of a few weeds and buds, when they ramble abroad poaching in the fields, and exposing themselves to debilitating cold, rain, and sleet." Most farmers allowed their livestock to roam the woods and forage for themselves; they gave little attention to sheltering them or feeding them a balanced ration. The Germans, on the other hand, gave considerably

Handmade wooden hay fork made from a sapling and its roots

Toy triangular harrow prepared farm boys for future work

better care to their livestock. They fed them in their large barns, which were amply provided with stables, and sometimes even built additional stables, probably to house sheep and hogs. Often large trees were kept in pastures to give shade from the heat of the sun. However, fencing pastures was not a common practice; not until the Revolution did advertisements of farms for sale stress that the land was "well fenced" or "in good fence." Taken as a whole, animal husbandry among the Germans in Pennsylvania, though by no means perfected, was clearly superior to that practiced by most other contemporary farmers.

Without such care for their animals, the Germans would not have raised so successfully the famous Conestoga horse, a particularly large and strong draught animal. Developed by Swiss Mennonites who had settled along the Conestoga Creek in Lancaster County, these animals attracted considerable attention because of their size and strength. The Germans seem to have been well supplied with good horses as early as 1755. In May of that year Franklin, in a letter to the Germans of Lancaster, York, and Cumberland counties, requested 150 wagons, with four horses for each wagon, and 1,500 pack or riding horses, for the use of Braddock's army in the French and Indian War. The response was so good that Braddock wrote a letter to the king praising the Germans. The Pennsylvania Germans supplied almost all the horses for the American army during the Revolution, as well as some horses and teamsters for the British

Cow hobble kept the milk cow from kicking

Farming Methods of the Pennsylvania Germans

Since manure was the only means of improving the soil during most of the colonial period, the oxen and cattle of the German farms were valuable in maintaining soil fertility. This was especially true in Lancaster County, where the fattening of beef cattle was an important industry from early colonial days. Straw, cornstalks, and stable refuse were thrown into the barnyard, where they were trampled by fattening cattle during the winter. The yards were cleaned once a year, and the refuse was spread over the fields and plowed under. The farmer with a barnyard full of manure was regarded as a prosperous landowner. Undoubtedly the Germans' careful stabling of their animals enabled them to collect the manure easily. A wide use of manure distinguished the German farmers from most others who, if they used manure at all, applied it only to maize and potatoes.

Artificial fertilizers came into use comparatively late; only lime appears to have been used to any extent before the Revolution. The use of grass crops, especially clover, to restore and maintain the soil did not come into regular practice until after 1800; only grasses produced in natural or irrigated meadows were part of German

Hand sickle for harvesting small amounts of grain

Hand-harvested wheat in Cumberland County. The wheat was cut using a grain cradle, and the individual sheaves were hand-tied.

husbandry before 1773, when "Lancaster County Red Clover" was first advertised in *The Pennsylvania Gazette*. Whatever land-restoring measures the Germans used, the area they farmed was not marked by the soil exhaustion found on a large tract near Philadelphia or by the desolation resulting from the land-skimming practices in the South.

Like other farmers of that time, the colonial Germans employed no uniform plan of rotating crops. Instead, they depended largely upon fallowing to restore the productivity of their fields. Usually, the plan of rotation involved letting the ground lie fallow for three years. Near Lebanon freshly cleared land was cultivated according to the following six-year cycle: (1) wheat, (2) wheat, (3) oats, (4) fallow, (5) wheat, (6) fallow. Land that had been in use for some time was cultivated according to a five-year plan: (1) wheat, (2) barley, (3) corn or oats, (4) fallow or buckwheat, (5) fallow if buckwheat in the fourth year. Perhaps the best plan of which we find any record was employed near Allentown late in the eighteenth century. This consisted of a four-year cycle: (1) wheat, (2) oats or corn or buckwheat, (3) clover, (4) plowing to sow. The idea of rotating crops has been attributed to the Philadelphia Society for Promoting Agriculture, but the Society was not established until 1785, several years after Schoepf and other visitors had observed the plans for rotating crops just described.

One of the most notable features of Pennsylvania German agriculture during the eighteenth century was its extensive use of irrigation. As early as 1754, Governor Thomas Pownall, on a visit to

Lancaster, expressed his admiration of the practice of irrigation as well as of the general appearance of the German farms:

> I saw some of the finest farms one can conceive, and in the highest state of culture, particularly one that was the estate of a Switzer. Here it was I first saw the method of watering a whole range of pasture, and meadows on a hillside, by little troughs cut in the side of the hill, along which the water from springs was conducted, so that when the outlets of these troughs were stopped at the end the water ran over the sides and watered all the ground between that and the other trough next below it. I dare say this method may be in use in England. I never saw it there, but I saw it here first.

Farm land was valued according to the amount that could be irrigated, and when land was divided, rights to the use and control of streams were carefully set forth in title deeds. Practically all advertisements of farms for sale stressed the acreage of watered meadow and the presence of strong springs or streams on the premises. That the investment of money and labor in careful irrigation was justified is shown by the extensive and profitable fattening of beef cattle, the superiority of farm animals, and the high yields of hay crops.

The Fruits of Their Labor

An early traveler observed that the Pennsylvania Germans, instead of relying on a single crop, "multiplied the objects of their culture." As early as 1753, Lewis Evans listed thirty-six varieties of crop, classified as grains, "roots," greens, melons, berries, and fruits, which were then being cultivated in Pennsylvania. The most common and apparently the most profitable crop was wheat. An important part of every plan to rotate crops, the grain of the Germans supplied much of the bread eaten by the contending armies of the Revolution. In addition to wheat, corn and rye were grown extensively; barley and oats appear to have been grown less often.

Dairying and butchering were important industries of the German farms. The milk, cheese, butter, and meat produced, besides filling the needs of the family, brought cash from the markets of Baltimore and Philadelphia. At least some butter was exported to the West Indies as early as 1754. The German Society, founded in 1789, offered a goldpiece to the farmer who produced the largest amount of English cheese, stipulating that the quantity submitted had to be at least 500 pounds.

Although there was little systematic cultivation of fruit in this country before 1800, an orchard appears to have been a significant part of a typical German farm. Peter Kalm, in 1748, observed that on every German farm there were some apple trees, the fruit of which was either sold or made into cider. Later travelers frequently

Winemaking

The Spirits of '76

In 1794 western Pennsylvania farmers challenged the new American government by refusing to pay a stiff excise tax on whiskey. Anyone who has heard of the Whiskey Rebellion is aware that the production of spiritus frumenti was a significant part of the economy of western Pennsylvania in the eighteenth century. Not so well known is the importance of distilling and brewing in the industrial life of the eastern part of the commonwealth, especially in the counties of York and Lancaster.

Small industries were a part of practically all farms. Along with looms and spinning wheels, operated by the women, there were blacksmith and cooperage shops, grist and aromatic oil mills, tanneries, and distilleries. Most numerous were the distilleries; malt-houses, malt-mills, "brandy houses," and stills were frequently advertised as special features of farms. At the time of the Revolution, by a conservative estimate, there were 353 distilleries in York County and 293 in Lancaster County. An article in the American Daily Advertiser stated that "It [distilling] is an effort made by those who are just rising from pressing circumstances . . . by which they can make something more than by the labor of cutting timber and digging the soil."

There were sound economic reasons for the flourishing of the industry. It was a way of securing ready cash with a small investment. It was also the best way to dispose of surplus grain and fruit with an adequate return. The fruits of the apple and peach orchards not preserved by drying could be turned into salable cider and brandy. Excess wheat, corn, barley, and rye could be distilled into whiskey or brewed into beer, both of which found a ready market. Operators of grist mills found the ownership of stills especially profitable, since their shares of grain brought to them for grinding could be turned into whiskey. An important stimulus to the industry was the difficulty of transporting raw farm products to markets in Philadelphia, Baltimore, or Wilmington. Distilling grain or fruit and transporting the liquor was not only easier but often more profitable. A Conestoga wagon typically carried four barrels, each containing approximately 150 gallons.

An account of one of the most enterprising distillers in Lancaster County is provided by the diary of Susanna Müller, who describes the prodigious industry of Peter Miller of Providence Township. His house, she states, was common among contemporary farm dwellings, the lower part being built of stone and used as a still. Here Miller distilled whiskey, applejack, brandy, cherry bounce, oil of sassafras, oil of peppermint, and oil of pennyroyal. According to tradition, he also extracted alcohol from potatoes. When he found that he had insufficient rye to keep his still going, he distilled sixty ounces of oil of peppermint. Storing the oil in flasks, which he packed in his saddlebags, he started for Philadelphia early in the morning, sold his oil for sixty dollars, and returned home before the end of the second day—having traveled 140 miles to reap a tidy profit.

It is doubtful that other farmers matched Peter Miller's diligence, business acumen, and attachment to his stills, but it is certain that many seriously engaged in the production of alcoholic beverages.

Bottles for rum, gin, and wine were either mold-blown or free-blown.

Making "cherry bounce," from the sketchbook of Lewis Miller, nineteenth-century Pennsylvania German folk artist of York County.

Copper whiskey still

Brewer

October 1.

TO BE SOLD,

Or rented for a Term of Years, A Commodious Brew-house, Malt-House and Dwelling-House contiguous, situated at the upper end of Water-street, between Race and Vine-streets, bounded on the river, and by two wide alleys, one being a public alley: The buildings & implements are all in good order, & every article wanted for carrying on the business, may be landed at the wharf, without the heavy charge of carting. The works are so calculated that they may be managed with as much ease, & as little expence, as any brewery in the city. Any person inclining to purchase, or rent the said premises, may inquire for further particulars of JOHN JONES. N: B: The business is carried on as usual; where may be and different kinds of BEER, at the customary prices.

"Graeme Park," built as a brew house by Governor Sir William Kieth

Large apple butter kettle on a stand, shown with a stirrer and a ladle

Split oak basket

spoke of the Germans' special concern with fruit-growing; apples and peach trees are mentioned most often, with occasional reference to cherry trees. Advertisements of farms for sale often mention orchards ranging from one hundred to five or six hundred trees, indicating that fruit-growing was a regular part of German husbandry. Fruit was extensively used in distilling brandy. Apples and peaches were also preserved by drying. The productivity of the orchards was probably increased by at least some systematic care, such as occasional grafting and pruning of trees and sometimes by seeding the soil between rows of trees with maize, rye, or oats.

Vegetable gardens were a necessary part of all farms at this time, and the Germans appear to have cultivated them assiduously. Benjamin Rush regarded the products of their gardens, in which they grew most of the vegetables then known to northern Europe, as an important contribution to the economy of Pennsylvania. To the German farmers settled near Philadelphia he gave credit for introducing the citizens of that city to a variety of vegetables. He ascribed the freedom from dermatitis enjoyed by Philadelphians to this element in their diet.

Flax and hemp were cultivated extensively. Flax was common on all German farms, but the greatest production of hemp was found in the valleys of the Susquehanna, the Conestoga, the Pequea, and their tributaries.

The quality of any husbandry must be judged, of course, less by its diversity than by its yield. Unfortunately there are no precise and comprehensive statistics about agricultural production throughout the Middle Colonies. There does seem to be sufficient evidence, however, to show that the yield of the Pennsylvania German farms was above average. The yield of wheat in the Middle Colonies during the eighteenth century has been estimated at between ten and fifteen bushels per acre, with the lower figure being the more common. The average yield for all of Pennsylvania has been estimated as low as six bushels. Corn yields in the Middle Colonies are generally put at from twenty to twenty-five bushels per acre, rye at ten to fifteen bushels; the average yield of hay in six counties in Massachusetts was less than one ton per acre. Contemporaneous observers of German farms in Pennsylvania indicated that their yields frequently exceeded these figures, especially in wheat. A usually reliable traveler gave the following wheat production figures for farms in various locations: Bethlehem, fifteen bushels; Allentown, twelve to eighteen bushels; vicinity of Kutztown, twenty bushels; near Reading, ten to fifteen bushels; Lebanon, fifteen to twenty bushels. Washington noted several instances at York and Lancaster where "between forty and fifty bushels of wheat have been raised to the acre." Competent later historians state that the production of between twenty and thirty bushels per acre was not uncommon among the Germans in Pennsylvania. There is evidence, too, that they were equally successful with corn and hay. Corn yields of between twenty-five and forty bushels were reported at Allentown, Reading, and Lebanon; and hay crops of from one to two tons per acre for two cuttings were cited for the same areas.

Pewter flask, or dram bottle

Transporting Goods—The Conestoga Wagon

Production alone, however, did not insure prosperity. Surplus wheat, corn, and other products had to be transported to a market. Since many farmers lived a great distance from urban centers, transportation presented a difficult problem. The rivers, especially the Susquehanna, Delaware, and Schuylkill, offered a partial solution, but each presented great difficulties and inconvenience: the Delaware was too shallow in some places and too swift in others, and both the Susquehanna and the Schuylkill depended on freshets to make them navigable.

Despite the deterrents of distance and bad roads, the Pennsylvania Germans soon found a satisfactory substitute for river transportation. They devised a large, sturdy vehicle that was capable of withstanding the jolting of rough roads and the wear of long trips: the Conestoga wagon. Usually associated with the romantic excitement of covered-wagon trains, marauding Indians, and the Gold Rush, it is seldom connected with the prosaic use for which it was created. Yet it played a vital part in the economy of these farmers and is one of the best monuments to their resourcefulness.

Hitching four or six large, powerful horses to their Conestoga wagons, the Pennsylvania Germans brought heavy loads of wheat and other produce from distances of fifty, a hundred, and more miles to Philadelphia. Writing in 1753, Lewis Evans stated:

> . . . the economy of the Germans has since taught us the method of bringing their produce to Market, from the remotest part at a small expense. The Method is this, evry Farmer in our province almost, has a Waggon of his own, for the Service of his Plantation, and likewise the horses for tillage, in the spring and fall of the Year . . . they load their Waggon and furnish themselves with beasts, and provender for the Journey. The Waggon is their Bed, their Inn, their everything, many of them will come one hundred and fifty miles without spending one Shilling.

In 1789 Benjamin Rush observed that "it was no uncommon thing, on Lancaster and Reading roads, to meet in one day fifty or a hundred of these wagons, on their way to Philadelphia, most of which belong to German farmers."

Conestoga wagon. The wagon jack is leaning against the front wheel, and the drag shoe can be seen in front of the rear wheel. The latter slowed the wagon on a downslope. The board extending from under the tool box is the "lazy board," the only place to sit or stand.

Grease bucket

Wagon tool box

The Conestoga Wagon

During the early 1700s English and German traditional craftsmen—wheelwrights, blacksmiths, joiners, and turners—in the Conestoga valley of Lancaster County began to combine features of earlier European wagons—the road wagons of England and the large farm wagons of western Germany—to produce familiar but new styles of freight-bearing vehicles. By mid-century these wagons were generally known as Conestoga wagons. They were also known as "Dutch wagons" because many of the farmers who owned the wagons and drove their produce from Lancaster area farms to Philadelphia markets were Pennsylvania Germans.

Some of these drivers became "regulars," professional teamsters who cut romantic figures, typically wearing full beards, leather or homespun clothing, and flat broad-brimmed hats. Many wagoners smoked cheap cigars, called "stogies," to reduce throat discomfort caused by road dust; they also consumed much liquor, purchased from the many taverns along the road to Philadelphia, to reduce the monotony of spending several days on the road. To drive his wagon the wagoner either walked along the left side of the team or rode the left horse nearest to the wheel. He steered the horses with a jerk line attached to the reins of the left leader horse, and he encouraged the team over rough spots on the pike with his seven-foot-long blacksnake whip, which he cracked over the heads of the Conestoga horses. Along smoother stretches of road, the wagoner might have chosen to sit on a thick oak board, called a "lazy board," which could be pulled out from under

the wagon box. In position, the lazy board allowed the driver to sit directly in front of the left rear wheel of the wagon. In any of these three positions— walking, sitting on a horse, or sitting on the lazy board—the driver drove the team from the left and steered his wagon to the right of approaching wagons, a custom many view as the origin of modern American traffic laws requiring drivers to drive on the right side of the road.

By 1776 Conestoga wagons had become the most important vehicles of overland freighting, although other wagons were also being made and used. Conestogas had been used for transporting farm products, iron ore, and other freight for over half a century. Their military utility was recognized during the French and Indian War when Major-General Edward Braddock, with the aid of Benjamin Franklin, hired one hundred and fifty Conestoga wagons to support his ill-fated march against Fort Duquesne in 1755. The Conestogas proved invaluable to the American cause during the Revolution, when Pennsylvania farmers supplied most of the wagons used by the American army. They were especially important in supplying Washington's troops at Valley Forge during the winter of 1777–1778. After the war, Conestoga wagons were to become even more important as they were adapted to the demands of the westward migration of families. Their presence on the American landscape would be most visible during the 1820s. By the mid-nineteenth century they would be almost entirely replaced by the railroads.

Combination claw hammer
and wagon pin

Wagon jack

The Breadbasket of America

On Wednesdays and Saturdays, which were market days, Philadelphia's High Street (later Market Street) was lined with the great covered wagons, filled with produce to be sold and rations for the farmers and their horses. Other cities and towns, particularly Lancaster and York, also furnished a market for their crops. The great market at Lancaster, resembling closely the markets of European German cities, attracted many farmers, especially of the Amish and Mennonite sects. In boxes and on small trestles, the farmers offered their bounty—butter, eggs, cider, apple butter, schnitz (dried apples), fowls, sausages, beets, corn, beans, carrots, turnips, lettuce, and much more. Not mere subsistence farmers, these husbandmen helped feed many inhabitants of towns and cities and realized considerable profit.

Certainly not all Pennsylvania Germans were good farmers. Such groups as the Moravians, Amish, Mennonites, and Schwenkfelders were more successful than others. By way of contrast, in the frontier lands lived Germans who were content as long as they had plenty to eat and drink, little work to do, and no taxes to pay. They complacently described their condition as "Wir machen just so aus" (We get along so-so). These, however, were few in number.

Even if we cannot accept at face value the assertion of Benjamin Rush that the millions of dollars produced by the German farmers made possible the foundation of the Bank of North America, their great contribution to the wealth of Pennsylvania is undeniable. Their industry, conservatism, and respect for the land fitted them well for the demands of eighteenth-century American agriculture. Their devotion to careful husbandry, capacity for hard labor, and thrift made for an agricultural prosperity unmatched anywhere else in America. To them must go much of the credit for giving Pennsylvania more economic independence than that enjoyed by the tobacco, sugar, and maritime colonies. Pennsylvania was known for a hundred years as the "breadbasket of America" largely through the productivity of the German farmers.

Workers in Penn's Woods

Pennsylvania was the workshop of the colonies as well as their breadbasket. Colonial Pennsylvania is most often pictured as a rich pastoral society, largely populated by pious Quakers, sturdy German farmers, and rugged, independent Scotch-Irish frontiersmen. There is enough truth in this popular image to explain its persistence, but it is far from the whole story. By 1776 Pennsylvania was the manufacturing center of North America, possessed the largest city in the new world, and was home to a sizable number of me-

Shoemakers

Smithery

chanics, craftsmen, seamen, and early industrial workers. An astonishing number of skilled trades were represented. Indeed, the variety of occupations indicates the diversity and sophistication of colonial Pennsylvania's commerce and industry. There were wheelwrights and millwrights, fullers and dyers, painters and carvers, gunsmiths and locksmiths, and a myriad of others. A vigorous iron industry employed the iron workers and miners who were the first industrial workers. Little attention has been paid to this diverse and important working class, perhaps because documentary evidence of its role in colonial life is difficult to find. Yet the contribution of these workers is evident in the edifices they built, the roads they laid, and other works of skill that have survived them.

They came from England and Ireland, Germany and Africa, from lands throughout the world. Most came of their own free will, some in chains as slaves, some as convicts, and an unfortunate few as a result of having been kidnapped in the immigrant shipping centers of London, Amsterdam, and Rotterdam. Many brought skills with them. Of 1,838 immigrants who debarked at the Philadelphia docks during a four-month period in 1709, 706 were skilled craftsmen, a surprisingly high figure when one makes allowances for the women and children who accompanied them, and a good indication of the needs of the colony, barely three decades old, for skilled nonagricultural labor.

Most of the immigrants became farmers and employed their skills as part of an integrated family economic unit. Others became itinerant craftsmen traveling from farm to farm trading their services for wages, a bed, and a place at the family table. A significant number made their way to the iron plantations scattered through south-

Button maker

Cooper

Sawing wood

eastern Pennsylvania, along the broad Susquehanna, and up the Juniata to the Alleghenies. Growing interior towns like Lancaster, Reading, York, Easton, and Middletown attracted a few. But most of those who did not take up farming settled in the bustling young metropolis of Philadelphia, where a man with skills and the will to work was in demand. The competitive availability of cheap land in the interior and the chronic shortage of labor combined to keep wages high in comparison with England and made the colonial period, for the most part, one of relative prosperity for workers.

Slave Labor in Pennsylvania

Slavery, never a strong institution in Pennsylvania, was on the road to extinction by 1776. True, slavery had existed in the Delaware River valley among the Swedes and the Dutch even before the settlement made by William Penn and the English Quakers, and many of the early Quaker settlers, including Penn himself, were slaveholders. Nevertheless, from the beginning Quakers fought the legality of slavery, and the number of slaves in Pennsylvania was never large compared with the southern colonies; only the New England colonies had fewer. As early as 1700 a merchant implored a slave supplier "to hand me no more negroes for sale, for our people do not care to buy." Exact figures are not available, but on the eve of the Revolution there were in Pennsylvania only about ten thousand slaves, around three percent of the colony's population. Most were in the area near Philadelphia, but by 1776 many could be found in southwestern Pennsylvania as well. They were owned mainly by the English and Scotch-Irish settlers; the Germans generally did not hold slaves. As has been noted, the farms of the Pennsylvania Germans were small, self-supporting family units which had no need for large numbers of unskilled slave labor. In addition, many of the German farmers rejected slavery as morally reprehensible, and by the Revolution the German counties had a ratio of four to five hundred whites to one black. What blacks there were, both free and slave, found employment as domestics, teamsters, porters, and carters or on the iron plantations.

Most of the slaves in Pennsylvania came not directly from Africa, but only after undergoing a "seasoning" process in the British West Indies. After entering through the port of Philadelphia, an adult usually sold for about forty pounds sterling. Pennsylvania slaves were usually housed in their masters' homes, well fed and decently clothed, frequently allowed to marry, and often instructed in the Christian religion. Quakers were encouraged to bring their slaves to meetings. About 1760 the Anglican Church appointed a "catechist" to teach Philadelphia Negroes the principles of Christianity. Although the treatment of slaves was comparatively mild in Penn-

I DO hereby advertise the publick that *Philip Henson* and *Mary* his wife, being largely indebted to *Alexander Baine*, for securing the same did enter into and execute a deed of mortgage for Negro *Pat, Joe, Jenny,* and *Sall,* and all their increase, together with sundry chattels. I understand one *Julius Saunders* has got possession of the said slaves, and may probably offer them for sale: I therefore give this notice of the mortgage, which is recorded in *Albemarle* court, and no part of it paid.   DAVID ROSS, for
                    ALEXANDER BAINE.

To be SOLD *for ready money, at* Halifax *court-house, on* Thursday *the* 15th *of* September *next, being court day,*

SEVERAL very valuable *Virginia* born SLAVES, by virtue of a deed of trust made to

JOHN WIMBISH, & Co.

sylvania, numerous advertisements for runaway slaves in colonial Philadelphia newspapers reveal that not all of them were happy with their lot; some of these ads described marks of mistreatment.

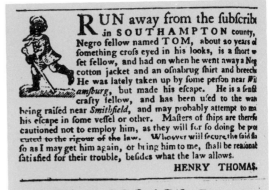

The slave trade and slavery itself were the subjects of much legislation by the provincial Assembly. A long series of laws placed taxes on the importation of slaves, originally for revenue but finally, as in 1773 when a duty of twenty pounds was levied, to discourage further importations. Beginning in 1700 the Assembly passed a series of restrictive laws, composing what might be called the colony's "black code." Negroes found footloose and idle could be bound out as servants. Liquor was not to be sold to them. Whites and blacks were subjected to different modes of trial and punishment. Negroes were denied the right of trial by jury. Slaves and Negro servants were forbidden to go more than ten miles from home without written permission from their masters and were required to be home by nine o'clock at night. They were not to meet in groups of more than four persons. Intermarriage between the races was forbidden. These discriminatory measures applied to all Negroes, whether they were slaves, indentured servants, or free.

On the other hand, as early as 1688 isolated Quaker voices had spoken out in denunciation of slavery and the slave trade. Francis Daniel Pastorius, George Keith, William Southeby, Benjamin Lay, John Woolman, and Anthony Benezet contributed to this movement in the pre-Revolutionary years. Their efforts culminated in 1776, when the Philadelphia Yearly Meeting of Friends provided that any member who refused to free his slaves should be disowned. In 1775 a group of Philadelphia Quakers founded the Society for the Relief of Free Negroes Unlawfully Held in Bondage. Only four meetings were held in 1775, and after that there are no minutes until 1784, but a committee was appointed to investigate reports of kidnapping and to render aid to free Negroes. In 1787 the society was reorganized as the Pennsylvania Society for Promoting the Abolition of Slavery, for the Relief of Free Negroes Unlawfully Held in Bondage, and for Improving the Condition of the African Race. Two prominent non-Quakers were chosen as officers, Benjamin Franklin as president and Dr. Benjamin Rush as one of the secretaries. The Pennsylvania Abolition Society, as it is generally called, was the first antislavery organization in world history, and it still exists, giving aid to black students.

The Pennsylvania Assembly on March 1, 1780, passed the first state law providing for the emancipation of slaves. (Vermont, not yet a state, had prohibited slavery by its constitution of 1777.) The Assembly voted thirty-four to twenty-one in favor of gradual abolition. Massachusetts and New Hampshire soon achieved emancipation through court decisions based on their state constitutions. The rest of the northern states followed Pennsylvania's example and passed laws freeing slaves. Although many believe slavery in the

Benjamin Lay, Quaker Abolitionist

Benjamin Lay, described by Franklin as "the Pythagorean-cynical-christian Philosopher," launched one of the earliest and most unusual anti-slavery crusades in colonial Philadelphia. An English Quaker hounded from his native country for involvement in political and religious controversy, Lay gained a new focus for his reformer's zeal during a short stay in Barbados, where the excesses of slavery caused him great anguish. Arriving in Philadelphia in 1732, he quickly became a gadfly to Quaker slaveowners. Although his wife was a member of the Quaker community, Lay's abrasive and persistent fulminations on the subject of slave ownership prevented his acceptance in the Friends Meetings. On one occasion, after his ejection from a Meeting by a brawny attendant, Lay remained sprawled in the gutter where he had been deposited— a gesture of protest for the violence shown him. His book All Slave Keepers that keep the innocent in bondage . . . *was printed in 1737 by Benjamin Franklin, who later expressed the opinion that Lay's efforts had been the origin of the anti-slavery movement in Pennsylvania.*

    In an engraved portrait the bearded hunchback is shown standing outside the cave that was outfitted with his library of nearly two hundred volumes, decorated with pine boughs, and used as a retreat for meditation and study. He holds a book by an earlier English Quaker, Thomas Tryon, The Way to Health, Long Life and Happiness . . . , *which contains practical and rational suggestions on food preparation, hygienic household management, and happy marital arrangements, and suggests Lay's professed aim of achieving a peaceful, healthful, and moral approach to living. Lay's interest in vegetarianism and a simple life style are indicated by the spring of water, the bowl, the basket of fruit, and the turnips scattered in the foreground of the portrait.*

    The print, issued probably in the early 1760s shortly after Lay's death in 1759, had wide popularity and was reprinted in numerous versions well into the nineteenth century. Both Franklin and Washington owned copies and Benjamin Rush commented in 1798 that the print was to be seen in many houses in Philadelphia. As a record of a colorful personality and as an image of the reforming zeal which often bursts upon the American scene, this print shows a unique aspect of the colonial experience.

BENJAMIN LAY.

Lived to the Age of 80, in the Latter Part of Which, he Observed extream Temperance in his Eating and Drinking, his Fondness for a Particularity in Dress and Customs at times Subjected him to the Redicule of the Ignorant, but Those who were Intimate with Him, thought Him an Honest Religious man.

North was abolished so peacefully because it was economically un-profitable, emancipation may have been largely motivated by the democratic spirit of the Declaration of Independence. This conten-tion is supported by the preamble to the Pennsylvania law:

> We conceive that it is our duty, and we rejoice that it is in our power, to extend a portion of that freedom to others, which hath been extended to us, and a release from that state of thraldom, to which we ourselves were tyrannically doomed, and from which we have now every prospect of being delivered.

It was not for men, the law went on, to inquire why in the creation of mankind the inhabitants of various parts of the earth had been distinguished by a difference in features and complexion. "It is sufficient to know that all are the work of an Almighty Hand."

The principal author of the law was George Bryan, a Scotch-Irish Presbyterian. It provided that children born to slaves after its pas-sage were to become free at the age of twenty-eight years. All slaves were to be registered by their masters with the county courts; those not registered by November 1, 1780, were to be free. The discrimi-natory legislation of the colonial period, including the ban on inter-marriage, was repealed. Negroes, whether slave or free, were to be tried and punished in the same manner as white people. A supple-mentary measure of 1788 provided for a fine of £1,000 for any Pennsylvanian found guilty of participating in the slave trade. By 1790 the census reported only 3,737 slaves in this commonwealth.

Spokesman for Black Americans:
Anthony Benezet

Anthony Benezet (1713–1784), a French Huguenot by birth but a Quaker convert, spent most of his life in Philadelphia. A teacher by profession, he opened an evening school for Negroes in his home in 1750. He campaigned against slavery and the slave trade through letters, newspaper articles, pamphlets, and books. Controverting the common charge that Negroes were inferior beings, he preached the natural equality of all men. His most substantial work, published in 1771, was Some Historical Account of Guinea, *a study of the African background of the slaves, in which he maintained that the West African peoples were peaceful and prosperous and enjoyed a high degree of civilization until corrupted by the incursions of European and American slave traders.*

Speaking of the Declaration of Independence, Benezet wrote: "If these solemn truths uttered in such an awful crisis, are self-evident: *unless we can show that the African race are not men, words can hardly express the amazement which naturally arises on reflecting that the very people who make these pompous declarations are slaveholders, and, by their legislation, tell us, that these blessings were only meant to be the* rights of white men, *not of all* men: *and would seem to verify the observation of an eminent writer: 'When men talk of liberty, they mean their own liberty, and seldom suffer their thoughts on that point to stray to their neighbors.' "*

Benezet visited every member of the Pennsylvania assembly to press for passage of the state abolition law of 1780. His death in 1784 was mourned by large numbers of people, blacks and whites alike. He left the bulk of his estate to be used for the education of Negroes.

Loading plan of slave ship

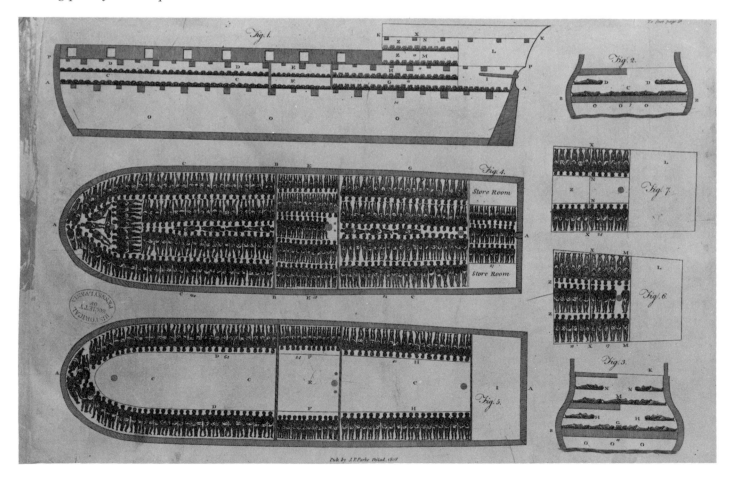

Indentured Servants

A practical deterrent to the growth of slavery was the widespread use of the system of indentured servitude. Although estimates vary, probably from one-third to one-half of the immigrants who came to Pennsylvania were indentured. Between 1735 and 1755, for example, 60,000 indentured servants entered the colony. England experimented with emptying its jails by sending convicts as bond servants, but Pennsylvanians discouraged the practice. Most bond servants came of their own free will, even if the picture Pennsylvania recruiters painted for them was a bit rosy. They sold their services for a period ranging from three to five years, in return for their passage. There was also a small home supply of indentured servants, consisting of bound out convicts and debtors who substituted terms of servitude to creditors for incarceration.

The overwhelming majority of indentured servants came from England, Ireland, and Germany. Although their condition was temporary, in many ways their lot was little better than that of slaves. The passage to America was a horrible experience. Packed together in holds of slow ships with no sanitation and inadequate rations, scarcely more than half survived the voyage. Once in Philadelphia, they were sold at auction—individually, even when such sales separated members of families. Those indentured immigrants not sold in the city were guided into the interior by "soul drivers," where they were offered for sale. Most were sold to farmers, but some had special skills making them valuable to master workmen in the various trades. They had more rights than the black slaves, but the incidence of runaways was high.

Apprentices

Aspects of indentured servitude were also found in the apprentice system. Usually an orphan or the son of poor parents (in the case of Benjamin Franklin, the youngest of ten sons), the apprentice was bound to a master craftsman or tradesman who provided training in his trade or craft in exchange for services. Often the employer took the child into his own home. The conditions of the apprenticeship were carefully set down, as can be seen in this contract:

> Jonathan Hurst, Jr., by consent of his mother Anne Hutchins, indents himself apprentice to James Gottier, of Philadelphia, cooper for eight years from this date to have six months schooling and six months evening schooling to learn to read, write, and cipher, to be taught the trade of cooper, and at the end of his time to have two suits of apparel, one of which is to be new.

The law required employers to care for their apprentices and retain them in hard times as well as good. The usual term was seven

SOME
HISTORICAL ACCOUNT
OF
GUINEA,
Its Situation, Produce and the general Disposition of its INHABITANTS.
WITH
An inquiry into the Rise and Progress of the SLAVE-TRADE, its Nature and lamentable Effects.
ALSO
A Re-publication of the Sentiments of several Authors of Note, on this interesting Subject; particularly an Extract of a Treatise, by GRANVILLE SHARP.

By ANTHONY BENEZET.

Acts xvii. 24, 26. God that made the World——hath made of one Blood all Nations of Men, for to dwell on all the Face of the Earth, and hath determined the——Bounds of their Habitation.
Eccles. viii. 11. Because Sentence against an evil Work is not executed speedily, therefore the Heart of the Sons of Men is fully set in them to do Evil.
Deut. xxxii. 34. Is not this laid up in Store with me and sealed up among my Treasure. To me belongeth Vengeance and Recompence, their Foot shall slide in due Time, for the Day of their Calamity is at Hand; and the Things that shall come upon them make haste.

PHILADELPHIA: Printed by JOSEPH CRUKSHANK, in Third-street, opposite the Work-house.
M,DCC,LXXI.

Black Pennsylvanians in the Revolutionary Era

The call for liberty and independence in the thirteen colonies was sounded by blacks as well as whites. The white colonists sought freedom from oppressors in Britain while blacks sought freedom from their oppressors in the colonies. Both movements reached a climax in the revolutionary era, establishing precedents that would determine the nature of race relations in the future nation. This dual development was dramatically played out in Pennsylvania.

At first black and white Pennsylvanians were fighting a common enemy. Men from both races enlisted in the Continental Army and served in Pennsylvania's navy. Although much is known about the role of whites, little is known about the gallantry of black Pennsylvanians in the Revolutionary War. John Pompey was among the seamen on the Burke *in 1776, and twenty of the two hundred crewmen on the* Royal Louis *were black sailors. One was James Forten, who later became a prominent leader in Philadelphia. He was an "inventor, manufacturer, philanthropist, and organizer of protest." Black Pennsylvanians also joined the army. One of them, Edward Hector, a member of the Third Pennsylvania Artillery, was recognized for his bravery in the Battle of Brandywine in 1777.*

After the Revolutionary War ended, the leaders of the new nation hammered out the political doctrines that would become the political foundation for an American republic, based on the concepts of freedom of the individual and human rights. The climax of this political drama took place at the Constitutional Convention in Philadelphia in 1787. However, the political, economic, and social privileges gained by whites were disallowed for blacks in the new nation. This inconsistency in the application of human rights became the basic cause of conflict between the races. The war for American independence had been won, but the "war" for the equality of Afro-Americans had just begun.

Richard Allen

Cliveden, where Richard Allen and his family served the Chew family. The battle of Germantown was later fought on the lawn.

The year 1787 was a crucial one. A few months after the Constitution was adopted, black Pennsylvanians initiated the drive for the rights of black people in the United States. Two leaders emerged during this period: Richard Allen and Absalom Jones, former slaves. Jones was born in Sussex County, Delaware, in 1746, but his master took him to Philadelphia. Allen was born in Philadelphia in 1760. The Allen family were slaves of the chief justice of Pennsylvania, Benjamin Chew, who sold the Allens to a family in Dover, Delaware. By 1786, Allen and Jones had purchased their freedom and settled in Philadelphia permanently. By this time also they were Christian converts and Methodist local preachers, and both were members of St. George's Methodist Church in Philadelphia.

As the numbers of free blacks increased after the Revolutionary War, so did discrimination against them. This was most noticeable in churches. At St. George's Methodist Church, for instance, blacks could sit only in the gallery. Because of the acceleration of discriminatory practices against free blacks, Richard Allen and Absalom Jones called for the formation of a Free African Society in 1787. It was the first Afro-American organization to be formed on the basis of the self-determination and self reliance of black people.

If there were to be dual communities in the new republic, one white and the other black, Allen and Jones felt that the latter should not be dependent on or subservient to the former. Thus blacks in Philadelphia were urged to join the Free African Society and contribute to the cost of providing social services for the city's black community, such as caring for widows, burying the dead, providing adequate housing for local people and fugitive slaves. On the other hand, the members of the society were not racial exclusivists. They believed that the two communities could work together. This conviction was realized during the yellow fever epidemic in Philadelphia in 1793. Allen, Jones, and other blacks in the city worked harmoniously with Dr. Benjamin Rush and the white community to alleviate the suffering and bury the dead.

Another idea that sprang from the Free African Society was the need for independent black religious institutions, where Afro-Americans could worship freely. This aspiration eventually caused conflicts in the rank and file of the society. By 1794 the society had spawned two independent black churches: the African Episcopal Church and the African Method-

Absalom Jones

ist Church. Allen became the leader of the Methodist group and Jones the head of the Episcopal group. By the eve of the Civil War the black Episcopalians had been incorporated in the Episcopal Church in the United States, but Allen's church became the African Methodist Episcopal Church. Today it is established throughout the United States, many Canadian provinces, the West Indies, and Africa. It is the largest independent black denomination in the world. Bethel A.M.E. Church in Philadelphia, now a national monument, stands as a symbol of the leadership Allen and Jones provided for their people in the revolutionary era.

years, and many new journeymen remained in their masters' employ after the apprenticeship ended. Though for the most part the system was humane, it was restrictive, and items like the following appeared frequently in colonial newspapers:

Youthful apprentice

Six Cents Reward

Ran away from the subscriber on Saturday evening, the 29th ult. an indented apprentice to the cabinetmaking business, named John Rimbey, between nineteen and twenty years of age. He had on when he went away a new black fur hat, blue coat, and corded pantaloons and striped vest. The public is hereby cautioned against employing or harboring said apprentice, as the law shall be enforced against any person doing so.

Free Labor

The importance of the system of bound labor emphasizes the favored position of free labor, for those who remained to practice their trades commanded high wages. It was not uncommon for a skilled tradesman to become an employer, purchase land, and construct a substantial house. Describing his situation in a letter home to England, one anonymous early settler declared that "It is a great deal better living here than in England for working people. Poor working people doth live as well here as landed men doth live with you thats worth twenty pounds a year. I live a simple life and hath builded a shop, and doth follow weaving of linen clothe, but I have bought 450 acres of land in the wood." Ships' carpenters were known to purchase a share in a vessel and become capitalists.

Shipbuilding

By the close of the pre-Revolutionary period, no other colonial city rivaled Philadelphia in the value and variety of her manufactures, and in that center of commerce free labor predominated. Since the main impetus for the economic development of the city came from her trade with England, continental Europe, and the West Indies, the maritime industries flourished first. By 1754 there were twelve shipyards at Philadelphia, and the industry, centered at Kensington, provided employment for hundreds of workers in the ropewalks, sail lofts, cooperages, smithies, and dozens of other enterprises necessary to the building of a great ship. As early as 1689 a Pennsylvania poet sang the praises of the industry:

> Within this six or seven year
> Many good ships have been built here
> and more, some say, will be built yet
> for here is timber very fit.
> Good carpenters who bravely thrive,
> And master builders to contrive
> Who can prepare the iron stuff.

By 1775 thirty percent of Philadelphia's property owners were artisans, and this included only heads of families owning real estate. One example of the growing sophistication of Pennsylvania's economy was the increased specialization of the labor force. Blacksmiths, who had performed almost all of the metalworking tasks in the early colonial period, now shared the work with ornamental ironworkers, anchor forgers, coppersmiths, tinplate workers, and others. Carpenters had the assistance of joiners, turners, cabinetmakers, carvers, and coachmakers. Building tradesmen included roofers, painters, glaziers, plumbers, plasterers, housewrights, stonemasons, and bricklayers.

Iron Workers

Workers found themselves in a very different world, however, on the Pennsylvania iron plantations like Cornwall, Hopewell, and Valley Forge, which dotted the eastern half of the province. Obtaining a sufficient supply of labor was a continual problem for the ironmaster. Skilled furnace and forge workers were hard to find, and in 1764 Thomas Penn sent a number of charcoal burners to Pennsylvania for the purpose of "teaching those employed at the Iron Works to make the coal [charcoal] with much less quantity of wood than they had hitherto consumed." For the most part, the labor force consisted of indentured servants, with a significant number of free Negroes and slaves. Women did not share in the production of iron as they did in England. The wives and daughters of the workers were employed as casual day laborers in the fields or in spinning thread and weaving clothes for the ironmaster and his family. Boys were often apprenticed as helpers at the forges or as workers in the secondary iron manufactories, such as the nail and tinplate works.

Hopewell Furnace as reconstructed in a modern drawing. The charge was carted to the furnace by way of the ramp at the right.

Life on these plantations achieved a degree of continuity, and frequently several generations of the same family worked at the same trade on the same plantation. A high percentage of bond servants stayed on after expiration of their indentures. An iron plantation was a complex economic unit requiring many specialized skills as well as a large number of common laborers. The characteristics of the iron plantation—its divisions of labor, its physical isolation, and the patriarchal relationship between the ironmaster and his employees—all persisted in the iron, steel, and mining industries in Pennsylvania even into the twentieth century.

Iron Plantations in Colonial Pennsylvania

Colonial Pennsylvania's iron plantations were similar to the tobacco plantations of Virginia and Maryland or even to the small feudal manors of medieval Europe. Because charcoal provided the fuel for the smelting of iron ore in the 1700s, a vast forest was required to support each furnace and forge. In isolated wooded areas, therefore, essentially self-sufficient ironmaking communities developed—consisting of an ironmaster's mansion house, homes for the workers, furnaces and forges, a general store, a grist mill, a sawmill, and a blacksmith shop. These settlements were sometimes surrounded by as much as 10,000 acres of forest land, which limited outside commerce. Consequently, the community needed to be agriculturally independent, so there were extensive grain fields as well as livestock pens, orchards, and gardens. Workers were needed to cut timber for the charcoal kilns, as about 400 bushels of charcoal were needed to produce a ton of hammered bar iron; they were also needed to quarry the iron ore and limestone, mostly by simple pick and shovel methods, to haul the raw materials to the furnace, frequently by oxcart from the far reaches of the plantation; and to produce food and animal feed on the farmland. In addition, there were the managers, bookkeepers, and overseers necessary to keep such a large establishment operating. Finally, there were expert teamsters to haul the iron products over tortuous woodland roads to nearby markets, or to the

Schuylkill and Delaware rivers, where the iron was floated downstream to Philadelphia by flatboat.

The wide availability of iron in the middle colony of Pennsylvania provided a vital industrial resource during the period of the Revolution. It is estimated that in 1776 the gunmakers of Pennsylvania alone could produce 100,000 stands of arms a year. Many of the iron forges—notably Hopewell, Cornwall, and Warwick—produced shot and cannon for the Continental Army. The importance of the Pennsylvania iron furnaces and forges to the Continental Army was well recognized by the British. For example, a British force in 1777 destroyed the Mount Joy Furnace at Valley Forge in order to reduce the production of war materials.

By the time of the Revolution many of the ironmasters had amassed fortunes and had become distinguished citizens of their areas. Some became leaders in recruiting companies of soldiers for the Continental Army. Mark Bird, ironmaster of the Birdsboro Furnace, outfitted a company of 300 men with uniforms, tents, and provisions at his own expense.

The production of iron in Pennsylvania, already large in 1776, was stimulated by war needs. At the end of the Revolutionary War the foundations had been laid for what was to remain the greatest single industry in Pennsylvania—the making of iron and steel.

Constructing charcoal kilns to convert wood into charcoal needed in making iron

Tapping an iron furnace

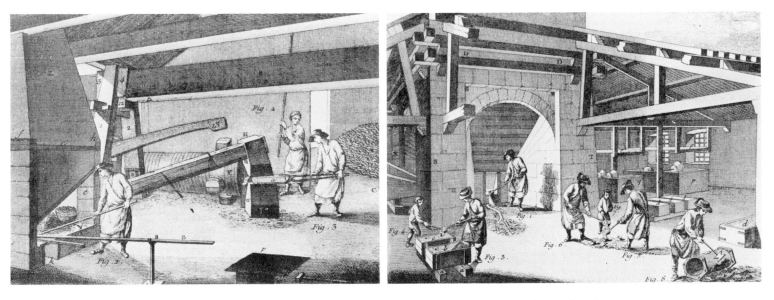

Forging cast iron into wrought iron　　　　　*Molding iron utensils on the casting floor*

Women in the Workforce

Single women were at a premium in the colony, and one contemporary observed that "even the meanest single women marry well and being above want are above work." Nevertheless, women were significantly represented in a variety of occupational roles. They found jobs as domestic servants at high wages, or in spinning and knitting, for which they were paid on a piecerate basis. This home-based textile production constituted a major industry in the province, and during the Revolution Philadelphia women boasted that they clothed the population without foreign aid. Although most tailors, furriers, and staymakers were men, women filled the jobs for milliners, menders, dyers, and wool scourers. Men dominated the trade of hairdressing for both men and women, but most of those engaged in the laying out and dressing of the dead were women.

Worker's Organizations

The availability of cheap land, the difficulty of communication, and the chronic shortage of labor militated against workers forming organizations resembling modern trade unions. Another obstacle was the British common law theory that economic organization to raise prices or wages constituted a criminal conspiracy. Nevertheless, there is evidence of rudimentary labor organization in colonial Pennsylvania. Most of these organizations were combinations of master workmen to secure and maintain a monopoly of business operations and regulate entry into their trades. In many ways they resembled medieval craft guilds.

Most notable of these was the Carpenters Company of Philadelphia, which built and owned Carpenters' Hall, where the first session of the Continental Congress convened. Chartered in 1724 for the purpose of "obtaining instruction in the science of architecture, and assisting such of their members as should be in need of support," the Carpenters Company soon concerned itself with the economic well-being of its members. Its activities included regulating prices for all carpentry as well as architectural and building work. A "book of Prices" containing the rates was directed at both employees and employers in order to assure fair wages and fair value. The company arbitrated disputes between masters and workers and regulated the relationship between master workmen and apprentices. As a mutual aid society it provided benefits for widows and orphans and furnished carriages for the funerals of members. A standing committee on vice and immorality also existed, although its activities and purposes are, unfortunately, lost to history.

Other early labor organizations were organized ostensibly as volunteer fire companies. Organized by trades, these seem to have had only a minor interest in fire fighting. The most notable company, the Cordwainers Fire Company, was organized in 1760 and was the forerunner of the first trade union in the United States. Founded by thirty-nine master shoemakers, the company regulated indentured servants and apprentices and set standards for entry into the trade. In addition to the usual benefits, the cordwainers made low-interest loans to needy members and issued traveling papers signifying good standing in the trade for shoemakers leaving Philadelphia. By 1776 there were seventeen such companies in Philadelphia, and in addition to protecting their trades, they took an active interest in politics. By the time of the Stamp Act they had worked out an elaborate system of intercolonial correspondence. Seamen in the coastal trade functioned as couriers in this undertaking. In Philadelphia the Carpenters and Cordwainers companies were active in mobilizing sentiment against the Crown. The printing tradesmen not only organized to exert political pressure but also published tracts encouraging resistance to British policy.

Despite the diversity of its enterprise, Philadelphia did not have a large resident class of unskilled workers that could be called a proletariat. Boatmen, watermen, fishermen, and common sailors constituted the largest group of common laborers. Dockside workers, carters, porters, and house servants could also be included. Though not a large group, most were free laborers dependent on their own devices to support themselves. In good times they benefited from the labor shortage, and some of them earned enough to provide well for their families and laid enough aside to become property owners. Nevertheless, in hard times they were most severely affected. Without any kind of organization, they were at the mercy of employers and had little or no protection against wage reductions and unemployment. When unemployment became widespread, as it did several times during the colonial period, the rudimentary provisions for public charity were unequal to the task. In addition, a pauper class consisting of widows, orphans, and the infirm existed at all times.

Had it not been for extensive private charity, the economic system might have broken down with possibly dangerous consequences for social stability. Philadelphia Quakers, the main supporters of public poor relief, took care of their own poor through their meetings. Private contributions built the greatest almshouse in the colonies in Philadelphia in 1767. Reflecting its cosmopolitan nature, Philadelphia was the home of a number of ethnically organized charitable societies. The St. Andrew's Society for Scots and the Deutsche Gesellschaft von Pennsylvanien for needy Germans are two examples. Citizens of Irish and English descent also developed benevolent societies, as did the workingmen's organizations. Although much still needed to be done, Philadelphia's efforts at poor relief were probably superior to those of any other American city of the time.

Commerce and Trade in Colonial Pennsylvania

Philadelphia's economy, like that of other leading colonial cities, rested primarily on the commercial activities involved in the handling of exports and imports, and the services, such as freight handling and insurance, associated with a maritime trade. Related to the maritime trade too were the city's manufacturing activities: shipbuilding, flour milling, and the cooperage industry.

The cargoes and ports of destination for Philadelphia's commerce provide a picture of the total Pennsylvania economy, and of how this economy differed from that of the other colonies. Pennsylvania's exports consisted primarily of wheat, flour, and bread. These three commodities comprised about half the colony's exports, and through them the colony's agricultural, manufacturing, and commercial activities were closely linked. Thus, although not the leading wheat producer (Maryland and Virginia, despite their emphasis on tobacco as an export staple, produced larger quantities of wheat), Pennsylvania developed into the major processor of wheat, with Philadelphia the port of origin for more than half the total colonial exports of flour.

Philadelphia also led in the export of lumber products. A cooperage industry developed to produce the barrels, casks, and hogsheads necessary for shipment of flour, bread, and salted meats. Boards, planks, staves, and shingles were also major exports of the colony. The most important nonagricultural exports were bar iron and pig

Port of Philadelphia as viewed from New Jersey

iron. These shipments reflected Pennsylvania's rise as the major iron-producing colony.

The colonies shipped "staples" to four principal areas—Great Britain and Ireland, the West Indies, southern Europe, and the Wine Islands (Madeiras, Azores, Canary Islands)—to earn the foreign exchange needed to purchase a great variety of manufactured goods, principally from Great Britain, and assorted tropical commodities, such as molasses, coffee, sugar, and salt.

England was the single most important source of imports for the colonies. They depended on her for clothing and dry goods, which represented about half of the imports; these were followed by hardware, principally wire and nails, assorted metal products, and a variety of other manufactured goods, from books to spices. Unlike Virginia and Maryland, however, Pennsylvania produced no cash crop, like tobacco, with a sufficient market in England to pay for its desired imports. Pennsylvania's exports to England, principally ore iron, augmented by occasional shipments of wheat and flour, were well below its imports of manufactured commodities. As a result, Pennsylvania commerce was largely devoted to finding markets for its native products and those which it obtained from coastwide trade, and then of using the earnings gained from this trade to pay outstanding deficits accrued in trade with Great Britain.

The West Indies (especially Jamaica) in the late eighteenth cen-

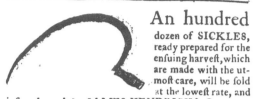
Advertisements

tury were becoming increasingly specialized in the production of sugar. As a result, these colonies were dependent upon outside sources for basic foodstuffs. Pennsylvania's agricultural produce, shipped via Philadelphia, became a major source of this supply. In one typical voyage, the *Elizabeth* sailed from Philadelphia to Kingston in 1764 carrying a cargo of 930 barrels of flour, 348 kegs of bread, 34 barrels of pork and gammons, 80,000 shingles, 3,000 staves, and assorted other commodities. The West Indies trade produced favorable trade balances, which were then used to repay balances owed to Great Britain. Pennsylvania also exported sizable quantities of wheat, bread, and flour to the Wine Islands and to Spain, Portugal, and Italy. In return, colonial ships received principally wine and salt. This trade also produced a favorable earnings balance.

In addition, Philadelphia was a major port for the coastwise trade among the colonies. The growth of this trade during the eighteenth century indicates both the economic specialization of individual colonies and their developing interdependence. Pennsylvania's principal products for foreign markets—flour, bar iron, and salted meats—also dominated its shipments to other colonies. Philadelphia engaged in an extensive re-export trade as well. It imported rum from New England and rice and naval stores from the southern colonies, which it then shipped to other countries.

Manufacturing in Colonial Pennsylvania

Pennsylvania produced a great variety of products. The farm regions supplied both raw materials and a final market for manufactured goods. Iron, zinc, and copper from mines within the colony led to the development of metalworking industries. Philadelphia's role as a leading port also served as a stimulus to manufacturing. Flour-milling, baking, meat-processing, and brewing developed as the economic link between the colony's agricultural regions and its overseas markets. The hides that were a by-product of the meat-processing industry became the raw materials from which developed a sizable leatherworking industry, producing shoes, gloves, and leather breeches. Cooperage and basketry were made possible both by the region's ample timber resources and by its ability to ship its agricultural products to foreign markets. The availability of timber was the basis not only for a lumber industry—planks, boards, shingles—but also for the shipbuilding, furniture, wagonmaking, and carriage industries. Merchants played a central role in these manufacturing activities, since they often provided the funds to construct the necessary gristmills or ovens used to manufacture commodities for export. The development of an urban merchant class also provided a market for products such as glass, clocks, paper, and fine household utensils.

By 1776 Pennsylvania had also developed the major iron industry within the colonies. Indeed, although primarily agricultural, the thirteen colonies developed before the Revolution into a major iron-producing region, accounting for approximately fifteen percent of total world production. From its inception in 1716 in the Schuylkill Valley, the iron industry in Pennsylvania moved west with the pace of settlement into the Delaware, Cumberland, and Susquehanna valleys. The colony was rich in iron ore and timber, the key raw materials for the production of iron. In size and technology, the colonial iron industry compared favorably with that in England. Pennsylvania had twenty charcoal blast furnaces and forty-five forges before 1776, more of either than any other colony. Furnaces in the colonies at Warwick and at Reading each produced 800 tons annually, sizable outputs for the period.

England sought to encourage the production of basic iron (pig and bar iron) in the colonies as a way of reducing the dependence of its iron manufacturing industry on the excellent Swedish ore, and in 1764 both pig and bar iron were admitted duty free. Iron manufactures were another matter. Hearings in the House of Commons in 1740 noted drastic declines in the English fabrication of bar iron, while in the colonies British axes and other iron products were no longer being bought. As early as 1738 restrictions on the manufacture of hardware in the colonies were debated, and in 1750 Parliament passed an Iron Act which encouraged continued import of basic iron but forbade establishment of new slitting mills (for making nails), plating works, or steel furnaces in the colonies.

QUARRY STONE, not inferior to any in this province, to be sold by NATHANIEL BROWN, and THOMAS FELTON, which they will deliver at any wharf, in the city or suburbs, at a most reasonable rate. Likewise a pair of mill-stones, bolting reels, one hopper, and several other utensils

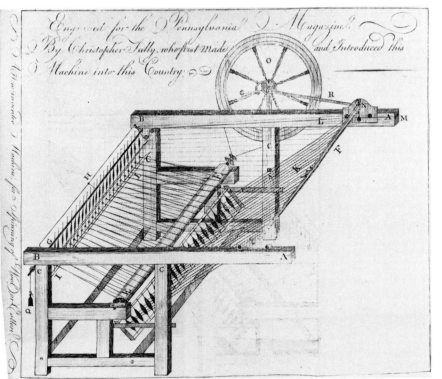

Spinning machine

139

Such legislation was more effective in raising American ire than in diminishing its competition with home industry, and the restrictive provisions of 1750 were widely ignored. By 1775 there were more furnaces and forges in the American colonies than existed in England or Wales. Meanwhile, in 1770 the Pennsylvania Assembly proceeded to encourage the making of steel, and American forges continued to turn out forbidden iron-derived implements and utensils in generous quantities. These consisted primarily of commodities for use on the farm (agricultural implements) and in the household (kettles), but the forges were also used by many other industries, such as wagon-making, shipbuilding, and gunmaking. Steel furnaces were built after 1750 in the Schuylkill Valley. Indeed, in 1762 Whitehead Humphries began producing steel in a furnace located at Seventh Street between Market and Chestnut streets in Philadelphia.

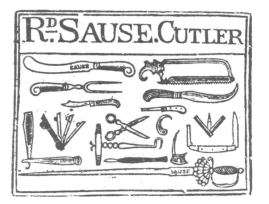

Advertisement

English Mercantilism in Colonial America

England imposed a number of political constraints upon economic activities in the colonies. The objective of these policies, generally referred to as mercantilism, was to insure that colonial activity contributed to the economic well-being of the mother country—at the expense, if necessary, of the colonies.

The colonies were seen both as sources of raw materials, particularly of strategic commodities (lumber) and luxuries (tobacco), which formerly had to be imported from other European countries, and as markets for British manufactured goods. The specific instruments of these policies were the Acts of Trade and Navigation, imposed in the middle of the seventeenth century, and a series of later decrees which sought to prevent development in the colonies of manufacturing activities. The intent of the Navigation Acts was to channel much of the international trade of the colonies through Great Britain. The principal provisions were that trade between Great Britain and the colonies had to be carried in vessels and by crews of English or colonial origin, that specific "enumerated" colonial exports (principally tobacco) could be shipped only to Great Britain (where a substantial portion was subsequently re-exported to other European countries), and that imports to the colonies from European countries had to be sent first through England before moving on to the colonies, again only on English or colonial vessels.

The Pennsylvania economy was not as seriously hurt by these British policies as were those of other colonies. Unlike Maryland and Virginia, for example, which bore the brunt of Great Britain's requirement that it receive all tobacco, Pennsylvania's principal exports were not on the enumerated list, and policies regulating commerce had little impact on its trade. It had a viable shipbuilding industry of its own, and the largest portion of its imports would likely have come from Great Britain even in the absence of the acts. It had been affected by the Molasses Act of 1733, but only in a minor way because rum-making was far less important to the economy in Pennsylvania than it was in New England, and because the administration of the act was so loose that it was widely circumvented. If any Pennsylvania industry was likely to be damaged by British policy, it was the iron manufacturing industry, particularly by the Iron Act of 1750. As we have seen, however, Pennsylvania ironmakers refused to take this act seriously.

Economic Self-Regulation in Pennsylvania

Although there was opposition in Pennsylvania to many of England's attempts to regulate economic conditions, this opposition was directed at the specific provisions of the regulations, not at the principle of governmental regulation. Rather, throughout most of the colonial period, there was general acceptance in Pennsylvania and the other colonies of the precept that a colonial government could regulate economic activity for the general good. In the early period of settlement, colonies adopted numerous measures calling for bounties, subsidies, premiums, and compulsory activities, designed to stimulate the production of manufactured goods or to encourage the construction of key processing facilities such as gristmills and sawmills. The hope was that these measures would reduce dependence on an uncertain flow of imports from Great Britain, but they appear to have had little impact.

The colony also regulated various aspects of trade and commerce. Philadelphia continued a practice of many British market towns, specifying weight, quantity, and prices for bread and beer. Other Philadelphia laws set prices for cartage and hauling. The most important colonial regulations, however, established compulsory inspection of commodities for export. Many merchants recognized that their ability to sell Pennsylvania products, primarily processed foodstuffs, in distant markets depended on their assumed quality. Efforts to establish an inspection system began early in the eighteenth century. With the development of major export demand for flour, these efforts intensified. The basic flour inspection law of 1725 provided that "no merchant or person whatsoever shall lade or ship any flour for exportation out of this province before he shall first submit the same to the view and examination of the officer who shall search and try the same in order to judge of its goodness." Similar inspection laws applied to barreled beef, pork, and lumber products. Comparable laws were passed in other colonies, but none appear to have been as rigorously enforced as those of Pennsylvania.

Life in Rural Pennsylvania

Although Philadelphia was the colony's and perhaps America's most famous community, relatively few Pennsylvanians tarried there. Colonists imbued with the pioneer spirit quickly moved beyond the ports of entry where their ships docked. Eager to get settled on their own lands and driven by the desire to eat their own produce, they paused only briefly to acquire a minimum of tools and supplies before setting off into the wilderness. A place to live was the first order of business; frequently a crude three-sided lean-to, with its opening downwind, sufficed temporarily. Trees were cut to clear land for planting, the felled timber made into notched logs with which to build a permanent cabin.

Daub-and-wattle, mud or plaster and woven wood used in construction

Building a Home

When materials were ready, and before cold weather came, a newcomer's neighbors gathered in the common cause of house-raising. Though hard work, it was also an occasion for savoring the support derived from neighbors and friends. At day's end, when the cabin was essentially completed, everyone feasted together in thankfulness and merriment. While near neighbors wended their way homeward by the light of pine or pitch torches, friends from greater distances often stayed on, extending the festivities to the daylight hours. In this way jobs too big for the single family became working parties, or "frolics."

Log cabins, first introduced by the Swedes in the early seventeenth century, continued to serve western settlers long after the Revolution. A family's first cabin was likely to be a crude, hastily erected, temporary home, limited in size by the time and strength of the building party, who had to cut, carry, and lift into position every unbarked log. Chinks were stuffed against draughts with whatever material—moss, bark, or clay—lay conveniently near. Hewn log houses, designed for permanent dwelling, required more careful selection of logs, skillful trimming and notching, and the laying of a firm foundation of flat stones. Two-story hewn-log houses,

Broad axe used to hew logs

their chimneys drifting white smoke through Pennsylvania's valleys, were a tribute to the American axe and a symbol of the transition of the frontier from wilderness to settlement. Stone houses, too, might be found, but like stone bridges they would remain a luxury in a region where wood was so abundant, time so pressing, and labor so dear.

Recreated settler's house at the Pennsylvania Farm Museum at Landis Valley is typical of a German permanent frontier house.

Recreated thatched log barn at the Pennsylvania Farm Museum at Landis Valley

The Boggs Family: Central Pennsylvania Pioneers

Throughout the 1770s central Pennsylvania was a transitional zone between two stable but very different ways of life. To the west the older social order of the Indians had changed very little from that of their ancestors. To the east colonists had firmly established a rural society with many small towns and extensive farmsteads. Between them was the frontier. Remaining Indian villages on the frontier represented numerous tribes: villagers usually were recently dispossessed from their lands to the east and already accustomed to such colonial habits as wearing ruffled shirts and cooking in metal pots. The settlers included former tenant farmers, recent European immigrants, social outcasts from eastern urban areas, and the very poor. Together these people developed their own lifestyle, based on both Indian and colonial customs, and a social order founded on tolerance and mutual support.

Andrew Boggs was one of the earliest colonial settlers in central Pennsylvania. With his wife, seven children, and an indentured servant, he established his home near the present site of Milesburg in 1769. Boggs' estate included three hundred acres of land (ten cleared), three head of cattle, three horses, and some pigs and dogs. So remote was frontier life at this time that Boggs was forced to make a two-day trip to the Juniata River simply to obtain flour. All other supplies which he could not produce himself he brought by canoe from Philadelphia once a year. We get an early glimpse into Boggs' life from the diary of a traveling minister, who describes the evening of July 31, 1775, in Boggs' cabin: ". . . We dined on fish—suckers and chubbs and on venison. It is a level, rich, pleasant spot, the broad creek running by the door. . . . Soon after we had dined two Indian boys bolted in (they never knock or speak at the door) with seven large fish, one would weigh two pounds. In return Mrs. Boggs gave them bread and a piece of venison. Down they sat in the ashes before the fire, stirred up the coals and laid on their flesh. . . . When they were gone . . . I sat me down on a three-legged stool to write. This house looks and smells like a shambles; raw flesh and blood in every part, mangled wasting flesh on every shelf. Hounds licking up the blood from the floor; an open-hearted landlady; naked Indians and children; ten hundred thousand flies; oh! I fear there are as many fleas. . . . Seize me soon, kind

sleep, lock me in thy sweet embrace. . . . For all this settlement I would not live here for two such settlements; not for five hundred a year."

Boggs was elected township supervisor in the first local elections in 1773. No doubt, this honor resulted from his reputation for treating all frontiersmen fairly. Local Indians regarded Boggs as a friend, a reputation which survived him and was responsible years later for saving the life of his son during an attack. Andrew Boggs died in 1776, two years before the Indian uprising known as the "Great Runaway" forced the abandonment of the frontier by colonists. Eight years later Mrs. Boggs and her family returned to the same cabin, where they helped other early settlers bring the stable social order of the east to central Pennsylvania.

Recent aerial view of Boggs' settlement site; the cabin was located to the right of the bend in the stream.

Heating the Home

Except in Philadelphia, where houses might include several fireplaces, a single hearth and its great chimney dominated the home. Here cooking and baking were done while life-sustaining heat poured from the open fireplace on wintry evenings. The problem of finding enough heat to sustain life in Pennsylvania's climate dominated rural life. In an attempt to focus heat more directly into a room, V-shaped fireplaces were introduced. German settlers brought with them an iron stove which could be set inside the fireplace—an innovation which probably helped inspire Benjamin Franklin's energy-saving "Pennsylvania fireplace" of 1742. It was a remarkably ingenious invention. Smoke and hot gasses passed upward over the top of a metal box, then dropped downward behind it before entering the chimney near floor level. Cold air from the floor was drawn into the box, passed between a series of baffles, and then forced out into the room by convection currents. Practical humanist that he was, Franklin observed that his invention was both good business and good for the community: "We leave it to the *Political Arithmetician* to compute how much Money will be sav'd to a Country, by its spending two thirds less of Fuel; . . . And to physicians to say, how much healthier thick-built Towns and Cities will be, now half suffocated with sulphury Smoke, when so much less of that Smoke shall be made, and the Air breath'd by the Inhabitants be consequently so much purer."

Lighting the Home

During the 1770s, factory techniques were introduced in the manufacture of candles, lifting one conventional household chore from many Pennsylvanians. In the country areas, however, most settlers still collected the fat of deer or bears, along with pork, beef, and mutton tallow, for candle-making. Spermacetti, which became available from the whaling ports at mid-century, provided several times the light of conventional candles. Bayberry candles were a welcome luxury because they burned more slowly and with less odor than tallow candles.

In the fall, every thrifty rural housewife saw to it that a full supply of candles was prepared and carefully stored for use in the dark months ahead. There was a knack to the candle-making; a good worker dipped candles slowly and evenly. If allowed to cool too fast, candles were likely to be brittle and would crack. The process also required care to avoid melting previous layers or congealing the fat unevenly. A candle frame, from which hung numerous wicks of tow, hemp, or cotton to be immersed simultaneously, helped to speed the process, and molds of as many as twenty-five units

Rushlight holder on a table in the Hans Herr House. Rushlights were cattails soaked in tallow.

Keeping Warm in 1776

Early settlers in Penn's Woods turned mostly to the forests for resources to combat the freezing cold and chilling dampness of the fall, winter, and spring months. In the forests were to be found firewood for heating the home; furs, skins, feathers, and down for protecting the body against the damp cold. Men and women alike wore fur-lined boots over heavy knitted woolen stockings. Undergarments were of homespun flannel worn in multiple layers, while outergarments were of wool, deerskin, or fur. Muffs were fashionable for men, and stocking hats protected both sexes from frozen ears. Children dressed like their parents, and infants enjoyed the warmth of blankets with which they were wrapped mummy-like.

Only the heavy outergarments were removed for sleeping. The German and Dutch featherbeds, spread both underneath and as coverings, were judged by travelers to be warmer than the canopied and heavily curtained bedsteads of the English. All members of a family often shared a bed; even visitors joined them, quite modestly, in kitchens turned bedrooms, close to the fireplace. In the larger houses, where separate bedrooms occupied the second floor, a central chimney often had multiple fireplace openings so that each sleeping quarter could be supplied with heat. Stones or bricks were frequently heated in the fires and then carried to the beds, wrapped in heavy coverings to preserve the warmth. Some homes boasted a warming pan, a long-handled, covered brass container in which hot charcoals could be carried from room to room and moved back and forth between the covers of each bed to remove the worst of the shocking chill before would-be sleepers climbed in.

Churches and meeting houses, unoccupied much of the time, usually were not heated. Hardy attendants at services sometimes carried footstoves fired by charcoal and placed beneath or between the pews. Pet dogs were allowed to lie at the feet of their masters and mistresses, the warmth of their furry bodies being much appreciated. Large pockets made from wolves' furs, into which parishioners could place their cold feet, were often attached to the seats. Meetings being lengthy, short recesses were observed during which those in attendance retired either to an adjacent longhouse with its roaring fireplace, or to a nearby tavern to partake of the dual comforts of a warm room and a warming drink.

In time a variety of stoves were invented and produced for sale. The earliest types, hardly more than large cast-iron boxes on legs, often protruded through a wall to the outside, where they could be refueled and tended as needed. Cannonmakers used their molds to build a heating device that looked like an upended weapon and was appropriately called a cannon stove. Many early stoves were charcoal fired and without flues. Wood- or coal-burning appliances owed much of their development to the inventive genius of Benjamin Franklin. His creations made possible the circulation of heat throughout a structure by means of vents and flues.

Keeping warm in 1776 was a year-round task. The natural warmth of the summer sun could be enjoyed only when it was accompanied by all the hard work necessary to assure warmth during the cold months.

Five-plate (five-sided) stove used to heat the parlor of a Pennsylvania German house. It was fed through an opening in the back of the kitchen fireplace.

Portable foot warmer, filled with hot coals, was used in wagons and carried to church in the winter.

*Bed warmers, filled with hot coals,
took the chill off cold bed clothes.*

German corner stove with wrap-around bench

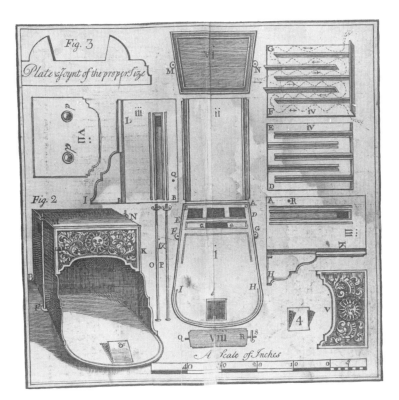

Franklin stove

*In large kitchen fireplaces several fires were often used at one time.
They were the equivalent of burners on a modern range.*

Brass candlesticks

Candlemold

greatly simplified it. Molds were tapered for easy removal of the candles. Often candles were made from treasured formulas, such as mixtures of beeswax and tallow, to be used in church or on special occasions. It remained for the early nineteenth century to introduce candle-making machinery, superior tallow components, and chemically treated self-trimming wicks. (In 1776 householders trimmed their candles with a simple scissors with broad-blades—perhaps into a metal box soldered to it to catch the trimmings.) Two hundred candles could be molded in a good day's work.

With so much work, or cost, having gone into candles, it is easy to see why the cone-shaped douter (called by later generations a "snuffer") was devised to put out the flame quickly. "Early to bed and early to rise," Poor Richard admonished his readers if they wanted to be wealthy, and although he promised health and wisdom as well, he may have been thinking of the cost of candles. We may recall that the frugal Franklin also advocated Daylight Saving Time.

Feeding the Family

In the autumn months the rural housewife and her children were busy preserving foods: slicing apples to be hung and dried, salting or smoking meat and fish, making jams, canning preserves, pressing cheeses into flat wheels. Meat and fish would then be packed and

From Lewis Miller's sketchbook

stored in barrels; on the farm there might be a springhouse where meat and dairy products could be kept fairly cool. The food was cooked in large iron kettles at the open hearth. The huge fireplaces in the farm kitchen were sometimes so large a man could walk into them. A small brick oven might be built into the side of the chimney. The fireplace foundations were often twelve feet square, and the extensive masonry above the fireplace supported hooks and cranes bearing heavy kettles, as well as gridirons, spits, skillets, andirons, and perhaps the favorite family firearm. The family diet consisted largely of pork and beef, cabbage, potatoes, and rye bread. Fish, deer, and wild turkey were occasionally added to the menu. Tea and coffee were scarce, but there was always plenty of cider, beer, and brandy for those whose religions permitted drinking them.

From Lewis Miller's sketchbook

Spinning and carding

Advertisement

JAMES CUNNING,

At the Sign of the SPINNING-WHEEL, in Market-ſtreet,

INTENDING to leave this for England ſome time in February, will ſell off at the loweſt price for Caſh, the large and general aſſortment of DRY GOODS he has now on hand; among which are, a quantity of ſuperfine and low priced broadcloths of divers colours, from 30ſ. to 6/8. with ſuitable trimming; Iriſh hollands and linens, from 7/6. to 18d. per yard, &c.——Likewiſe, a large aſſortment of JEWELLERY, conſiſting of ſet ſhoe, knee and ſtock buckles; hair pins; ſhirt buckles; ſilver lockets; ſilver ſeals, &c. plated ſhoe, knee and ſtock buckles; pinchbeck ditto; common yellow and white metal ditto; plated ſpurs; a few pair of beſt holſter piſtols; one hundred ſilver watches of different prices; with many articles too numerous for an advertiſement.

He returns his moſt grateful thanks to his friends and cuſtomers, by whoſe conſtant favours he hopes to be able to make connexions that will, when our unhappy differences with the Mother Country are ſettled, put it in his power to ſerve them on better terms than ever.

N. B. The houſe where he now lives, with a leaſe of eight years, either to be let of the intereſt to be ſold. Likewiſe four plantations in the New-Purchaſe to be ſold—all expences paid except patenting.

Clothing

On the frontier Indian methods of tanning hides of wild animals were imitated by early settlers. But the skilled tanners who landed in the province soon brought refinements. The settlers learned to clean hides with lye made by leaching wood ashes, placing them in a crude plank box imbedded in the earth, being careful to alternate them with crushed oak bark shavings, and finally soaking the mass in water. After several renewals of the solution and perhaps six months later, they removed the hides, washed and hung them to dry, then rubbed or rolled them to improve pliability. From these skins they made trousers, jackets, moccasins, shoes, and hats.

Linen could be prepared from the widely available flax plant, whose long fibers provided a strong cloth, though only after considerable time and effort. Organic material was rotted away from the fibers in running water for about two weeks, or by the slower action of dew. After this "retting" process, they were then dried in the sun or in ovens. The two wooden beams of the "flaxbreak" beat and broke up the fibers, which were then further cleansed by beating with a wooden knife and then drawn through a comb called a "hetchel." Such dressed flax could be spun in a specially designed flax wheel and woven in a handloom, then washed and bleached in the sun.

Cell at Ephrata in which a Sister would have spun, weaved cloth tape, and slept

What They Wore in 1776

In colonial America there was a great difference between the clothing worn by the wealthy and that of the middle and lower classes. While the servants and the poorer people usually wore clothing of rough homespun and cotton, the aristocracy mirrored the fashions of London and Versailles. Foot-high "fashion babies" were brought to America to display the latest styles. Warp-dyed taffeta, silk brocade, ribbed silk, hand-painted Chinese silk, heavy satin, velvet— these were just some of the magnificent fabrics that found their way into the colonies.

Styles of clothing on the farm were very different from those in the fashionable circles of Philadelphia. The country housewife wore a full skirt with a clearly defined waistband and a chemise, over which she wore a work bodice. She draped a scarf, called a "fichu," over her shoulders, crossing it in front at her waist. Always, inside and out, she covered her head, usually with the popular white gathered "mob cap."

Ladies of fashion wore ankle-length skirts, made fuller by bone hoops. Their undergarments included stays, linen or cotton breeches, and several petticoats, including at times a quilted one. When the weather turned warm, the fashionable lady would don a thin shawl or scarf of muslin, damask, silk, or cotton. Her head might be covered by a "calash," or collapsible bonnet, or perhaps by the more elegant Gainsborough, with its large graceful brim trimmed with plumes. Underneath she wore a wig or a high, fancy hairdo, even if she had to sleep on a block of wood to keep it in place. To protect her skin, she might cover her face with a silk or velvet mask, and pull long white kid gloves, richly embroidered, over her arms. Her shoes, unlike the sturdy, mannish ones her country cousin wore, were extremely dainty, with thin, narrow soles and perhaps two-inch heels.

Men's clothing showed the same class differences. The farmer wore linen or leather pantaloons (often without a flap so they could be turned around) and a checked shirt of heavy linen or wool. He could also be seen in a frock, resembling an artist's smock, which in the summer he could wear without a shirt. In the winter he wore a coat of coarse woolen cloth. The fur of raccoon, wolf, bear, or fox supplied the material for his hat.

The man of high fashion, on the other hand, could dress like a dandy. His sleeveless waistcoat would be made of imported satin, velvet, or brocade, and

Fashionable gown

Dressmaker's shop

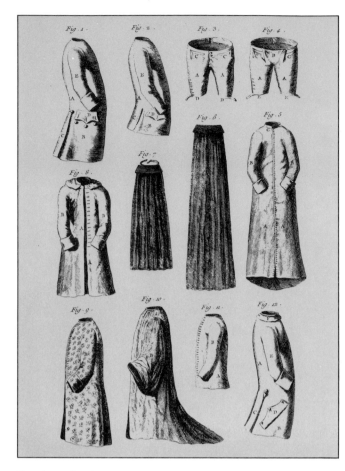

Gentlemen's clothing

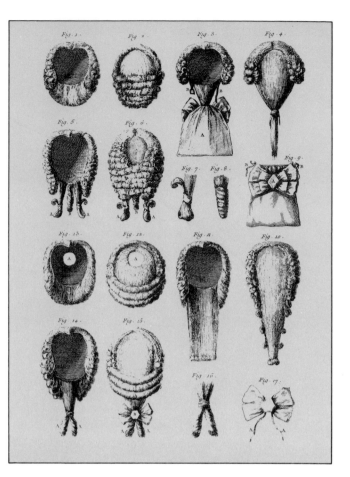

Gentlemen's wigs

Gentlemen's tailor

might be embroidered with flowers. His coat would be laced and ruffled and would sport double rows of gold buttons. His breeches, perhaps light blue or yellow, were made of fine cotton and Chinese nankeen. If knee-length, these breeches were called "small-clothes," and worn with white silk stockings.

Men's shoes were square-toed, and all classes wore buckles—pewter and brass for the poor; silver, gold, and cut steel for the rich. Left and right shoes were the same and interchangeable.

The most popular hat for men was the cocked hat, worn as a three-corned "tricorne" on the aristocratic gentleman, usually black with perhaps a gold braid adorning it or feathers or fur along the edge. The hats of the working class were usually not cocked; farmers preferred a wide brim to shield them from the sun.

Wigs were a standard item of dress throughout the colonial period—from the 1650s to about the 1800s. Men of high fashion wore wigs made from a variety of materials—including actual hair from humans, goats, and horses, or from calves' and cows' tails, as well as mohair, thread, silk, and fine

Typical common dress

wire. At home, these hot, heavy wigs would be removed, and men would cover their shaved heads with
turbans. To complete their costume, they would wear
a full-length silk dressing gown called a banyan.

Children's dress after the age of five usually resembled that of their parents. Long chemises and
caps were placed on both boys and girls under five.
Thereafter, boys wore the waistcoats and tight knee
breeches seen on their fathers, and girls the same
tight bodices and full petticoats worn by their
mothers. After they were seven or eight, boys of the
wealthier families had their heads shaved for wigs;
girls, from the age of three or four, were sometimes
expected to wear corsets reaching from their knees to
their underarms. To keep their skins fashionably
white, these girls like their mothers wore linen masks,
sunbonnets, and long gloves.

The last part of the century saw some changes.
Boys were allowed to wear more comfortable one-
piece suits over linen shirts, and by 1800 little girls
were able to dress more like little girls and less like
little women. The revolutionary movement helped to
democratize clothing styles. The importation of fancy
materials was discouraged in favor of homemade
cloth, and men who had worn wigs began to wear
their hair tied back with a single ribbon in a simple
queue. Less ornamented dress became a sign of
patriotism, and clothing among the rich became
more practical and comfortable.

Wigmaker and barber

ETHAN SICKELS
Leather-Dreſſer and Breeches-Maker

George Bartram,

At the Sign of the Naked Boy, half Way between Cheſtnut and Walnut Streets, in Second-Street, HAS a general Aſſortment of DRY GOODS, imported in the laſt

John White

Stay-   Maker,

Who formerly lived in Strawberry-Alley, has now removed into Walnut-ſtreet (almoſt oppoſite Mrs. Hopkinſon's) near Fifth-ſtreet, WHERE he continues to carry on the Staymaking buſineſs as uſual.

Pennsylvanians added woolen garments to their simple wardrobes by raising sheep. Wool was scoured with weak lye and soap, then carded to straighten and intermingle varying lengths of fiber for added strength. (In 1777, Oliver Evans, only recently launched on his own career as inventor and steam engineer, developed a card-making machine capable of producing 150 pairs of cards a day.) Next, the wool was combed to extend the fibers. It was then spun and woven, which involved complex machinery and technical know-how. Fulling or felting was more rapidly done when in 1698 a mill using rollers and soapy water was introduced in Pennsylvania. Dyeing and shearing, both operations requiring additional technical experience, followed.

Family and Community

Life in Pennsylvania, then, was for the most part primarily the experience of home and family. Family members joined in clearing the land, preparing soil, and cultivating crops, and in all the chores of domestic living. Such sharing of tasks was often in evidence around the hearth in the home on a wintry night as the father might be carving or whittling a tool. Nearby was the mother, busily engaged in one of the numerous steps in converting garden products into threads or yarns, cloth and clothing. Children's hands were kept from mischief by jobs that required threading slices of fruits, vegetables, or meats to be dried and preserved. It is little wonder that the fireplace and hearth became symbols of the close-knit family of America's frontier.

Gradually, as the wilderness gave way to the settlers, communities evolved. Scattered homesteaders cooperated not only in cabin- and barn-raisings, but in a wide range of activities which contributed to their common good. Before long, schools and churches, gristmills, sawmills, and the shops of blacksmiths, tanners, and cabinetmakers dotted the countryside and marked the hamlets as service centers for their communities. General stores emerged to provide a setting for social intercourse, as well as to supply the settlers' material needs. Roads slowly replaced the paths within and among the communities. Inns were built along the way to serve travelers, but they served the local people as well by connecting them with the outside world, bringing them news and current events, information and ideas.

Growing Up in a New Nation

Growing up in early Pennsylvania was no simple matter for most children. There was as great a spread as there is today between deprivation and advantage—from the earthen floored huts on the edge of the Endless Mountains to the gracious mansions of Philadelphia. The great majority of Pennsylvania families, however, shared a common experience and economy, mostly agricultural and self-sufficient, in which work was important for children as well as adults. This work was paid for not in cash but in comfort gained for daily life. Virtually everything that a person touched in the course of the day was made by someone in the family, who was also responsible for its maintenance and repair. That the child was expected to do his share is indicated by the various entries of fifteen-year-old Noah Blake in his journal: "Finished the winters lot of nail making and put the forge to rights." "Day spent in forge barn fashioning trunnels for bridge. Did forty." "Shortest day of the year, Midwinter Day. Finished Sarah's rocking chair. Made mother a candle stick." Still another entry, one of many revealing the close involvement of children with adults in everyday work: "Still working on the bridge floor. Father splits while I saw."

Like few children today, the child of 1776 was fully involved in the rhythms and cycles of nature: maple sugaring in March, preparing the ground in April and planting the garden in May, haymaking in June, harvesting in July and August, cider-making in September, gathering nuts in October, husking corn in November— and so it went through all the years of a child's life. The Almanac, read as regularly as the Bible, registered the hours of sunrise and sunset, the phases of the moon, the tides, the proper times for planting and harvesting. These regularities, together with printed aphorisms and folk wisdom, some of it superstition but much pragmatic and founded on natural truth, made life orderly, predictable, lawful. The few available books were greatly treasured, and the more common newsheets, broadsides, and pamphlets were in some families read aloud by the children.

Undoubtedly there was more moralizing both by and for children then, and the child of 1776 was perhaps more acquainted with danger, certainly with illness and death, than the child of today. Nevertheless, then as now, children were mischievous, reluctant to go to school, fond of pranks sometimes breaking over into vandalism, unhappy over punishments, eager for food and play, new clothing, and small treasures—at least such is the testimony of letters and diaries and the later recollections that have come down to us. How familiar is Anna Green Winslow's unhappiness concerning her black hat and red jacket: "Dear Mama, you dont know the fation here—I beg to look like other folk."

The German tradition of decorating a tree at Christmas was brought to the colonies by immigrants. This Lewis Miller sketch is thought to be the first American picture of a Christmas tree.

Then as now children relished holidays, the more perhaps as there were so few of them, like Training or Muster Day (for the volunteer militia) and the community harvest festival. The new nation at once added two more: Election Day and Independence Day. All recollections of childhood reveal the importance of special days to children, particularly the break in the usual routines. One early American re-

Infancy

Manhood

The Revolutionary Family

The early American family was quite different from the modern one in size, composition, and psychology. According to the Federal Census of 1790, the average Pennsylvania family consisted of six persons—two more than the average today and one more than the average in England then. Frontier families tended to be somewhat smaller than those in the towns, because of the larger proportion of male, unmarried, and newly married settlers on the frontier. Since infant mortality in the 1700s was relatively high, an average family size of six meant that married couples typically produced eight children. A family often contained not only nearly full-grown children but also an unweaned infant. Life expectancy being considerably shorter than now, one parent was likely to be dead and the other elderly before the last of their offspring left home.

The family of 1776 was usually neither what sociologists call "nuclear" (one set of parents and their children) nor "extended" (related sets of parents with assorted offspring). Few households contained pairs of grandparents, and brothers or sisters almost never lived together after marrying. Married sons in rural areas often lived near their fathers, although not with them, while waiting to inherit land. The colonial family is best described as a "modified extended" one, since many households included a few special relatives (frequently one grandparent),

as well as apprentices, lodgers, servants (free or indentured), and slaves (rarely in Pennsylvania).

Despite minor variations in structure, depending on whether a household was headed by a farmer, merchant, artisan, or laborer, the family was patriarchal. If fathers were benevolent despots, then mothers were sources of comfort, especially for the very young. Beyond the toddler stage the young were perceived as adults in miniature, and were expected to act older than their age. Adolescence in the modern sense was not part of the life cycle; maturing was a gradual ascent from infancy to adulthood. Living quarters were cramped, lacking the privacy that moderns demand, so the control of aggression among family members often was a pressing problem.

The revolutionary-era family's most striking characteristic was its religious outlook. Every member's behavior had a divine warrant, and all aspired to salvation. Preachers warned parents that their children were bound to be damned unless their wills were broken, so the elders drummed deference and obedience into children either by manipulative loving or by sheer force (to spank or not has been one of America's longest running debates).

Colonial families would have been uncomfortable for most moderns, but they produced their share of competent human beings, fitted for the challenges of their time and place.

The Peale Family, 1773, by Charles Willson Peale, showing his wife, mother-in-law, several of his children and their spouses, the family nurse, and the dog.

BLINDMAN's BUFF.

BEREFT of all Light,
I ſtumble along ;
But, if I catch you,
My Doom is your own.

MORAL.

How blind is that Man,
Who ſcorns the Advice
Of Friends, who intend
To make him more wiſe.

membered: "I always liked 'training day' because then I could go a fishing. Fished all day till dark, and felt sorry when night came."

The excitement of these days was observed by children in ways appropriate to their interests, but children always remained on the fringe of adult activities, which invariably included speeches. In fact, one of the effects of growing up in revolutionary times, with their emphasis on public expression and speech making, was the training of the boy in declamation, a practice which lasted through the next century, even creeping into the girl's world as "elocution." Every boy would be asked in any gathering to "speak a piece" for the benefit of his elders. Such a "piece" was selected from classics of oratory from Spartacus and Cicero to Shakespeare and even Logan, the pre-Revolutionary Indian Chief. Because it would be bad form to refuse, every boy had a couple of such pieces "on tap." Contemporaries believed these speaking pieces gave children concepts which served as guiding ideals—perhaps through them they would learn to become model citizens.

Pages from a children's book illustrate popular games combined with moral lessons.

THREAD *the* NEEDLE.

HERE Hand in Hand the Boys
unite,
And form a very pleaſing Sight ;
Then thro' each other's Arms they fly,
As Thread does thro' the Needle's Eye.

RULE *of* LIFE.

Talk not too much ; ſit down content,
That your Diſcourſe be pertinent.

HOOP *and* HIDE.

GO hide out, and hoop,
Whilſt I go to ſleep :
If you I can't find,
My Poſt I muſt keep.

MORAL.

With Carefulneſs watch
Each Moment that flies,
To keep Peace at Home,
And ward off Surprize.

Life in Philadelphia

The lives of colonial Philadelphians differed radically from those whose homes were in the hamlets or on scattered farmsteads. After the initial pioneering days, many Philadelphia area families were affluent enough to import the finest furniture, fabrics, silver, and pewter to furnish town houses and country estates. The town houses were two or three stories high, made of brick with many windows. A stoop before the door was almost universal, and most houses had balconies along the entire length of the second floor. Wives of the wealthy concerned themselves with household duties, their dress, and with embroidery of all kinds. Women of fashion wore the finest and most expensive imported silks and satins, with elegant bracelets, necklaces, and other jewelry. Affluent men's garments were just as elaborately made of elegant fabrics trimmed with silver buttons and buckles. Some clothing was bought ready made, but typically fabrics and trimmings were supplied to the family seamstress or tailor, whose work the housewife supervised.

Fashionable Philadelphia ate well. It was not uncommon to see fourteen separate courses served at dinner. In the wealthier homes, imported madeira, burgundy, and claret would be served, and a caller could expect to be offered a drink of rum punch from a crystal or china bowl in the drawing room. Coffee, tea, and chocolate, as well as beer and ale, were the popular drinks. Philadelphians had a choice of meats: beef, ham, pork, mutton, lamb, duck, chicken, and some wild game. Fish dishes, including oysters in hot shells and turtle soup, might also be found on their tables. A breakfast dish which is still unique to Philadelphia was scrapple, a sausage-like combination of pork and corn meal. Several desserts might be served at dinner, including syllabub (milk or cream mixed with wine and sweetened), floating islands (combinations of custard and meringue, sometimes topped with floating pieces of jelly), trifles (rum or sherry-soaked cakes, with jam and whipped cream), fools (cooked and mashed fruit with cream), flummery (pudding made with boiled oatmeal or flour, with milk, eggs, and sugar sometimes added), and a variety of melons, jellies, and sweetmeats. As a rule, the colonists ate four meals a day: a light breakfast of coffee or tea with a roll

Chinese export punch bowl. Punch was the forerunner of the cocktail. In elegant homes punch was served in individual vessels dipped from the bowl. In taverns the bowl was often passed from person to person.

Fashionable dress

159

View of Chestnut Street in Philadelphia

Friends Meeting House and Academy in Philadelphia

around 7:00, breakfast or lunch about 11:00, dinner at 4:00 P.M., and then supper before they went to bed.

The Athens of America

In many ways, Philadelphia and its environs dominated the entire province. The city and nearby counties maintained political ascendancy, despite the interior's increasing population. For the most part, eastern Pennsylvania staffed the governor's council, provided the judges, and controlled the provincial Assembly. In Philadelphia lived the "merchant princes," grown wealthy through local and foreign commerce, who gave the city its social as well as its political primacy. Their wealth contributed to Philadelphia's prominence in education, reflected in schools for all ages and purposes, even a medical school founded in association with its Pennsylvania Hospital. The city and its surrounding area sponsored several publishing enterprises, including Franklin's *Pennsylvania Gazette*, Sauer's *Geschicht-Schreiber*, and William Smith's *American Magazine*, which became the vehicle of expression for leading artists and poets, such as Philip Freneau, Charles Willson Peale, and Benjamin West, the "Raphael of America." Philadelphia's American Philosophical Society, founded in 1743, gathered the intellectual elite of the colonies. The city's Georgian architecture helped make it the most beautiful community in the province. Indeed, it was known as the "Athens of America."

Life and Politics in the City

As in the ancient Greek metropolis, of course, not everyone lived a life of cultured luxury. Most eighteenth-century Philadelphians were engaged in the heavy everyday work on which the life of the city and the colony depended: building, hauling, making and fixing things, or cleaning up the debris of human activity. But, unlike the slaves of classical Athens—or most of the European working people of their own time—Philadelphians could "raise themselves in the world." They could follow Dr. Franklin, the former printer who had sat in the provincial Assembly and who held honorary degrees from Oxford and St. Andrew's. Many tradesmen and shopkeepers became fairly prosperous, despite frequent periods of economic depression between 1760 and 1775, and no inherited patent of nobility was required to become a professional man, a banker, or even a merchant prince.

Although Philadelphia was a "city of opportunity" with little class struggle in the modern Marxist sense, many urban artisans shared the western farmers' resentment of the eastern gentry's power and privilege. Both frontiersmen and city workingmen felt that the

The Mifflins of Philadelphia

When the superb double portrait of Thomas Mifflin and his wife was painted by John Singleton Copley, the couple were on a visit to Boston to communicate with Samuel Adams and other leaders of the revolutionary movement. The year was 1773, and having at this time an important client as politically radical as Thomas Mifflin was a mixed blessing to the artist. Copley was the foremost artist in the colonies, and this was a lucrative commission, but three months after the picture was finished, a raging mob threatened Copley and smashed the windows of his father-in-law, Edward Clarke, a prominent Tory. Clarke was a consignee of the taxed tea which had arrived from England only to be dumped in Boston harbor. In 1774 Copley left for England, never to return.

Whatever his misgivings, Copley was evidently attracted to the contrasting personalities of his two sitters. He considered this double portrait a challenge to the skills and authority which came as a climax to his American career. Compositionally, he juxtaposed two three-quarter length portraits, placing Mrs. Mifflin in the prominent foreground plane in front of her husband, who casually leans on the back of a Chippendale chair. Copley lightened the faces and bodies against a dark background to achieve harmony in color, space, and design; the result is one of his masterpieces.

Mifflin as a teen-ager had been the subject of a portrait by Benjamin West and, after the Revolution, he sat for Gilbert Stuart. Yet neither of the other likenesses has the impact of the Copley work, which is a remarkable characterization of two unusual people. Mifflin at the time was a radical Whig, active in Pennsylvania avant-garde politics, and a member of the Provincial Assembly. He was to go on to become a member of the Continental Congress, a major general and quartermaster general under Washington, and, under the new constitution, the first governor of Pennsylvania. Half a dozen Pennsylvania place names are testimonials to Mifflin's years of service to his native province and state.

Yet some of the ambiguities and uncertainties which marked his life seem evident in Mifflin's face as he turns to his strong-willed wife. John Adams once referred to Sarah Morris Mifflin as "a charming Quaker girl," but as we look at this powerfully projected woman, she seems to return our scrutiny coolly and objectively, as if she were assessing the viewer. Sarah Mifflin was the anchor of her husband's existence, and her death in 1790 left him bereft as he assumed the duties of governor of the new state of Pennsylvania.

Thomas and Sarah Morris Mifflin, by John Singleton Copley, 1773

affluent suburban counties were overrepresented in the colonial Assembly, so the two groups gravitated toward a political alliance culminating in the Assembly's reapportionment act of March 1776. This developing alliance was foreshadowed in 1764 in the affair of the "Paxton Boys"—a group of five hundred frontiersmen who, impatient with the failure of the Quaker-dominated assembly to protect them against the Indians, had killed a score of peaceful Conestoga Indians before marching on Philadelphia. These frontier activists were "invited and Encouraged by many Considerable persons in Philadelphia," according to an observer. The good works of well-to-do Quakers and Moravians among the "poor natives" were twisted in many minds, urban as well as rural, into "excessive regard manifested to Indians, beyond his Majesty's loyal Subjects." The treaty rights of poor natives meant little either to frontiersmen, whose families' lives were threatened by the Indian counteroffensive following the French and Indian War, or to city workingmen, whose families' well-being seemed neglected by "the opulent merchants and gentry."

That phrase is from a letter of "Tom Trudge" complaining in the *Pennsylvania Chronicle* that the poor paid more than the rich to the Philadelphia street commissioners for removal of rubbish, garbage, and dung. Tom also charged that the rich got better scavenging and street-paving service. Regardless of inequities, the six elected commissioners kept Philadelphia's streets so clean and well paved that visitors marveled. The street commissioners protected their pavements with restrictions on the weights, speeds, and tire widths of carts and wagons. Property owners, even the holders of vacant lots, were required to pave "with good well burnt Bricks, or good square flat Stones, the Footways and Gutters." The street commissioners also provided brick-arched sewers for waste water and regulated the digging of private wells or privies. Elected city wardens made sure that hundreds of public water pumps and whale oil lamps were spaced along the streets. Regulators of "party walls, buildings, and partition fences" imposed safety standards with the cooperation of the Carpenters Company. Chimney-sweeps were licensed, and they were fined if a fire occurred in a flue within a month after its cleaning. The city government maintained four hand-drawn fire engines, but most citizens relied more on the seventeen private fire companies, which served also as political clubs comprising both gentry and craftsmen—increasingly united in opposition to British policy.

Vital to all Pennsylvanians was Philadelphia's seaport, largest in the New World, with its ninety wharves on a three-mile waterfront. Thus the nine wardens of the port, responsible for the construction and repair of piers and lighthouses as well as the licensing and regulation of pilots, were leading merchants and mariners appointed by the Pennsylvania Assembly. Agricultural products from the hinterland either moved through the port or were offered in Philadelphia's

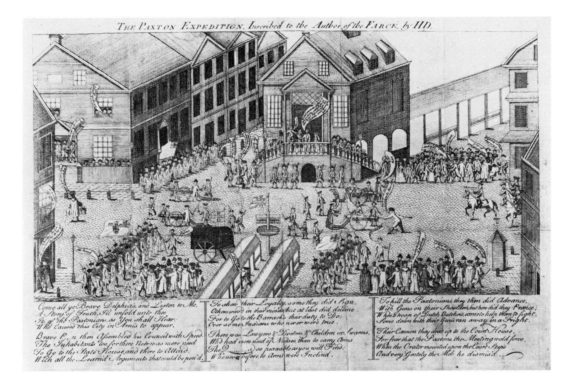

Come all ye Brave Delphia's and Listen to Me.
A Story of Truth I'll unfold unto thee.
So of the Paxtonians, as You shall Hear.
Who Caused this City in Arms to appear.

Brave P___n then Assembled his Council with Speed.
The Inhabitants too, for there Nedr was more need
To Go to the State House, and there to Attend.
With all the Learned Arguments that could be pen'd.

To shew their Loyalty, some they did Sign
Others would in thir minds, but at last did decline
For to Go to the Barracks thir duty to Do;
Over some Indians who never were true.

There was Lawyers & Doctors & Children in Swarms,
Wh'd had more need of Nurses, than to carry Arms
The D___d so persuade as you will Find.
Who never before to Arms were Inclind.

To kill the Paxtonians, they then did Advance,
With Guns on their Shoulders, but then did they Prance;
Wh'n a troop of Dutch Butchers comets help them to fight,
Some down with their Guns ran away in a Fright.

Thir Cannon they drew up to the Court House,
For fear that the Paxton, the Meeting wold force
When the Orator mounted upon the Court Steps
And very Gentely the Mob he dismiss'd.

The Paxton Boys' March on Philadelphia

After nearly ten years of sporadic Indian warfare, a group of settlers in and around Paxton Township (now Harrisburg), dissatisfied with the Quaker-dominated Assembly's measures against Indian attacks, took matters into their own hands. On December 14, 1763, they attacked a settlement of Indians on Conestoga Manor, in Lancaster County, and killed six of them. Fourteen Indians who were away from the settlement at the time of the attack were taken to the town of Lancaster and lodged in the workhouse for their own protection. To complete their work the "Paxton Boys" broke into the Lancaster workhouse on December 27 and killed all the remaining Conestoga Indians.

There was widespread support for the Paxton Boys throughout the colony, especially among the Scotch-Irish settlers. When the provincial government attempted to press the search for the murderers, the Paxton Boys decided to march on Philadelphia, confront the Assembly, and demand redress of their grievances. The specter of these "white savages," as Benjamin Franklin called them, marching on Philadelphia sent the residents into a panic. A defense of the city was organized and included a number of Quakers who, to the surprise of many, took up arms.

A contemporary cartoon portrays one of the embarrassing moments of this general mobilization.

During the night of the fifth of February 1764, an alarm was sounded and wild rumors flew that anywhere from five hundred to two thousand Paxton Boys were converging on the city. Units marched up and down the streets and, in the incident portrayed here, the artillery was just about to fire upon a contingent of supposed Paxton Boys when the gunners discovered that it was a company of German butchers (far right in cartoon) marching to the city's defense.

The Paxton affair demonstrated many of the religious, social, and political antagonisms that had been developing over the years. In the ensuing pamphlet warfare, the Quakers were accused of failure to provide adequate frontier defense. In turn, the Quakers attacked the Presbyterians for being behind the murder of the Indians. One result was that for the first time the Presbyterians coalesced into an effective political force within the colony. The Paxton affair also established a precedent for a pattern of action that would be followed repeatedly as the colony prepared for the Revolution—immediate, extemporaneous responses which were often extralegal and outside the structure of established government. This approach to problem-solving was typical of local politics in colonial Pennsylvania, and was used successfully by the radical leaders to bring Pennsylvania into the Revolution.

Fire capes worn to protect the firefighters from falling debris. 1775 refers to the date the company was organized.

A hand pumper. A bucket brigade kept the tank filled.

Leather fire bucket used in bucket brigades

Firemark indicating insurance coverage. Firefighters, funded by the insurance companies, would let houses burn if they did not bear the firemark of their company.

Salvage bags were kept in the home. They were used to lower valuables out the window.

Firefighting and Fire Insurance in Philadelphia

While the revivalists of the Great Awakening were saving souls from otherworldly fire and brimstone, Benjamin Franklin busied himself with saving the material wealth of Philadelphia from earthly flames. In 1736 Philadelphia's "men of property" accepted Franklin's proposals and formed America's first volunteer fire department, the Union Fire Company. According to Franklin's Autobiography, thirty citizens compacted "for the more ready extinguishing of fires, and mutual assistance in removing and securing goods when in danger." The members of this first company were expected to supply and maintain their own leather buckets, linen salvage bags, and baskets. Moreover, they were required once a month "to spend a social evening together, in discoursing and communicating such ideas as occurred to us upon the subject of fires." Absentees and late arrivals were fined—the proceeds going toward the purchase of ladders, hooks, and engines.

Philadelphians quickly realized the common sense and utility of the volunteer fire company. Using the Union's design as a model, civic-minded men from every district of the city established comparable firefighting units. By the middle of the eighteenth century at least eight more companies were formed: the Fellowship, 1738; the Hand-in-Hand, 1742; the Heart-in-Hand, 1743; the Friendship, 1747; the Star, 1749; the Britannia, 1750; the Hibernia, 1752; and the Northern Liberties, 1756. Each of the local forces had a "Fireward," who wielded a long wooden and brass staff as an emblem of his authority. Engineers, foremen, and their assistants minimized the tumult and confusion at a fire by shouting directions through "work horns" to the bucket brigades, the ax-men, the hookmen, and the pumpers.

Although rivalry rather than cooperation often characterized the relationship among companies before mid-century, by 1788 Franklin could proudly ask in his Autobiography "whether there is a city in the world better provided with the means of putting a stop to beginning conflagrations . . . the city has never lost by fire more than one or two houses at a time." Through the establishment of the Philadelphia Contributorship, America's first successful fire insurance company, Franklin discovered a method of coordinating the efforts of the various companies for the "Utility of the Inhabitants in

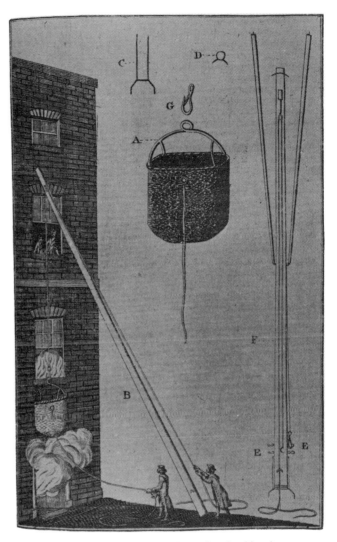

Apparatus for rescuing people and valuables from burning buildings

General." At a meeting of the Union Fire Company on July 26, 1751, Franklin requested that two delegates from "the other Several Fire Companies" be appointed to meet at the Royal Standard in Market Street to discuss the formation of a fire insurance company. On February 18, 1752, after two years of organizational preparation, Franklin displayed at the Court House the thirty-two articles of the Philadelphia Contributorship's Deed of Settlement. By April 13 seventy-five of Philadelphia's leading citizens, including James Hamilton, governor of Pennsylvania, agreed to be "Contributors unto and equal Sharers in the Losses as well as the Gains." As Franklin had shrewdly anticipated, the losses were fewer than the gains, and the company thrived.

markets, the great original one in High (now Market) Street or the two newer ones in the "South part" and the "Northern Liberties." Weights and measures, cleanliness, and certain prices (notably those of bread and firewood) were regulated by the market clerks, appointed by the city government, known as the "corporation."

Along with its merchants and artisans, colonial Philadelphia had its poor and criminal classes, including sailors without berths, discharged soldiers, insolvent debtors, unwed mothers, and transported convicts from England. A seventeen-man watch, appointed by the city's dozen constables, patrolled the streets at night. The constables were themselves appointed, along with the town crier, by the eight aldermen who, together with twelve common councilmen, comprised the city government. The aldermen also served as justices of the peace.

The disadvantaged were assisted by charitable organizations in the City of Brotherly Love. Richard Wistar and other Friends formed, in February 1776, the Philadelphia Society for the Relief of Distressed Prisoners, whether confined for crime or for debt. Both municipal and Friends' almshouses provided shelter for the homeless, as well as food, firewood, and medical care for "indigents." Several private benevolent organizations were primarily for the purpose of helping needy immigrants on national lines: notably the St. Andrew's Society (Scottish), the Deutsche Gesellschaft von Pennsylvanien (German), the Friendly Sons of St. Patrick (Irish), and the Society of the Sons of St. George (English). Other charities were occupational, such as the Society for the Relief of Distressed Masters of Ships, their Widows and Orphans. Hardly anyone was completely neglected.

As the threat of a British invasion grew in the fall of 1776, Philadelphia's elaborate system of administration, governmental and private, largely collapsed. Many Quakers withdrew from the government because of pacifist convictions, and many civil servants, as well as members of fire companies, joined the militia. By December 2, when the British took Brunswick, New Jersey, thousands of Philadelphians were fleeing the city (it is estimated that the population was cut almost in half, to less than 22,000) and the Continental Congress moved to Baltimore. Although that emergency lasted barely a month—until Washington's Christmas victory at Trenton—Philadelphia had been stripped of both manpower and funds, taxes being due in December with nobody to collect them. The new Commonwealth of Pennsylvania declared martial law in the city on December 8, and four days later General Israel Putnam arrived, at Washington's orders, to become military governor.

Pierced tin lantern, often used by watchmen and constables

Policing Eighteenth-Century Philadelphia

The first watch in Pennsylvania was formed in Philadelphia in 1684 for daytime hours only. Apparently as a result of complaints, such as that of a grand jury that called the Court's attention to the "Great rudeness and wildness of the youth and Children in the town of Philadelphia. That they dayly appear up and down the streets, gaming and playing for money," the city's Common Council appointed the first night watch. One watchman had the whole city as his charge. At the time of his appointment, this watchman's duties were "to go round the town with a small bell in the night time, to give notice of the time of the night and the weather, and if anie disorders or danger happen by fire or otherwise in the night time to acquaint the constables thereof."

In 1704, the Council ordered that the city be divided into ten constabulary precincts, and that an equal number of watchmen be assigned to each constable. (As the population increased, so did the number of constables and watchmen.) Every able-bodied housekeeper was supposed to take his turn at the watch or to find a substitute, as was the custom in England. By 1743, the grand jury was complaining that the watch was a much greater expense than necessary, and bore hard upon the poor. Perhaps because of the persistence of such complaints, and reports of "some pitiful Night Robberies" in the city, in 1750 an act was passed granting power to a board of six wardens to provide a permanent paid watch. The act purported to be "of great importance for the Preservation of the Persons and Properties of the Inhabitants, and very necessary to prevent Fires, Murders, Burglaries, Robberies and other outrages and Disorders." Watchmen were authorized "to apprehend all Night-Walkers, Malefactors, Rogues, Vagabonds, and disorderly Persons, whom they shall find disturbing the Public Peace, or shall have cause to suspect of any evil Design, and to carry the Person or Persons so apprehended, as soon as conveniently may be, before one or more Justices of the Peace of the said City."

On his hourly rounds, the watchman carried a lantern, a rattle in case he needed to call for assistance, and a club. Besides crying the hour and the weather, the watchman often spread information and alarms. It is said that the news of the British surrender at Yorktown, in 1781, was brought to one

part of the city by a German watchman, crying the hour and adding, "unt Cornwalish ist daken!"

This system continued relatively unchanged until 1845, when Pennsylvania's General Assembly passed an act which laid the foundation for the organization of the modern city police force.

Ratchets were carried by watchmen to call for help and to alert the citizenry.

Watchmen and constables wore ordinary clothing. When not on patrol they could be found in their watch boxes.

The Walnut Street Gaol (prison)

This fellow is luckier than most; he has a bench and a violin.

Ducking stools were especially used to test the innocence of women accused of witchcraft.

Crime and Punishment in Eighteenth-Century Pennsylvania

Pennsylvania's response to crime can be divided into three periods: William Penn's "Great Law," enacted in 1682; the English code that replaced it in 1718 and prevailed until 1786; and the post-Revolution criminal laws.

Penn, in his First Frame of Government, made clear that, in contrast to the English system of punishment, his would be "a liberal and humane" commonwealth. Quaker reform called for the substitution of imprisonment in a house of correction for the English penalty of capital or corporal punishment. Nevertheless, Quakers took a severe and moral view of the law. In the main, crimes of violence against the person were punished by imprisonment at hard labor. For assaulting a parent, the child was to be confined during the pleasure of the parent. Murder was the only capital crime. But many offenses, particularly sexual crimes, were harshly punished. "Defiling the marriage bed" was penalized by whipping and one year's imprisonment for the first offense and life imprisonment for the second. Even the first offense of bigamy was punished by life imprisonment.

In 1718, the reign of Quaker law came to an end. The English code that replaced it provided for thirteen capital crimes: various degrees of treason, murder, manslaughter by stabbing, serious maiming, highway robbery, burglary, arson, buggery, rape, concealing the death of a bastard child, advising the killing of such a child, and witchcraft. Larceny was the only felony not made a capital crime. The practice of whipping, branding, and mutilation was the punishment for lesser crimes. At Third and Market streets in Philadelphia, opposite the prison, stood the whipping-post, pillory, and stocks, where convicted persons were publicly whipped or otherwise punished. The city had a public whipper until just before the Revolution.

Such extreme penalties could not, however, deter the crime which followed the economic collapse after the French and Indian War. Urban prisons were filled with criminals and debtors alike. The years before the Revolution witnessed an alarming increase in robbery and violent crimes. Harrowing accounts of holdups on the highways and stories of seaport gangs roaming the streets, along with tales of housebreaking and pilfering, filled the newspapers. Current stories also told of pitiful conditions in the jails and of unjust and severe sentences for minor offenders. Enlightened opinion was revolted by the harshness of the criminal code. The Revolution and the reform ideas of the time left an imprint on the Pennsylvania Constitution of 1776 by requiring "the future legislature" to "reform" the "penal laws." Punishment must be made "in some cases less sanguinary, and in general more proportionate to the crimes." Pennsylvania followed this constitutional admonition with significant changes in its penal structure, and continued thereafter to be a leader in penal form.

Hand-wrought shackles

The Birthplace of Party Politics

Philadelphia emerged from the Revolution battle-scarred but still intact. Along with physical destruction and neglect, bitter factional disputes had torn the city before, during, and after the hostilities. But by 1789, the year the nation got a new Constitution and a new President with widespread support, Philadelphia got a new Charter and a new Mayor with citywide backing. Pennsylvania has been called the birthplace of modern party politics: that is, the art of compromise among coalitions. Although the idea of a political party was distasteful to most eighteenth-century minds—Washington's Farewell Address still spoke of the "baneful effects of the spirit of party"—Pennsylvanians had been forced by their heterogeneity to engage in party politics. Nor is it a coincidence that America's first paid political advertisements appeared in Philadelphia newspapers in 1744. Looking back over his century in 1797, the Quaker historian Robert Proud observed that Pennsylvania "appears never to have been without a discontented and murmuring party in it," but adds that "parties were very free with each others conduct, yet, they are said mostly to have kept within the rules of decency and order." As a Friend, Proud plays down the occasional resort to arms of political factions like the Paxton Boys. On the other hand, a government delegation led by Benjamin Franklin persuaded those frontiersmen to turn back without entering the city, leaving behind two representatives to draw up a statement of grievances for consideration by the governor and Assembly. Perhaps Franklin said the final word when he wrote in his *Autobiography* that "there is no liberty without faction, for the latter cannot be suppressed without introducing slavery in the place of the former."

An eighteenth-century "smoke-filled room"

A New Song Suitable to the Season,
To The Tune of Good English Beer.

Of Good Honest Souls, our Songs lets Raise,
  We've Right at our free Elections:
To Vote for all those that Most doth Please,
  Nor Value New Ticket Objections,
                                    Spoke.
Of those Honest Hearts loud Fame hath
  They'll neer be Enslaved By P——n Sir.
They'll secure all our Rights, by the L..d it's no joke,
  In Council with Honest Old Ben Sir.
        Chorus.
    Then to them Crown our Bowls,
      Our Plenteous Brown Bowls,
    And toss them of Clever, to All true British Souls,
    To all True Loyal Souls, and Old Ticket, Old ticket for ever,
    Huzza Old Ticket, Huzza Old Ticket,
    Huzza Old Ticket, Old Ticket for Ever.
        2
    The Election's now Past We've Got the Day,
    Hark, Hark, to the New Ticket cries Sir;
    They're down in the Mouth they South & Say,
    "We've lost it by Telling of Lies Sir."
    They're future Attempts We will Disdain,
      We're fixt in Our Resolution:
    Come let us Agree, and Our Agents maintain,
    Then Safe is Our Constitution.

        Chorus.
    Then, to them Crown our Bowls,
      Our Plenteous Brown Bowls:
    And toss them of Clever, to all true British Souls,
                                              ever
    to all true White Oak Souls & Old ticket, Old Ticket for
    Huzza Old Ticket, Huzza Old Ticket,
    Huzza Old Ticket, Old Ticket for Ever.
        3
    To them let us fill a Glass and Sing,
      We Old Ticket Men are Hearty:
                                          sore
    Four Hundred and more we've Bang'd them
      So I care not a Figg for their Party,
    Come now Drink about lets see it all Out,
      With Hearts as light as a Feather:
    And Chearfully Laugh, at the Author a (Calf)
    Of the Bombastich Piece Bellweather.
        Chorus.
    Then to them Crown our Bowls,
      Our Plenteous Brown Bowls
    And toss them of Clever, to all true British Souls,
                                        for ever
    To all Heart of Oak Souls, th' Old ticket Old ticket
    Huzza Old Ticket, Huzza Old Ticket,
    Huzza Old Ticket, Old Ticket for Ever.

        FINIS.

Political cartoon

173

Entertainments and Diversions

Despite their many responsibilities in organizing their society, Pennsylvanians were not always serious. Indeed, they enjoyed a wide variety of recreations, some of which emerged directly from their work. When jobs were too big and tedious for a single family, neighbors would get together to turn them into parties, usually called frolics from the German *fröhlich* or bees probably from the Middle English *boon*. In this way corn husking and shelling, apple peeling and slicing, flax pulling and quilting, maple sugaring and the making of apple butter, house-building and barn-raising—all became social events. Weddings, funerals, and baptisms lasted all day and sometimes longer; they were occasions for renewing acquaintanceships and regrouping friends and relatives—with food and drink in abundance.

Individual sports too—swimming, skating, fishing, and hunting—were always popular among Pennsylvanians. The location of Philadelphia on the Delaware and Schuylkill rivers made swimming and ice skating especially popular. Some of Pennsylvania's early leaders were excellent skaters. Thomas Mifflin, General John Cadwalader, and Charles Willson Peale were among the most graceful, but Charles Massey, a biscuit maker, won recognition as Philadelphia's most skillful skater. An unknown black man was reputedly the fastest. One of the city's grandest winter attractions was the New Year's Day ox roast on the ice. Sleighing parties were another part of Pennsylvania's wintertime frolic. Sleigh caravans paraded across the countryside, occasionally stopping at a tavern for singing and dancing.

The tavern was a popular center of entertainment for many Pennsylvanians living in large as well as small communities. In addition to providing the atmosphere for song and dance, the tavern offered many other recreational and sporting activities. The table and board games of cards, dice, shuffleboard, and backgammon were common. Bowling greens for nine pins and shooting ranges for turkey shoots were generally located at or near an inn. The tavern sports of cockfighting and bull- and bear-baiting attracted many followers. Philadelphia's Timothy Matlack, an activist in the Revolutionary move-

Fishing

Bull baiting

the Bear-Beat, on the Common, 1809.

Bear-baiting, A barbarous Custom.

From Lewis Miller's sketchbook

ment, was an ardent cockfighter. His bouts with James DeLancy of New York drew the wrath of Francis Hopkinson, Pennsylvania's poet laureate and a signer of the Declaration of Independence. Hopkinson denounced this gruesome and brutal activity in a satirical poem, "The Cock-Fighter, an Elegy":

> That ere our pretty Cocklings learn to crow,
> To pamper Lust they must to Market go?
> But will you thus, on fatal Mischief bent,
> For our destruction cruel Sports invent?

In spite of such denunciations, cockfighting continued to attract large followings. Only horseracing exceeded it in popularity as a spectator sport in colonial Pennsylvania.

Horseracing prospered in Philadelphia largely through the efforts of the Philadelphia Jockey Club, founded in 1776 by seventy-one gentlemen to promote the pleasures of the turf. Lieutenant Governor Richard Penn presided over this body, and some of Pennsylvania's distinguished citizens patronized the track. John Dickinson—although a member of the Society of Friends, whose leadership traditionally discouraged the "sport of kings"—found the races a healthful diversion from his law practice. Local interest in racing grew so keen that the city bellman traveled about town asking Philadelphia residents to keep their dogs at home on racing days, presumably to keep them off the track. Horseracing in Philadelphia not only captured the fancy of local residents but also attracted racing enthusiasts from as far away as Maryland and New York.

Hunters, from Lewis Miller's sketchbook

175

Pony race in Rickett's Circus, January 14, 1797

In Philadelphia horseraces were held at Centre Square (where City Hall now stands) on a track outlined by ropes. The races enabled Pennsylvania's fashionable citizens to exhibit their wealth by making large wagers and by wearing expensive clothes. Although most popular among the wealthy, horseracing was enjoyed by all social classes. Society's lower orders viewed the races from the commons at Centre Square, where enterprising peddlers provided them with food, drink, and incidental entertainment. The lower classes regarded racing days as a time for revelry, and their drinking occasionally turned merriment into a drunken fracas.

Like racing days, fairs and circuses brought great excitement to Philadelphia's masses. Local inhabitants flocked to the gaming booths, trying their luck at various games of chance. Jugglers, tight and slack rope dancers, minstrels, and other performers gave Philadelphians much pleasure. Animal shows and wild beast displays, however, were the most intriguing, for they brought before the populace creatures rarely seen in the city and some not found in the colony.

Although fairs and circuses were a source of entertainment for some members of the elite, the wealthy class, by and large, turned to private social and sporting clubs for their recreational pleasures. There were excellent facilities for fishing and fowling at the Colony in Schuylkill, and the Gloucester Foxhunting had ample acreage for hunting. Thomas Willing, Benjamin Chew, and other Philadelphia notables joined Dickinson, Mifflin, and Cadwalader in these exclusive organizations. Equally selective was the Philadelphia Dancing Assembly, which offered another form of recreation to the aristocratic class. The assembly held dances and balls at the State House

Fair and market stalls in the Borough of York, 1801. This scene is typical of fairs held throughout Pennsylvania.

"Sea Captains Carousing in Surinam," by John Greenwood, 1758, is the most important visual document of eighteenth-century tavern life. Note the use of punch bowls and the absence of women, who seldom, if ever, appeared in the public rooms of taverns.

Colonial Pennsylvania's Inns and Taverns

Pennsylvania had more inns in the eighteenth century than any other colony. Philadelphia was a major commercial center, and roads reaching north, south, and especially west from that city were lined with hundreds of inns, taverns, wagon stands, and tap rooms. At least a dozen Pennsylvania villages were named for inns or taverns: Temple in Berks County (for the Solomon's Temple), Lionville and White Horse in Chester County, Bird-in-Hand and Blue Ball in Lancaster County, Broad Axe and King of Prussia in Montgomery County, and Red Lion in York County are just a few. Many rising artists—Edward Hicks, Gilbert Stuart, and Benjamin West, for example—were hired to paint the colorful signs that graced most inns.

The stagecoach traveler from New England or New York would have been impressed by one characteristic of Pennsylvania inns: most were of stone, in contrast to the wooden inns characteristic of the northern colonies. Among these sturdy and beautiful buildings are the Jolly Post Boy in Frankford, the Brickerville House in Brickerville, the Black Bass in Lumberville, the Red Rose in West Grove, and

the Court in Newtown, all surviving into the twentieth century. In the eighteenth century the typical country inn was surrounded by a small farm and orchard which helped to stock the inn's larder. In the public rooms of Pennsylvania inns a patron could drink locally made beer, ale, and cider, as well as a limited array of expensive wines and spirits. The proprietors of many Pennsylvania inns were of German descent, and their hearty fare was widely known and admired throughout the colonies.

The inn or tavern served two important functions. First, it was a place of lodging and refreshment for travelers who could afford these amenities. Second, it was the secular center of its neighborhood or community: sports, social gatherings, and more serious community activities centered at the inn. In rural areas the innkeeper and his family were likely to be among the most influential citizens of their community.

As the Revolution approached, some inns tended to be Whig, or patriot, and others Tory, or loyalist. After the war began, several changed their names from Royal George to George Washington, while others altered British symbols—for instance, by showing the imperial lion in chains. At Bristol, when American troops riddled the sign of the King George with bullets, the prudent innkeeper adopted a neutral device, the Fountain. One Philadelphia tavern went all the way, the Golden Lion becoming the Yellow Cat.

The public rooms of inns were doubtless scenes of high-spirited conviviality as recorded by the American painter John Greenwood. As community centers, however, the inns also saw serious and significant gatherings. Before attacking the British in Philadelphia, Captain Allan McLane assembled his troops at the Jolly Post Boy. Earlier McLane had captured Streeper's Tavern (now the General Wayne Inn) in Merion to use as his headquarters. Washington and his staff dined at the Old Ferry Inn before crossing the Delaware, and leaders of the Continental Congress took meals at the Golden Plough Tavern while meeting in York. The signers of the Declaration of Independence conducted many of their deliberations at Philadelphia's City Tavern. In fact, the political and military decisions of the late eighteenth century were more likely to emanate from inns than from any other place, and those decisions do not appear to have suffered from the ambience in which they were made.

Conestoga wagon approaching a roadside inn, or tavern

Many taverns were named for the heros of the revolutionary period. This sign is attributed to Jacob Eicholtz.

Kitchen of the Golden Plough Tavern, York

Dancing "Sir Fopling's Aires," about 1710

Interior of the New Theater on Chestnut Street in Philadelphia, 1794

every week from January to May. Its exclusiveness disturbed some members of the middle and lower classes, whose reactions indicated a growing hostility toward the elite class.

The theater, though a popular form of entertainment for many, reflected the same feeling of class antagonism and resentment during this period of unrest. The middle class became incensed at the theater because it, like horseracing, served as an outlet for aristocratic vanity. The privileged class used the theater to display its wealth, as its members arrived in elaborate carriages and wore luxurious garments. They also sat in the best seats. The separation of the boxes from the gallery was a great social divider which the Sons

of Liberty, an organization agitating for American independence, found particularly galling.

The revolutionary movement disrupted pastimes and amusements in Pennsylvania. As Anglo-American tensions became strained beyond the point of reconciliation, a large number of Pennsylvanians put aside their recreations and directed their energy to the awesome task of preparing for war. The success of the revolutionary movement in Pennsylvania brought with it the direct suppression of many sports and amusements. Leaders of the revolutionary wartime government attempted to purify society by purging it of all vice and frivolity. The radicals banned such sports and amusements as horseracing, cockfighting, animal-baiting, shooting matches, gambling games, and stage plays because they considered these activities immoral, frivolous, and unproductive. In the austere atmosphere enveloping Pennsylvania at the onset of the war for American independence, interest in recreation sank to a low ebb.

The marvelous discovery of electricity was at first of no practical use. The sophisticated Philadelphians, who loved diversions, playfully turned electricity into a tingling new parlor game.

Frontispiece to Merry Fellows Companion, *1797*

The American Jest Book and The Merry Fellow's Companion

Beginning in 1789, when the Philadelphia publishing firm of Carey and Spotswood brought out The American Jest Book *and* The Merry Fellow's Companion, *and through the next decade, colonial publishers issued eleven editions (six in Pennsylvania) of these collections of American humor. Editions varied in size, from the twenty-six pages of* the Merry Fellow's Pocket Companion *to the two hundred and forty-page Boston editions of the 1796* American Jest Book. *The anecdotes recorded in these books were sometimes topical and probably reflect the humor making the rounds during the political events of the revolutionary era. The following story is told in* The Merry Fellow's Companion *or* American Jest Book *of 1797, published by John Wyeth for Mathew Cary of Philadelphia:*

"Dr. Franklin, as agent for the province of Pennsylvania, being in England at the time the parliament passed the stamp-act for America, was frequently applied to by the ministry for his opinion respecting the operation of the same, and assured them that the people of America would never submit to it. The act was nevertheless passed, and the event showed he had been right. After the news of the destruction of the stamped paper had arrived in England, the ministry again sent for the doctor, to consult with him, and concluded with this proposition, that if the Americans would engage to pay for the damage done in the destruction of the stamped paper, the parliament would then repeal the act. To this the doctor answered, that it put him in mind of a Frenchman, who having heated a poker red hot, ran into the street, and addressing an Englishman he met there, 'ha, monsieur, voulez-vous give me de plaisir et de satisfaction,—and lete me runi dis poker only one foote up your backside?' 'What!' says the Englishman—'Only to lete me runi dis poker one foote up your backside.' 'D—n your soule,' replies the Englishman. 'Welle, den, only so far,' says the Frenchman, pointing to about six inches of the poker.—'No, no,' replies the Englishman—'d—n your soule, what do you mean?' 'Welle, den,' says the Frenchman, 'will you have de justice to paye me for the trouble and expence of heating de poker?'—'d—n me, if I do,' answered the Englishman, and walked off."

"*Flax Scutching Bee*," *by Linton Park. Flax scutching, or swingling, a combined working and social occasion similar to corn husking and quilting, remained prevalent until the twentieth century. The dried flax plants were beaten and scraped with swingles (wooden staves shaped like sharp knives) to separate the fibers. In Park's painting the people are as much engaged in rustic horseplay and courting as in the work at hand. The background illustrates the frontier craft of building with logs.*

The Theater in Colonial Philadelphia

The theater in Philadelphia was a microcosm of Pennsylvania society during the years leading to the American Revolution. It reflected Pennsylvania's internal political turmoil, social class conflict, and religious pressures during this period of confusion and disorder. After more than a decade of harassment, the Philadelphia theater became active in 1760 and thrived until the eve of the Revolutionary War.

Strong political and religious opposition nearly extinguished the theater during the late 1750s. Several religious denominations—the Society of Friends, the Presbyterians, the Baptists, and the pietistic Lutherans—objected to the theater as frivolous and incompatible with their social ethic of piety, industry, and productivity. These religious groups, campaigning long and hard, urged the Pennsylvania legislature to ban the theater. Simultaneously, a political dispute erupted between the legislature and the Philadelphia Academy. The lawmakers planned to deny the Academy its primary source of revenue by abolishing lotteries. To generate support for their cause, the antagonists of the Academy included a ban on theaters in their anti-lottery bill. Governor William Denny, a friend of the theater, saw through this political scheme. He signed the bill in June 1759, but only after the lawmakers had agreed to a six month delay before the law took effect. This delay gave the building contractors ample time to complete the Southwark Theatre, which was under construction during the controversy. It also enabled the king of England, a proponent of the theater and the final authority on all laws adopted in Colonial Pennsylvania, to veto this statute before it was ever enforced.

As relations between the colony and the mother country grew strained beyond the point of reconciliation during the 1770s, political and social tensions heightened among Pennsylvanians. Large numbers of the colony's middle class, chiefly Scotch-Irish Presbyterians, were frustrated because their insufficient wealth prevented them from reaching the mainstream of Pennsylvania politics and social life. They expressed their frustration by opposing the theater, which they resented because it served as an expression of aristocratic pretentions. The wealthy sat in the most expensive seats, separated from the gallery by partitions. This seating arrangement, acting as a visible barrier, so incensed the Sons of Liberty that they tore down the partitions.

When the middle and lower classes gained control of Pennsylvania's political reins during the revolutionary movement, they prohibited the theater in the new Commonwealth. The gloom and austerity of war squelched dramatic production, for its supposed frivolity had no place in the minds of the Pennsylvania revolutionaries as they entered the struggle for American independence.

The New Theater

This conjectural drawing of the Southwark Theater as it looked in 1766 was based on research by Charles Durang, a nineteenth-century performer and promoter.

"Penn's Treaty With the Indians," by Benjamin West, 1771

Religion

William Penn, motivated not only by his "Holy Experiment" in good government and freedom of conscience, but also by reasonable calculations for increasing the value of his royal grant, wanted to provide asylum for the persecuted members of the Religious Society of the Friends of God, derisively called "Quakers." Having traveled on the Continent, he was moved also by the plight of Protestant sectarians in Germany, and perceived the utility of attracting some of them to the wilderness of Penn's Woods. They came, increasing their numbers through successive waves of immigration. The Protestant sects proliferated, some of them becoming extremely radical in their ways of thought and living. The commonwealth that William Penn founded on principles of perfect equality and universal religious freedom resulted in such a generous policy that Pennsylvania soon became a dissenter's paradise, appealing strongly to the downtrodden, who were encouraged by liberal grants of land. Later, with similar encouragement, members of Europe's established churches came to Pennsylvania. The result was the greatest variety of religious groups in the colonies.

The Varieties of Religious Belief

America has often been blessed by astute foreign observers, such as Crèvecoeur, de Tocqueville, and Schaff, but none has so picturesquely described the American situation as did a little-known German observer who came to Pennsylvania in 1750 as an organist and schoolmaster. Gottlieb Mittelberger returned to his homeland after four years and wrote an account of his *Journey to Pennsylvania* for his fellow countrymen in 1756:

> It [Pennsylvania] offers people more freedom than the other English colonies, since all religious sects are tolerated there. One can encounter Lutherans, members of the Reformed Church, Catholics, Quakers, Mennonites or Anabaptists, Herrenhueter or Moravian brothers, Pietists, Seventh Day Adventists, Dunkers, Presbyterians, Newborn Separatists, Freemasons, Freethinkers, Jews, Moham-

187

American Friends going to meeting in the summer.

Buckingham Friends Meeting House in Bucks County. Construction began in 1763.

Quaker Meeting House in Columbia County. It was typical to have separate doors for men and women.

Quaker Meeting House in York

medans, Pagans, Negroes and Indians. . . . There are several hundred unbaptized people who don't even wish to be baptized. . . . It is possible to meet in one house among one family, members of four or five or six different sects.

Left out of Mittelberger's description were the Baptists (except the German Baptist Brethren, known as Dunkers or Dunkards), Amish, Schwenkfelders, members of the Society of the Woman of the Wilderness, New Mooners, Inspirationists, Anglicans, and Deists like Franklin and Paine. George Whitefield, noted English evangelist, observed in 1739 the presence of sixteen different religious groups in Germantown alone.

There was a close correlation between Pennsylvanians' religious and ethnic backgrounds. Most Anglicans were English; Presbyterians, Scotch-Irish; and Mennonites, Amish, Schwenkfelders, and other comparatively small sectarian groups, German. Several religious groups were cosmopolitan. Friends' meetings had English,

Baptism at church meeting

A WESTERN VIEW OF THE Catholic Chapel AT CONEWAGO near HANOVER Pa

1. Represents the Chapel. — 2. Parsonage residence — 3 — Superintendant Farmers dwelling — 4 — Barn — 5. work Shop — 6 — Hermitage house.

Catholic Chapel near Hanover

The "Old Gemein House," built in 1742, was the second house constructed in Bethlehem

Welsh, Dutch, and German members. Although most Moravians were German, some were English and Swedish. Members of Reformed congregations were primarily German, but a few were Dutch. While many Lutherans were German, some were Swedish. Nevertheless, most members of these religious groups formed congregations which were ethnically exclusive.

Count Nicholas von Zinzendorf in
conference with the Indians of the Five Nations

Corner of a common room at Ephrata arranged for use by a member of the writing school

Ephrata Kloster: Camp of the Solitary

The Ephrata Kloster (Cloister) is a unique symbol of the religious excitement and confusion that gripped the Pennsylvania colony in the middle decades of the eighteenth century. Founded in 1732 by Johann Conrad Beissel, a strange but charismatic mystical pietist, the Kloster village flourished for nearly a century as a religious agricultural-industrial commune of the Seventh Day Dunkers. At its height it served paradoxically both as a cultural center and as a disruptive force for Pennsylvania Germans.

Conrad Beissel, an orphan of the German Palatinate, and a baker, was seized by the pietistic revival of the late seventeenth and early eighteenth centuries and joined the Schwarzenau Dunkers, a radical pietist group which migrated to Germantown in the decade 1719 to 1729. There he witnessed such Schwarzenau practices as celibacy, the communal holding of goods, the Agapé or love feast, and baptism by triune immersion. He absorbed the sect's mystical pietism and Rosicrucian lore. He also read the Bible in literalist fashion and became enamored of certain Hebraic doctrines and customs, especially the dietary laws and Sabbatarianism.

An ascetic at heart, Beissel withdrew from the Germantown Dunkers to the Conestoga wilderness to live a hermit's existence and to woo the "Virgin Sophia" in quietness, according to the lyrics of one of his hymns:

> O blessed life of loneliness!
> Where all creation silence keeps;
> Who so can serve in quietness
> His God, and never from him creep
> Has won the goal of blessedness.

But he was an ardent evangelist, so his solitude was soon invaded by comrades who longed to live a life of voluntary poverty and scorn for the institution of marriage. In 1732 the "Camp of the Solitary" was begun, and buildings soon arose along a "haunted stream" which the Indians called Koch-Halekung, Den of Serpents, and white men pronounced Cocalico.

At its height in 1745, the Ephrata community consisted of some three hundred persons. After the death of Conrad Beissel in 1768, the community rapidly declined and by the turn of the century the celibate orders were practically extinct. In 1814 the surviving householders organized the Seventh Day German Baptist Church, which continued as a congregation in the Ephrata Cloister until 1934.

The historical and cultural significance of such utopian movements which dotted the American landscape is often hard to assess. Fortunately, in the case of Ephrata, there are some tangible remains, particularly in printing and architecture. The Ephrata Press was the second oldest German press in America, established in 1743, and

Sleeping cell at Ephrata showing the sleeping bench with a block of wood for a pillow

Two pages from the Ephrata hymnal
Paradisisches Wunder-Spiel, *1754*

The Ephrata Cloister

The years 1735 to 1749 marked the zenith of the Ephrata community. During this period the members organized themselves into three orders. Two orders of solitaries practiced a rigid monastic discipline: the Roses of Saron, nuns or sisters, and the Zionitic Brotherhood, monks or brothers. They adopted the Jewish custom of beginning the day at sunset with supper, the only substantial meal of the day for the devout. Then followed a strict rhythm of work, meditation, reading and writing, and singing practice, with a religious office of two to four hours at midnight (mette), consisting of psalms, hymns, and prayers. The third order comprised the householders or seculars, who were married and were to practice continence, not celibacy, as well as obedience, charity, and voluntary poverty, and whose property and income were at the disposal of the leader. On Friday nights and Saturdays there were services of worship in which all members participated, the brothers sitting in a choir, the sisters out of sight in the gallery, and the householders on the floor area, with Conrad Beissel seated between the monks and the householders. The members adopted ecclesiastical names and designed a habit which resembled Capuchin apparel. The solitary wore white pilgrim garb and the householders gray, as a Sabbath vestment or uniform.

Singing was fostered as an expression of a theology and a vocation. Many of the hymn manuscripts have been preserved in the artistic penmanship of the Kloster sisters. Beissel, though untrained in music, invented a mysterious and unique system of harmony and composition, which was used in over a thousand hymns and anthems. In four, five, six, or seven parts, his music was designed for two or three choirs singing antiphonally. The singers practiced three nights per week from eight to midnight, when the tower bells would toll for the night watch. To inculcate the necessary purity of heart, the singers were required to appear in their white garments, and were placed on a distinctive diet which Beissel thought would improve the vocal chords and develop particular ranges. The Turtel-Taube (1747) ("Song of the Solitary and Deserted Turtle Dove, namely the Christian Church") was the first original hymn book printed in the colonies. A manuscript copy was later presented to Benjamin Franklin by Peter Mueller.

The restored interior of the Saal (chapel)

The colonial struggles did not leave the Ephrata community unaffected. As a work of charity the Kloster gave refuge to victims of the Indian raids in 1755. As pacifists the members were opposed to the Revolution but sympathetic to the Patriot cause. Peter Mueller was an ardent worker for liberty and in December 1775 received a contract to print four hundred copies of "Rules, Regulations and Articles of Association" and also to print Continental paper money. During the Revolution the army confiscated, over the solitaries' protests, large quantities of paper for cartridge wadding, quilts, blankets, grain, and other supplies. After the Battle of Brandywine in September 1777, Washington sent five hundred soldiers, ravaged by typhus, "camp fever," and scarlet fever, to the Camp of the Solitary. There they were nursed by the sisters. One hundred fifty soldiers and some of the solitary died, and three of the original buildings later were razed to prevent the spread of the diseases. For none of these good works did the members of the Ephrata community receive either compensation or thanks.

Grapes growing above the windows in the German tradition provide fruit and shade the windows.

Protestant German gardens often have a Yucca (Lord's Candle) in the center of the traditional cruciform layout.

View of the Ephrata Cloister before the recent restoration

it published many works of religion, tracts, and broadsides. One of its most memorable accomplishments is the *Mennonite Book of Martyrs* (*Märtyrer-Spiegel*, or *Martyrs Mirror*), the largest book printed in colonial America, which took three years to produce. Calligraphy was developed into the fine art of *fraktur-schriften*, and there still survive hand-illuminated Ephrata songbooks and inscriptions.

In a flurry of building activity the community, between 1735 and 1749, constructed nine buildings according to designs they recalled from their Rhenish-Palatinate homeland. The surviving complex represents some of the best copies of medieval German architectural style in America. These early buildings were built of log and stone, with mortar of clay and grass, the walls covered with thick layers of lime. The architectural design is expressive of the religious principles of the society. The low doorways are reminders of humility; the lack of adornment symbolizes the importance of spiritual beauty; the ascetic beds are board benches with wooden blocks

Ephrata calligraphy

195

Spiritual virgin dressed in the Ephrata habit, used to illustrate the flyleaf of a manuscript hymnal of 1745

for pillows. The stairways are so narrow that the mystics needed a guide rope to go up and down. There are long, narrow halls to the cells, which have doors only twenty inches wide. The surviving buildings include the Saron (Sisters' house), the Saal (chapel), the Almonry, Beissel's log cottage, a householder's cottage, three other cottages, and the 1837 Academy building.

Ephrata represents an incongruous messianic vision for America: a monastic order on a Protestant frontier. Peter Mueller, Beissel's successor, sensed that a new mood had come; that cloister living was not likely to appeal to the new American generation. He wrote to Benjamin Franklin in 1771, "The genius of the Americans is bound another way." The mystical asceticism and pietism of the Ephrata experiment was out of step with the affirmative mood of "the pursuit of happiness" and the life-embracing optimism of the new world. It belongs to a romantic past.

The Academy building in the Ephrata complex, however, reminds us of the pioneering efforts at education among Pennsylvania Germans struggling to understand the world. Of Conrad Beissel himself, perhaps the title given him by his followers, *Vater Friedsam* (Father Peaceable), is all that needs to be said. There was also Peter Mueller, a graduate of Heidelberg University, a speculative scholar, a highly gifted minister and theologian, and a member of the American Philosophical Society. And there was Michael Wohlfahrt, known as Michael Welfare, who in spite of his enthusiasm, impressed Franklin with his lack of dogmatism.

Religious Liberty in Colonial Pennsylvania

In Pennsylvania, members of all religious groups were able to worship freely, for religious liberty was a fundamental principle in Penn's "Charter of Privileges to the Provinces and Counties of Pennsylvania" (1701). The charter guaranteed freedom of faith and worship to all believers in God, including Jews, although political privileges were limited to Christians. Under British pressure, but with the acquiescence of the provincial government, the charter was modified in two significant respects: the Roman Catholics were politically disenfranchised in 1705 (although on the eve of the Revolution, Pennsylvania was the only place where Mass could be celebrated publicly), and the Provincial Council, alarmed at the large German immigration, passed an ordinance in 1717 requiring all immigrants to take an oath of allegiance to the king and government. Nevertheless, the government permitted Mennonites and Friends who could not in good conscience take oaths to provide equivalent assurance in their own way. Formed under the principle of noninterference in religion, Pennsylvania expanded so rapidly and haphazardly that it became the first experiment in radical pluralism, testing whether a society with so many churches and sects could survive. All the tensions of religious pluralism which were to characterize nineteenth-century American religion were in full force in eighteenth-century Pennsylvania, where the number of coexisting sects showed that diversity need not be a threat to order and authority. Rather, the churches and sects of Pennsylvania acted as voluntary societies competing on an equal basis in a free society.

Clergymen, Laymen, and Lay Preachers

The settlers often migrated before their ministers, finding themselves scattered in small groups in remote frontier areas, where they joined with their neighbors to organize a congregation, purchase land, and build a church. Only then did they send out a call for a minister, whom they tended to regard as hired help performing a service. When the minister arrived, he found himself isolated from the status-giving context of church authority, with no control over the congregation except by the force of his character and the astuteness of his political sense. Gottlieb Mittelberger was shocked by the situation:

> Throughout Pennsylvania the preachers do not have the power to punish anyone, or to force anyone to go to church. Nor can they give orders to each other, there being no consistory to impose discipline among them. Most preachers are engaged for the year, like cowherds, in Germany; and when anyone fails to please his congregation, he is given notice and must put up with it. So it is very difficult to be a conscientious minister; especially since one has to tolerate and suffer a great deal from so many hostile, and to some extent vile, sects. Even the most exemplary preachers, especially in rural districts, are often reviled, laughed at and mocked by the young and old, like Jews. I myself would, therefore, rather be the humblest cowherd at home than be a preacher in Pennsylvania. . . . They have a saying there: Pennsylvania is heaven for farmers, paradise for artisans, and hell for officials and preachers.

In those established churches which recognized educated and ordained ministers, there were not nearly enough clergymen to supply each local church; as a result, between the visits of the parish circuit-riding priest or preacher, laymen were often asked to lead local congregations. The unestablished sectarians, who tended to be suspicious of the clergy as a distinct class, often elected lay preachers from the membership. Led by one of their own, these local congregations debated their way through to a collective understanding of standards for personal and community behavior relating to the common good. In this way, these scattered churches became seedbeds for the development and testing of democratic principles, later to be transplanted into the governmental theory of the emerging nation.

The Great Awakening in Pennsylvania

In an obscure way, the wave of revivalism that swept the colonies during the eighteenth century, known as the Great Awakening, had its beginnings in Pennsylvania. William Tennent, a Presbyterian, starting with the idea of educating his three sons, founded a "Log College" on his farm in Neshaminy and trained twelve others who all became fiery evangelists. The Tennents, with Theodorus Jacobus Frelinghuysen in New Jersey, split the Presbyterian Church into "New Lights" and "Old Lights," thus establishing new congregations. Fed up with traditional orthodoxy, the Tennents frequently turned their services into bedlam. While the congregation shouted and rolled on the floor, the revivalist preachers raged and stamped to convey their immediate experience of God. At the height of the movement, George Whitefield came to Philadelphia to lend his prodigious talents. Soon the revival cut across all ecclesiastical lines. Benjamin Franklin, both amused and impressed by Whitefield, observed that "multitudes of all sects and denominations" attended his services, developing a great sense of community and overcoming divergences among churches and sects. The Great Awakening had tremendous impact on the whole of American life. Especially on the frontier, where German pietists and Scotch-Irish Presbyterians were mingling, it had not only religious but political implications. From its emphasis upon the worth of the individual in the sight of God, there was no great jump in logic for the frontiersmen to see their equality in the sight of men.

Religion and Politics

The separation of church and state did not mean the divorce of religion and politics. Pennsylvanians, by and large, have always accepted the hazard of merging religion and politics and have been willing to use political means to implement their deepest moral and religious concerns. In 1776, therefore, the religious diversity of the colony made it inevitable that there would be a variety of political responses to the idea of independence.

Most of the Friends and members of the German pacifist groups—Mennonites, Dunkers, Moravians, Schwenkfelders—remained neutral during the revolutionary period, although they were active in humanitarian causes. They had a difficult time because their positions were easily misunderstood. The Methodists, led by John Wesley, were mostly Loyalists, and many Methodist preachers returned to England. Francis Asbury, the only one of Wesley's preachers to remain active in the colonies, was a noncombatant on principle.

Most Anglican clergymen in Pennsylvania were also strongly Loyalist. For example, the Reverend Jacob Duché, Chaplain of the Continental Congress, finally declared for the Loyalists and im-

Trappe Church

Muhlenberg's Church at Trappe

Most Pennsylvania German colonists had received their religious training from educated clergymen in the well-established Lutheran and Reformed churches of Germany. The conditions they found in Pennsylvania, however, were very different. There were few competent pastors, and worshipers usually assembled in barns or private homes. For Lutherans, the situation began to change in 1742 when Henry Melchior Muhlenberg arrived to serve as pastor at Philadelphia, New Hanover, and Providence, now known as Trappe. A pious Christian and a persuasive leader, Muhlenberg organized congregations, enforced spiritual discipline within them, and regularly led them in worship.

In addition, Muhlenberg urged his people to construct facilities appropriate to the worship of God. For the congregation at Trappe, Muhlenberg designed a building patterned after the rural churches which he had known in Germany. Parishioners hauled stone to the site, hewed the timbers, raised the walls, and built the pews. They imported only the red walnut pulpit and the pipe organ. Muhlenberg be-

gan to hold services in the church in 1743. Members of the congregation's governing body, the vestry, sat facing other worshipers in the pews along the front wall. The pastor's family sat opposite the pulpit. Wealthy members rented commodious pews in the front of the church. Indentured servants and other poor people sat in the rear gallery, most distant from the pulpit.

During the Revolution, the grounds around the church were sometimes occupied by American soldiers. On one occasion when Muhlenberg entered the sanctuary, he found that the troops had stacked their rifles on the altar and were lounging irreverently about the building. It is likely that this incident confirmed his doubts about the validity of the Revolution. The building has been restored with few changes to its appearance during Muhlenberg's ministry, and the Augustus Lutheran Church of Trappe still holds services here on historic occasions, during the summer months, and by candlelight on Christmas Eve.

Simple and austere interior of the Augustus Lutheran Church

John Peter Gabriel Muhlenberg, the "Fighting Parson"

On October 1, 1746, Henry Melchior Muhlenberg, patriarch of the American Lutheran Church, became the father of a son—John Peter Gabriel—born in Providence, Pennsylvania. John Peter's interests were military, not ecclesiastical. His tendency to idle away his youth in hunting and fishing brought his father to the brink of despair, although he gratefully noted that at least his son did not add to his other vices an interest in "womanizing." After a stormy adolescence, which included an ill-conceived apprenticeship to a merchant in Lübeck, Germany, from whom he ran away, John Peter settled down, was ordained an Anglican minister, and accepted a parish in Woodstock, Virginia, in 1772. The young minister, however, was soon caught up in the political upheaval that would end in revolution.

When Great Britain imposed the so-called Intolerable Acts on the citizens of Boston to punish them for their "Tea Party," Muhlenberg served as chairman of a citizen's group in Frederick County, Virginia, which wrote a formal protest. He continued his anti-British agitation as chairman of a local Committee of Correspondence and, as a delegate to the Virginia Convention, was swayed by the patriotic oratory of Patrick Henry. Much to his father's annoyance, John Peter exchanged his clerical garb in January 1776 for the uniform of a colonel in the Eighth Virginia Regiment. There was, he explained, a time for everything, and the time had come to fight.

After service in Georgia and South Carolina, where he helped repulse a British attack on Charleston, Muhlenberg was appointed brigadier-general attached to Washington's army. He fought with the commander-in-chief at Brandywine Creek, where he helped save a brigade under General Anthony Wayne from destruction, and at Germantown, and he suffered through the desperate winter of 1777–1778 at Valley Forge. General Muhlenberg played an important role at the Battle of Stony Point, where he supported Wayne's successful assault on the key stronghold. Then, as second in command to von Steuben, he was sent to Virginia to raise another army for the Southern campaign. In January 1781, Benedict Arnold, now a turncoat, invaded Portsmouth with 1,000 men. Muhlenberg was sent to invest him with but 700 troops. When Arnold was reinforced by 2,000 men Muhlenberg became the

prey. The American retreat was orderly. On April 25, Muhlenberg made a gallant, if hopeless, stand outside Petersburg, holding the field for two hours until British cannon drove him back. The last act in Muhlenberg's military career was played when he was second in command to Lafayette at Yorktown. After crossing the James River to destroy all boats and provisions, thus cutting off a British escape, Muhlenberg commanded the attack on a major British redoubt. Five days later Cornwallis surrendered.

Muhlenberg retired from the army as a brevet major general to spend the remainder of his days in politics. He was elected to the Council of Pennsylvania, served as vice-president of the Commonwealth from 1785 to 1788, and actively campaigned for the Federal Constitution. After representing a Montgomery County district for three terms in the House of Representatives, he was elected to the United States Senate in 1801. He served but a month, resigning the post to become collector of customs for the port of Philadelphia, a position he held until his death in 1807.

plored George Washington to lead the colonies back to Britain. The Reverend William White, rector of Christ Church, Philadelphia (who was to become the first Episcopal bishop), was the only Anglican priest to continue to serve in Pennsylvania during the war. Nevertheless, many lay members of the Church of England became rebels; in fact, two-thirds of the signers of the Declaration of Independence were Anglicans.

Few Lutheran clergymen were eager to become involved, perhaps as a consequence of the traditional Lutheran doctrine of the separation of religion and politics. Like many Germans, Henry Melchior Muhlenberg, the "Father of American Lutheranism," was loyal to the house of Hanover. Moreover, he had become a British subject in 1754. Yet his two sons were active politically, one becoming a major general in the rebel army, and the other the first speaker of the House of Representatives. Like the Anglican lay members, however, most of the Lutheran and Reformed laity supported the revolution. In Philadelphia, the governing bodies of the Lutheran and Reformed congregations issued an appeal to their co-religionists in New York and North Carolina, urging them to advance the cause of independence.

Members of other religious groups in Pennsylvania supported the revolution without reservation. Presbyterians, who had long opposed the Friends' pacifistic policies toward the Indians on the frontier, condemned their neutrality and urged independence, partially perhaps to reduce even further the Friends' political influence in Pennsylvania. Baptists (except Dunkers) also wholeheartedly supported the revolution. Roman Catholics generally were on the revolutionary side in the hope that greater civil liberty would lead to greater religious liberty. In this hope they were justified, for Pennsylvania's new Constitution of 1776 removed all political disabilities from the Roman Catholics.

Education

Although Pennsylvania was a religious haven in an age of widespread intolerance, serious educational problems resulted. What has been called "the first large community since the Roman Empire to allow different nations and religious sects to live under the same government on terms of equality" became the home of a bewildering diversity of nationalities and religions, all with differing views about formal education. It was inevitable that Pennsylvania would become in its early schools the outstanding example of "Middle Colony Parochialism."

Quaker Schools

William Penn was well educated and widely traveled, a linguist of parts, a graduate of an English grammar school and a student at Oxford for two years, before his complete conversion to the Society of Friends in his late twenties. That conversion included acceptance of Quaker views about education. Since the Friends, unlike Calvinists, Lutherans, and Anglicans, felt no need for a highly educated clergy, or for any clerical class whatsoever, Penn saw no place for a college in the province of Pennsylvania. Quaker institutions of higher education were not founded until mid-nineteenth century. Even secondary schooling was viewed with suspicion by the early Friends. However, a high premium was put upon literacy for both sexes. The Quaker meeting house in Pennsylvania would either serve a dual purpose for worship and elementary schooling or have a separate elementary school building nearby. The most famous Quaker elementary school was the William Penn Charter School. Founded in Philadelphia in 1689, it flourishes today in Germantown, rivaling in fame the Boston Latin Grammar School dating from 1635.

Colonial Quaker schools, whether started by Friends of English, Welsh, or Irish background, were "liberal" for their time in several respects. They admitted pupils from other denominations, levied no tuition fees upon the poor, and had no objection to women teachers, who were historically limited to conducting "dame schools," fre-

The presence of girls in a schoolroom was rare. From Lewis Miller's sketchbook

Going to School in 1776

Going to school was only one form of education in colonial Pennsylvania. The main responsibility for children's learning rested in the hands of individual families and, to a lesser extent, in the apprenticeship system. The school year was short—only two or three months in some rural areas—and few children advanced beyond the elementary level. In the entire province of Pennsylvania before the Revolution only some twenty secondary schools existed; most of these were tiny and church-related, exceptions being Franklin's Academy and the community-sponsored schools in Carlisle, Strasburg, and Warminster Township. In eastern Pennsylvania, especially among the Quakers and Germans, elementary school was held in or near the church or meeting house. The interdenominational neighborhood school of the frontier was usually a one-room log cabin. The idea of free tax-supported schools was introduced into the Wyoming valley of northeastern Pennsylvania in 1773 by settlers from Connecticut.

Elementary schooling consisted mostly of memory work and drill in the Four R's: Reading, 'Riting, Religion, and 'Rithmetic. Schoolbooks were scarce.

Texts in the language arts—primers, spellers, and copybooks—blended rules for reading and writing with religious information and moral instruction. Arithmetic was taught almost entirely through problems dictated by the teacher. Recitation—the parroting of prescribed answers—and copywork occupied most of the school day. Pupils copied from their texts or their teachers' dictation, and a premium was placed on good penmanship. (Penknives were essential to keep quills well sharpened.) A bit of colonial doggerel sums up the curriculum:

> Here are the schools of divers sorts,
> To which our youth daily resorts,
> Good women, who do very well
> Bring little ones to read and spell
> Which fits them for writing, and then
> Here's men to bring them to their pen,
> And to instruct and make them quick
> In all sorts of Arithmetick.

The typical elementary schoolmaster was chiefly a disciplinarian. (Women teachers were rare, although the Friends and the Wyoming settlers had a few.)

Except in the better church schools, the schoolmaster was likely to be untrained and underpaid. Lacking job security or social standing, he was often foot-loose and irresponsible. Pupils were punished for minor errors by being called "lazy" or "foolish," for more serious deficiencies with the dunce's cap and stool, and for major offenses with cracks of the hickory switch.

There were enlightened educators in colonial Pennsylvania, such as Francis Alison, Samuel Blair, Alexander Dobbin, Daniel Francis Pastorius, and Robert Smith. Christopher Dock, "the pious schoolmaster on the Skippack," wrote the earliest American treatise on school management, in which he argued for a central role for music in the curriculum, a modified monitorial system of instruction, and a humane discipline. Although educational reform lagged behind the political revolution of 1776, its beginnings could be seen.

Children's books

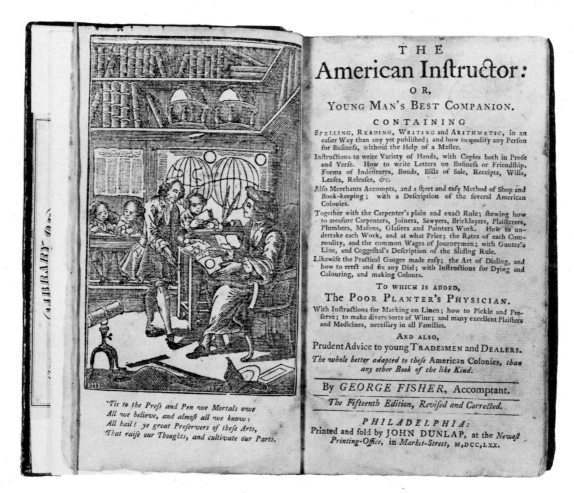

Schoolbook for young men

quently in their own kitchens. The Friends also took seriously the loosely enforced "apprenticeship system," placing orphans for trade training under members of the Society. The Friends' attempts to provide schools for Indian children were unsuccessful, but they did establish and endow one for Philadelphia Negroes. The Society experienced a serious blow before the Revolution when a sizable group seceded to the Anglican church, but by 1776 the Quakers had established from forty to fifty schools.

The Moravians and Education

They were never among the largest colonial denominations, but the Moravians were educational trail-blazers. An historical phenomenon, they had changed their nationality (from Bohemian or Czech to German) to retain their religion. Their Bishop Comenius was the towering educational figure in seventeenth-century Europe. In Pennsylvania, the Moravians founded the first nursery school, established in 1749 a famous boarding school for girls at Lititz, gave to music a prominent place in school as well as in church, and won for Bethlehem and Nazareth high educational reputations. They also had at least one well-regarded school in Philadelphia.

From Lewis Miller's sketchbook

Of all the early settlers, the Moravians were the most devoted and successful missionaries and teachers among the Indians. For some twenty years their work prospered. At Gnadenhutten, thirty miles from Bethlehem, they had an Indian congregation of five hundred persons. But their remarkable achievements there, and in several other settlements, ended in failure. As Wickersham, a standard authority on Pennsylvania education, says: "It will be one of the saddest pages in the history of Pennsylvania that shall truthfully tell how all the efforts of the Moravian Brethren for the welfare of the Indians were frustrated and rendered abortive, how town after town founded for their converts had to be abandoned and new homes sought for them and how at last . . . Zeisberger and his . . . colaborers accompanied with hearts full of sorrow the little band remaining under their guidance across the borders of Pennsylvania toward the setting sun, to meet more sorrows to the end."

Other Sects and Parochial Education

Other groups also established parochial schools. The Scotch and Scotch-Irish Presbyterians, wherever they established congregations in the East, set up elementary schools, an estimated fifty in all. And, no less than the New England Puritans, they believed in a well-educated ministry. That need was partly supplied by the famous "Log College" conducted at Neshaminy, in Bucks County,

Classroom discipline was a problem even then.

from 1726 to 1742 by William Tennent. Before the founding of Princeton, in New Jersey, it was considered "the foremost intellectual training ground for future Presbyterian preachers." There were also a number of Presbyterian grammar schools in the colony, emphasizing the classical disciplines to set the course for young men who would go on to the ministry. Parochial and clannish in the first half of the eighteenth century, the Presbyterians were destined to be leaders in the "neighborhood school" and the genuinely public school movements. Like the nineteenth-century Methodists, they were to be "by schisms rent asunder, by heresies distressed," but they never lost their proverbial Scotch faith in education.

The Anglicans' Society for the Propagation of the Gospel, with ambitious plans for a network of schools in Pennsylvania equaling or exceeding its good showing in New York, was doomed to failure. Several of the German sects opposed it vigorously and whatever popularity it enjoyed at first naturally tapered off as political unpleasantness with England developed. The S.P.G. had only about a dozen schools at the peak of its work in colonial Pennsylvania.

Both the Lutheran and the Reformed churches, which included a majority of the German and Dutch colonists, were zealous in establishing elementary schools for teaching their Three R's: Reading, 'Riting, and Religion. Their leaders were all for emphasizing English, but many of their followers were not, agreeing with such groups as the German Baptists, the Brethren, the Mennonites, and the Amish, all of whom were bitterly opposed to the idea. Lutheran schools numbered around forty; Reformed, about twenty-five.

Roman Catholics, now largely synonymous with parochial schooling in Pennsylvania, are reported by some historians to have set up two or three schools by 1776.

The Seventh Day German Baptists, whose community was in part monastic, established Writing and Singing schools at the Ephrata Cloister (founded in 1732), primarily for its celibate members, an elementary school for children of the lay congregation, a Sabbath school open to all poor children of the vicinity, and a secondary boarding school, whose curriculum is reported to have included Latin and higher mathematics.

The Methodists, destined to become one of the largest denominations after the Revolution, were just beginning to get organized when the war started. They stand out as a group that apparently never established parochial schools to any appreciable extent and were virtually unanimous in supporting the public school movement when it finally got under way.

Parochial schools by no means account for all of the formal education in colonial Pennsylvania. There were also private schools with offerings running the gamut from scholarship to quackery. Clergymen frequently tutored or even conducted schools on the side.

Between 1750 and 1783 as many as 175 private schools were in business, whether with only two or three or with a dozen or more pupils. Most specialized in mathematical and scientific subjects or in vocational training (such as navigation and surveying), and a surprising number emphasized French.

Franklin, The Academy of Philadelphia, and the Beginnings of Higher Education

Franklin had attended the famous Latin Grammar School in Boston and decided that it simply would not do as a model for secondary schools in mid-eighteenth-century America. Something more practical was needed, a type of institution from which the classical languages need not be excluded, but one of special service to a rising middle class in an age of social, industrial, and political change. Supported by a large group of ardent and able supporters, Franklin drew up a plan for The Academy of Philadelphia.

This new type of secondary school was officially nonsectarian, although three-fourths of its twenty-four trustees were Anglican, some eager to have the institution identified with that church. It was chartered in 1749 and received its first students in 1751. The curriculum included history, geography, surveying, navigation, and merchants accounts, to single out a few subjects that set it off from the Latin Grammar School. It made provision for physical education exercises and games and even committed itself to a modicum of teacher training. Franklin felt strongly that Americans should be taught to speak and write English well and deplored the common neglect of English in many of the German sects, so he personally set down in detail the English courses of study. Within a few years the Philadelphia Academy was to become the College of Philadelphia, and by 1779 it was the University of Pennsylvania. Its medical school, the first in North America, was established in 1765.

Neighborhood Schools: Augury of the Future

The Philadelphia Academy was just opening its doors when another highly important type of educational institution was launched. It has been called, with only slight exaggeration, the link in the chain between parochial and public schools. In central and western Pennsylvania, generally less conservative than the eastern part, and in areas thinly settled and without churches, the so-called neighborhood school appeared, the first around 1750. These schools were established when several religious groups cooperated to form a community school in neighborhoods where each sect by itself would have had difficulty finding enough students to justify a separate

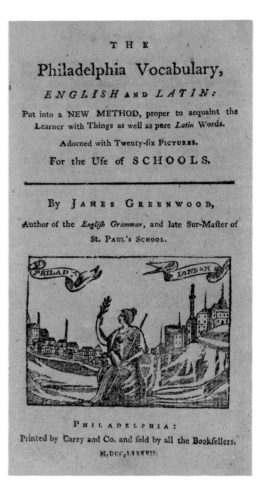

THE

Philadelphia Vocabulary,

ENGLISH AND LATIN:

Put into a NEW METHOD, proper to acquaint the Learner with Things as well as pure *Latin* Words.

Adorned with Twenty-six PICTURES.

For the Use of SCHOOLS.

By JAMES GREENWOOD,

Author of the *English Grammar*, and late Sur-Master of St. PAUL'S SCHOOL.

PHILADELPHIA:

Printed by Carey and Co. and sold by all the Booksellers. M,DCC,LXXXVII.

The old academy buildings in Fourth Street as originally constructed. The building at the left, the original structure, was built for George Whitefield.

denominational school. The idea of the neighborhood school took hold quickly in frontier regions, more slowly but firmly in the east. By 1836 there would be at least four thousand schools in the state, supported by the contributions of Pennsylvanians in their own neighborhoods. In spite of all the educational problems arising from its heterogeneous and scattered population, Pennsylvania had done fairly well in providing a direction for education in the new state when the Declaration of Independence was adopted.

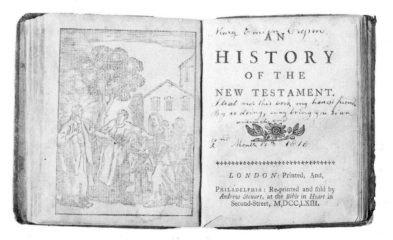

The earliest children's Bible printed in America

The College of Philadelphia

Recalling with satisfaction his role in the life of Philadelphia during the 1740s, Benjamin Franklin remarked: "There were, however, two things that I regretted, there being no provision for defense, nor for a complete education of youth; no militia, nor any college. I therefore, in 1743, drew up a proposal for establishing an academy."

Three years earlier, the move to establish a school for the education of poor children had been initiated by a group of "plain men, mostly mechanics," and when George Whitefield, the renowned English evangelist, returned to Philadelphia to continue his ministrations, and needed a building in which to preach, the two objects were combined: "to erect a large Building for a Charity School for the instruction of Poor Children gratis in useful Literature and the Knowledge of the Christian Religion: and also a House of Public Worship. . . ." Early in 1740, land was obtained, the foundation was laid, and building was begun.

The "New Building" at Fourth and Arch streets was completed late in 1741, after a series of financial problems were solved by obtaining "subscriptions" to ensure that the structure could be roofed. Money problems also beset the intended Charity School, and nearly a decade later, no masters had been engaged and no classes held. Then, largely as a result of Franklin's pamphlet Proposals Relating to the Education of Youth in Pensilvania, *some fifty Philadelphians pledged contributions so that a "Public Academy" could be founded. Twenty-four of the most generous donors, who agreed to serve as Trustees, met on November 13, 1749, signed the "Constitution" that had been drawn up by Franklin and Tench Francis, Attorney General for the province, elected Franklin their president and William Coleman their treasurer, and began negotiations for the purchase of the New Building. In December 1750 the Trustees announced that classes would begin next month, and shortly thereafter one hundred forty-five pupils had paid their fees and had begun their studies. The original concept of school for those who could not pay was not forgotten, and four months later the Free School was established in the building originally erected for that purpose, and within a year had enrolled more than sixty boys.*

To obtain official approval of the new institution, Tench Francis drew up a charter to be sent to England for signature. Thomas and Richard Penn sup-

ported the action—and also the school, with a donation of £500. In April 1753 the charter, addressed to "The Trustees of the Academy and Charitable School in the Province of Pennsylvania," was engrossed and sealed.

One step remained. Dr. William Smith of Aberdeen was engaged in 1754 as Master to teach "Logick, Rhetorick, Ethicks, and Natural Philosophy," and in the following year he proposed to the Trustees that the Charter be amended to approve formally the right of the school to grant a college degree. This was accomplished in June 1755, as reported by Philadelphia newspapers: "A College in the most extensive sense of the word is erected in this city and added to that collection of Schools formerly called the Academy."

Franklin's vision had become reality, a dozen years later than he had wished and not without difficulties—the financial problems already mentioned and others (the first master of the Free School, George Price, was dismissed because of drunkenness and abuse of his pupils; the redoubtable William Smith was later to be charged with Toryism and mishandling of finances). A generation before the Revolution the College of Philadelphia was established and thriving, developing into what was to become in 1779 the University of the State of Pennsylvania and eventually into the modern and prestigious University of Pennsylvania.

George Whitefield preaching

Science and Medicine

Secluded as Pennsylvania may have appeared to be in the remote North American wilderness, and preoccupied as the settlers were with the concerns of a new country—dealing with the Indians, meeting the wants of daily life, earning a living, erecting churches, schools, and taverns—the colony actually shared the fruits of an era of Western European intellectual progress perhaps unparalleled in history. The slow and arduous passage, over oceans not yet conquered by the newly found energies of steam, neither discouraged the floods of new settlers nor thwarted the drift of this eighteenth-century "Enlightenment" into the thriving seaport of Philadelphia and on to the west. Intellectual life in Pennsylvania reflected the scientific and technological interests of the Old World. Her citizens, in turn, contributed to both areas of knowledge in a manner not readily to be expected of a colony supposedly on the fringes of European civilization.

Pennsylvanians on the eve of revolution were the heirs of a new spirit of inquiry which had been eroding the complacencies of European thought since the Renaissance. Science—theoretical or applied as technology—thrived only when men's minds could divorce the behavior of nature from the inconsistencies of supernaturalism. It was but a short space of time, after all, which separated the mentality that hanged witches in New England from that which encouraged Franklin to explore the practical uses of electricity in Pennsylvania.

Influence of Bacon and Newton

This scientific mentality had its stimulus in the work of Sir Francis Bacon, born in 1561 in England on the very eve of the modern era of thought. Bacon's emphasis on cautious inductive thinking based on careful observation of nature would eventually dominate the method of American scientists well into the nineteenth century. His admonitions would set Pennsylvanian amateur scientists to careful study of weather changes, geological formations, and the exciting

Works of the astronomical clock David Rittenhouse made and used in his observations of the transit of Venus in 1769

new botanical discoveries of the North American continent. All of this must then be systematically tabulated, collated, and classified. "Baconianism" became a kind of secular religion in the New World.

The researches of another Englishman, Sir Isaac Newton, represented a polar influence in science which would affect all aspects of eighteenth-century thought. Newtonianism ventured beyond the confines of Earth and introduced to the excited imagination the wonders of a universe guided by mathematical law rather than supernatural whims. Newton in 1687 published (for that era, quite properly, in Latin) his *Mathematical Principles of Natural Philosophy*—a new Bible for the skeptical scientific mind. Its explanations of the cohesive nature of gravity, of the beautiful order and balance in a universe disciplined by mathematical relationships, offered new keys to understanding man's place in the eternal scheme. Newton, as had Bacon earlier, urged the direct investigation of the properties of things by careful experiment. But Newton also counseled inquirers to hypothesize explanations, not to be content with only massive collections of data. Observation must lead to generalization and experimentation—the essence of the scientific method in modern times.

Bacon and Newton together suggested that these inquiries into Nature should ultimately be applied to useful purposes, a goal readily welcomed by Americans such as Benjamin Franklin. Man as Nature's greatest creation was endowed with the capacity to investigate, to explain, and hence to solve all mysteries—and in the process to improve his own condition. It was a philosophical position in striking contrast to traditional New England puritanism, which had stressed the depravity of man in a world of the supernatural. Pennsylvania, with its rich mixture of cultures, was not New England. If even the stern Protestantism of the northeastern colonies was beginning to respond to the persuasions of the new world-centered philosophy, how much more readily might Pennsylvania succumb to its blandishments?

Books and Libraries in Pennsylvania: Carrying the Word of the New Science

The rich burden of Western European scientific thought was carried to the New World in various forms. Imported books, intended to adorn some ambitious colonial private library, were certainly major means. James Logan, William Penn's confidential advisor and Chief Justice of the Pennsylvania Supreme Court, imported the latest books in science and mathematics including the first known copy in America of Newton's *Principia*. His personal library of some three thousand volumes was kept in a small building near his home in Philadelphia, where it might also be used by studious

James Logan bookplate

acquaintances, for it was one of the best colonial libraries on classical and scientific subjects. It was here that young Thomas Godfrey, a close friend of Logan, was able to expand his own limited formal education. His strong talent for mathematics encouraged Godfrey's interest in optics and astronomy, and he is said to have learned Latin in order to be able to read the *Principia*. The importance of libraries for the promulgation of interest in science was exemplified in the subscription library organized by Franklin in 1731 as the Library Company of Pennsylvania. Included in this library's first shipment of books from abroad were volumes on geography, chemistry, botany, mathematics, agriculture, and architecture.

Perhaps no foreign work could have excited the interest of practical-minded Pennsylvanians as did Denis Diderot's twenty-eight volume *Encyclopedia*, the work of nearly two hundred specialists, completed only four years before the Declaration of Independence. Its detailed and beautifully illustrated pages scanned a vast variety of technological processes ranging from armaments manufacture to rope-making. Here, indeed, was embodied the Baconian ideal of utility, which would be a keynote of American science for two hundred years.

Pennsylvania and Europe: Exchanging Information

European scientific societies, particularly the Royal Society of London for the Improvement of Natural Knowledge, also stimulated American scientific curiosity. In pursuit of his own interests in the new and fascinating field of electricity, Franklin scanned regularly the Royal Society's *Philosophical Transactions*. He was one of twenty-six Americans honored by election to membership in the Society, and, along with the Pennsylvanian botanist John Bartram and Dr. John Morgan, founder of the first medical school in America at Philadelphia, also contributed to the *Transactions*.

A vigorous correspondence between dedicated specialists and interested amateurs alike in the years preceding the Revolution represented another powerful means of transferring the scientific enlightenment to American shores. Thus both Franklin and Bartram exchanged many letters with the London Quaker merchant Peter Collinson, a member of the Royal Society and an amateur deeply interested in natural science. Philadelphia by mid-century was a thriving entrepot for the exchange of ideas as well as commercial products. Merchants often acted as couriers between British scientists and Pennsylvanians, the former eager for data and specimens relating to the unique American natural history, the latter equally desirous of scientific materials, books, and instruments not available in the colonies.

Of course, people as well as letters crossed the Atlantic to ex-

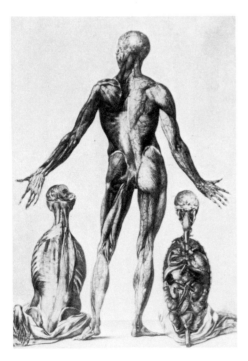

Anatomical drawing brought to America by William Shippen, Jr., and used at the first American medical school

change information and ideas. The best known American traveler was Franklin, whose frequent and often lengthy visits abroad afforded opportunities for contact with the practitioners of advanced European science which so attracted him that only the threat of war tempered his reluctance to return from England to America in 1775. Nevertheless, his departure for the Continent in 1776 as emissary to France provided for Franklin delightful new opportunities to explore the sources of scientific thinking, as well as to test his diplomatic strategy. In these various ways, data, ideas, and inspiration were carried to the colonies in the prewar decades, proving an unmeasurable stimulus to scientific progress in Pennsylvania.

Establishing the Intellectual Climate: The Junto and the American Philosophical Society

Pennsylvania and the other English colonies in America were breeding a widely scattered group of intellectually alert amateurs—merchants, clergymen, physicians, lawyers, government officials, and craftsmen—with strong scientific interests. What they needed was some clearinghouse through which they could share their own peculiar scientific interests. Once again, Benjamin Franklin provided impetus for such an organization when in 1727 he gathered a group of these citizens into a discussion club named the Junto. Its monthly meetings emphasized natural philosophy and tried to carry on a useful correspondence with like-minded men in the other colonies. The original Junto included specialists in botany, mathematics, medicine, geography, and mechanism. In 1743 Franklin expanded his concept of an intellectual mart by proposing a new society whose goals would stress useful knowledge within all the British American colonies. The result was the American Philosophical Society, which chose Franklin as Secretary, although he complained that it included too many "very idle gentlemen."

Meanwhile, an energetic Scotch-Irish immigrant teacher and merchant named Charles Thomson generated in 1766 a new American Society for Promoting and Propagating Useful Knowledge to succeed the Philadelphia Junto. Thomson stressed the goal of American self-sufficiency and urged it upon the new group. Emphasizing the great resources of Pennsylvania in particular and of America in general, Thomson related the causes of patriotism and of achievement in science. He argued that since Philadelphia was the intellectual center of the colonies and her citizens notable for their practical accomplishments, the American Society should provide scientific leadership for all the colonies. A merger in 1769 of the new Thomson group and the old Franklin group produced the American Philosophical Society Held at Philadelphia for Promoting Useful Knowledge. In 1771 the new society began its own collection of pub-

Benjamin Franklin organized the Junto to further the education of his fellow journeymen.

The Rules I drew up requir'd that every Member in his Turn should produce one or more Queries on any Point of Morals, Politics or Natural Philosophy, to be discuss'd by the Company, and once in three Months produce and read an Essay of his own Writing on any Subject he pleased. Our Debates were to be under the Direction of a President, and to be conducted in the sincere Spirit of Enquiry after Truth, without Fondness for Dispute, or Desire of Victory. . . .

Franklin on the Junto,
in his *Autobiography*

Experimental model of a harvester

lished *Transactions*, which provided an American equivalent of the envied series of the Royal Society.

As might be expected, the orientation of the American Philosophical Society was strongly utilitarian. Attention to surveying and mapmaking, mechanical inventions for saving labor, animal breeding, gardening improvements, and methods of preventing and curing diseases intermingled with discussions of fossil and archeological finds, mathematical innovations, and discoveries in chemistry. At last the American colonies, on the very eve of Revolution, had found in Pennsylvania a common medium for their scientific interests—combined, for many, with an expression of patriotic independence of England.

Popularizing Science in Early America

One did not have to be a member of an ambitious scientific society or to read its publications in order to pick up an acquaintance with science. The American zeal for popular lectures on such subjects—a zeal that would culminate in the Chautauquas of the late nineteenth century—existed in mid-eighteenth-century Pennsylvania. For example, Ebenezer Kinnersley, an itinerant Pennsylvanian Baptist preacher and talented amateur in science, began in the 1750s a thirty-year career of lecturing on such scientific topics as Franklin's experiments with electricity until, it is said, Kinnersley was more widely recognized in the popular mind as a scientist than was Franklin himself.

Science, too, entered the new colleges in Pennsylvania and elsewhere in the colonies, with results not always congenial to young men with humanistic or theological interests. One such collegian lamented:

> Now algebra, geometry
> Arithmetic, astronomy,
> Optics, chronology, and statics,
> All tiresome parts of mathematics,
> With twenty harder names than these
> Disturb my brains and break my peace.
> We're told how planets rolled on high,
> How large their orbits, and how high;
> I hope in little time to know,
> Whether the moon's a cheese, or no.

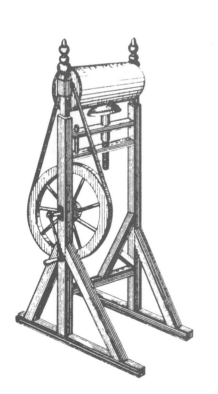

Franklin's electrostatic machine resembled a spinning wheel. The electric charge was generated by the friction of a cloth-covered plate against a revolving glass cylinder.

The Study of Weather

Weather and climate were of immediate concern to the colonists of Pennsylvania. Indeed, weather was a frequent topic in correspondence with one's friends, and voluminous notes were taken concerning

Benjamin Franklin, Experimental Scientist

In 1743, after attending a series of lectures on the new science of electricity, Benjamin Franklin (1706–1790) was stirred to action. A year later, after having heard that experimenters were charging glass tubes by rubbing them with silk, he not only duplicated the experiment but went beyond it. As he wrote a friend, he was very "engrossed" in this work, "what with making experiments when I can be alone, and repeating them to my friends and acquaintances, who . . . come continually in crowds to see them." Within a decade Franklin had discovered the chief properties of electricity and had proved electricity and lightning to be identical— feats described by Joseph Priestley as the "greatest" scientific advances since the time of Isaac Newton. These were heady years for Franklin, lecturing on electricity throughout the colonies, describing his experiments in papers published in leading magazines and in his own Experiments and Observations on Electricity. *Franklin enunciated a unified concept of electricity and originated the terms still used to describe electrical phenomena: positive and negative, charge and discharge, conductor and condenser.*

What is remarkable is that Franklin was able to do so much from so little. Apparently his first experiments were done with the Leyden jar, a corked bottle filled partly with water, electrically charged through a wire set into the cork. Franklin recognized that "at the same time that the wire and top of the bottle, and so on, is electrised positively or plus, the bottom of the bottle is electrised negatively or minus, in exact proportions: i.e., whatever quantity of electrical fire is thrown in at the top, an equal quantity goes out at the bottom." His "doctrine of points" held that lightning could be attracted during a storm by pointed pieces of iron. During a storm in 1752, in order to test his theory, he put up a kite to which was attached a pointed wire at the top, with a metal key at the bottom of the string. As the world knows, he succeeded in attracting lightning and producing sparks from the key. Fascinated by all areas of physics, as well as meteorology, Franklin investigated such questions as why breath is visible in cold air, why hail is formed in summer, and why snow on the mountains in hot climates never melts. He deserves his reputation as a scientist of the first rank—the "American Newton."

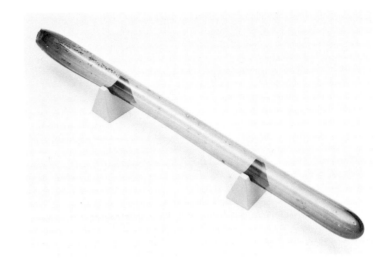

Green glass tube (2 inches by 28½ inches) was probably used by Franklin and Rittenhouse in generating static electricity.

Franklin's famous kite experiment

Franklin's battery of Leyden jars. Fifteen of the thirty-five jars appear to be original.

Benjamin Franklin by English artist Mason Chamberlin, 1762

temperature, atmospheric pressure, humidity, the force of the wind—often with the aid of home-made instruments where imported gauges of superior quality could not be obtained. All such observations, in turn, encouraged classification and analysis. Physicians weighed the relationship between weather changes and disease. Hugh Williamson, one of the first graduates of Franklin's College of Philadelphia, where he then taught mathematics before studying medicine abroad, prepared a paper relating the settlement of the country to climatic changes. Benjamin Franklin published a paper in the *Philosophical Transactions* in 1765 on "Physical and Meteorological Observations, Conjectures, and Suppositions" in which he sought to explain rain, fog, and winds in terms of the influence of varying temperatures on air particles and the revolving of the planet.

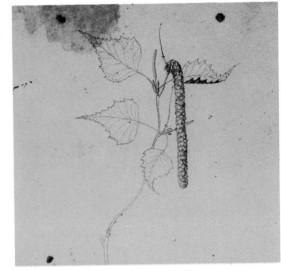

Geology and Botany

Pennsylvania's varied terrain challenged surveyors, mapmakers, and geologists alike. Lewis Evans in 1749 published a map of the Middle Colonies which outlined major roads of migration through the Lancaster, York, and Carlisle areas and soon found his expertise involved in boundary disputes. John Bartram, the widely wandering botanist, knew Evans well and shared his geological interests. Bartram conceived a plan to test mineral resources by boring into the earth. Pragmatically, he recommended that his hypothesis concerning submerged mountain ranges in the oceans implied good fishing banks wherever their peaks neared the surface. He also revised notions about the nature of limestone, with which Pennsylvania was plentifully endowed, by arguing its marine origin. His wanderings suggested to him the usefulness of preparing a geological map. Also interested in paleontology, Bartram provided the most useful suggestions for mounting the exciting find of mastodon bones which George Croghan, a Pennsylvania Indian trader, had discovered in the Ohio country.

Early botanical drawings of oak and paper birch.

Among the natural sciences botany was especially popular in Pennsylvania, with its rich variety of plants. In fact, European scientists drew heavily upon colonial contributors for descriptions and specimens. This was the century of Carl Linnaeus (1707–1778), the Swedish scholar whose *Systema Naturae* of 1735 had introduced Americans to a novel system of classification of plant life based on sexual characteristics. The idea of associating vegetable matter with male and female, shocking to many contemporaries, was widely promulgated by Linnaeus' students. Among them was Peter Kalm, who disembarked at Philadelphia in 1748 with intentions to extend the compliments of the master to John Bartram, to visit Bartram's fabulous botanical garden, and to begin a visit that lasted nearly two and a half years and provided European botanists with a treasure of knowledge about the flora of the Middle Colonies. One Pennsylvanian, Adam Kuhn, became the only colonial to study directly under Linnaeus at the University of Uppsala during 1761–1764. His experience resulted in the first college botany course in America, which Kuhn taught at the College of Philadelphia.

James Logan, at the height of his many-faceted career in politics and science, also pursued serious botanical studies. Maize especially intrigued Logan, whose experiments with pollination confirmed the sexual functions of plant organs. Logan's findings were published in the Royal Society's *Transactions* within a year of the publication of Linnaeus' own *Systema*.

A close friend and something of an intellectual ward of James Logan was a much younger Pennsylvanian whose name was to become synonymous with botany in America: John Bartram (1699–1777), born near Marple in Delaware County. Although his personal behavior remained strongly influenced by his Quaker heritage, the scientific revolution, of which he was also an inheritor, inclined him toward Deism. Bartram's early interest in the natural world impressed Logan, who encouraged the young man. Learning Latin in order to read Linnaeus, Bartram remained less interested in systems of classification than in wandering about the colonies in quest of new plants and distributing them to curious European and American scholars. His long correspondence with Peter Collinson in England finally aided him in obtaining the post of Botanist to the King in 1765.

Bartram's botanical garden, begun in 1729, was often visited by notables such as Benjamin Franklin and George Washington, and eventually became part of the Philadelphia park system. An inveterate traveler, Bartram visited the colonies to the south, where his careful observations helped to enrich the botanical lore and collections of scientists at home and overseas. Linnaeus praised him as "the greatest natural botanist in the world" and honored the American by naming a genus of moss *Bartramia*. The simple homespun Quaker personality of the Pennsylvanian is suggested by a letter from Collinson—also a Quaker—that John would do well to dress with somewhat greater refinement when, in 1738, he planned a botanical expedition in the South: "the Virginians are a very gentle, well-dressed people—and look, perhaps, more at a man's outside than his inside." An opponent of slavery, Bartram is said to have dined with his own freed slaves regardless of the presence of visitors.

At home in Pennsylvania Bartram pursued various scientific interests, tracing the course of the Schuylkill River in 1736, recording the annual devastations of the tent caterpillar as well as the existence of locust cycles, and preparing an article for the *Philosophical Transactions* in 1745 on "An Account of some very curious Wasps Nests made of clay in Pensilvania." John Bartram may have lacked certain professional qualifications—"to give the title of King's Bota-

TRAVELS

THROUGH

NORTH & SOUTH CAROLINA,

GEORGIA,

EAST & WEST FLORIDA,

THE CHEROKEE COUNTRY, THE EXTENSIVE
TERRITORIES OF THE MUSCOGULGES,
OR CREEK CONFEDERACY, AND THE
COUNTRY OF THE CHACTAWS;

CONTAINING

AN ACCOUNT OF THE SOIL AND NATURAL
PRODUCTIONS OF THOSE REGIONS, TOGE-
THER WITH OBSERVATIONS ON THE
MANNERS OF THE INDIANS.

EMBELLISHED WITH COPPER-PLATES.

By WILLIAM BARTRAM.

PHILADELPHIA:
PRINTED BY JAMES & JOHNSON.
M, DCC, XCI.

How John Bartram Became a Botanist

Colonial Pennsylvania was a museum of natural history awaiting exploration by citizens whose closeness to her fertile fields and primeval forests piqued their imaginations and trained their skills. Among such naturalists was John Bartram, whose initiation into the science of botany is here described—perhaps somewhat fancifully—by Michel-Guillaume Jean de Crèvecoeur, French-born writer of Letters from an American Farmer (1782).

" 'Pray, Mr. Bartram, when did you imbibe the first wish to cultivate the science of botany; was you regularly bred to it in Philadelphia?' 'I have never received any other education than barely reading and writing; this small farm was all the patrimony my father left me; . . . [O]ne day I was very busy holding my plough (for thee see'st that I am but a ploughman), and being very weary, I ran under the shade of a tree to repose myself. I cast my eyes on a daisy; I plucked it mechanically and viewed it with more curiosity than common country farmers are wont to do, and observed therein very many distinct parts, some perpendicular, some horizontal. "What a shame," said my mind, or something that inspired my mind, "that thee shouldest have employed so many years in tilling the earth and destroying so many flowers and plants without being acquainted with their structures and their uses!" This seeming inspiration suddenly awakened my curiosity, for these were not thoughts to which I had been accustomed. I returned to my team, but this new desire did not quit my mind; . . . I thought about it continually, at supper, in bed, and wherever I went. At last I could not resist the impulse; for on the fourth day of the following week, I hired a man to plough for me and went to Philadelphia. Though I knew not what book to call for, I ingenuously told the bookseller my errand, who provided me with such as he thought best and a Latin grammar beside. Next I applied to a neighbouring schoolmaster, who in three months taught me Latin enough to understand Linnaeus, which I purchased afterward. Then I began to botanize all over my farm; in a little time I became acquainted with every vegetable that grew in my neighbourhood, and next ventured into Maryland, living among the Friends; in proportion as I thought myself more learned, I proceeded farther, and by a steady application of several years, I have acquired a pretty general knowledge of every plant and tree to be found in our continent. In process of time I was applied to from the old countries, whither I every year send many collections.' "

John Bartram's home, built by him in 1730

nist to a man who can scarcely spell, much less make out the characters of any one genus of plants, appears rather hyperbolical," observed one distinguished contemporary. Nevertheless, his keen observation and ability to collect and preserve living specimens in his garden, and above all his wide-ranging scientific association and correspondence, combined to make John Bartram, as a recent scholar expressed it, "the field agent par excellence of the colonial era." His death in 1777 was one more sign of the end of that era.

John Bartram's son, William, born in 1739 in the old stone house in the botanic garden at Philadelphia, was well known for his skillful drawings in natural history. "Very elegant," Collinson called them, and William's talents, in an era when the sketcher-portraitist was an essential predecessor of the camera, were drawn upon by English sponsors of an exploring trip to the southeastern area even while war raged in 1773–1777. William, who made his way safely back to Pennsylvania in 1778, prepared a popular, frequently translated account of his travels. His list of 215 American birds remains a landmark in American ornithology.

Astronomy in Colonial Pennsylvania

Newton's notion of a mechanistic universe strongly influenced a growing interest in astronomy among Pennsylvania scientists, whose daytime concern with weather or the collection of plants yielded at nightfall to curious and careful observations of the skies. Astronomy appealed to the rational mind, compelling a desire for precise knowledge about the mysterious bodies that sailed through the heavens. The transit of Venus across the face of the sun in the year 1769 marked an astronomical event of the greatest curiosity throughout the colonies. For Pennsylvanians the closest point for studying the full period of the transit was in the Lake Superior area, but for reasons of cost and convenience the provincial assembly generously supported construction of a wooden observatory in Philadelphia's State House Square. Something of a holiday atmosphere prevailed in which the citizens shared the excitement of professional observers. Not far from Philadelphia, at Norriton, David Rittenhouse had set up an observatory equipped with his own instruments, including a 144-power refracting telescope. A nearly perfect day greeted all observers, and the usually meticulous Rittenhouse was so entranced by the event that he nearly botched his calculations. American observations drew wide and favorable attention abroad and encouraged a growing recognition that colonial science was coming of age.

David Rittenhouse was a tall and slender man of pleasant and extremely modest demeanor—a clock and instrument maker of splendid talent. His great grandfather was a Mennonite minister who had built the first paper mill in the colonies on Paper Mill

David Rittenhouse's "Projection of the Transit of Venus" was published in the first volume of the Transactions of the American Philosophical Society.

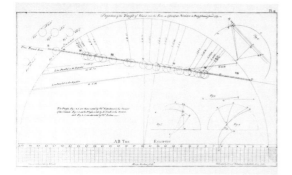

David Rittenhouse, Pioneer
Planetarium Builder

Consistent with the Newtonian "system of the world," in which the planets and satellites of the solar system were held to move in mechanically precise paths, mechanical planetariums were constructed as early as the seventeenth century. In England the most significant model was built by John Rowley for Charles Boyle, fourth earl of Orrery. As a result, Rowley's planetarium was referred to as an "orrery." Philadelphia's David Rittenhouse (1732–1796), who believed that an orrery could be made to reproduce apparent rather than real motions, viewed from inside the orrery, was at work on such a machine as early in 1767. In this year he wrote out for the first time his revolutionary and almost completely new design.

Rittenhouse's aim was not to "give the ignorant in astronomy a just view of the Solar System: but would rather astonish the skillful and curious examiner, by a most accurate correspondence between the situations and motions of the bodies, themselves." In his plan the planets would revolve about the sun in a vertical plane. In addition, desiring more accuracy than had been seen before, he stipulated that the planets must revolve around the sun in elliptical paths, not in circles; that the speed of rotation of the planets on their axes must be precise; and that each planet's orbit must be in proper relationship to the orbit of every other planet. For a "mechanic"— in Rittenhouse's case, a skillful clockmaker— this project represented a challenging task. Thus David Rittenhouse, by the time his orrery was completed, was an accomplished astronomer, physicist, and mathematician. Recognition of his scientific standing came when the College of Philadelphia conferred on him an honorary master of arts degree in 1767.

The first orrery built by Rittenhouse, strictly astronomical in concept and execution, had three faces, the largest of which contained a brass ball for the sun and ivory balls for the planets, which were made to revolve around the sun by the turning of a crank. In turn, pointers set on graduated plates showed the day, month, and year, over a period of 5,000 years with 1767 as the midpoint. A telescope, pointed from the sun at the planet under study, would give the planet's position with relation to the earth; when the telescope was placed on the earth, one could place a planet's geocentric position in the solar system. In addition, it was possible to reproduce a solar eclipse,

*David Rittenhouse
after a painting by C.W. Peale*

the phases of the moon, and the apparent motion of the sun as it moved in relation to the earth. The first orrery was virtually finished in 1771 and sold to the College of New Jersey (now Princeton University). Because this sale angered his friends at the College of Philadelphia (now the University of Pennsylvania) he agreed to make a duplicate for them.

Although Rittenhouse's need to make a living and desire to serve his country led him to decline the honor, it is a tribute to him that Thomas Jefferson in 1783 proposed that he construct an orrery for the king of France. Recognized internationally in scientific circles, the name of this Philadelphia clockmaker became synonymous with integrity and precise science used for human betterment. In short, David Rittenhouse was "the American mechanic rising to greatness."

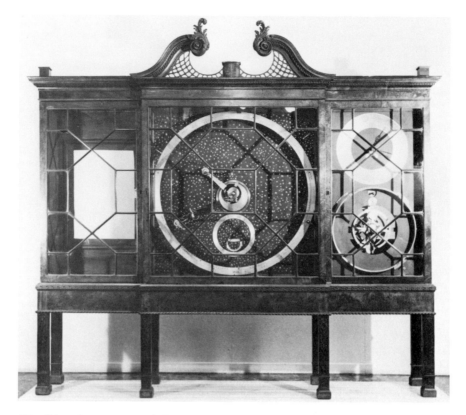

The Rittenhouse orrery (planetarium) at the University of Pennsylvania. The mechanism for the left panel was never completed. Note the stylistic similarity between this housing and that of the Rittenhouse clock on the opposite page.

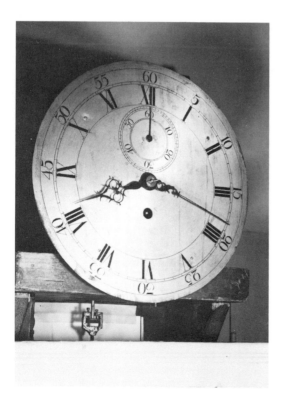

Face of the Rittenhouse astronomical clock

The Rittenhouse astronomical transit telescope used in the observation of the transit of Venus.

Run near the Wissahickon Creek. Like John Bartram, David Rittenhouse overcame a deficient early education by constant study and the professional guidance of admiring counselors, such as the Reverend Thomas Barton of Lancaster. Moving to Philadelphia to be in the main current of colonial science and public life, he entered upon a career of intense research and public service. His skill in surveying persuaded even the English astronomers Charles Mason and Jeremiah Dixon to accept his calculations in establishing the previously disputed Pennsylvania-Maryland border. River and canal surveys, often made with instruments of his own design and manufacture, also occupied much of his time.

Rittenhouse embodied the eighteenth-century ideal of the eclectic scientist-citizen. He studied the compressibility of water, researched electricity with Franklin, invented a collimating telescope, and developed a compensating pendulum, using his self-won knowledge of mathematics to help demonstrate "a very elegant theorem for determining times of vibration of a pendulum." His orrery (a small planetarium) plotted the motions of heavenly bodies with an accuracy still astonishing to mechanicians. One of the most widely respected scientists in colonial America, David Rittenhouse would soon apply his patriotism and talents to Pennsylvania's war effort.

Among the many other Pennsylvanians also interested in astronomy were Hugh Williamson, a physician who would become a member of the Continental Congress, and Humphry Marshall. Williamson's opinion that comets were probably inhabited, terrestrial-like objects was well received abroad, suggesting that Pennsylvania amateurs were not alone in mistaken astronomical enthusiasms. Franklin found Marshall's conscientious observations of the velocity, shape, and location of sunspots worthy of passing on to the Royal Society itself.

Physics and Chemistry

The branch of physics which most fascinated the eighteenth-century man of science was electricity. Here of course Franklin took the lead, but he was in constant touch with other colonists who shared his interest. Pennsylvanians Hugh Williamson, David Rittenhouse, and Ebenezer Kinnersley at the College of Philadelphia were the most prominent among them.

Chemistry, too, won a good share of the prevailing interest in science. In Pennsylvania, Dr. John de Normandies made careful tests of mineral waters found near Bristol to settle arguments about the value of mineral springs, and soon men like the physician Benjamin Rush were involved in comparing the virtues of newly found mineral springs in Philadelphia with the water at Bristol and else-

The Rittenhouse clock in the Drexel Institute of Technology is housed in an outstanding Chippendale style case by a Philadelphia craftsman.

Visit to the doctor from Lewis Miller's sketchbook.

Dr. Benjamin Rush's medicine chest. It is owned today by his descendant Alexander Rush, M.D.

where. One result was publication in 1773 of extensive experiments which Rush performed on medicinal effects of varying water sources. In 1770 the energetic if controversial physician also published his *Syllabus of Chemistry*, the first in the colonies.

Medicine in Colonial Pennsylvania

The health sciences practiced in Pennsylvania on the eve of the American Revolution were a combination of advanced medical science and empirical folk remedies, medical fantasies, and simple hokum. Even shrewd Benjamin Franklin allowed that "metallic tractors" made of special alloys could lure disease from ailing flesh. The powers of "animal magnetism" were widely accepted in Europe, where Franz Mesmer's patients linked themselves by a conductor to a central tub of that element. Men fascinated with electricity inevitably speculated about its potential curative powers. Franklin participated in experiments with electric shock treatments in paralytic cases, reporting only temporary benefits. It was an optimistic age, and the bridge between gullibility and the rationalist's faith in open-mindedness could be of short span. Why, indeed, should not men of genius evolve new methodologies and devices for curing diseases based on magnetism, the shape of one's face, exotic plants, or the disturbance of the blood? Benjamin Rush, certainly one of the

A Pennsylvania Physician in 1776: Benjamin Rush

Practicing medicine was by 1776 already a lucrative calling, as attested by the number of late and unpaid bills. Quacks aside, colonial medical men were respected members of the community, many serving in provincial and national congresses on the eve of revolution; at least five doctors of medicine signed the Declaration of Independence, among them Benjamin Rush.

Dr. Rush provides a useful example of the colonial physician in the process of transition to a new era in medicine as well as politics. Born near Philadelphia in 1745, Rush attended the College of New Jersey. He shifted his goals from law to medicine and studied with Dr. John Redman, a fellow Philadelphian who had trained at Edinburgh and Leyden. Redman was consulting physician at The Pennsylvania Hospital from 1751 to 1780, a member of the American Philosophical Society, and a devoted advocate of saline purgatives in medical practice. Both Rush and John Morgan had been Redman's apprentices.

Rush, too, completed his training at Edinburgh and later at London, where he met Benjamin Franklin. Upon returning to Philadelphia in 1769, he accepted the position of Professor of Chemistry at the College of Philadelphia and soon published the first American textbook on that subject. A prolific writer, Rush also profited from his association with Thomas Jefferson and Thomas Paine, and became a champion of the causes of abolition and independence. In June of 1776 he was elected to the Pennsylvania provincial conference concerned with the issue of independence, and shortly thereafter he signed the Declaration of Independence as an elected member of the Continental Congress.

After being appointed surgeon-general of the armies of the Middle Department, Rush, a determined if also dogmatic individual, protested the administrative deficiencies of a fellow Pennsylvanian, Dr. William Shippen, Jr. Congress supported Shippen. Rush's indiscreet participation in the so-called Conway Cabal against George Washington's leadership led to the doctor's resignation and return to Philadelphia.

The revolutionary spirit of change and reform fed Rush's liberal opinions, and he used his considerable literary abilities to advocate reforms such as temperance, abolition of slavery, and more progres-

Dr. Benjamin Rush, painted by Charles Willson Peale, 1776

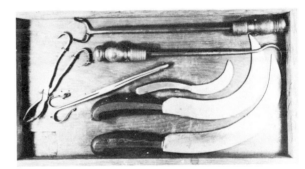

Operating instruments from physician's field bag

sive procedures in education. He was active in behalf of the new Federal Constitution as a member of the Pennsylvania ratifying convention, and joined the cause of liberalizing his state's own constitution as well. When a merger of colleges in 1791 created the University of Pennsylvania, Rush continued as a teacher of extraordinary popularity with students, if not with his competitors. As a scientist his weakness was inadequate clinical observation and too complete a confidence in bleeding as a cure-all. But, whatever his faults of personality and method, Benjamin Rush greatly encouraged interest in the advancement of medicine both in Pennsylvania and the new United States to the time of his death in 1813.

Glass and tin suction cups for drawing blood, and scarificator for making surface lacerations

Spring-loaded lancet

Surgical knives

best known and most highly educated Pennsylvania physicians, possessed such great faith in single-treatment blood-letting that one contemporary called it "one of the great discoveries contributing to the depopulation of the earth."

Those who did not patronize trained physicians had a range of other alternatives available. The local minister might also practice medicine in an attempt to cure the body and the soul together. The German pow-wow practitioner of a medicine based on religion and magic also thrived—as did the outright quack. Transvestite Charlotte Hamilton (posing as Charles Hamilton) ministered to eighteenth-century residents of Chester County. Charlatan Francis Torres bilked Philadelphians into purchasing "Chinese Stones" guaranteed to cure toothache, cancer, and the bites of mad dogs and rattlesnakes. Pennsylvania, honored for its many medical firsts, also produced the earliest patent medicine, *Tuscavora Rice*, developed by Mrs. Sybilla Masters.

Still lingering in the colonies were the superstitions and folk remedies common to a highly religious and essentially agrarian people. Disease and other ailments were frequently attributed to heavenly punishment or the purgation of sin. Home remedies, tested by experience real or fancied, were colorful in nature and terminology. What seemed more probable than a relationship between snake root and snake bite? Oil of turkey buzzard soothed sciatica; "Jerusalem Oak" when mixed with water would grieve intestinal worms. And even the plague, in one suggested colonial remedy, fled before a proper preparation of live toads baked in an overturned earthenware pot, then pounded in an iron mortar when cold. All of man's common ailments abounded in Pennsylvania, each with its remedies recommended by physicians who never saw a college lecture room. A Quaker physician left posterity this memorial of his methods:

> When patients come to I
> I physicks, bleeds and sweats 'em,
> Then—if they choose to die,
> What's that to I—I let's 'em.

Pennsylvania's health problems remained essentially constant from the seventeenth through the nineteenth centuries. Smallpox was an especial scourge which even accompanied William Penn on the *Welcome*—killing about thirty passengers. Even though inoculation for smallpox was well known, it was little practiced and smallpox was a major killer. Pennsylvanians were also plagued by the common cold, children's diseases (chickenpox, measles, mumps, and whooping cough), and huge numbers of other infectious and communicable diseases including scarlet fever, malaria, diphtheria, typhoid, typhus, cholera, dysentery, influenza, yellow fever, and tuberculosis. Syphilis and gonorrhea were also common. Well into the nineteenth century, a man wasn't considered a man in rural Pennsylvania unless he had the "chills," and it was only with the large-scale clearing of land and the use of pesticides that malaria became rare. Malignant and degenerative diseases, usually being internal, were not generally recognized. Cancer of the breast was a feared exception. Since there were few old people around, most of today's common geriatric complaints were rare.

Possibly no more than five percent of colonial physicians in 1776 held university degrees of any kind, but as more young men sought training at Edinburgh, London, Paris, and Leyden, a nucleus of professional expertise developed in the colonies. European-trained Pennsylvanians, for example, included Dr. William Shippen, Jr., Dr. John Morgan, Dr. Benjamin Rush, Dr. William Logan, Dr. Thomas Cadwalader, and Dr. Adam Kuhn—all of whom set up practice in Philadelphia, Pennsylvania's medical center. Meanwhile, many others attended lectures abroad and observed hospital practice without obtaining degrees.

Who were the other ninety-five percent of colonial physicians? Anyone who wanted to call himself doctor and could convince his neighbors of his distinction. It wasn't until the end of the nineteenth century that physicians were licensed in Pennsylvania. One could question the true qualifications of a Dr. Ludwig, who came to Philadelphia in 1775 and announced that he had studied physic and surgery "at the most renowned Universities in Germany." Other doctors who materialized from abroad, like James Graham, specialized. He offered his services "in all the disorders of the Eye and its Appendages; and in every Species of Deafness." Upon his later return to London, Graham opened "a temple of Health and Hymen," which offered a "celestial bed" to childless couples.

Most doctors were much less colorful. Some, like Dr. William Shippen, Sr., began as apothecaries and simply raised themselves to the rank of physician. In rural areas it was common for the local doctor to also be a farmer or a minister. Most doctors, whatever their training, also dispensed drugs. Perhaps the only meaningful difference between eighteenth-century apothecaries and physicians aside from the university-educated elite was that physicians charged for their services and dispensed medicine. The apothecary sold medicine and donated his advice. Doctors practicing in rural areas generally charged both a fee and a mileage rate for visiting a patient.

Hospitals and Medical Training

Philadelphia also became a colonial nucleus of hospital care and, closely associated with it, of formal and clinical medical training. Dr. Thomas Bond founded the Pennsylvania Hospital, the first in America intended for the sick, injured, and insane. In 1762 Dr.

Doctor's saddlebags. The bag in the foreground is fitted as a medicine chest.

Venesection (vein opening), shown in this old European woodcut, was widely practiced in colonial America. It was the most common form of therapeutic bleeding, remaining in practice into the nineteenth century.

William Shippen returned from European training to begin a series of anatomical lectures in the State House at Philadelphia, many illustrated with fine colored pictures by the Dutch painter Jan Van Rymsdyk. These had been presented as a gift to The Pennsylvania Hospital by John Fothergill, the English physician who in 1774 would help Benjamin Franklin draft a fruitless plan of reconciliation between the colonies and England. Shippen, however, relied more on human dissection than on pictures for his expositions, with the unhappy result that he barely escaped alive when his laboratories were invaded by angry mobs, horrified at such desecration of the "temple of God."

Formal medical training in the colonies was initiated at the College of Philadelphia by Dr. John Morgan, a graduate of its first class in 1757. Pursuing his training in London, Paris, and Italy, Morgan earned an M.D. at Edinburgh. Returning to Philadelphia, Morgan in 1765 prepared as his commencement address at the College *A Discourse upon the Institution of Medical Schools in America.* This stressed the importance of scientific training for physicians and the need to separate surgery and the apothecary's trade from the practice of medicine. One result was the founding of a medical school, an action which persuaded Benjamin Rush, still in London, to observe, "Methinks I see the place of my nativity becoming the *Edinburgh of America*," thus liberating American students from the perils and tediousness of the long voyage abroad.

In Pennsylvania, as elsewhere in America, the colonial Assembly made efforts to regulate matters of health and treatment, stressing quarantine laws and keeping a wary eye on quacks. American physicians early felt a common bond and joined societies, one of which—the Philadelphia Medical Society, established in 1766—might have endeavored to license and regulate physicians had Dr. John Morgan's efforts on that behalf succeeded.

Invalid's feeding cup

Dentistry

Dentistry is often considered the first American medical specialty, but, although toothaches were a common, universal, and dreaded occurrence, the important rise of professional dentistry is only a nineteenth-century phenomenon. In 1776 the dentist shared his practice with doctors, apothecaries, and even barbers, and the most common remedy was extraction, accomplished usually with the use of a "tooth key." One eighteenth-century American dental chair, preserved at the Temple University School of Dentistry, is a windsor chair with a headrest. Dentists often lanced gums and on occasion filled large noticeable cavities with gold inlay. Most people simply lost their teeth. "Women," it was observed, "lost a tooth for each child." With large families teeth were soon depleted. Poorer people just gummed their food. Those who could afford them had

Tooth extractor, used by most physicians and dentists, and by many barbers

The original building of the Pennsylvania Hospital soon after its completion

Colonial Philadelphia's Hospital and Medical School

Even John Adams, who found Philadelphia morally, religiously, and educationally inferior to Boston, was forced to admire the Quaker city's charitable institutions and especially its great Pennsylvania Hospital, the first true hospital in America. Soon after its inauguration the hospital attained international renown. Between 1751 and 1763, its first twelve years, it cared for an average of four hundred patients annually, with a mortality rate of about ten percent—probably half the rate then prevailing in European institutions. In 1762 The Pennsylvania Hospital established America's first medical library. The east wing of the old complex of The Pennsylvania Hospital was built about 1755, the west wing about 1796, and the center between 1794 and 1805. The central pavilion houses the first operating amphitheater in America.

Philadelphia also had the first medical school in America, founded in 1765. Because so many influential American physicians had studied medicine at the University of Edinburgh, America's pioneer institution was allied to the arts faculty of the Col-lege of Philadelphia rather than to The Pennsylvania Hospital, as in the London tradition. At the time of the Revolution there were only two places in America where one could study medicine, Philadelphia and in New York. Despite the patriotic reputations of the medical school's founder, Dr. John Morgan, and his principal protégé, Dr. Benjamin Rush, the alleged Loyalist sympathies of a majority of the faculty of the College of Philadelphia led the patriot-dominated state legislature to found the rival University of the State of Pennsylvania, which thereupon established its own medical school. In 1791, when tempers cooled, the two schools merged and the modern University of Pennsylvania was formed.

With unification the new medical school grew rapidly and needed new quarters. It found them in the President's House. In 1791 the Pennsylvania General Assembly authorized the building of a house to be donated to George Washington for use as an executive mansion—with the hope that Philadelphia would remain the national capital. After many de-

Medical students of colonial America bought tickets for admission to courses directly from their instructors.

Dr. John Morgan, the founder and first professor of America's first medical school

lays and the expenditure of over $100,000 the building was finally finished in 1797 and offered to President John Adams on a rental basis. He refused. The next year the University of Pennsylvania bought the building for use by the college and the medical school, and hired Benjamin Henry Latrobe to remodel it. In 1805 he added the domed pavilion next door for the exclusive use of the medical school.

Once offered to President John Adams, this building was known as "The President's House" after it became the home of the University of Pennsylvania Medical School.

The Mentally Ill in Colonial Pennsylvania

In Colonial Pennsylvania, mental illness was not considered a large problem. The population was sparsely settled, communities were rural and agricultural, and mental illness was not widespread (or widely reported). Medical literature emphasized the nature of mental illness rather than its treatment; physicians were limited in numbers and in skills; and medical attention was focused on those common illnesses and epidemics which affected a much larger proportion of the population.

Until 1750 there was no hospital in Pennsylvania that provided treatment or custodial care for the mentally ill, and the best they could expect was humane care by family, friends, and community. The mentally ill were generally not treated separately from other dependent persons. The family was the most important institution, and every attempt was made to maintain dependent persons within the family and the community. Families with insufficient resources to provide for the mentally ill were often subsidized by the community, and the mentally ill without families were usually boarded in an unrelated household. The mentally ill were sometimes treated harshly or inhumanely, and local officials often discouraged the dependent insane from settling within communities. However, confinement of the mentally ill in jails or almshouses was infrequent and limited to those whose illness was incapacitating or sufficiently severe to constitute a social danger or public nuisance.

Institutionalization of the mentally ill became more common in the last half of the eighteenth century; as Pennsylvania became more densely populated, the number of sick persons increased, and the mobility of the population made family and community care more difficult. The movement toward institutional care began in Philadelphia in 1750 with the founding of The Pennsylvania Hospital, which provided care for all sick persons who were indigent and without family and might otherwise have been placed in the Philadelphia Almshouse. Although the hospital was the first American institution to treat the mentally ill, it actually cared for very few such people in its early years, and curative methods remained rudimentary.

One physician who was interested in mental health even then, however, was Benjamin Rush, who has been called the "father of American psychiatry." (Among his writings is a brief psychological study of the impact of war on the minds of the populace.) In his concern for treating the mentally disturbed, he developed a "gyrator" (a revolving machine to be used in "torpid madness") and a "tranquillizing chair" complete with a box to be placed over the patient's head, straps for the wrists and arms, and stocks for the feet. Rush argued that the mentally deranged should be treated as sick people who could nevertheless contribute to society. In an era when the public attitude toward mental health was largely indifference, Dr. Rush and The Pennsylvania Hospital helped shape new attitudes toward treatment of the mentally ill.

Restraining chair devised by Dr. Benjamin Rush for calming violent mentally ill patients.

Leg amputation,
from Lewis Miller's sketchbook

dentures made, of bone or horn set into metal supports. Perhaps the best known surviving eighteenth-century dentures were made by Dr. John Greenwood for George Washington.

Surgery

In the British tradition the surgeon was considered a lesser creature than a physician—a mechanic rather than a theoretician. In America this distinction simply did not become an important one—although some European-trained physicians did look down their noses at surgeons, for in an age before antiseptics and anesthetics were known the surgeon's role was very limited. They would reduce simple fractures, and in cases of complex fractures they would amputate limbs, their most common operation. Speed, not delicacy, was the trademark of the good practitioner—some surgeons bragged of being able to excise a leg in less than a minute. Surgeons additionally extracted teeth and perhaps most dramatically trephined the skull. The only operation normally attempted that went within the body's cavities was "cutting for a stone," or the removal of bladder stones. The patient was "prepped" with a strong shot of alcohol and perhaps some opium and four strong men held him down while the surgeon operated. Medical men did not generally concern themselves with problems of women during childbirth—that was left almost entirely to the midwife.

The Revolutionary War was a major test and opportunity for American surgeons, providing a chance to learn from European doctors attending the British forces. The first American textbook on surgery, Dr. John Jone's *Plain, Concise, Practical Remarks on the Treatment of Wounds and Fractures*, was published as a result of the author's military observations and as a guide to his less well trained colleagues. Senior surgeon of the Continental Army was Dr. Bodo Otto, whose three sons, also trained as surgeons, assisted him during the war years. In the early decades of the eighteenth century, enlightened Pennsylvanians were debating the advances of theoretical science in their clubs and letters, but with the outbreak of hostilities the advances of science and medicine had more immediate applications.

Technology

Technological improvements introduced into eighteenth-century Pennsylvania were practical and ingenious responses to the challenges of turning the wilderness into farms and villages. Examples already have been given of the Pennsylvania colonists' domestic technology in their daily lives, as they built their homes and went about meeting their daily needs, making candles and turning flax into linen. The ethnic diversity of the colony influenced the direction of its technology. As the industrial revolution in England shaped the skills of immigrants from the British Isles, so the German settlers in Pennsylvania continued middle-European traditions in agriculture and crafts. It was a conventional German stove which inspired Benjamin Franklin's invention of the Pennsylvania fireplace. Henry William Stiegel brought skilled German technicians to operate his elaborate glass manufactory at Mannheim. Meanwhile, American ingenuity was fostered by rewards, bounties, and subsidies of money or land. The Pennsylvania Assembly encouraged citizens to duplicate British inventions and offered grants for that purpose. Inventors were provided patent protection. Private societies offered premiums and prizes to encourage innovation.

The Technology of Transportation:
Traveling on Land

One of the earliest and constant problems confronting colonial Pennsylvania was communication. The province's many streams and rivers seemed to offer ready highways, yet the frequency of drought, shallow water, and debris-cluttered streambeds posed serious hazards. Nor was all good land located near navigable waters, so inland farmers had to travel through valleys and over mountains on road ways of varying quality.

Indian paths—about eighteen inches wide and well trodden—crossed Pennsylvania's ridges and were especially useful for packtrains. A few major roads were constructed before 1776, among them the "King's Highways" authorized about 1700. These were earthen

To the PUBLIC.
THE FLYING MACHINE, kept by John Mercereau, at the New-Blazing-Star Ferry, near New-York, sets off from Powles Hook every Monday, Wednesday, and Friday Mornings, for Philadelphia, and performs the Journey in a Day and a Half, for the Summer Seafon, till the 1st of November, from that Time to go twice a Week till the first of May, when they again perform it three Times a Week. When the Stages go only twice a Week, they set off Mondays and Thursdays. The Waggons in Philadelphia set out from the Sign of the George, in Second-street, the fame Morning. The Paffengers are defired to crofs the Ferry the Evening before, as the Stages muft fet off early the next Morning. The Price for each Paffenger is *Twenty Shillings*, Proc. and Goods as ufual. Paffengers going Part of the Way to pay in Proportion.

As the Proprietor has made fuch Improvements upon the Machines, one of which is in Imitation of a Coach, he hopes to merit the Favour of the Publick.
                                        JOHN MERCEREAU

roads about fifty feet wide and hacked free of trees and underbrush. As early as 1687 a road extended from New Castle, Delaware, toward Chester and Philadelphia. The Old York Road connected Jenkintown with New Hope, and the Great Conestoga Road from Philadelphia to Lancaster provided access to that large inland community. Military roads suitable for wagon use in the French and Indian War had been pushed through the wilderness west of the Susquehanna by Generals Edward Braddock and John Forbes. As these roads deteriorated, packtrains at least could still make their way along them.

Travel by wheeled vehicles beyond the periphery of larger towns was most likely a bone-shaking and mud-mired experience. By 1730 stagecoach travelers leaving Philadelphia might reach Lancaster in less than two days, or New York and Baltimore in two to four days. For purposes of local traveling after 1700, options included two-wheeled carts with wide-rimmed wheels; two-wheel, two-passenger American-style sedan chairs; and light, open one-seat carts called "gigs."

Conestoga wagon

By 1760 the famed Conestoga wagon, named after a stream and valley near Lancaster, had been perfected by German settlers. Its high wheels with four-inch treads and its tightly constructed body adapted this sturdy vehicle to rutty lanes and river fords. A major design innovation was its sixteen-foot-long wagon bed which, by sloping from both ends to the middle, helped to keep loads—often of two to four tons—from shifting on inclines. The linen or hemp cloth tops, bound over six or eight hoops or bows, offered shelter from wind, rain, and sun. The wagons' blue bodies, pinched in the center because of their wider end-bows, and their great red wheels rumbling beneath round white tops, gave them a kind of grandeur as they paraded along Pennsylvania roads on their historic mission of transport and emigration that eventually converted them into the famed "prairie schooners" of the distant West. To all such vehicles local inventors added their own innovations. A log or chain cast behind them provided additional braking on hills, and tar and tallow were used to grease and toughen axles.

Building Bridges

If rugged terrain and forested slopes complicated road-building in much of Pennsylvania, myriads of small streams and several larger rivers posed major problems. Ferries were one obvious solution, but these were crude, slow, and hazardous during flood season. Smaller streams might be crossed by felling tree trunks across them in Indian fashion, then binding several together. In a region where wood was plentiful and craftsmen were in short supply, European-style stone bridges were costly exceptions. Pragmatic Americans worried less about permanency and aesthetics than about getting the job done quickly and with an economy of materials.

In colonial Pennsylvania, bridge building often followed the proven technique of Roman engineers: piles were driven into stream beds to support heavy timber girders, with transverse beams carrying the wooden planks of the deck. Timbers also were used for floating spans resting on beds of spiked planks locked between piles. Farmers discovered for themselves the rudiments of truss construction, employing stout beams to form two triangles united at their common side by a "king post." They used this strong and stable geometrical design to support barn floors and mills, and it was only a step to using the king-post truss to support bridge spans from above or below. Since Pennsylvania was the heart of colonial iron manufacture by 1776, the newly arrived Tom Paine dreamed of iron bridges and later prepared several models of a 400-foot cast iron span. Not until 1836, however, was the first American iron bridge constructed at Brownsville, Pennsylvania.

Waterways and Marine Construction

In 1776 most Pennsylvania commerce moved southeasterly toward Philadelphia and Baltimore. Even settlers on the tributaries of the Allegheny and Monongahela looked eastward to these major ports for the disposition of their surplus. Philadelphia, as Pennsylvania's outlet to the sea, was also a shipbuilding center. The age of sail required lumber in many forms, and Pennsylvania's great oak forests

Grey's Ferry and pontoon bridge on the Schuylkill River

Robert Fulton
after a portrait by Benjamin West

provided masts sixty and seventy feet tall. By 1776 Philadelphia's craftsmen were supplying much of the sail and rigging that were once the monopoly of England. Indeed, by that time Philadelphia was building almost half of the vessels constructed in the colonies, and these in turn constituted a third of the British merchant fleet. Locust and hickory wood nails, soaked in tar and tallow, fastened structures exposed to salt water. Without conventional heavy superstructures, colonial ships were built to be stable and fast, and despite the high prices of American labor, the ready availability of virgin forests made American shipbuilding strongly competitive in the age of wooden navies.

Inland waters encouraged other types of marine construction, ranging from hastily assembled log rafts and flat boats, valuable mostly for their resalable lumber, to the sturdy "Durham Boats," named after the Durham Iron Works in upper Bucks County near Easton. Often sixty feet long by eight feet wide and with a draft of only two feet, the Durham boats could carry as much as fifteen tons of furnace and forge iron on the Delaware to Philadelphia. They were pointed at both ends and could be poled upstream on the Delaware, Lehigh, and Schuylkill rivers.

America's canal age lay in the future, although James Brindley's engineering of the first independent canal in England in 1760 attracted the interest of visiting Americans such as Robert Fulton, and after 1765 several colonial canal schemes were broached. The port of Philadelphia, especially, saw in canals a means of tapping Pennsylvania's rich hinterlands. Thomas Gilpin, a Quaker merchant and landowner, surveyed a canal route from Head of Chester to Duck Creek on the Delaware. Commercially minded members of the American Philosophical Society supported study of a canal project proposed by Gilpin in 1769, and citizens of Philadelphia subscribed funds for the initial route surveys. When the Pennsylvania assembly made the canal project a special interest in 1771, Baltimore citizens lost interest as they foresaw all benefits going to Pennsylvanians. Meanwhile, Franklin recommended that skilled European engineers be invited to participate in what seemed a technologically complex task. The threat of war dashed all such hopes until 1828, when the Susquehanna-Schuylkill Canal came into being. The idea of steam navigation of Pennsylvania's inland waters was a dream held by many citizens, but it was not realized until the following century. In 1763, William Henry's abortive attempt to operate a stern-wheel steamboat on Conestoga Creek was applauded by his contemporaries.

Glassmaking in Old Pennsylvania

Glassmaking became an important Pennsylvania industry by 1776.

William Henry's model of
his early land yacht

An American Inventor: William Henry
and the Birth of the Steamboat

*Born in Chester County of an Irish immigrant father
and Huguenot-descended mother, William Henry
was at fifteen apprenticed to a Lancaster gunsmith.
His natural talent for mechanics led him to open his
own workshop, where he manufactured the famous
Pennsylvania rifle. Bringing skill and ingenuity to
the making of weapons, he built a prosperous and
highly respected firearms manufactory, which served
colonial troops called upon to quell Indian distur-
bances on the frontier after 1755. Entrepreneur-
inventor that he was, Henry created labor-saving
devices for his factory: a screw augur, a steam-heat-
ing system, a unique "sentinel register," which used
heated air to open and close a flue-damper on his
furnace.*

*During a visit to England Henry discussed the
mysteries of high-pressure steam with James Watt.
Presumably he applied this knowledge two years
later, in 1763, when he attempted to operate his own
stern-wheel steamboat on Lancaster's Conestoga
Creek. The experiment failed, but it was the first
of its kind in the colonies. Largely because of Henry,
several of America's steamboat pioneers found in
Lancaster the inspiration and technological know-
how which one day would telescope distances to the
Old World and open the fertile river valleys to millions of settlers.*

*Robert Fulton, born in 1765 in what is now
Fulton Township in Lancaster County, absorbed the
local enthusiasm for gun craftsmanship and became an admirer of Henry. Perhaps while painting
Henry's portrait, young Fulton also picked up his
dream of steam navigation before leaving Lancaster
for Philadelphia at age seventeen. John Fitch also
visited Henry in Lancaster. Clockmaker, skilled mechanic, engine-builder, Fitch abandoned Connecticut
for Bucks County in 1782 to pursue his own dreams
of a steam-propelled vessel and was dismayed to
find Henry had long anticipated his speculations.
But Henry, who had not yet submitted drawings of
his experiment to the American Philosophical Society, was generous: "Although I am many years
before you in the scheme, yet as long as I have not
brought it to the public view . . . I will lay no
claim to it." Fitch later confessed that "it chagrined
me considerably to find that I could think of nothing
but someone would be before me in the thought." In
1787, nonetheless, Fitch launched his first peculiar*

*twelve-paddle steamboat on the Delaware, while
curious members of the Federal Constitutional Convention lined the river bank.*

*It would not be until 1807 that Robert Fulton—
once the curious neighbor lad of William Henry in
Lancaster—sailed the now celebrated* Clermont *up
the Hudson and into technological history.*

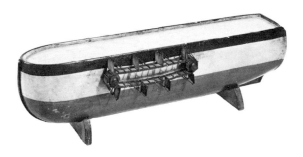

*Model and two versions
of John Fitch's steam-driven boats*

Glass blower

*Blown glass flask attributed
to the Stiegel Works of Manheim*

Caspar Wistar, a German emigrant to Philadelphia, where he manufactured brass buttons, built a glassmaking factory in neighboring West Jersey in 1740. Wistar developed improved techniques and stimulated good workmanship in the industry, bringing European glassmakers and introducing the practice of dividing shares in the business with his craftsmen. (His grandson, whose name was the same, gave greater distinction to the family by his career in medicine in Philadelphia, succeeding Benjamin Rush as professor of chemistry at the College of Philadelphia and becoming an energetic president of the American Philosophical Society. It is after this Wistar that the wistaria, usually called wisteria, vine is named.)

Another German immigrant—the dapper "Baron" Henry William Stiegel—remained in Pennsylvania to become America's most widely remembered manufacturer of glass. Having prospered in the iron industry, Stiegel in 1762 plotted out the town of Manheim in Lancaster County and two years later began building his extensive glass plantation there. Stiegel visited glass plants in England and, following the example of Wistar, imported to the colonies English and German workmen with the latest knowledge in enameling and other refinements of their craft. Stiegel glassware was to become widely renowned for its clarity and variety—collectors items for the future. Unfortunately, the self-anointed baron was led by his baronial tastes into bankruptcy and the sale of his business in 1774.

The Iron Industry in Penn's Woods

No industry has been more closely identified with Pennsylvania than ironmaking. Pennsylvania's rich ores encouraged a rate of expansion which made it the leading American iron producer by 1776. By then ironmaking reached up the Schuykill and Susquehanna valleys and branched into that of the Juniata. Philadelphia, as the colony's mercantile center, provided capital for the early entrepreneurs: men like Thomas Rutter, who in 1716 established a bloomery and furnace at Coalbrookdale in Chester County; "Baron" Stiegel, who in 1750, eight years after his emigration from Germany, assumed control of what was to become Elizabeth furnace; and Peter Grubb, who in 1740 founded Cornwall furnace near one of the continent's richest deposits of ore. The Durham Iron Works, beginning in the 1720s, shipped boatloads of bar iron down the Delaware for export at Philadelphia, where cargoes reached nearly three thousand tons yearly by 1770. At least fifty Pennsylvania iron furnaces helped to meet rising demands by 1771. By 1776 ironmaking had expanded west of the Susquehanna, where scattered but rich ore deposits were neighbor to plentiful limestone and timber.

The beginnings of the Pennsylvania iron industry were rooted in the "bloomery," which was built like a wide and deep blacksmith's

The blast furnace was charged with loads of charcoal, iron ore, and limestone.

forge, was economical to erect, and was simple to operate. Pieces of ore were shoveled into the forge on burning charcoal. Each ton of iron required an average of about four hundred bushels of charcoal, and a furnace could use an acre of hardwood in a single day. A hot blast generated by a bellows, which was powered by a water wheel, smelted the iron as a workman puddled it with his long bar to gather it into a lump. The glowing mass was moved to a neighboring anvil and fashioned into wrought iron, usually in bar form.

In Pennsylvania, however, the blast furnace was introduced early and soon predominated. It was usually located on the side of a hill, with a casting shed below it to catch the molten iron as it flowed from the furnace hearth into molds formed in sand. Iron ore, limestone for purifying it, abundant hardwood groves, and a sprightly stream were essential nearby resources. Furnace construction usually was of limestone, with a lining of harder sandstone and a filler of clay to provide some insulation against the great heat. Beginning as a pyramid perhaps twenty-five feet square at the base, the furnace tapered upward an almost equal distance. Loading and firing the furnace was a careful, time-consuming, and laborious process. Iron ore—which might be first baked into pellets—was loaded into wagons, as were the required layers of sledge-shattered pieces of limestone and the necessary charcoal. A bridge or platform spanning hilltop and furnace stack permitted laborers to trot basketloads of ore, limestone, and charcoal across the gap and to dump them into the chimney in alternate layers. Once fired, furnaces were kept in

A ruined blast furnace, typical of the many eighteenth- and nineteenth-century relics of the charcoal iron industry.

239

operation as long as weather and demand permitted, for several days were required to work up a melt. The limestone acted as a flux to which impurities clung, rising to the surface as slag while the heavier iron sank to the bottom of the furnace. There it was tapped off into sand-bedded long gutters with branching arms—the "sow and pigs" in popular parlance.

In the neighboring casting sheds, molten metal also could be poured into special molds designed for various utensils. Refinement of the pig iron took place in a smelting furnace where heavy timber hammers pounded out the basic bar iron shape at the forge before any necessary cutting into desired lengths, usually about fourteen feet long by two inches wide and one-half inch in thickness, a convenient size for blacksmiths and for export.

America was still in its technological infancy and, given the uncertainties of wind, the energy of Pennsylvania's swiftly flowing streams drove the machinery for hammering and slitting iron, as well as operating the large double bellows supplying the furnace blast. The waterwheels required were impressive, and in the 1750s some Pennsylvania wheels were forty feet in diameter.

The clank of iron could be heard throughout the colony. To the chagrin of British manufacturers and merchants, foundries fashioned domestic pots, pans, kettles, plowshares, gardening tools, and rims of cart wheels. Baron Stiegel's Elizabeth furnace cast such diverse items as stoves, soap kettles, and equipment for making sugar. Here too might be forged the American axe, an implement so popular that British manufacturers were said to attempt selling their own less efficient product as "American made." Nails, bolts, rivets and similar necessities were often produced in farm homes, especially during the long months of winter. In this newly developing "iron age," the blacksmith was a highly esteemed craftsman, whether he hammered out Franklin-styled lightning rods or fashioned other useful implements. When James Galloway, a Westmoreland County blacksmith, went to war in 1776, his neighbors thought his work so indispensable that they collected money, a rifle, and a butcher knife to hire his replacement.

Steel, already in demand in 1776, was produced in small quantities by the cementation process. Bar iron was dusted with powdered charcoal, ashes, and horn shavings, then heated in a blast to what appeared as the right color, and left in the furnace to cool for a week or more. The favorite Pennsylvania approach, picked up from German workers, treated pig iron with careful selections of wood. Steel manufacture, if small, provided Pennsylvanians with sharp-edged tools and, when the break with England resolved into warfare, with swords and bayonets.

Wrought iron plate for keyhole

Folk Arts in Pennsylvania

Much of what remains to remind us of colonial Pennsylvania, from tools to buildings, consists of products that the colonists constructed with their own hands. Works of "folk" origin remain relatively stable in style, form, and function. Period styles—such as Queen Anne, Chippendale, or Victorian—have no parallels in a folk tradition. The everyday utensils, the houses and outbuildings, the dress and food of the rural Pennsylvania farmers during the Revolution were adaptations of earlier European peasant cultures, not new American styles. Many products of Pennsylvania regional folk culture have endured with little change during the two hundred years since the Revolutionary War. For example, the "plain" clothes of present Amish folk are essentially the same type of garments worn by many Pennsylvania farmers, as well as their European counterparts, throughout the seventeenth and eighteenth centuries. It is thus through folk tradition and the objects of folk material culture that the eighteenth century can most easily be revisited today.

The Pennsylvania Rifle and the Conestoga Wagon

Some of the hand-crafted items produced in Pennsylvania had assumed such importance by the end of the eighteenth century that they are not usually thought of as folk objects. The inaccurately termed "Kentucky" rifle was developed by Pennsylvania gunsmiths from the clumsy European rifles already known to the settlers earlier in the eighteenth century. At about the same time, by 1730, the Conestoga wagon was developed in the Conestoga Valley of Lancaster County. Since these wagons were handmade by individual blacksmiths and wheelwrights, no two were exactly alike. The Conestoga wagon combined features of the eighteenth-century English road wagons and the large wagons of western Germany—a striking illustration of the British and German ethnic synthesis. Unlike the covered wagons which took settlers further west, the Conestoga wagon was designed to carry only freight. Instead of riding inside the wagon, the driver rode one of the horses or stood or sat on a

The Pennsylvania Rifle

After Andrew Jackson's Kentucky and Tennessee riflemen defeated the British at New Orleans in 1815, the deadly accurate long rifles they carried were immortalized in song and legend as Kentucky rifles. In fact, the basic American form of this weapon was developed primarily in Lancaster County, Pennsylvania, during the eighteenth century. The developers were immigrant German gunsmiths, who previously had made short, heavy flintlock guns with distinctive rifled barrels for big game hunters in central Europe. Daily life on the frontier required the most efficient weapon that could be made. The German heavy rifles were clearly superior to the smooth-bore muskets brought by the English settlers. Not satisfied with this advantage, the Pennsylvania German gunsmiths gradually improved their European models, producing a lighter and longer rifle that was more accurate over a longer range and yet required less powder and smaller caliber shot.

As the colonial frontier expanded, the innovative Pennsylvania rifle was gradually diffused, as Lancaster County gunsmiths or their apprentices moved into surrounding counties and colonies. At the start of the War of Independence gunsmiths already were making Pennsylvania rifles in Maryland, Virginia, North Carolina, and Georgia. When hostilities began, the Continental Congress placed controls on the prices and distribution of guns, directing them to the Patriot armies. The Pennsylvania rifle played no small part in the final outcome.

The revolutionary era was the beginning of the rifle's golden age, and much attention was given to artistic as well as functional detail. Finest specimens of native walnut, maple, and curly maple were sought for the stocks. These were often painstakingly carved into intricate patterns and inlaid with brass, silver, or even gold. Patch boxes—cut into the right sides of stocks to hold the greased patches that were wrapped around the muzzle-loaded rifle balls—had hinged covers made of brass or silver. These were usually engraved with intricate decorative motifs. Some owners considered their rifles to be such personal treasures that they gave them poetic names.

Efficiency rather than beauty was what counted among the riflemen of the Continental Army. Both they and their British foes had a deep respect for the Pennsylvania rifle.

Pennsylvania rifle leaning against the settler's cabin at the Pennsylvania Farm Museum at Landis Valley.

Rifling machine. The term rifling refers to a pattern of grooves cut into the interior of the rifle barrel. This imparted a spin to the bullet which made it far more accurate than a bullet fired from a smooth bored weapon.

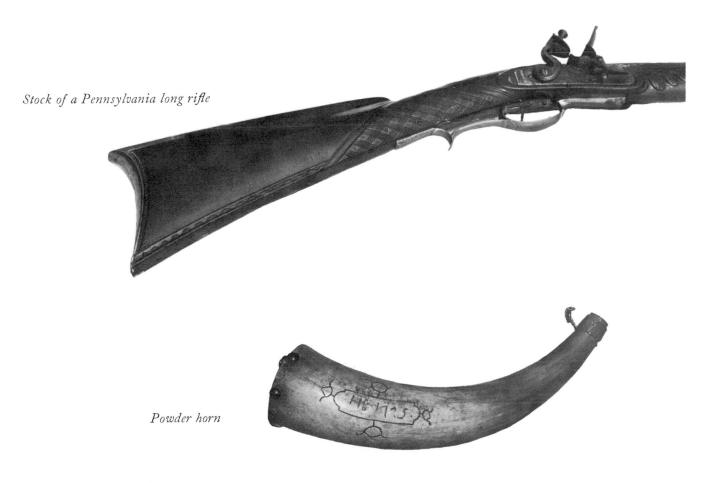

Stock of a Pennsylvania long rifle

Powder horn

"lazy board" that slid out from underneath the wagon. He would usually decorate his horse with bells, and when his wagon was mired in the mud, it was the custom of the road for him to give his bells to the fellow teamster who pulled him out. Even today, when we are confident nothing can hinder us from being someplace, we promise to "be there with bells on."

Barns and Houses and Housewares

Like the Conestoga wagon, much of Pennsylvania folk culture by 1776 had evolved from a blending of English and German designs, although in most cases the German influence was the stronger. Such was the case with the Pennsylvania German "bank barn"—also called "Switzer barn," "Sweisser barn," "Swisser barn," and "Overshot barn"—which by the late eighteenth century was steadily replacing the earlier, smaller British and central European styles of barn. Such an impressive architectural feat was the Pennsylvania barn that in 1789 the British traveler Thomas Anbury wrote in his *Travels Through the Interior Parts of America:* "The farmers in Pennsylvania, and in the Jerseys, pay more attention to the construction of their barns than their dwelling houses."

Pennsylvania rural dwelling houses, too, by the Revolution had developed their own styles, based chiefly on British "I houses" and German houses of the Rhine Valley. Like the barns, the Pennsylvania farm houses are often banked, with only half of the cellar underground and a ground level entrance in the back. A German peasant house in the English Georgian mode has more or less symmetrical window and door openings. Two stories tall, two rooms deep, and two rooms wide, Pennsylvania folk houses were made of log, stone, wood frame, and brick.

Most of the traditional housewares were made of readily available materials, such as wood and clay. Although domestic folk objects were primarily functional, they can reveal a highly developed sense of decoration. Blanket chests and "dower" chests were painted in bright colors and elaborate motifs. The owner's name and the date of construction were a part of the decoration. Clothes were stored in these lidded chests and in larger wooden wardrobes, called *schrank* by the Pennsylvania Germans. Chests of drawers were not important in the rural household of the late eighteenth century.

Different kinds of storage cabinets for kitchenware were in use by the end of the eighteenth century. Pewter cupboards had all open shelves, usually about five, with strips of wood fitted across the upper shelves to hold in the pewter or china plates that made a decorative display. A variant of the simple pewter cupboard was the Welsh "dresser," composed of a series of open shelves set on a deeper closed cabinet. In this type of cabinet double grooves were

Dry sink displaying redware pottery and hand-whittled clothespins

cut along the upper shelves for displaying plates. A variant of the Welsh dresser was the Dutch cupboard, which had enclosed cabinets in both the upper and lower sections. Corner cupboards usually had two parts like the Dutch cupboards and Welsh dressers. The top section might have solid wooden doors, like the bottom section, or it might have panes of glass in the doors, or it might have open shelves with scalloped frames.

Chairmaking was a traditional craft in rural Pennsylvania. Perhaps the most common country chair after about 1700 was the ladderback, or slat back, chair. It derives its name from the ladder of three to six slats morticed into posts to form a concave back. This comfortable chair usually had a rush or a splint seat. The ladderback chair was found throughout the colonies as an adaptation of an English folk chair. Another chair made in Pennsylvania in colonial times was the plank peasant chair. Gothic in appearance, this chair was made by the Pennsylvania Germans. Traditional motifs and dates often were carved into the back. The legs were wedged into holes drilled completely through the plank and angled out to give maximum stability.

Delaware Valley slat ladderback armchair, made of hickory and maple

Pine plank chairs, often called "Moravian chairs," were cheap and easy to construct. This is a direct copy of the traditional German form.

The adjustable back and rush seat of this daybed mark it as a rare example of comfort-oriented rural furniture.

Made in Lebanon County, this dower chest is English Chippendale in form and German in decoration. Drawers and closets were rare in rural Pennsylvania. Most clothes were folded and kept in chests.

Corner cupboards, like this arch-doored example, held the best china and glassware in fine homes.

The most ubiquitous motif painted or carved on Pennsylvania folk objects is the tulip. This design element was known after the sixteenth century in Europe and may have been associated with the Holy Lily as a folk art motif. Often the tulip was blended with other flowers and with fruits, such as the pomegranate, to create a richer and more varied pattern. Other motifs commonly found are figures, of birds, including the parrot, pelican, swan, rooster, peacock, and *distelfink* (goldfinch). After the Revolution the eagle became an especially popular bird design in Pennsylvania folk art. Human figures, standing or mounted on horseback, were also used as decoration on various objects.

Fraktur and Tulipware

A Pennsylvania German folk art employing the full array of traditional designs was *fraktur-schriften* (literally "fracture-writing"), usually shortened to *fraktur*. This type of script, in which words were broken up with curlicues and other decorations, developed in sixteenth-century Germany and Switzerland—probably in imitation of medieval illuminated manuscripts. Fraktur was used especially in household documents commemorating rites of passage: birth and baptismal certificates, wedding certificates, and to a lesser degree death certificates. Family registers, house blessings and mottoes, and book plates also were often rendered in fraktur. A number of religious books were in fraktur, notably the hymnals of the Ephrata Cloister, and the sisters there produced a guide for fraktur writers entitled *The Christian A B C Book* (1750). Along with the ornate lettering illuminated with colored inks, fraktur documents have elaborate borders using the typical floral and fruit patterns, the tulip and the bird, and other symbolic motifs such as angels holding trumpets, children and mermaids, crosses, crowns, and hearts.

Tulipware, the common general term for Pennsylvania German decorated pottery, includes pieces produced by three different processes: slip, polychrome, and sgraffito. To slip-decorate a piece of pottery, a potter took a piece that had been molded but not fired and, with a cup of liquid clay attached to a quill through which the "slip" flowed in a tiny stream, worked out a design. If he used several cups containing slips of different colors, he got a polychrome effect. In the sgraffito process red Pennsylvania clay was beaten or rolled flat, until half dry, and then shaped. A slip of white New Jersey clay was then poured over the concave side of the pottery. After further drying, the desired designs and inscriptions were scratched through the slip, exposing the red clay underneath. When dry, the piece could be glazed and fired. Sgraffito pottery was decorated with the familiar Pennsylvania folk motifs. A design found chiefly on pottery is the rider on horseback. Inspired by Continental troopers, this motif was the only common one directly affected by the American Revolution. George Washington is the most frequently identifiable rider on post-Revolutionary pottery.

Cooking and Quilting

Grains of various kinds made up a large portion of the rural diet. Cornmeal was used to make Bannock bread; a thick batter of the meal was either baked or fried. Dried corn was also used to prepare a type of gruel. Breads were made from corn, pumpernickel (unsifted rye), rye, buckwheat, and oats, as well as wheat. What modern Pennsylvania housewives call "scrapple" probably stems from an early Pennsylvania German dish called pan-hash, leftover meat broth cooked with corn meal. Fried meatballs, or *fricadells*, were favorites; sauerkraut and *speck* (fat pork) and *knepp* (dumplings) were also common food items. Dumplings were sometimes prepared with fruit, either apples or a wild fruit. Dried apples, or *schnitz*, were eaten by the earliest German immigrants and have persisted as a favorite, virtually a symbolic food among Pennsylvania Dutch people. Pies of all kinds, jams, and sweet or sour relishes were almost staples among the German settlers.

The high cost of imported textiles in the colonies contributed to the manner of production and use of domestic fabrics in eighteenth-century Pennsylvania. Home spinning of flax or wool was a tedious process, so every bit of cloth was used and reused. A logical use of fragments of cloth was the quilted coverlet. Random piecing together of assorted bits of cloth produced the "crazy quilt." Not surprisingly, however, the same sense of design that fostered carved furniture or implements and painted barn decorations also led to the use of brightly colored geometrical motifs in quilt design. Although old patterns, such as the log cabin design, can be found throughout the eastern United States, the bright hues of a Pennsylvania German quilt are often quite distinctive. Some of the same patterns seen in other items of Pennsylvania folk art—the star motif, for example—can also be found pieced or appliqued in the quilt.

After synthesizing the ethnic features of the two dominant folk traditions, the English and the German, the folk art of Pennsylvania assumed a character of its own. It was conservative and stable, rather than progressive and faddish, and it was little influenced by the political events which were soon to rock the colony. The later industrial and demographic revolutions of the nineteenth and twentieth centuries have resulted in the relatively recent decline of this traditional heritage, but at the time of the American Revolution objects produced in Pennsylvania were mostly traditional, or folk, in nature.

This pierced tin and pine "pie cabinet" was used for cooling and storing pastries and bread. It is a direct descendant of the livery cupboard (larder) of the seventeenth and early eighteenth centuries.

The quilting party represented a common practice of combining work with a social occasion. The tedium of hand stitching scraps of leftover fabric was relieved by making the job a community effort and an occasion for families to get together for good talk and cheer. The painting depicts the older women hard at work on one side of the table, while the younger women are more easily distracted by the young men at their sides. Other men have left the women to themselves as they talk business or politics around the stove. A mother proudly watches as her baby is admired by grandfather, who is unaware of the dog and cat in uneasy relation around his chair. Keeping the animals in view, however, is a little boy who munches on an apple while staying close to his mother at the quilting table. Although painted in the nineteenth century by an unknown folk artist, the painting's childlike simplicity makes it timeless.

A dower chest was presented to a girl around the age of nine for collection of household items and clothes she would take to her new home after marriage. This chest, made in Pennsylvania, is one of the earliest examples to survive.

This massive walnut schrank (wardrobe) is decorated with inlaid hard wax. Made by a Lancaster craftsman in 1766, it can be taken apart for easy moving like many other German wardrobes.

Music in Pennsylvania

The musical expressions of the early settlers of Pennsylvania reflected their diverse cultural backgrounds and religious beliefs. English ballads, love lyrics, and dialogue songs; Irish courting ballads and dance tunes; Scottish or German hymns and work songs —all have been assimilated into the rich treasuries of Pennsylvania folk culture. In the mountains, valleys, and fertile fields, each cultural group transplanted and adapted its native heritage to the conditions of life in the New World. While religious idealists who hoped to "build Zion in the woods" brought their hymn tunes with them— or, like Beissel and Kelpius, composed their own—the more sophisticated "gentleman amateurs" of Philadelphia sought to reconstruct a musical life mirroring that of their native England.

Music in Rural Pennsylvania

Pennsylvania was geographically in a unique position as the folk song repertory of the English-speaking settlers developed, for Pennsylvania was the common ground where two different strains of the folk song met in eastern North America. The colonists of New England, on one hand, and those from southern New Jersey to Georgia, on the other, each had distinctive forms, different from each other in musical settings, rhythms, repertory, wording, and singing mannerisms. For example, a tradition of hymns and spirituals became common to the South, not the North, whereas sea chanteys were found mainly in the North. The Irish highly ornamental melodism was more current in the North, as were the strict "waltz-time" rhythms, while "dwelling" arbitrarily on unaccented notes was characteristic of the South. Sandwiched between these two areas, Pennsylvania shows traits of both. Play-party songs, work songs, and love ballads—now associated with the South and lovingly preserved by folk singers like Kentuckian Jean Ritchie—can be found in Pennsylvania; so can the various forms of informal social dancing associated with New England. At the same time, Pennsylvania's musical inheritance fused, transformed, or subtly blended both traditions.

Singing group with dulcimer and violin, from Lewis Miller's sketchbook

Fifes and Drums in Pennsylvania

From the end of the Crusades to the twentieth century in Europe, the fife and drum provided the chief music of the infantry, according to the musicologist Curt Sachs. The same was true in North America from the earliest settlements until the Army and the Marines discarded their fife corps in the late nineteenth century. This military use has dominated writing about fifes and drums, disregarding the fact that fifing is also an established folk practice: one of the ways of making traditional music. Folk fifing (and drumming) has long been practiced in Switzerland and Alpine Austria—also, it would seem, in Britain and North America. Folklorists cannot definitely trace folk fife bands in Pennsylvania back to the 1700s; yet it is practically certain that such music-making occurred. It is hard to believe that, when the Revolutionary forces disbanded, fifing disappeared with them, only to revive and undergo great local development some time later. The Mattatuck fife and drum corps of Connecticut traces its existence back to 1767, and similar groups must have existed in Pennsylvania at that time. Some seventeenth- and eighteenth-century tunes played only by fifers (and absent from early fife-music publications) indicate a long independent regional tradition.

The sparse records of traditional fifing in nineteenth-century Pennsylvania, and the reminiscences of surviving twentieth-century players, are quite revealing. Towns, hamlets, or neighborhoods over much of rural Pennsylvania used to resound with fife and drum music. Bands were everywhere—recruiting, disbanding, reorganizing, holding contests a bit like fiddlers' contests, and competing with adjoining communities' bands like local ball teams today. These so-called martial bands met and celebrated Independence Day—and, later, Decoration Day—in county seats, with parades and all-day playing. They were convinced that in doing this they were rendering patriotic service to their country by perpetuating the music which had led our forces to victory. The bands also played at political meetings, rallies, and celebrations (or "pole-raisings"); at county fairs, weddings, wedding "serenades," church dedications and socials, cornerstone-layings, funerals, memorial rites, welcomes to distinguished visitors—in short, on every occasion that gave them an excuse to perform. Migrant farm laborers who could play joined local bands wherever they were working. Oldsters taught youngsters how to fife or drum, and many players never affiliated with any martial band, but fifed simply for their own enjoyment. Long-lasting local bands sometimes evolved peculiar drumming styles, by which they could be identified by ear before they were visible.

The decline of fife and drum music began early in the twentieth century; and, between the two world wars, bands and activities both virtually disappeared from Pennsylvania countrysides. Today, occasional "revivals" are not in the older tradition: now the fifers, formerly musically unlettered, play "by the notes" from printed music books, and most of the tunes previously remembered are no longer known. The fifers played tunes of all sorts—any melody that could be used as a march. Yet old British folk march and dance tunes formed the bulk of their repertories. The illustrated marches exemplify music played in Pennsylvania exclusively by fifers, tunes current in the British isles during the seventeenth and eighteenth centuries. In Pennsylvania they were known so commonly, and in such diverse forms, that the likelihood of their being survivals from the 1700s is great.

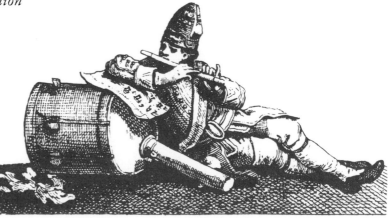

Detail from "The Invasion," engraved by William Hogarth, 1756

Three fife tunes

The Music of the Pennsylvania Germans

In Pennsylvania, the Anglo-American musical traditions coexisted with the often more sophisticated music of the Pennsylvania Germans. The great diversity that characterized the musical life of Pennsylvania before 1790 can be illustrated by the practices of just a few of the German-speaking groups who sought refuge in the colony.

As early as 1694, one group of about forty persons, led by Johann Kelpius, brought at least seven musical instruments with them to their settlement on the Wissahickon Creek near Philadelphia. Although little is known of the music performed by this sect, Kelpius' compilation of ten hymns, *The Lamenting Voice of the Hidden Love at the time She lay in Misery and Forsaken* (1705), contains some fairly sophisticated harmony. His small congregation—called the Wissahickon mystics or hermits—participated in the ordination of the German Lutheran Justus H. Falckner in Philadelphia's Old Swedes' Church (*Gloria Dei*), where an ensemble of viols, oboes, trumpets, and kettledrums was accompanied by a recently installed

Trumpet players of Lititz,
from Lewis Miller's sketchbook

pipe organ. Falckner reflected the attitude of many Pennsylvania German ministers when he argued that music was indispensable "in spreading the Gospel truths among the sects . . . to say nothing of the fact that the Indians would come running from far and near to listen . . . and might be willing to accept our language and teaching and remain with people who had such agreeable things."

Although the Moravians—who settled in Bethlehem, Nazareth, and Lititz—were one of the smallest groups of German immigrants, they contributed significantly to the musical life of Pennsylvania before 1776. They established the first American *Collegia Musica*, whose performances of choral and instrumental music achieved an excellence seldom matched by ensembles anywhere else in the colonies. The small Moravian communities possessed excellent libraries of European instrumental music, and their ensembles used a wide variety of instruments: viols, trumpets, oboes, trombones, flutes, and kettledrums. The finest and, for at least three decades, the only art music composers in the colonies were the descendants of the Moravians. The works of some of these Americans of German descent, such as John Antes (1741–1811), show strong stylistic ties with the musical styles of their homeland. These ties were reinforced by the constant infusion of European-trained composers into the Moravian communities.

To meet their need for musical instruments for ensemble playing, Moravian craftsmen produced some of the finest instruments available in the colonies. David Tannenberg (1728–1804), the Lititz organ builder, constructed nearly fifty instruments for Roman Catholic, Lutheran, Reformed, and Moravian churches. Tannenberg's workshop provided training for native apprentices, and the few surviving organs of his construction give eloquent testimony to his skills.

David Tannenberg and his journeymen installing an organ in the Old Lutheran Church, from Lewis Miller's sketchbook

David Tannenberg, Organ Maker of Lititz

An important contributor to the musical heritage of colonial Pennsylvania was the Moravian organ builder David Tannenberg. Tannenberg came to Pennsylvania in 1749 from Berthelsdorf, Saxony, to pursue the trade of joiner. He lived for a while in Nazareth and Bethlehem, where he worked both as a carpenter and as town business manager. After serving his apprenticeship under the older Moravian organ builder Johann Gottlob Klemm, he finally settled in the Moravian community of Lititz in 1765, where he lived and pursued his craft until his death in 1804. He left a legacy of forty-one organs, eight of which still survive (in addition to three organ cases), to remind us of the active musical life of the Moravian communities of Pennsylvania.

Every detail of life in a Moravian settlement was strictly regulated. In fact, the town elders at one point expressed the view that Tannenberg should not pursue the career of organ building because it was "tied up with a good deal of disorder." But evidently Tannenberg convinced them to drop their objection. He even convinced them that the composer John Antes, who had begun making harpsichords, should make only stringed instruments, so as not to compete with Tannenberg's keyboard instrument business. Tannenberg's relationship with the strictness of the Moravian community seems to have been characterized by both conflict and accommodation. Once he asked a tailor to make him a pair of red trousers (for what occasion we can only guess), and the elders denounced the idea for setting a dangerous precedent of "clothing foolishness." In spite of such conflicts, Tannenberg remained an active member of the religious and secular life of Lititz, serving as treasurer, township assessor, executor, and assistant in the worship services. He also participated in the extraordinarily rich musical life of Lititz as organist, violinist, and vocalist. The town had many musical instruments and groups, including a trombone quartet, used to announce public and religious events like weddings and funerals, and an orchestra called the collegium musicum, *whose library contained chamber works by important European composers like Handel, Haydn, Mozart, and Boccherini.*

Tannenberg's organs were of the old-fashioned tracker variety, instruments noted for their flexible, mellow action and fine tone. Tannenberg's organ cases were also recognized for their beauty. They were usually white, with gold trim to set off the na-

tural metal of the exposed pipes. His keyboards were the reverse of the modern style: the naturals were black and the sharps white. The Tannenberg organ in the Trinity Lutheran Church, Lancaster, dates from 1774 and is a particularly fine example of his art. Its works were replaced in 1854, but its case (enlarged by a tower and flat at either end) was retained. The awe and respect which Tannenberg's creations inspired are revealed in the slightly exaggerated description of this organ by Thomas Anburey, a lieutenant in the British Army of General Burgoyne, who thought it excelled the best in London.

Tannenberg organ in the Trinity Lutheran Church

Because the Moravians, the Wissahickon mystics, and other German communities like Conrad Beissel's cloistered camp at Ephrata remained isolated by customs and language, their influence on the course of later American music was small. But they helped to plant the seeds of a thriving musical life in Pennsylvania. Their love of music, their traditions of excellent performance, and their belief in music as an expression of the joy of work and faith were retained by their descendants after the early communities were assimilated.

Music in Colonial Philadelphia

The musical life of Philadelphia before 1790 was largely the creation of a small group of dedicated amateurs. Realizing that the cultivation of the arts in America would depend on private philanthropy rather than on public revenue, these "gentleman amateurs" devoted themselves to such professions as business, politics, various crafts, or the law. They considered music an edifying diversion and a means of benefiting a number of favored charities.

Philadelphia's most important musical figure, and America's first native-born composer, was Francis Hopkinson (1737–1791). Together with Lieutenant Governor John Penn, James Bremner, and a handful of other friends, Hopkinson helped to organize benefit concerts such as the one advertised in *The Pennsylvania Gazette* on April 4, 1765, for the College of Philadelphia. Even before his graduation from the College in 1759, Hopkinson and his friends had established the first public concert series. George Washington attended the second concert of that first season on March 25, 1757.

Concerts were undoubtedly given before 1757, but records of such events are scanty because in Philadelphia most of the newspapers and most of the residents seem to have ignored the performances of ballad operas, instrumental music, and secular vocal music which had already become the most common ingredients of the concert programs in the other colonial cities. Most of the public concerts, it seems, were casually organized. Programs were selected at the last minute, and some concerts, though advertised weeks in advance, were never given. Of greater importance than the subscription or benefit concerts were the informal evenings of chamber music and social dancing. Governor Penn regularly presided over such sessions at his home on Third Street, and Benjamin Franklin mentions such events in his correspondence. Franklin's improved glass harmonica, the Glassychord, which first charmed a Philadelphia audience in 1764 (at the Assembly Room in Lodge Alley), was probably the featured novelty at many of Philadelphia's musical *soirées*. The tradition of domestic music-making was one of the most important elements in the early musical history of Philadelphia.

Public concerts in Philadelphia were not annual events. There are

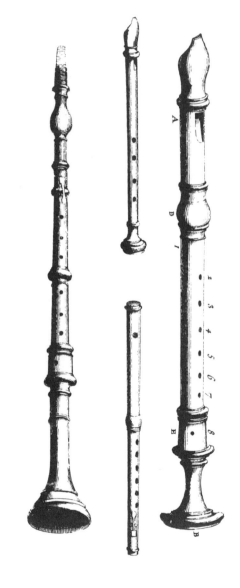

Wind instruments

Franklin's glass harmonica became a continental favorite. Even Mozart composed for it. Sound is produced when the performer touches his water-moistened fingers to the glass bowls, which are kept rotating by an assistant.

no records of any in 1766–1767, when Francis Hopkinson was in England. In 1769, however, Giovanni Gualdo, a musician and wine merchant, placed an advertisement in *The Pennsylvania Gazette* for a concert devoted to performances of his own works, probably the first such concert in the colonies. Gualdo seems also to have been the first maestro to conclude a concert with a ball, during which members of the audience could perform quadrilles, hornpipes, minuets, cotillions, and other popular dances of the period. Gualdo, however, only incorporated into the format of the subscription concert one of the most popular private diversions for early Philadelphians.

Public concerts were given in warehouses, taverns, lofts, meeting rooms, theaters, or at the College auditorium. The programs contained works, or excerpts of works, by many of the best known European composers—Handel, Telemann, J.C. Bach, Vivaldi—and,

Pennsylvania's Pioneer Composer: Francis Hopkinson

One day in 1788 little Polly Jefferson burst into tears while sitting before the fire. Her father, Thomas, thought perhaps she was ill, but she soon assured him she was not; it was only that the song her sister Patsy had been playing on the harpsichord was so sad! Francis Hopkinson, composer of the song about a weary traveler, must have been very pleased to hear that one of his own favorite compositions had so touched his friend Jefferson's small daughter.

Composed in the "Heights of a Storm" and "forcibly pathetic" according to Hopkinson's description, "The Traveller Benighted and Lost" was added to the collection Seven Songs for the Harpsichord or Forte Piano *after the title page had been engraved, thus becoming the eighth of the* Seven Songs *published in Philadelphia in 1788. Although quaint, it is one of our self-proclaimed "first composer's" duller efforts. In fact, most of Hopkinson's songs are unexceptional; what distinguishes them is the collection itself, for the* Seven Songs *is universally acknowledged as the first group of secular solo songs composed and published by a native American in America. George Washington, to whom the volume was dedicated, lamented his inability to further Hopkinson's career as a composer: "what alas! can I do to support it?—I can neither sing one of the songs, nor raise a single note on any instrument to convince the unbelieving."*

The best Hopkinson songs combined pretty Italianate melodies with rather unimaginative basses. Inner parts and harmonies had to be supplied by the keyboard player—a performance practice typical of the time in England and on the Continent. One of the loveliest songs in the collection, "Beneath a Weeping Willow's Shade," is reproduced as it originally appeared. The naive, lilting melody and musically pictorial accompaniment—suggesting the mockingbird's trill wafting away upon the breeze—still have the power to charm, if not to move us to tears.

Beauty may the Heart controul. But Musick elevates the Soul.

Frontispiece to The Vocal Companion, *1796*

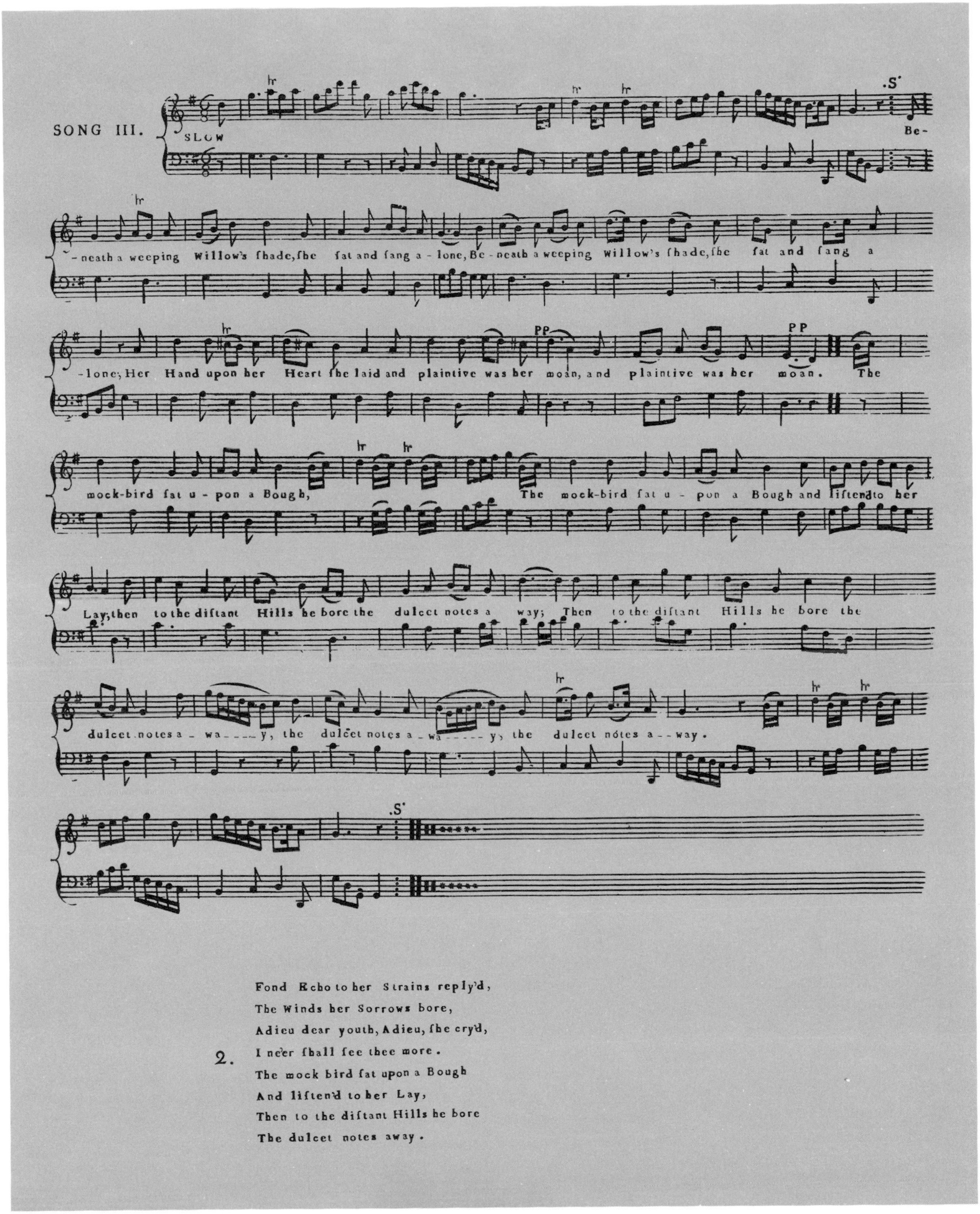

"Beneath a Weeping Willow's Shade," by Francis Hopkinson

*Fashionable dances were learned
from European sourcebooks*

because of the nature of the benefit concert, works by local composers, most of whom are now forgotten. Although the number of performers was never very large, the variety of instruments featured in some of these programs shows that Philadelphians were familiar with instruments from every orchestral family. Like European concerts of this era (1750–1776), Philadelphia programs contained songs (patriotic, parodistic, lyrical), overtures, readings, solos, and pieces for various small ensembles. Certainly the fondness for novelty motivated many of these early concerts. To take but one example, Mr. H.B. Victor informed the local "musical gentry" of his intention to offer a concert during which he would play "the first and second trumpet and a pair of annexed kettledrums with the feet, all at once."

Philadelphia concerts and balls depended on amateur as well as professional musicians. A 1769 issue of the *Gazette* carried the following item:

> The Orchestra, on Opera Nights, will be assisted by some musical Persons, who as they have no view but to contribute to the entertainment of the public, certainly claim Protection from any manner of Insult.

"Opera Nights" probably featured the popular English imports—ballad operas like Gay and Pepush's *Beggar's Opera*. Although such "theatricals" were constantly subjected to harassment by public officials or by certain local residents, there are records of performances in 1749, 1751, and 1754. In 1754, the Old American Company of Comedians, led by William and Henry Hallam of London, engaged William Plumstead's warehouse for a season that proved to be a dismal failure. The opposition to ballad opera, farce, and pantomime in 1754 seems not to have lessened in succeeding years: there are no records of performances between 1760 and 1766. Although advertised performances did occur later, the Pennsylvania legislature followed a recommendation of the Continental Congress and banned "theatricals" from 1778 to 1789. This official action did not deter enterprising Philadelphians, who devised misleadingly euphemistic titles, like "Lectures: Moral and Entertaining," to disguise the true nature of the entertainments offered at Plumstead's warehouse or at the Southwark Theater (completed in 1776). After 1789, the musical theater flourished under the direction of professional musicians from England and Germany. With the foundations laid by Hopkinson, Gualdo, Bremner, and others, these immigrants began establishing the musical organizations, the regular concert series, and all the institutions which made the next sixty years (1790–1850) the "Golden Age of Music" in Philadelphia.

Before 1776, musical performances were an edifying diversion for many Philadelphians. The benefit concerts, the ballad operas, the *soirées* of Francis Hopkinson and his friends, and the evenings of dancing were a significant part of the cultural life of the city. In rural Pennsylvania, the instrumental and choral music of the Moravians, the songs and hymns of the Pennsylvania Germans, and the ballads of the English and Scotch-Irish provided a much richer musical life than might have been expected by a twentieth-century observer.

Printers and Printing

Printer's type tray

Unlike the artifacts of folk culture or the ballads of rural Pennsylvania, the development of a native literature depended on the work of a professional artisan: the printer. An event of symbolic significance to printing in America occurred in 1723, when seventeen-year-old Ben Franklin left Boston for the South after "differences" with his half-brother James, to whom he had been apprenticed. Within a very few years after Ben's arrival in Philadelphia, the growing printing presses of that city became the most prolific in the colonies, issuing the greatest variety of printed matter and displaying the highest quality of artisanship in printing accuracy and design on this side of the Atlantic. Appropriately, it was a Philadelphia printer, John Dunlap, who produced the official text of the Declaration of Independence for distribution among the colonies.

William Bradford had established the first press in Pennsylvania in 1685, and five years later, in partnership with Samuel Carpenter and William Rittenhouse, had built the first American paper mill in Germantown. But after a falling out with local authorities, he moved to New York, where he became the "Official Royal Printer." In 1723, he was visited by the young Franklin, seeking employment. With the help of Bradford and his son Andrew, Ben found his job in Philadelphia in the printing house of Samuel Keimer.

Inside the Printshop

"Keimer's printing house," wrote Franklin in his *Autobiography*, "consisted of an old damaged press and a small worn-out fount of English types." Keimer's ineptness dismayed the young printer, who had learned his trade well in Boston and who had already written and set in type his "Silence Dogood" essays: "I endeavoured to put [Keimer's] press into order fit to be worked with," wrote Franklin. He succeeded, and thus began his Philadelphia career as America's most famous printer.

The equipment Ben Franklin found in Keimer's shop closely resembled the sort he had learned to use in James Franklin's estab-

Print shop

*Paper was handmade from a pulp
derived from linen rags.*

lishment. Almost without exception the colonial American printer
employed materials and machinery he had been taught to work with
in English print shops, or by printers who had emigrated from
Britain. The first presses were of a wooden variety described in 1683
by Joseph Moxon as that "makeshift slovenly contrivance." The
first type, imported like the presses, came from Holland—until after
the middle of the eighteenth century, when the type cast by William
Caslon in England and Alexander Wilson in Glasgow began to replace the older faces. Much of the ink came ready-mixed from England or Holland, although Franklin and certain other printers

Copper plate printer

bought the ingredients—lampblack and linseed oil boiled with rosin —and mixed their own.

Common paper, the lightweight stock used for newspapers and magazines, was made locally in the papermills of Pennsylvania and Massachusetts, but the finer book papers of heavier weight were customarily ordered from Holland. Both kinds were hand made from linen rags and were "laid"—that is, made in a mold in which fine wires, running from end to end, and heavier wires, crossing from side to side, left their impress on the finished product. Held up to the light, a sheet of paper revealed the fine wire's "wire lines" and coarser wire's "chain lines" as translucent patterns within the paper.

Pennsylvania Paper Mills in the Revolution

"Paper bullets" are often said to be the stuff of revolution, but the metaphor took on reality in Pennsylvania at the beginning of the American Revolution. One consequence of the Declaration of Independence was a sudden shortage of paper, not only for the ordinary business of printing, but also as wadding for bullets in muzzle-loading rifles—and, quite basically, for currency. Pennsylvania had been the pioneer colony for paper making. As early as 1690, a Mennonite minister, William Rittenhouse, financed by printer William Bradford, set up the first paper mill in the American colonies in a small ravine leading to Wissahickon creek. His first mill was swept away by a flood in 1701, but Rittenhouse and his descendants went on producing paper. His mill was succeeded by several others, notably that of Thomas Willcox, an Englishman who, starting in 1729, was busy producing paper for various enterprises of Benjamin Franklin from the Ivy Mill on Chester creek.

Until the imposition of the Stamp Act in 1765, the Pennsylvania mills and those in the other colonies could meet only a tiny proportion of the demand for paper, which was mostly imported, but the Crown duties on paper led to a growth in the colonial industry. Yet the fifty-three American mills which existed in 1775 were not enough, so the Continental Congress took early action; on July 18,

1776, it passed a resolution "that the paper makers in Pennsylvania be detained from proceeding with the association to New Jersey," where artisans were already enlisting in the armed forces. At Willcox's Ivy Mill, paper stock for currency was soon exhausted, and the English-made paper molds were worn out. Nathan Sellers, who re-faced molds for Willcox, had already enlisted and was on his way to Long Island. A special petition to the Congress got him back in two days, and he spent at least three months re-facing molds, for which he was paid directly by the Continental Congress. By August 9, 1776, the Council of Public Safety of Pennsylvania re-emphasized the resolution of the Congress requiring Pennsylvanian paper makers to pay strict regard to the order prohibiting them from joining the army. After currency, the most pressing need was for cartridge paper, since each bullet fired from a muzzle loader was rammed into the barrel with paper and powder. Because Rittenhouse's mill was unable to supply all the bullet wadding needed, two wagons and six soldiers were sent to the mill at the Ephrata Cloister. Finding Ephrata out of paper stock, the soldiers seized unbound sheets of The Martyrs Mirror, *which had been printed there in 1748. Similar stories abound to illustrate the consistent need for paper, as well as the rags from which it was made, during the American Revolution.*

Rittenhouse Mill was built in 1751, enlarged in 1787, rebuilt in 1859, and was demolished with the dwelling in 1875.

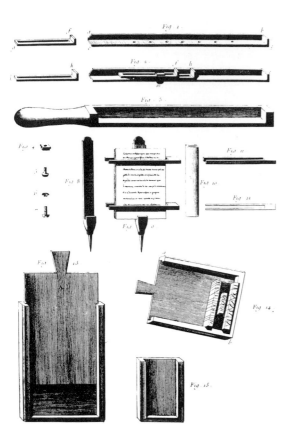

Printer's tools

The furnishings for a printshop, consisting of cases for the type, composing sticks, imposing stones, chases, and other paraphernalia, were either bought in Europe or manufactured locally by village cabinetmakers. Inventories preserved from late eighteenth-century printshops suggest that the total value of the equipment and furnishings required for a well-organized printing establishment would be about $5,000. Yet most printers began, as did Ben Franklin's nephew, with a one-press shop and a limited inventory of type, at a total cost of approximately $2,000, with the hope that they could do enough business during their first two or three years to be able to expand into a two- or even three-press shop and to buy additional fonts of type.

Even with a single press and limited supplies of type, the newly established printer could contract to produce a share of the thousands of blank forms, tickets, vestry notices, advertisements, certificates, promissory notes, receipts, and bills that were entered as orders in printers' work books surviving from the 1760s and 1770s. More material success could be achieved if the printer received orders to publish sermons, catechisms, or school primers, or, better yet, if he were fortunate enough to issue a successful newspaper, general magazine, or that phenomenon of colonial American printing history: the almanac.

The Colonial Almanac

Even before *The Bay Psalm Book*, considered the first book composed and printed in America (1640), Stephen Daye had published *An Almanack for New England for the Year 1639*, compiled by William Peirce. John Tulley of Connecticut added proverbs, jests, and "notices of remarkable events" to the calendar and meteorological and astrological tables in his almanac of 1687, and James Franklin produced the first Rhode Island almanac the year after he moved his press from Massachusetts to Newport. By the time of the skirmishes at Lexington and Concord, every city and many a town in British America had its own almanac. One enterprising publisher used gravestone inscriptions instead of verse to touch his readers' sense of the comic:

> Here lie the remains of Samuel E———
> Untimely joined to his Maker
> By the Fall of a Chimney
> In a Windstorm.
>
> He left behind, Jane, his comely Widow,
> Whose Address is 23 Bedford Street,
> Whose Disposition is One
> Willing to be Comforted.

But he also included some prose drolleries:

> When Thomas Jefferson came to the Court at Paris as the new American Minister, he was introduced to a nobleman, who said, "Ah, yes. You replace Dr. Franklin, I believe." "I succeed Dr. Franklin," Jefferson replied. "No man can replace him."

These almanacs were issued annually and literally read to pieces— so that very few copies of the numerous almanacs published before 1800 have survived.

It was of course Franklin who made Pennsylvania the home of the most famous almanac of all: *Poor Richard's Almanack*. It was extremely popular, reaching one person out of every hundred in the colonial population. It lasted an extraordinary twenty-five years, concluding with the issue for 1758 which contained the famous preface, "The Way to Wealth." The preface is in the form of a speech by Father Abraham, who answers a series of questions about the nature of the times by quoting those maxims from Poor Richard which preach industry, frugality, and virtue. This was only Father Abraham's Poor Richard, however, for not all of the almanac's sayings were so clearly moral. Observations like "There's more old

Drunkards than old Doctors" were probably just as responsible for the success of Franklin's almanac as "God helps them that helps themselves"; yet most of us know Poor Richard from the many reprintings of "The Way to Wealth," and Father Abraham's Poor Richard has also become ours.

The almanac, however, was much more than a source of amusement and moral uplift. This was especially so among the Pennsylvania German farmers, for whom it was the standard reference work on farming, homemaking, cookery, and even haircutting and household medicine. Christopher Sauer's German-language almanac, first published in 1738, took its place beside the Bible and the hymn book on the shelves of German settlers throughout Pennsylvania and as far away as Georgia. Other printers including Franklin published almanacs in German for brief periods, but none came close to the forty successful years of Sauer's almanac.

By 1776 Pennsylvanians could choose from among sixteen almanacs—including one in German—thirteen printed in Philadelphia and three in Lancaster. Ranging from *Poor Richard Improved*—the successor to the famous annual Franklin had sold in 1758—to *Father Abraham's* by Abraham Weatherwise or to *The Philadelphia Newest Almanack for 1776* by Timothy Telescope, these immensely useful volumes appeared in pocket or regular editions of sixteen to twenty-four pages. Along with seasonal, astrological, and weather data, almanacs often printed medical or other scientific material, trenchant homilies, and humorous verse. However, for more timely information and news than an annual could provide, Pennsylvanians and other colonists depended on pamphlets and weekly newspapers.

The Printing of Books

The sternest challenge for the early American printer was posed by the production of a book, and as a result he produced relatively few. Whereas the apprentice could learn quickly to set up and run off minor jobs (invoices, tickets, forms of various sorts, even broadsides), it took a craftsman—an experienced journeyman or a master printer—to design, set up, print, and perhaps also bind a book of any considerable number of pages. Nevertheless, the best books that were produced by eighteenth-century American printers compared quite favorably in quality with those issued by London pressmen.

A large part of colonial Pennsylvania's output of books was in the German language. The first German book published in Pennsylvania was a devotional work by Conrad Beissel, issued by Andrew Bradford in 1728. In 1730, Franklin published a small collection of German hymns, and in 1739 Christopher Sauer brought out a large one, directed chiefly to the Dunkards. Sauer subsequently published

Printed by Franklin

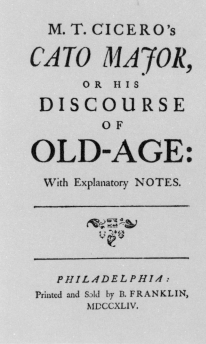

M. T. CICERO's
CATO MAJOR,
OR HIS
DISCOURSE
OF
OLD-AGE:
With Explanatory NOTES.

PHILADELPHIA:
Printed and Sold by B. FRANKLIN,
MDCCXLIV.

The German Reformed Hymnbook

Because of the absence of hymn writers in the German Reformed Church in America during the eighteenth century, the first hymnal used by that denomination was a German one. The Neu-vermehrt und vollständiges Gesang-Buch, *a reprint of the popular Marburg Reformed hymnbook, was first published in Pennsylvania's Germantown by Christopher Saur in 1753 and again in 1763 and 1772. To the second and third editions Saur (also spelled Sauer) added an appendix of thirty hymns of German origin. Ludwig Baisch of Philadelphia in 1774 printed a fourth edition to which he added an appendix of fifty hymns.*

From the beginning the Reformed Church placed importance on psalmody. Both Zwingli and Calvin had held that the Word of God must be preeminent and that human productions should have no part in public worship. Accordingly, the first hymnbooks of the Reformed Church were metrical versions of the psalms. For many years the most popular of these psalters was a rhymed rendition by Ambrosius Lobwasser, a professor of law at Königsberg and a Lutheran.

The first part of Saur's edition of the Gesang-Buch *consisted of Lobwasser's metrical version of the Psalms of David. The second part included the covenant hymns of Pastor Joachim Neander, the father of German Reformed hymnody. Because more than a third of the hymns also appeared in the Lutheran Marburg hymnbook, Saur's edition was especially desirable for use in the many union churches of Pennsylvania. The third part consisted of the Heidelberg Catechism, the common confession of the German Reformed Church, published in the New World for the first time in Pennsylvania. The catechism was followed by prayers of private devotion, the gospel and epistle lessons for Sundays and festival days, and the history of the destruction of Jerusalem.*

This hymnal exemplifies the complete dependence on Germany by a large segment of the colonial Pennsylvania population for its sacred literature, yet it also represents a publishing venture of considerable magnitude.

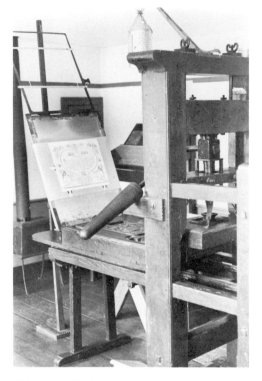

The third Ephrata press,
still in operation

hymnals for the Mennonites and the Amish, the Schwenkfelders, and the Lutheran and Reformed denominations. Sauer's German quarto Bible was the first Bible printed in the New World in any language. The largest book published in the American colonies was the German translation of the Mennonite *Martyrs Mirror*, produced at the Ephrata Cloister in two volumes in 1748 and 1749. Heinrich Müller, a printer and publisher trained by Sauer, became the first printer of Congress.

In the years just after the war, Thomas Dobson of Philadelphia brought the craft of printing in America to the high point of its hundred and fifty-year history when he published the third edition, the first American edition, of the *Encyclopaedia Britannica* in eighteen large quarto volumes, set in type made especially for it by John Baine & Grandson of Philadelphia, printed on paper manufactured in Pennsylvania, and containing more than five hundred copperplate engravings by American artists of the era. The first book produced on this side of the Atlantic on such a scale, Dobson's *Encyclopaedia* marked both the end of the colonial era in American printing and also the beginning of an industry that was, by 1850, to publish as many books in that one year as the colonial printshops produced in the entire century and a half before the Treaty of Paris recognized the United States of America as one of the family of independent nations.

The Martyrs Mirror, *printed at*
Ephrata, was the largest book published
in Colonial America.

The Literary Scene

Most likely the Reverend Jacob Duché spoke truly of Philadelphia citizens when in 1772 he observed: "Such is the prevailing taste for books of every kind that almost every man is a reader." By the 1770s Philadelphia printers could offer readers throughout the colonies not only a wide assortment of imported and reprinted books but also locally produced pamphlets, almanacs, newspapers, and magazines. Furthermore, residents of Philadelphia and visitors alike could use well-stocked public libraries or, for a small fee, purchase circulating subscriptions, the precursors of today's rental libraries. As colonists began to find leisure after the rigors of establishing home and province, they turned to varied reading materials—as well as concerts, lectures, and plays—for instruction and entertainment. The serious concerns of the Revolutionary era, moreover, provided a greater stimulus for the written word than for any of the other arts.

Before the nineteenth century, pamphlets served as the chief public forum later provided by newspapers and magazines. Throughout Europe, especially in France and England, social, political, and moral disputes involved writers like Milton, Voltaire, and Swift in the classic era of the pamphlet during the seventeenth and eighteenth centuries. In colonial America too, pamphlets—often in the guise of "letters"—appeared in burgeoning numbers whenever controversy arose. (In fact, popular political commentaries had proved so convincing that by 1775 conservatives feared the mob effect of pamphleteering.) The recognition of a common cause and a receptive readership were important stimuli for the eventual production of a national literature. The common cause, not individual literary ambition, was the impetus behind such Pennsylvania literary figures as John Dickinson, Tom Paine, Francis Hopkinson, and Hugh Henry Brackenridge.

Colonial Spokesmen: Dickinson and Paine

Philadelphia lawyer John Dickinson stands among the most successful of political essayists. From his protests against the Sugar Act

Our *vigilance* and our *union* are *success* and *safety*. Our *negligence* and our *division* are *distress* and *death*. They are *worse*—they are *shame* and *slavery*. Let us equally shun the benumbing stillness of *overweening sloath*, and the feverish activity of that *ill informed zeal*, which busies itself in maintaining *little*, *mean*, and *narrow* opinions. Let us, with a truly wise *generosity* and *charity*, banish and discourage all *illiberal distinctions*, which may arise from differences in *situation*, forms of *government*, or modes of *religion*.

Dickinson in *Letters from a Farmer in Pennsylvania*

. . . as in absolute governments the King is law, so in free countries the law ought to be king; and there ought to be no other.

Paine in *Common Sense*

and the Stamp Act to his carefully reasoned *Letters from a Farmer in Pennsylvania* (1768), Dickinson advocated legal redress, boycott, and—these failing—armed rebellion. Following publication of his "Farmer's Letters" in Europe, Dickinson became an international celebrity to whom verses were dedicated, commendations voted, formal toasts lofted.

Persuaded by Franklin to leave England for America, Tom Paine arrived in Philadelphia in 1774, and with Franklin's help became the editor of *Pennsylvania Magazine*. He used its pages to advocate many progressive positions: abolition of slavery, women's rights, the folly of dueling, the humane treatment of animals, the need for international arbitration. When his *Common Sense* was published in 1776, he became the leading spokesman for the revolutionary cause. As John Adams said, "Washington's sword would have been wielded in vain had it not been supported by the pen of Paine." In *Common Sense* Paine argued that "the universal order of things" precluded the colonies' subjection "to any external power," and he argued not for reform but for "an open and determined Declaration of Independence." *Common Sense* sold a hundred thousand copies within ninety days. When the revolution broke out, Paine joined the army and, to bolster the soldiers' morale, wrote the first of his sixteen *American Crisis* pamphlets. It is said that George Washington read Paine's words to inspire his troops before their surprise victory at Trenton.

Pennsylvania Wits: Hopkinson, Brackenridge, and Franklin

A signer of the Declaration of Independence and a gifted humorist, Francis Hopkinson first displayed his talent as a political satirist in a pamphlet called *A Pretty Story* (1774), written under the pseudonym of Peter Grievous. "Once upon a time," wrote Peter, "there lived a certain Nobleman, who had long possessed a very valuable Farm, and had a great number of children and grandchildren." An immense tract of land far from the mansion house is but poorly valued by the noble Father because he considers it uncultivated and "overrun with innumerable wild beasts very fierce and savage." Peter, more fittingly surnamed Mischief, was of course Francis Hopkinson, whose urbane allegorical satire on the relations between Old Farm and New Farm, or England and the American colonies, dramatized issues facing the first Continental Congress, just then assembling in Philadelphia's Carpenters' Hall. The pamphlet went through three editions by 1775.

In time Hopkinson followed this early success with popular revolutionary ballads—satiric verses and camp songs. He is best remembered as author of "The Battle of the Kegs" (1778), a comic poem based on the British soldiers' panic at seeing barrels floating down

Philadelphia's John Dickinson, "Penman of the American Revolution"

On July 4, 1768, John Dickinson of Philadelphia sent James Otis a copy of a song for American freedom, written by Dickinson and Arthur Lee of Virginia. The song, with its famous line "By uniting we stand, by dividing we fall," was designed to help unite the colonists against the oppression of England. Set to the tune of the familiar "Hearts of Oak," this "Liberty Song" achieved widespread popularity. Throughout the colonies, cavalcades of the Sons of Liberty heartily sang the tune under the local liberty tree, accompanied by the discharge of cannons and shouts of joy. The entire party would then repair to a nearby tavern for a festive celebration and rounds of toasts.

Toasts inspired by Dickinson's writing were becoming much the rage by 1768. The "Liberty Song" had appeared a few months after his tremendously popular "Letters from a Pennsylvania Farmer." This series of twelve letters, written in response to the Townshend Acts, appeared in the Pennsylvania Chronicle *from December 1767 to February 1768. So popular were these "Letters" that they were promptly reprinted in nearly every colonial newspaper, and "To the Farmer" soon became a favorite toast of the colonists.*

In the "Letters," Dickinson denounced the Townshend duties as unlawful taxation by Parliament for the sole purpose of raising a revenue. Although different in form, the Townshend duties, he argued, were no less a danger to colonial rights than the Stamp Act Taxes had been. He bolstered his argument with quotations from the "Declaration of Rights and Privileges" (a document which he had principally authored), adopted by the Stamp Act Congress of 1765. The purpose of the "Letters," Dickinson asserted, was to convince the colonists that they were "exposed to the most imminent dangers; and to persuade them immediately, vigorously, and unanimously, to exert themselves, in the most firm, but most peaceable manner, for obtaining relief."

For his powerfully persuasive contributions, such as the "Letters," Dickinson has been appropriately named the "Penman of the American Revolution." However, his role as revolutionary was restrained. He preferred pen to sword, reconciliation to independence. He urged defiance of British injustice but felt the cause of liberty "a cause of too much dignity to be sullied by turbulence and tumult."

THE PATRIOTIC AMERICAN FARMER.
J-N D-K-NS——N Esq.r BARRISTER at LAW:
*Who with Attic Eloquence and Roman Spirit hath Asserted,
The Liberties of the BRITISH Colonies in America.*

*'Tis nobly done, to Stem Taxations Rage,
And raise, the thoughts of a degenrate Age,
For Happiness, and Joy, from Freedom spring
But Life in Bondage, is a worthless Thing.*

Printed for & Sold by R. Bell Bookseller

Only reluctantly did he finally give up his hopes for reconciliation. At the Second Continental Congress, his pen produced both the "Olive Branch Petition," unanswered by the King, and the "Declaration on the Causes and Necessity of Taking Up Arms," cheered by the colonial armies. Although he eventually came to see the break from England as inevitable, he felt that the colonies needed more time to prepare for the conflict. The lack of complete colonial unity, full military preparations, and definite foreign alliances convinced Dickinson that the Declaration of Independence was an error in timing. It is one of the ironies of history that the "Penman of the American Revolution" was actually a reluctant revolutionary who did not sign the Declaration of Independence.

Tom Paine's First Forum,
The Pennsylvania Magazine

It appeared in only nineteen monthly issues (from January 1775 to July 1776). Its readers probably numbered no more than five thousand for any one issue. Yet the Pennsylvania Magazine *occupies a conspicuously important place in the history of journalism in America and might even now be cited as one of the most influential periodicals in the national experience.*

One man—Thomas Paine—accounts for both its influence and its reputation. For, as Paine wrote from Philadelphia in February 1775 to his friend and sponsor, Benjamin Franklin, then in London, "a printer and bookseller here, a man of reputation and property, Robert Aitkin [sic], has lately attempted a magazine, but having little or no turn that way himself, he has applied to me for assistance. He had not above 600 subscribers when I first assisted him. We now have upwards of 1500, and daily increasing. I have not entered into terms with him. This is only the second number. The first I was not concerned in."

And so the Pennsylvania Magazine *became Tom Paine's forum, the platform from which he addressed to the American colonists those searingly eloquent polemics that were the seedbed of his* Common Sense *and, later, the* Crisis Papers. *Publisher Aitken's statement in his prospectus that he would exclude both religious and political controversy, except "as the subjects of philosophical disquisition," became an early casualty of Paine's revolutionary zeal. Under a variety of pseudonyms, Paine attacked monarchy and sang of liberty in ringing tones. John Witherspoon, president of the College of New Jersey, joined him in these assaults on authority. In articles, in poems, in songs, the* Pennsylvania Magazine *drew the issues that were to culminate in revolution.*

Yet, despite the urgency of political issues in 1775–1776, much of the content of the Pennsylvania Magazine *was concerned with other matters. Paine addressed himself to such problems as women's rights, the evils of dueling, cruelty to animals, and the perils of marriage. Witherspoon joined in this latter discussion and also wrote a series of letters on education, which were widely reprinted. A scientific flavor was added by the articles of Benjamin Rush, David Rittenhouse, and Matthew Wilson. Much attention was given to mechanical subjects,*

sometimes illustrated by engraved plates. In subject matter, the Pennsylvania Magazine *was a veritable potpourri.*

"On the whole," writes Frank Luther Mott, the historian of American journalism, "it was a good magazine, containing a larger proportion of original material than most other eighteenth century American magazines." But the import of the Pennsylvania Magazine *was much greater than this modest claim for it suggests, chiefly because it had as editor for most of its short life a remarkable man—Thomas Paine.*

Tom Paine

Title page of Pennsylvania Magazine

These are the times that try men's souls. The summer soldier and the sunshine patriot will, in this crisis, shrink from the service of his country; but he that stands it *now*, deserves the love and thanks of man and woman. Tyranny, like hell, is not easily conquered; yet we have this consolation with us, that the harder the conflict, the more glorious the triumph. What we obtain too cheap, we esteem too lightly: it is dearness only that gives everything its value. Heaven knows how to put a proper price upon its goods; and it would be strange indeed if so celestial an article as FREEDOM should not be highly rated.

Paine in *The Crisis*

the Delaware River in 1777. Convinced the kegs concealed armed men—they were actually mines intended to destroy British ships—the king's forces opened fire, thereby amusing onlookers and thousands of patriots who learned of the incident through Hopkinson's song.

Hugh Henry Brackenridge—clergyman, lawyer, editor, writer—came to America when he was five. An ardent advocate of the Revolution, he served as a chaplain during the war. He then went to the frontier town of Pittsburgh, where he established its first bookstore and its first school, and in 1786 helped found its first newspaper, *The Pittsburgh Gazette*. In his last years he served as a justice on the Pennsylvania Supreme Court. He is best remembered for a remarkable comic novel published in 1792, *Modern Chivalry*. "The great moral of this book," Brackenridge says at its conclusion, "is the evil of men seeking office for which they are not qualified."

The major literary figure in Pennsylvania, however, was Benjamin Franklin. By the time he launched the career of Tom Paine in 1774, he had already completed a half-century of significant writing on political, educational, religious, philosophical, and scientific subjects.

Men & Melons are hard to know.

If your head is wax, don't walk in the Sun.

Many Foxes grow grey, but few grow good.

Would you persuade, speak of Interest, not of Reason.

In Rivers & bad Governments, the lightest Things swim at the top.

He that builds before he counts the Cost, acts foolishly; and he that counts before he builds, finds that he did not count wisely.

Franklin in
Poor Richard's Almanack

Many of these essays were published in his own newspaper, *The Pennsylvania Gazette* (1729–1766), or in his *Poor Richard's Almanack* (1733–1758). During the pre-Revolutionary years Franklin wrote vigorously concerning Britain's relationship to the colonies, arguing initially for a Royal Charter and the rights granted all British subjects. But by 1773 his manner had turned satirical: *Rules by Which a Great Empire May Be Reduced to a Small One* is ostensibly addressed to a minister who wants to make his kingdom more governable by making it smaller. The rules parallel those actions which England had been taking in her colonies: don't fail to levy unfair taxes, don't send qualified governors, don't pay attention to grievances.

In the years that followed, Franklin's public responsibilities as a diplomat abroad, as a participant in the Continental Congress, as a negotiator of the Treaty of Paris somewhat curtailed his political writing, although during the 1770s he still found time to compose witty bagatelles and to work on his *Autobiography*.

The Literature of the Pennsylvania Germans

Not all the writing done in colonial Pennsylvania was in English. From 1683—when the first Germans arrived in Penn's Woods through the American Revolution, most Pennsylvania German literature was written in standard German by individuals who had been educated in German universities and who were influenced by the mystical-pietistic tradition of seventeenth-century Europe.

Some controversial tracts were produced from the beginning, but the Pennsylvania Germans' first concerns were hymns, prayers, and other devotional literature. Sects which finally had found release from European religious persecution and literary censorship enthusiastically seized the opportunity to create religious literature suited to their particular spiritual needs. Accordingly, most of the early writings appeared in the form of poetry and were written by religious sectarians and separatists, many of whom were motivated by a profound *"Innerlichkeit."* Frequently the poems were meant to be sung, but some were not suitable as hymns. In colonial Pennsylvania the German hymnals were used as devotional literature in the home as well as for congregational singing.

Pennsylvania German literature begins with Francis Daniel Pastorius, the leading founder of Germantown. Although some of his poems may be classified as *"Kleindichtung,"* and are of questionable literary merit, his works as a whole demonstrate his forcefulness as a writer of both prose and poetry. They reveal a comprehensive knowledge in a broad spectrum of subjects and a command of eight languages, including English. Pastorius was a deeply religious man, but he was not swept along by the mystical, otherworldly religious fever that typified some of the other early Pennsylvania German poets. His writings were consistently more rational than mystical; he was a practical man. Pastorius' most important literary work was his "Beehive," an encyclopedic collection of verse and prose covering a variety of topics, written in several languages and employing a wide range of images, many of them from nature. A large portion of this huge collection is still unpublished but is now being edited for publication.

Mystical subjectivity among the early Pennsylvania Germans reached its zenith in the hymns of Johannes Kelpius and Conrad Beissel. Kelpius was highly educated, but as a young man he became disillusioned with European civilization. To escape from the seemingly decadent society and apostate established religion of the fatherland, he led a small band of millennialists to Pennsylvania in 1694. On the banks of the Wissahickon Creek near Germantown he spent most of the remaining years of his short life in relative seclusion. Instead of trying to adjust to the new American culture he exhorted his followers to train their eyes on Jesus and to be on guard against the subtle wiles of Satan. He was concerned almost exclusively with man's spiritual welfare. All of his hymns are characterized by the poet's longing for the "unio mystica," for eternal union with God.

In 1720 Conrad Beissel came to Pennsylvania with the intention of joining Kelpius and his small celibate society known as "The Woman in the Wilderness." However, Kelpius had died in 1708 and his followers had subsequently scattered. After a few years of searching and a brief association with the German Baptist Brethren, or Dunkards, Beissel founded his own celibate community, the Ephrata Cloister, where he and his followers—both brothers and sisters—wrote an extraordinarily large number of hymns. It has been estimated that Beissel, whose formal education was limited, wrote as many as one thousand hymns.

Few critics regard Beissel's poetry as great literature. Nevertheless, his poems did fill a religious need in their time. Like Kelpius, Beissel made no effort to absorb or adjust to the emerging American culture. Instead of breaking new literary ground in a new land he invested his artistic energies in continuing the poetic heritage of seventeenth-century German religious poetry, steeped in the mystical tradition of Jakob Böhme's philosophy. Unfortunately, Beissel's voluminous writings on a small number of themes and in a few simple poetic forms inevitably resulted in considerable repetition and monotony.

Although the Schwenkfelders, who came to America in 1734, wrote some hymns and odes in this country, the great majority of their vast body of religious poetry was written in Europe. As a despised sect, the Schwenkfelders had not been able to have their writings published on the Continent. Upon their arrival in free America they therefore directed their literary efforts primarily toward copying, transcribing, compiling, and publishing their existing literature.

Title page of Christopher Dock's classic book, School Management

The Mennonites and Amish historically have been a reticent people. It is probable that some of the countless anonymous colonial religious poems were produced by them, but it is almost certain that they were never prolific writers. Moreover, they had brought their Bibles and hymnals with them from Europe and thus were not pressed into writing new songs and devotional literature. (It should be recalled, however, that at their request and under their supervision the monumental *Martyrs Mirror* was translated from Dutch into German and published in 1748 and 1749 at Conrad Beissel's Ephrata Cloister.) The one distinguished Mennonite author of eighteenth-century Pennsylvania was Christopher Dock, a schoolmaster. Even today his *Schulordnung*, a treatise on school management, is considered a classic by educators in America. Although it was written in 1750, Dock's modesty compelled him to ask that the work not be published until after his death; thus it was published by Sauer in 1770.

Although the so-called church people—the Lutheran and Reformed denominations—soon far outnumbered all other Pennsylvania Germans, relatively few hymns and other devotional literature were produced by them in colonial America. Both groups were content with Luther's translation of the Bible and with the *Marburger Gesangbuch*, which was reprinted several times in America.

From the 1730s to the American Revolution the Moravians produced an incredible number of religious poems. During his brief stay of some fourteen months in the New World, Count Nikolaus Ludwig von Zinzendorf, the founder of the Moravian community in America, wrote a tremendous volume of poetry. Moreover, he inspired many of his followers to cultivate their poetic talents as well. Unlike Kelpius and Beissel, whose dominant theme was an uncontrolled yearning for the marriage of the spiritual bride and bridegroom, Zinzendorf—like his fellow leader and biographer, August Gottlieb Spangenberg, and their followers—was inclined to write for specific occasions and about particular groups of people. Thus many of their poems are unmistakably rooted in American soil. Of the Moravians in America, Spangenberg wrote, "Nowhere else have been composed such beautiful and edifying hymns for shepherds, ploughers, threshers, reapers, spinners, knitters, washers, sewers, and others as among them and by them." To be sure, some of their hymns also treat purely religious topics and could just as appropriately have been written in Europe as in America; yet in many cases the Moravian poets, more than any other Pennsylvania Germans, drew their subject matter and their inspiration from the world around them. The Pennsylvania of the mid-eighteenth century is often realistically depicted in their poetry.

Language has played a significant role in the production, development, and reception of Pennsylvania German literature. Although standard German was the language of church and school and of the early intellectuals, the common folk always found it more natural to converse in their own dialects. At first their linguistic world was exceedingly small, as each sought to use the dialect of the area in Europe from which he had come, but through a gradual leveling and blending process those features that had made each dialect distinct from all others were slowly eliminated until one common dialect emerged. This process was greatly facilitated by the Revolutionary War, which virtually stopped immigration for about fifteen years, thereby permitting the various dialects to coalesce. Today this common dialect is popularly known as Pennsylvania Dutch. Although the dialect continued to serve as an exclusive means of oral communication among Pennsylvania Germans for almost seventy-five years after independence, it was not until the middle of the nineteenth century that the first of a vast body of dialect writings began to appear.

If Pennsylvania German literature in the first half of the eighteenth century reflects a primarily religious outlook, the literary productions in the second half of the century, and especially in the years following the War of Independence, reflect a mood of transition. By then the first great religious leaders and teachers were dead, and, even among the Pennsylvania Germans, society was showing definite signs of becoming more secular. Newspapers, magazines, almanacs, and a variety of pamphlets played an increasingly dominant role as vehicles of literary communication.

The poetry and prose of the Revolutionary era tried to meet the practical needs of a people bent upon improving personal and political conditions. In the spirit of Franklin, who believed in working at self-betterment, Pennsylvania citizens sought reading material to increase their understanding and their skill. For example, officials of the fledgling Philadelphia Library Company noted with surprise the numbers of mechanics and tradesmen seeking self-improvement through reading. Of the eight thousand volumes housed in Carpenters' Hall in 1774, the vast majority were practical and informative. Most Pennsylvania writers, speaking to such ends or to the common cause of liberty, admirably met the needs of history. In the next century, the shaping genius of writers like Cooper, Hawthorne, and Whitman would emerge to transform the colonial experience into a national literature of distinction.

Newspapers and Magazines

In 1776 the seven newspapers issued in Philadelphia staggered publication so that at least one appeared every weekday except Wednesday. In addition, the Pennsylvania *Evening Post* came out Tuesday, Thursday, and Saturday nights. Although every colony except Delaware had its own newspaper by 1765, those from Philadelphia circulated by subscription not only throughout Pennsylvania but in the other provinces as well. Modeled on their English counterparts and frequently copying material from them, colonial newspapers nevertheless gradually assumed a distinctive character. From its tenuous beginnings in 1704, the newspaper had included moral and political commentary; by the 1770s essays on current events commonly supplemented news, advertising, and the traditional weather reports begun earlier by Franklin in his *Pennsylvania Gazette*. By 1775 the *Pennsylvania Mercury* even contained a poet's corner, to which many women contributed verse. Early in its notable history, the *Pennsylvania Packet* issued a supplement including literary and scientific offerings. Two colonial Pennsylvania newspapers were published in the German language, including one founded by Christopher Sauer in 1739.

It was through the Philadelphia papers, beginning with Benjamin Towne's *Pennsylvania Evening Post*, that on July 4, 1776, word was first carried that "This day the Continental Congress declared the United Colonies Free and Independent States." All the city's papers carried stories of the event, and both the *Evening Post* and Dunlap's *Pennsylvania Packet*—later the first to print Washington's "Farewell Address"—published the entire text of the Declaration. Heinrich Müller translated it into German and published it in his *Pennsylvanischer Staatsbote*. Although not as politically effective as the pamphlet, the newspaper nevertheless provided a convenient medium for spreading opinion and civic information, or for advertising goods and skills.

Colonial magazines struggled to survive during the Revolution. In 1741 Philadelphia printers had established two of the first periodicals published in the colonies, but, because of unstable social and political conditions, only three magazines were launched between 1760 and 1774. The most significant periodical of the era was Robert Aiken's *Pennsylvania Magazine*, for which Tom Paine served as editor from February 1775 to May 1776. In its final issue, that of July 1776, this sprightly magazine printed the Declaration of Independence. Livelier than its predecessors, the *Pennsylvania Magazine* carried current dispatches on the war, accepted a large number of original literary contributions, and printed "An Occasional Letter on the Female Sex"—an essay which is currently earning Thomas Paine recognition as an early advocate of women's rights. The magazine also carried Paine's *Common Sense* and *Crisis* tracts, as well as verses to Washington written by the New England black poet Phillis Wheatley. While other colonial periodicals published poems by Philadelphia's Francis Hopkinson and New Jersey's Philip Freneau, until later in the Revolution these rival magazines rarely achieved the originality of the *Pennsylvania Magazine*.

The Artists
of Colonial Pennsylvania

In the eighteenth century, the center of professional painting in Pennsylvania, like that of music and publishing, was Philadelphia. There art supplies were available, and at least a few art collectors could be found—William Shippen, James Hamilton, and especially Judge William Allen, whose contributions to the American art world have been largely played down because of his Tory leanings. Allen's collection of antique paintings and copies of old masters provided inspiration for several budding American artists, and Allen fostered the career of the most influential American artist of 1776, Benjamin West.

Early Eighteenth-Century Painters

As early as 1712, Philadelphia had attracted a European-trained professional painter when Gustavus Hesselius (1682–1755), who had accompanied his pastor brother to a calling in Delaware, moved on to Philadelphia to practice his art. After some travel, Hesselius returned to Philadelphia in the 1720s; he remained active there until his death, producing portraits in a realistic style that he had learned in his native Sweden. Perhaps the finest extant works by Hesselius are the portraits of two chiefs of the Delaware Indians. The paintings of *Lapowinsa* and *Tishcohan* were commissioned by Thomas and John Penn and are the first successful likenesses of North American Indians by an artist in the New World. In spite of his talents, like most other painters in the colonies Hesselius had to supplement his income from easel painting by performing other tasks. These included painting the interior of the new State House in Philadelphia.

The attraction of Philadelphia for portrait commissions brought other artists, often on short stays. John Smibert (1688–1751), the Scottish-born painter of Boston, traveled to Philadelphia in the summer of 1740 and produced fourteen portraits before departing. The American-born portrait painter Robert Feke (1707–1752) made trips from New England to Philadelphia in 1746 and 1749. Feke's portrait of *Mary McCall*, probably painted in Philadelphia in 1746, expresses the taste of the wealthy class that had developed in the colonies in the eighteenth century.

The rather bold and honest baroque naturalism evident in the likenesses produced by these artists gave way around mid-century to a more elegant, decorative style related to the rococo tradition of European portraiture. An Englishman, William Williams (1727–1791), established himself as a portrait painter in Philadelphia about 1747 and remained there for two decades before moving to New York and eventually returning to England. Williams was one of the first artists to introduce to America the conversation piece, a form of informal group portraiture on a small scale that had become popular in Europe. Besides his career as a painter, Williams, at various times, was a seaman, a musician, and a novelist. In addition, he was connected with the theater and was the first professional scene painter in America. Perhaps something of his talent as a scene painter is to be seen in the conversation piece of *Husband and Wife in a Landscape*, painted in 1775. This painting shows the increased desire for mannered decorativeness in the third quarter of the century.

A more sophisticated practitioner of society portraiture was John Wollaston (active in America, 1749–1767), an English-trained painter who came to America and worked in the principal centers of the colonies, including Philadelphia in 1758, before returning to Europe. He influenced the younger American-born painters, such as John Hesselius (1728–1778), the son of Gustavus.

Benjamin West (1738–1820)

The first American artist to achieve an international reputation was Benjamin West. A student of William Williams, before he was twenty he produced his acknowledged American masterpiece, a portrait of fifteen-year-old *Thomas Mifflin*, the future governor of Pennsylvania. Another example of West's work in America is the portrait of *Elizabeth Peel* painted about 1758, which, especially in the rhythmically stylized highlights of the drapery, suggests the influence of Robert Feke and John Wollaston. By the time he was twenty-one, West's youthful works brought him to the attention of a group of Philadelphia and Lancaster merchants, most notably Judge Allen, who made it possible for him to go abroad to study. He never returned.

In 1760, West arrived in Italy, where he came in contact with the neoclassical ideas that were transforming European taste in the arts. He settled in England, became the favorite painter of King George III, and was elected President of the Royal Academy. In England he was able to abandon portraiture, which was the only

Benjamin West, after becoming President of the Royal Academy in London

Thomas Mifflin, by Benjamin West, 1758. By the time West went abroad at the age of twenty-one, he had already been painting with considerable success for half a decade. This portrait shows young Mifflin, the future Revolutionary soldier and governor of Pennsylvania, in all the pride of his scant fifteen years, posed with a large fowling piece and some birds. West was only twenty when he painted this portrait.

variety of high-style painting colonial America supported, and could devote himself to historical and biblical subjects. Typical of the work he was doing in 1776 is *The Raising of Lazarus*. Although he was now an English resident, West's emotional ties with his native land were always strong, and he was greatly troubled by the war. It was probably to reaffirm his Americanism in a safe fashion that he painted his *William Penn Treating with the Indians* in 1771, and his studio became the unofficial headquarters of American students who wished to study painting.

"The First Fruits," by John Valentine Haidt

According to Otto Uttendörfer and Walther E. Schmidt, in Die Brüder (*Gnadau, Germany, 1914), the names of the subjects are as follows: (1) Christiana Guly, a Persian; (2) Thomas Mammucha, a Mingrel; (3) Kajarnak, from Greenland; (4) Sam, an Indian from New England; (5) Christian Zedmann, an Armenian; (6) Gratia, a Negro; (7) Rachel, a mulatto from St. John; (8) Anna Maria, from the Virgin Islands, the daughter of missionary Freundlich and his wife, Rebecca, a mulatto; (9) Catharina, a gypsy; (10) Oly Carmel, or Joshua, from St. Thomas; (11) Jupiter, or Immanuel, from Carolina; (12) Andreas, father of Michael, from St. Thomas; (13) Anna Maria, from the Virgin Islands; (14) Michael, her nephew, from Silesia; (15) uncertain; (16) Francesco, from Florida; (17) a child, from Berbice; (18) Kiboddo, a Hottentot; (19) Ruth, a Mohican Indian; (20) Thomas, a Huron Indian; (21–23) uncertain; (24) Wasamapah; and (25) Johannes.*

John Valentine Haidt, Bethlehem's Moravian Artist

Although painting in eighteenth-century Pennsylvania, like that in other areas along the eastern seaboard, was largely confined to portraiture, one artist, John Valentine Haidt, was in a position to paint nearly as many canvases of religious subjects as those that recorded the likenesses of his fellow Pennsylvanians, for Haidt became in effect the official painter of the Moravian Church.

Haidt was born in Danzig, Poland, in 1700, the son of a goldsmith. In spite of his early interests in the Lutheran ministry and in painting, paternal wishes determined that he too would become a goldsmith. After completing his training, he traveled through Italy and France before establishing himself as a goldsmith in London in 1724. There he married, and in the late 1730s became interested in the Moravians. In 1740 he traveled with his family to the Continent and settled in the Moravian community at Herrnhaag in Saxony, where in the years that followed he devoted himself principally to church work, including service as a lay preacher. About 1746, through the encouragement of Count Zinzendorf, the patron and bishop of the Moravian Church, he turned to painting, producing religious paintings for the Moravian communities in Europe.

It was in America, however, that Haidt was to spend his most productive years as a painter. In 1754 he and his wife arrived in Bethlehem, Pennsylvania, the center of the Moravian Church in America. After serving as a pastor in Philadelphia for over a year, he returned to Bethlehem, which remained his principal residence in spite of duties which often called him to other Moravian communities.

In Bethlehem, painting seems to have become his major duty. Besides his numerous portraits of fellow Moravians, Haidt painted many religious subjects, which in his own mind were visual counterparts of his sermons. "The First Fruits" is a subject that is of special significance to the Moravian Church and one that Haidt had painted in an earlier version in Germany. The variety of peoples included in the painting reflects not only the Moravian emphasis on worldwide missionary work but also Zinzendorf's belief that only a few key individuals rather than great numbers of people in each pagan society are prepared for conversion. Thus each of the figures depicted beneath the seated figure of Christ represents the initial convert or "first fruit" of a particular society. This is confirmed by the banner carried by the angel, on which a passage from Revelations reads, "These have been redeemed from men as first fruits for God and the Lamb."

In style the religious paintings of Haidt are provincial New World counterparts of the late Baroque manner of European art. His frequent use of emotionally charged figures arranged along diagonals receding into the pictorial space are echoes of more competent works he must have seen in Europe.

Haidt's painting career lasted until the eve of the Revolution, when ill health forced him to curtail his activities. When he died in 1780, he left behind more than seventy paintings, most of which are still in the Moravian communities of Pennsylvania.

"The Artist in His Museum," by Charles Willson Peale, 1822

Charles Willson Peale—
"The Artist in His Museum"

With a sense of history, a young captain serving during the Revolution, Charles Willson Peale, painted miniature portraits of his fellow officers. Repainted to life size, these portraits were to become the cornerstone of America's first true museum— The Philadelphia Museum. The museum, originally housed in Peale's home, was founded in 1786. In 1794 it was moved into Philosophical Hall, and in 1800 it was expanded across the State House Yard into the State House itself, which had recently been vacated when the Pennsylvania Legislature had moved out to begin its trek to Harrisburg. Today that vacated structure is revered as Independence Hall. To citizens in 1800 it was just an excess public building.

"The Artist in His Museum"—painted in 1822 when Peale was 81—is set in the Long Room on the second floor of the State House, and is a combination of description, symbolism, and theatrics. The proud proprietor dramatically lifts a drapery to reveal the layout of the Long Room, which was used for the display of birds. Peale was a pioneer of modern taxidermy and also a pioneer in the technique of displaying subjects against naturalistic backgrounds. The birds are set against appropriate painted backgrounds. Each case is a forerunner of the modern natural history diorama. On the extreme left one sees the mounted paddlefish which was the first gift to the museum. Above the cases are some of Peale's collection of Revolutionary War portraits.

Now symbolism takes over. In the left foreground is a mounted turkey. Many Americans felt that the food-giving turkey should be the emblem of the new nation. Displayed in front of the bird are several implements Peale used in practicing taxidermy. In the right foreground are the supposed mammoth bones which were loaned to Peale in 1784. These bones are credited with interesting him in developing a natural history museum. On the table are his palette and brushes. Mostly hidden behind the drapery is Peale's most famous museum acquisition, the mastodon skeleton which he exhumed in Ulster County, New York, in 1801. In reality this attraction never was displayed in the Long Room; it remained at Philosophical Hall, where an extra fee was charged to see it.

In 1810 Peale turned over active control of his museum to his son Rubens. The founder lived in semi-retirement until his death in 1826. After Rubens took control, the museum's character changed, profit becoming increasingly important as entertainment overshadowed science. The museum finally closed in 1845, and its collections were largely dispersed or destroyed. The largest remaining segment of the museum is the portrait collection displayed in the Second Bank of the United States Building in Independence Hall National Historical Park. Thus ended the story of a pioneer American institution, which in its day reflected the variety of interests in the life and customs of the new nation, and which was the progenitor of both the pseudo-museums and the true scientific institutions that have followed it.

Benjamin West and "The American School" of Painting

In 1776 the most influential artistic force in America was represented by a painter who had not lived in the colonies since 1759, Benjamin West (1738–1820). Born into a Quaker family near Swarthmore, Pennsylvania, West reputedly learned to mix colors from local Indians. He also studied painting with a visiting English artist named William Williams. Through the application of his learning, he painted a series of portraits, including one of the young Thomas Mifflin, which won him recognition as an artist of extraordinary talent.

By 1759 West's paintings had received such widespread acclaim among a group of Pennsylvania merchants, notably William Allen (for whom Allentown was named), that West was sent abroad for further study. After residing in Italy for three years, he visited England. His paintings caught the eye of George III and led to West's appointment as court painter. West also became president of the Royal Academy and served in that capacity for twenty-eight years.

Although West realized that his artistic goal of "painting history" could never be achieved by returning home, he became teacher to two generations of American painters. One of his earliest students was Mathew Pratt, who arrived from America in 1764 with West's fiancée. Pratt painted "The

American School" portraying West at work teaching his protégés—a scene that would be replayed for over fifty years. Two other Americans taught by West in England were the revolutionary patriot Charles Willson Peale and Rhode Islander Gilbert Stuart, who later made a career from his portraits of George Washington.

Although West was a royal official and friend of the king, he always considered himself an American. His patriotic sentiment is reflected in his painting of William Penn negotiating with the Indians, completed during the years of turmoil preceding American independence. This painting represents a significant departure from conventional art since his characters here wear contemporary dress rather than the drapery that tradition required.

Writing to Charles Willson Peale shortly after the Treaty of Paris recognizing American independence, West lucidly stated his feelings regarding the Revolution: "let me congratulate you and my countrymen in general, on the event of the Peace and the fortitude they have shown during the unhappy war. Thier [sic] wisdom and unshaken perseverance, must enrole them for ever among the greatest characters of antiquity, and transmit that name which nothing but their Virtues could have achieved."

"The American School," by Matthew Pratt, 1765. Matthew Pratt, of Philadelphia, had been in England barely a year when he painted this pleasantly informal group of young artists in West's studio. Standing on the left, West comments on a drawing held by Pratt, while other pupils listen attentively. No other known picture bears Pratt's signature, which appears at the lower left of the canvas on the easel.

Matthew Pratt (1734–1805)

A painting of West's London studio was made by Matthew Pratt in 1765. *The American School* shows Pratt and other Americans studying with West. Pratt was born in Philadelphia, where he received early training under James Claypoole, Sr., a glazier and house painter, before beginning his career as a painter of portraits. In 1764 he sailed for England, where he worked with Benjamin West in London and painted portraits in Bristol before returning to Philadelphia in 1768. Pratt found it necessary, after his return, to supplement his artist's income. As a result, he helped beautify Philadelphia with his skillfully wrought and painted signs.

Charles Willson Peale (1741–1827)

C.W. Peale
after a painting by Rembrandt Peale

Perhaps the most interesting figure among the eighteenth-century painters working in Pennsylvania was Charles Willson Peale. Born in Queen Anne's County, Maryland, he was first trained as a saddler and a painter of signs and coaches. A person of great curiosity, eager to try his hand at all forms of craftsmanship and creativity, Peale became interested in portrait painting and received his first lessons from John Hesselius, who had moved to Maryland from Philadelphia. In 1767 his interest in painting took him to London to study under Benjamin West. After he returned to Maryland in 1769, his commissions carried him on trips to Philadelphia, Baltimore, Williamsburg, and Mount Vernon, where he painted his first portrait of George Washington in 1772. After serving in the Continental Army, Peale settled permanently in Philadelphia in 1778, and for a time was a member of the Pennsylvania Assembly.

During the war and later, he painted portraits of the principal figures of the Revolution, both civil and military, many of which he exhibited in the gallery attached to his studio. But painting was only one area of interest for the inventive Peale, and in 1782 he built a museum of natural history, the first in America, which eventually grew to such proportions that it had to find room in the State House (Independence Hall), remaining there until its dispersal in the mid-nineteenth century.

Charles Willson Peale, painter, engraver, inventor, naturalist, statesman, museum proprietor, and scientist, combined, like Franklin, that sense of Yankee practicality with a youthful enthusiasm and curiosity which seemed to express perfectly the aspirations and potentials of the new republic.

Colonial Pennsylvania Architecture

O f all the arts, none reveals more about the manners, mores, and events of an era than its formal architecture. Architectural history usually charts a progression of stylistic modes, each flowing into the next while remaining distinct. Such history emphasizes the great homes and important public buildings, which illustrate style most evidently. But in everyday houses and service buildings, in barns and local churches, the folk tradition prevails—and it is conservative. Whereas buildings constructed in academic styles can usually be dated within ten years, folk structures, like the objects of folk material culture, are almost impossible to date within fifty years. Pennsylvania has played a significant role in both the development of formal architectural styles and in the maintenance and adaptation of traditional folk forms.

Typical farmyard pump

Frontier Housing

Before 1776, when large areas of Pennsylvania still could be called frontier, many of the colony's structures were temporary. The most common first shelter was a hut built of forked sticks covered with grass, bark, and mud, whose prototype was the temporary agricultural shelter of the English and European countryside. (The very first Pennsylvania settlers had lived in caves—either enlarged natural ones or new artificial ones—in the banks of the Delaware and Schuylkill rivers.)

The Swedes were the first Europeans to make a lasting architectural mark on Pennsylvania. They brought with them the *Port*, that homely structure, so adaptable to the wilderness of North America, which we call the log cabin. The Swedish cabin, made of hewn logs laid horizontally with chinking between them, was tight and warm. Nailless, held together by the corner notching of the logs, it could be constructed with a few simple tools, chiefly a felling axe and a broad axe, from the material found on any wooded tract. A chimney built in a corner within the dwelling added a distinctively Swedish touch to the cabin. Often the gable ends were framed and

Froe and mallet used to split shingles

A Chester County wainscot, or joined chair, near the fireplace in this recreated Pennsylvania German kitchen

sheathed with boards, because in a gable, where notching was impossible, logs could not be firmly held together. The roofing was of shingles cut with froe and mallet, and the windows were small, unglazed openings fitted with sliding shutters. The "Lower Swedish Cabin" in Darby is an altered remnant of Swedish construction in Pennsylvania, probably dating from the 1640s. Although log construction is usually associated with simple domestic structures, the first European capital within what was to be Pennsylvania, *Printzhof*, erected at Tinicum under the direction of Governor Johan Printz, was built of logs. Because the Swedes were never numerous in Pennsylvania, the Swedish tradition of log construction quickly died out, and the practice of using timber in this fashion had to be reintroduced into Pennsylvania by the Rhineland Germans, who arrived in large numbers beginning in the 1730s.

It was into a version of the German log cabin, adopted by the English and Scotch-Irish, and in some measure adapted by them, that Abe Lincoln was born. The Bertolet-Herbein Log House of 1738, recently moved to the Daniel Boone Homestead near Reading, epitomizes the simple log structure. Larger buildings, sometimes with two stories and sometimes built in several sections or modules, also were developed. As people became more prosperous, log buildings were rendered more fashionable—and also more weatherproof—by sheathing them with siding. In this disguise many log houses still stand, revealed to the knowing eye only by a characteristic sag and a thickness of wall. Some log structures, like General Arthur St. Clair's home in the Ligonier Valley, were not meant to be left unsheathed. They represent a frontier version of an elegantly framed house.

Pennsylvania German Rural Architecture

Both the Swedes and the Germans considered log construction a temporary expedient to be replaced, if possible, by stone or brick. The Zeller House (1745) in Newmanstown, for example, has the same floor plan as a typical log house, but is constructed in stone two feet thick. As James K. Paulding said: "If a German builds a house, its walls are twice as thick as others—if he puts down a gatepost, it is sure to be nearly twice as thick as it is long." Fort Zeller, as it was erroneously called by later generations because of its characteristic thick walls and small window openings, is built over a spring. The main floor has two unequal rooms: a living chamber over the spring room and a kitchen. A large chimney provides a fireplace for the kitchen and a stove connection for the other room (in many other German houses this second space is divided into two). As is typical in German construction, the chimney emerges at the center of the roof, rather than along one of the end walls, as was common in English structures.

Located about a mile from the Zeller House is the Georg Muller House (1752) at Milbach, the best remaining upper-middle-class German domestic structure in America, and perhaps the one most imbued with the tradition of the German Renaissance. There once were "stoeps" with flanking benches by each entrance, and a pent roof ran around the building at the first-story level as it still does at the two levels in the gable ends. Topping the house, which is built of local limestone trimmed with red sandstone, is a very Germanic piled-up gambrel roof with a "kick" or bellcast on each of its four levels. The interiors, now in Philadelphia's Museum of Art, are unparalleled examples of Germanic internal design in this country. Their feeling of heaviness arises from their use of the square and the rectangle as decorative motifs. The German influence is also clearly seen in the fireplace arrangements and the pent roofs of the Potts House at Pottsville, in Germantown's Grumblethorpe, and in hundreds or perhaps thousands of less elaborate stone farmhouses that dot the rich farmland of eastern and central Pennsylvania.

German religious institutions also have added to Pennsylvania's architectural heritage. What has been called "the most distinctively Germanic church in Pennsylvania" was constructed in Trappe, probably about 1743, from a plan of a stone church drawn by the great Lutheran leader Henry Melchior Muhlenberg. Augustus Lutheran Church, with its characteristic high gable roof, has been little altered over the years. Communal groups of German origin also made their contributions. In Ephrata, Seventh Day Baptists, under the leadership of Conrad Beissel, built their Cloister and imbued it with the feeling of medieval Germany. Constructed of log, wood, and stone, the Saron (Sister's House) and the Saal (Church) show their Gothic heritage, with roofs medieval in height and steepness and the kick or bellcast always at the eaves. The Moravian buildings at Bethlehem, dating mostly from 1742 to 1770, are of stone and reflect the more gracious and less austere life led by Count von Zinzendorf's followers. Their Germanic gambrel roof lines, again with the familiar kick, proclaim the buildings' origin.

Perhaps the greatest German contribution to Pennsylvania architecture was in the introduction of refinements to Old World barn types—most notably in the bank barn, with its cantilevered overhanging loft. Early barns were generally of wood, but as means allowed, brick and especially stone were employed. Settlers moving south and west carried the Pennsylvania barn idiom with them.

The City: Architecture in Philadelphia, 1776

The cultural center of Pennsylvania in the eighteenth century was Philadelphia, which by the middle of the century had become the largest city in the colonies. The city had been carefully laid out according to a gridiron plan drawn up in 1682 by Captain Thomas

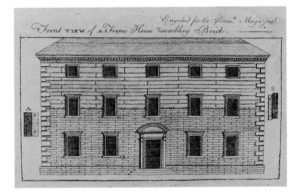

Symmetry was important in a Georgian house. Wood was often cut to resemble more costly brick and stone.

The Pennsylvania German House

In Europe what was to become the traditional Pennsylvania German house was often found in the corner of the cowbarn, with man and beast housed under one roof. Buildings like this were probably known in eighteenth-century America, but none survive. Moreover, it is probable that, given the abundant land and materials in the New World, the barnhouse custom soon died out.

The traditional Pennsylvania German house had a three-part floor plan. The entrance door led into the kitchen, a room that usually ran the entire width of the house. A huge walk-in fireplace stood along the inside kitchen wall. The remainder of the house was divided into a front parlor and a back bedroom. Many of the houses, particularly those built in the nineteenth century, had two front doors side-by-side, one to the kitchen and one to the parlor (leading many a casual observer to wonder what a "double" house is doing in the middle of the countryside). The parlor was heated by a five-plate stove fed through an opening in the back of the kitchen fireplace. The bedroom was unheated. Often a closed-in stairway, located in a corner of the kitchen, led to a loft or, if it were an especially fine house, to upstairs bedrooms. Floors in early houses were often hard-packed earth; in more substantial houses, wide random-width floorboards were the rule. Outside walls were usually of plaster over log or stone, and interior partitions were of vertical boards.

Paint, which was scarce, was used sparingly. Customarily, however, the interiors would be whitewashed each spring.

Two of the most noted Pennsylvania German houses are the log house at the Ephrata Cloister and the Hans Herr House, the oldest house in Lancaster County. The words "log" and "cabin" seem to go together. A cabin is generally a one-room house, and people are often surprised at the size log structures can attain. The Ephrata log house has the typical three-part floor plan, with the parlor used, as parlors often were, as a weaving shop. Many visitors do not realize at first that it is a log building, because the logs are covered. German log houses were seldom meant to be left uncovered. Sheathing made the houses more airtight and extended the life of the logs—and the owners avoided rechinking each spring. The Hans Herr House is a four-room variant of the more familiar floor plan in that there is a back room carved out of the rear portion of the kitchen. The high pitched roof is medieval in character and covers a two-story loft. The lower level of the loft was used for sleeping quarters and the upper level for storage. The roofing consists of hand-split oak shingles common to German houses, although thatch, clay tile, and slate were also used. The Ephrata log house and the Hans Herr House are only two of the hundreds of eighteenth-century German houses surviving in Pennsylvania.

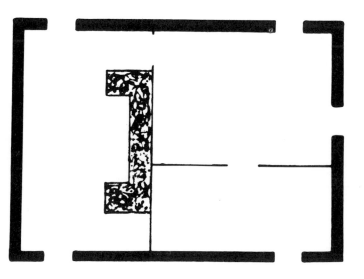

Floor plan of a typical
Pennsylvania German three-room house

The Hans Herr House in Lancaster County served for many years both as a home and as a Mennonite meeting house. It is now a museum.

Log house at the Ephrata Cloister

Modest row houses on a narrow Philadelphia street

Holme, William Penn's Surveyor General. The plan provided for the city to stretch from the Delaware River on the east to the Schuylkill River on the west, a distance of approximately two miles, while from north to south the city extended about one mile. Along the streets, which intersected at right angles and divided the city into 170 rectangular blocks, could be found paved sidewalks and some fine brick row houses rising as high as three stories and reflecting in style the London row houses that had been built following the great fire of 1666.

Although very little remains of the row houses, some excellent examples of the larger, free-standing homes of the eighteenth century are still to be seen in Philadelphia and the surrounding area. Such large, elegant, and well-constructed houses reflect the security and settled conditions in the eastern part of the state and remind us that by the eighteenth century the frontier had moved much farther to the west. They express, too, the rise of a wealthy class of merchants, ship owners, land proprietors, and the like, who sought to emulate the gracious living of the upper classes of English society. Along with their New England counterparts and the Southern tobacco growers, they became the principal source of art patronage in the colonies, especially in the areas of architecture and painting.

As the eighteenth century progressed, the influence of contemporary English architecture, in a style derived from the Italian Renaissance, became predominant in the city. Although not obvious in the ever-multiplying rows of ordinary houses, which customarily were not stylish, the new spirit marked the elaborate town houses of the

Second Street and Christ Church in Philadelphia

well-to-do merchants and professional leaders. Often simple in classical restraint outside, they were lavishly finished within. Perhaps the grandest surviving example of this genre is the Steadman-Powel House of 1765, located on South Third Street. The house's interiors are now divided among the Philadelphia Museum of Art, New York's Metropolitan Museum, and the house itself, which has been carefully restored. The rooms are of elegant Louis XV rococo design, rendered by Philadelphia craftsmen expert in woodworking, paneling, and carving. The excellent interior trim, which characterized Philadelphia town houses, is apparently the result of the practice of entrusting it to carvers and joiners rather than the builders of the house.

Georgian Philadelphia

The style of architecture prevalent along the eastern seaboard in the eighteenth century is usually designated by the term "Georgian" and is a late expression of the classical form of architecture that had been developing since the Renaissance. More often than not the design of eighteenth-century American homes was the work of an amateur or gentleman architect, often the owner himself, who was assisted by a master mason and guided by the numerous illustrated architectural handbooks imported from the Continent or, especially, from England. The engraved illustrations of such books provided him not only with ideas for the arrangement of the rooms but also with details of fireplaces, stairways, overmantles, windows,

Columb's Mag.

A South East View of Christ's Church.

300

Georgian Architecture in 1776

The American colonists acted out their rebellion in a Georgian architectural setting. The style that was modern and popular among the colonials had already become passé to the English, from whom the style had been borrowed. American Georgian architecture was a simplified version of the dominant style of Renaissance England, which was in turn a variation of Italian Renaissance style. Andrea Palladio designed carefully symmetrical neoclassical structures which had enormous influence on Sir Christopher Wren. After the Great Fire of London in 1660, Charles II charged Wren to design a number of churches as well as the Garden Front of Hampton Court Palace. Wren's subsequent influence in America is evident in the colonial tradition of church architecture.

Colonial towns and cities especially prized their stylish churches, of which Christ Church in Philadelphia was one of the most celebrated. The main body of this structure was built between 1727 and 1744; the steeple was added in 1754. During the deliberations that led to the drafting and signing of the Declaration of Independence, numerous delegates worshiped here. The building is a veritable catalogue of Georgian forms: the symmetry in window and door placement, the central great arched window flanked by two Venetian or Palladian windows, the heavy dentil molding along the eaves, and the balustrade at the roofline. The church's bell tower rose to a height of 196 feet—making it one of the tallest structures in colonial America and surely the city's most prominent landmark for those arriving at Philadelphia by ship.

By 1776, the style had become so popular that many of the great events of the Revolution took place in or around Georgian structures: the First Continental Congress met in Carpenters Hall; the Declaration of Independence was signed in the State House (Independence Hall); the Battle of Germantown was fought around Cliveden; and Benedict Arnold was motivated to turn traitor—at least in part—by the expense of Mount Pleasant, a great house he had extravagantly bought for his wife.

In short, the American Georgian style underlined the colonists' debt to English architecture, which paralleled their debts in music, literature, and political philosophy. The popularity of a modified Georgian style at a time when the English were more tempted toward neo-Gothic, Adamesque, and Baroque underlines not only the inevitable culture lag, but also the increasingly evident differences in American and British tastes.

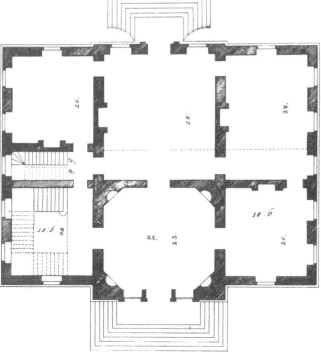

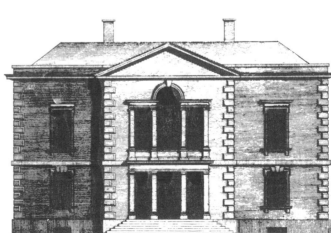

Drawings from English pattern book used by American architects

State House and street scene

doorways, and such, which could be copied exactly or adapted to suit his individual taste and needs by the skilled craftsmen responsible for the construction.

This high architectural style, reaching perfection within the colonies, is based on English interpretations of the Italian Renaissance forms. Although it is not entirely contemporary with the Georges, it is best known as the Georgian.

Buildings constructed in the Georgian idiom, in the so-called Golden Age of about 1725 to 1775—whether churches, public buildings, or homes—were marked with a devotion to symmetry and an attention to the refined, heavy detail so characteristic of the style. Among the most elegant Georgian structures constructed in Pennsylvania were the great country mansions built in and around Philadelphia. Most spectacular of all, on a hill high above the Schuylkill River, is Mount Pleasant, the masterpiece of the "Colonial Chain," a unique series of suburban estates which have been preserved in what is now Fairmount Park.

Captain John MacPherson's country seat of Mount Pleasant, built in 1768, is a veritable catalogue of Georgian forms. The building placements are a testament to the eighteenth-century worship of balance. The main house is flanked by two dependencies which, in turn, are flanked by two barns. Although the mansion stands in splendid isolation, there are no windows on the sides—presumably because such apertures would interfere with the balance of the room interiors. Two stories high, Mount Pleasant is finished in stucco and trimmed in brick; a belt course of red brick delineates the first and second floors. The corners of the central pavilion and of the building itself are emphasized and given a sense of strength with the use

This nineteenth-century watercolor recalls the Friends Meeting House and the Courthouse as they would have appeared in 1776.

of exposed large stones, or quoins. Its projecting central bay is pedimented, and above the doorway is the Palladian window so beloved by the builders of fine Georgian mansions.

Just as American building forms lagged behind their English counterparts, so the building styles of western Pennsylvania followed earlier trends in the east. This is perhaps nowhere better illustrated than in "Mt. Braddoc," the Isaac Meason House near Uniontown. Although built in 1802, the mansion reproduces many of the high fashion conceits of great houses built a quarter of a century earlier in the east.

Public Buildings in Colonial Philadelphia

Facades of homes were simple, but exterior architectural elegance was expressed in ecclesiastical and secular public buildings. An exception was the Friends' meeting house, which reflected simple Quaker tastes. Such structures as the Greater Meeting House in Philadelphia, built in 1755, or its country counterpart, Buckingham Meeting House in Lahaska, resemble large plain houses. The Anglicans, however, felt no such restraint. When Christ Church was designed, consciously to be *the* Church of the Episcopalians of Philadelphia, its designers (most notably the physician John Kearsley) looked to the London churches of Christopher Wren for their inspiration, as an earlier generation had looked to other Renaissance sources when the State House was constructed between 1732 and 1756. The State House, better known today as Independence Hall, was designed by Andrew Hamilton, a lawyer and speaker of the Pennsylvania Assembly, in a form that resembles an elongated Georgian house. The tower and steeple, completed after his death, are reminiscent of Wren's church towers and give a welcome relief to the building's largely horizontal lines.

One of the most important buildings of the revolutionary period was Carpenters' Hall. Originally built in 1770 as headquarters for the Carpenters Company, a guild of the city's master carpenters and builders, it is a modest but elegantly decorated structure, built in the form of a Greek cross, with plenty of light wood trim, handsome arched windows, and balustrades. Carpenters' Hall was the meeting place of the first Continental Congress in 1774. A tablet outside is inscribed: "Within these walls, Henry, Hancock, and Adams inspired the delegates of the Colonies with nerve and sinew for the toils of war."

Interiors and Furnishings in Colonial Pennsylvania

Throughout the eighteenth century the interiors of Georgian houses were richly decorated. The focal point of the large central hallway was usually the staircase, with its lathe-turned balusters culminating in a newel post. The walls of the individual rooms were sometimes covered from floor to ceiling with handsomely carved wood paneling, most often on the fireplace wall, which was the aesthetic focal point of each room. More frequently, paneling extended from floor to waist height, with plaster walls above.

The style names attached to the furniture of the period are Queen Anne and Chippendale. Both reflected the influence of the baroque and the rococo. Whereas earlier furniture emphasized the straight line, these styles incorporated the curve. Carving became fashionable. The most favored furniture woods were walnut for Queen Anne furniture and mahogany for Chippendale. Furniture made in Philadelphia was especially desirable, and the names of William Savery and Benjamin Randolph are associated with furniture of the highest quality.

The furnishing of an elegant home in 1776 would present a few surprises. Venetian blinds were common. Wall-to-wall carpeting was used in the parlors of the wealthy. This was highly patterned imported Wilton carpeting, laid in narrow strips. Most of the other rooms in the house had bare wood floors or floors partially covered by rag rugs. Occasionally oriental carpets were used on floors, or painted canvas treated with varnish, the forerunner of linoleum. Everywhere deep colors were used. The poor whitewashed their walls out of economic necessity, but the rich used paints of deep reds, blues, and greens. For practical reasons, baseboards were often painted black. If possible, imported wallpaper, often with oriental motifs, was hung in the principal room. This paper was usually hand

Philadelphia Chippendale side chair

A fine example of a Chippendale highboy, probably made in Northumberland County

This trade card advertises elaborate Chippendale style furniture made by a Philadelphia cabinetmaker.

The Port Royal Parlor was moved to the Henry
Francis du Pont Winterthur Museum, reassembled,
and furnished with a fine collection of Philadelphia
Chippendale furniture.

Advertisement for Windsor chairs

Colonial Pennsylvania's Furniture

While eighteenth-century Pennsylvania became a significant American center for the production of elegant and elaborate furniture designed to appeal to affluent followers of fashion and high style, the bulk of the furniture produced during the colonial period—probably at least eighty percent—was of the timeless, simple, and utilitarian sort that was serviceable to the average family.

The Windsor or "stick" chair originated in England in the seventeenth century, and was first produced in the colonies about 1725. But the Windsor style eventually came to be regarded as among the most typically American and graceful kinds of cheap furniture. Pennsylvania versions of the Windsor chair were acknowledged to be especially well-made so that Philadelphia chairmakers found a demand for their wares in the other continental colonies as well as in the West Indies. Characteristically lighter than their English counterparts, American Windsor chairs and benches were painted—frequently a dull green which ages until it is almost black—because they were invariably made of several different kinds of wood. The spindles might be made of hickory (favored as a strong wood that had "spring" and would not splinter), the seats of oak or maple, and the legs of maple, birch, ash, or chestnut. The Windsor chair, the sturdy stretcher-based table, the blanket chest, durable benches and stools, and simple bedsteads were mainstays of the average

eighteenth-century Pennsylvanian's furnishings—and such pieces were often to be found in the less public rooms of the fashionable house as well.

The pieces most prominently on display in fashionable Pennsylvania homes during the revolutionary era were likely to be in styles that reflected the rise of the Baroque in Europe: Queen Anne and Chippendale. Queen Anne furniture was characterized by cabriole legs, curvaceous, flowing vertical lines, and the widespread use of the shell motif. Most high-style Pennsylvania Queen Anne furniture was made of walnut. Chippendale, the later of the two styles, was named for Thomas Chippendale, an English furniture maker who in 1754 issued the first edition of his influential work The Gentleman and Cabinet-Maker's Director, being a collection of the most Elegant and Useful Designs of Household Furniture in the Most Fashionable Taste. Chippendale incorporated into furniture design such elaborate and exotic elements as the yoke back of the mandarin chair. As might be expected, the finest Pennsylvania Chippendale furniture was produced in Philadelphia, and the grouping in the Port Royal parlor represents the finest of the fine. Collectors of eighteenth-century American furniture especially prize Philadelphia Chippendale (much of which was done in imported mahogany) for its graceful lines and rich, ambitious carving.

Windsor "stick" chairs have clean, functional lines

This Queen Anne chair is attributed to William Savery, an important Philadelphia cabinetmaker.

Chair used in the sickroom of the Moravian Brethren's house in Bethlehem is typical of Moravian wing chairs with Queen Anne legs.

colored and came in sheets rather than rolls. To imitate the expensive wallpaper, walls sometimes were decorated with stenciled designs.

There were no dining rooms in the modern sense. The wealthy ate their main meals in parlors on gate-leg or drop-leaf tables that were set up and extended at meal time. The tableware was especially interesting. Forks had two or three tines and were still primarily stabbing implements. Knives were broad-bladed, and food, including peas, often was lifted to the mouth on them. People in fine homes ate off pewter or china dishes and drank wine from glasses, sometimes mended by the insertion of brass rivets. Glass was very precious. Although some glass was American-made at places like Baron Stiegel's glassworks, most of it was imported. Elegant homes also used silver on the table. Silverware and serving pieces had a special value before the days of banks. People were very conscious of how many pounds of silver they had "laid in plate" or made into silver utensils. Having a silversmith form silver into useful items would identify one's wealth, making it less tempting to thieves.

In the less affluent houses most people ate from wooden or redware plates, in the kitchen. Kitchen implements in rich houses and average ones greatly resembled one another. A more affluent house might have a clockwork jack to turn the roast before the open fire, but in all houses the common kitchen utensils were made of wrought iron, wood, or clay. Red clay, common throughout Pennsylvania, was lead-glazed and known universally as redware. It was cheap and could be formed into storage jars, mixing bowls, and jugs. Salt-glazed stoneware made from white clay was more durable, though less common, and served the same functions as redware. Baskets were indispensable; most were made of split oak or ryegrass and hickory splits. Bowls carved out of burls were especially prized for their lightness and durability.

Furniture in the kitchen was less fashionable than that found in the parlors. The timeless stretcher-based table and ladderback or Windsor chairs (often called "stick furniture") were common. In the ordinary house a "settle," or high back bench, stood near the fireplace. It was an especially desirable place to sleep during the winter. In the average house beds were rare, often only one or two in a household. Children shared beds (three or four to a bed was not uncommon), or they slept on stuffed ticks on the floor: in front of the fire in winter, in the loft in summer.

In the average home, chairs were much less common than today. In many houses there was only one—for father. Everyone else sat on benches or stools. Chairs, by and large, were a mark of status, and the middle class might have several in the parlor. Floors in the average home were bare, although some rag carpets were used. In the Pennsylvania German household some of the furniture would be brightly painted in traditional design to brighten the plain interior.

One or two beds, a chair, stools, benches, a table or two, and several storage chests on bare floors—these comprised the worldly goods of a typical family. Although the house and goods of the rich man in Philadelphia in 1776 might be opulent, the surprise to modern eyes is how little the average colonial Pennsylvanian owned, and how spare was his life.

Pewter sugar bowl.
Bowls of this type were often used as
Communion vessels.

This pear shaped, or Queen Anne,
pewter teapot is one of the most delight-
ful shapes of all pewter hollow ware.

A pewter flagon (left) and coffee pot (right) made by William Will. Pewter is an alloy of tin and copper with a low melting point. It often contains small amounts of lead and antimony. Pewter items are made by casting in bronze molds. A pewterer usually had only a few molds, and therefore used the cast parts interchangeably on various vessels. Note the similarity of the individual parts of the above two pieces.

310

William Will—Patriot and Pewterer

William Will, the "Paul Revere of American pewter," was born in the Rhine Valley of Germany in 1742 and migrated with his parents to New York in 1752. As a young man he went to Philadelphia and established himself as a pewterer. An honest and robust man, Will was quick to gain the respect and confidence of his fellow Philadelphians. He was a distinguished soldier, patriot, and craftsman who served his community and country during and after the War for Independence. In 1776, the youthful Will hastened to organize an infantry group known as "Captain Will's Company of Associators." The following year he was appointed, along with Charles Willson Peale, Commissioner for the Seizure of Personal Effects of Traitors in Philadelphia. Between 1777 and 1780 he served as Lieutenant-Colonel of the First Battalion and as Commander, first of Colonel Jacob's Third Battalion and later of the Third Regiment of Foot. In 1779 Will also served as Commissioner for Collecting Salt. Will's distinguished service led to his election as high sheriff of Philadelphia in 1780, 1781, and 1782. In 1785 the citizenry of Philadelphia elected Benjamin Franklin Councilor and sent as representatives to the General Assembly Robert Morris and William Will.

William Will's distinguished career as a servant of the American Revolutionary Cause and in the government of the young Republic was paralleled by his accomplishments as a pewterer. He was a superb and inventive craftsman. His work is invariably fine, and it illustrates a distinction and individuality rarely encountered in the work of other American pewterers. His flagons are without parallel and his coffeepots are among the most elegant which have survived. In American pewter, those rare examples of marked flagons made before 1790 fall into two distinctive types: the Lancaster, Pennsylvania, and the William Will types. Will's inventiveness can be seen in both the flagon and coffeepot here. The design of these two pieces is borrowed from the customary form of eighteenth-century silver coffeepots. The flagon, with its elegant beading and dramatic adaptation of the coffeepot form, challenges the more ordinary straight-sided flagons which are usually encountered. The design of the handle of this flagon is English in origin. The spout, however, is from a Germanic tradition. By incorporating elements of different traditions into a single piece, Will achieved his daring designs.

A similar adaptation of design can be seen in the coffeepot. That elegant piece, standing nearly sixteen inches tall, is graced by a square base and finely proportioned finial. It embodies the finest elements of American eighteenth-century pewter. The other coffeepots, teapots, and the several tankards seen here display the great range of Will's accomplishment. The quality of William Will's craftsmanship and his daring use of ambitious designs set a standard by which the products of other American pewterers are measured.

Corner cupboard with pewterware attributed to William Will

311

The Road to Independence

Paul Revere came riding into Philadelphia on May 19, 1774, bearing dispatches and letters from Boston. At the London Coffee House at Front and Market streets he found a curious and eager crowd, who already knew that the British Parliament had determined to punish Massachusetts for the destruction of East India Company tea by closing the port of Boston and placing the city under military rule. Revere brought a copy of resolutions of a Boston Town Meeting and letters for important Philadelphians, notably Thomas Mifflin, Joseph Reed, and Charles Thomson. All these messages were immediately read aloud. The resolutions urged an intercolonial boycott of importations from Britain until the obnoxious measures were repealed—the tactic which had proved successful in destroying the Stamp Act in 1765. The letters described the details of the British actions, and pointed out the danger to all if Parliament could close off trade and set up military rule in a colony without encountering local resistance.

Excitement and apprehension mounted as the implications of the documents became clear. British action at Boston threatened everyone, and effective response demanded unified action by the colonials. That meant some kind of intercolonial congress, and as British troops formed part of the threat, the prospect loomed of an ultimate confrontation between these and some type of colonial troops. But first a response had to be made to the Boston resolutions; and to ascertain the sense of the people, Reed, Thomson, and Mifflin called a Philadelphia town meeting. The invitation appealed most to those who were hot for resistance and who sought to exclude pacifists and those who thought Boston ought to be punished for the hoodlumism of the Tea Party. But the radical separatists knew they needed the support of the political element then strongest in Philadelphia and in Pennsylvania as a whole: the moderates. Of these, John Dickinson, author of the famed *Letters from a Farmer in Pennsylvania*, stood as the acknowledged captain. To give the town meeting political respectability, he had to be on the platform. The three radicals, on the morning of May 20, set out for Dickinson's home, Fairhill, to persuade him to chair the meeting that evening.

BENEVOLENCE *of temper towards each other*, and UNANIMITY *of councils*, are essential to the welfare of the whole— and . . . for this reason, every man amongst us, who in any manner would encourage either *dissension*, *diffidence*, or *indifference*, between these colonies, is an enemy to *himself*, and to *his country*.

John Dickinson

The Repeal—
Or The Funeral of Miss Ame-Stamp

After a morning's discussion, Dickinson acceded, but he changed his mind over the lunch hour and by late afternoon still resisted all the arguments of his callers. Thomson told Reed and Mifflin to go into the city to stall the opening of the meeting until he arrived with Dickinson. In the Long Room of the City Tavern on Second Street near Walnut, a crowd of some three hundred jammed together, representing everyone from the restrained Quakers to the most violent of the radical partisans. As the time to call the meeting to order passed, arguments on the floor became louder and more bitter. People shouted for Reed to open the meeting, and it was all he could do to prevent the pair who were to serve as co-chairmen, Thomas Willing and Edward Pennington, from sounding the gavel. At length, after what seemed an endless delay, the door opened and Charles Thomson came in, bringing John Dickinson with him.

The meeting then began with Reed explaining the messages from Boston. Thomson was supposed to follow with a fire-and-brimstone speech in support of Boston's plea for help, but he was so exhausted from two days' exertions without sleep that he spoke only a sentence or two. All should make common cause with Boston, he said, then fainted and had to be carried out. At this point, John Dickinson took command. As he arose to speak the hall grew quiet, for the assembly recognized him as a wise and cautious leader and as the one whose

Repeal of the Stamp Act, a political broadside published in England in 1766, shows "Mr. Stamper" (George Grenville, author of the Stamp Act) carrying the tiny coffin of "Miss Ame-Stamp," dead after just one year. The other mourners were all proponents of the act in England. The family vault, in which the coffin is to be placed, houses the remains of previous unpopular taxes, while bales of stamps, returned from America, and black cloth for mourners sit on the wharf.

advice they valued. An epitome of Pennsylvania, he was thought too radical by the conservatives, and too conservative by the radicals. He expressed the sympathy of all for Massachusetts, asked the meeting to adopt resolutions calling on the governor to convene the Assembly, and urged the Assembly to take "every legal step" to redress colonial grievances. With these modest proposals the meeting broke up, to the dissatisfaction of some and the relief of others. Before adjourning, the meeting set up a committee, composed of both moderates and radicals, to draft Pennsylvania's reply to Massachusetts. Their letter proposed that England should rescind its punitive acts, and that to cool the current crisis it might be wise for Boston to pay for the tea its inhabitants had destroyed. An intercolonial congress would deal officially with Britain, holding a boycott on British goods as a measure of last resort. This document, so typically middlish, so typically Pennsylvanian, infuriated some of the ardent, arrogant Bostonians, but gave a sense of prudence and sanity to the slowly unfolding drama of revolution.

Arousing the "Peaceable Kingdom"

Pacific Pennsylvania indeed would be hard to arouse to the point of wishing independence from the mother country, much less of bearing arms against fellow countrymen loyal to the Crown. Many factors combined to make Penn's province slow to respond to revolutionary overtures. The politically dominant Quakers, allied with the German sectarians, abhorred violence and foreswore war. They realized that the very charter of 1681, which created the colony, had stated that both the provincial government and the British Parliament had the right to tax the inhabitants. Moreover, the hand of British rule had rested very lightly upon colonial Pennsylvania from the day of its founding. No royal governors flaunted their privilege, nor did the Church of England carry much influence here. The German settlers had almost no contact with the British government, while the Scotch-Irish held less hostility toward Parliament than they did toward the politically dominant Quakers, who resisted protecting the frontier settlements against Indians.

At the same time, William Penn's sons, who had returned to the Anglican fold, held influence in the royal Privy Council—especially Thomas Penn, who often gained favors for his colony. After unsuccessfully fighting against the Iron Act of 1750, he made no great effort to see it rigidly enforced in his province, where ironmaking was a major industry. In 1751, he won Pennsylvania's exclusion from the restrictions placed on the issue of paper currency in other colonies, a privilege he could gain because his colonial government had scrupulously backed its paper issues by silver bullion and refused to print notes above its ability to redeem them in metal. Ex-

MAGNA Britania her Colonies REDUC'D.

EXPLANATION

The above Prophetical Emblem, of what wou'd be the Miserable State of Great Britain and her Colonies, Should She persist in restraining their Trade, destroying their Currency, and Taxing their People by Laws made by a Legislature, where they are not Represented.

The Author, with a Sagacity and Invention natural to himself, has compriz'd in one View, under the Character of Belisarius, the late Flourishing State of Great Britain, in the Zenith of Glory and Honour; with her Fall into the most Abject State of Disgrace Misery and Ruin. Belisarius was one of the Greatest Heroes of the Antients, He lived under Iustinian the Emperor. He Gain'd a Victory over and concluded an Honourable Peace with Cabades King of Persia; Took Carthage and Subdued Gilimer the Usurper of the Crown of the Vandals, Overthrew Vitigas and refused the Throne of the Goths when offer'd to him; Rebuilt the Walls of Rome after they were distroy'd by Totila, and performed many other Military Atchievments too tedious to enumerate. In this Part of his Character is represented the late Succesful and Flourishing State of Great Britain, which aided the King of Prussia against the Powerful Armies of Hungary and Russia; Supported Portugal against the Spaniards, and reduc'd France and Spain to the most Advantageous Terms of Accommodation.

By the latter Part of Belisarius's Life is represented the Unhappy and Miserable State of Great Britain, should the late Measures against America take Place. This General at length being Accused of a Conspiracy against Iustinian, That Emperor barbarously Ordered his Eyes to be pulled out, which reduced him to the Greatest Poverty, and Obliged him to Subsist on the Alms of others. The Motto is also Striking, and elegantly Expressive of this Truth Date Obolum Belisario-Give Poor Belisarius a Penny.

View the Countenance of Great Britain under this Character, and you Percieve nothing but Abject Despondency; Her Eyes, and the Stumps of her mangled Arms raised towards Heaven in Vain. Behold her Colonies; the Source of Her Commerce, Wealth and Glory, Separated from her Body, and no longer Useful to her. The Famous English Oak Deprived of its Wide Extended Top and late flourishing Branches, save a few, and those with its Body wither'd and Decay'd. The Ground Beneath it producing nothing but Bryars and Thorns. The British Ships, the Instruments of her Trade, with Broom on their Topmasts, denoting that they are Advertized for Sale, being no longer either necessary or Useful to her People. Her Sheild which she is incapable of Weilding, laying useless by her. The Laurel Branch droping from the hand of Pennsylvania, which She is render'd unable to retain. And in Fine, Britania herself Sliding of the World, no longer Courted by the Powers of Europe; No longer Able to Sustain its Ballance; No longer respected or Known among Nations.

Moral.

The Political Moral of this Picture is Now easily discovered, History affords us many Instances, of the Ruin of States, by the Prosecution of Measures, ill Suited to the Temper and Genius of its People, The Ordaining of Laws in favour of one Part of the Nation to the Prejudice and Oppresion of Another; is certainly the most erroneous & Mistaken Policy. An Equal Dispensation of Protection Rights Priviledges and Advantages, is what every Part is entitled to, And ought to enjoy: It being a Matter of no Moment to the State whether a Subject grows Rich and flourishing on the Thames or Ohio, in Edinburgh or Dublin. These Measures Never fail to Create great and Violent Jealousies and Animositys between the People favoured and the People Oppressed. From whence a total Separation of Affections Interests, Political Obligations and all manner of Connections necessarily Ensue, by which the whole State is Weakened and perhaps ruined forever.

Engraved in Philadelphia.

A political cartoon designed by Franklin in 1776

cept for a brief awkwardness during the French and Indian War over the funding of military measures, the relations between Pennsylvania and the home government had been peaceful and untroubled. Meanwhile, the local economy was thriving. Philadelphia had become the largest city in North America and led all others in ocean commerce. The Germans had made a garden plot of the interior farms, and the Scotch-Irish pushed the frontier ever westward, opening up new land to cultivation. Life had been good to Pennsylvanians. They had neither need nor cause to revolt.

Uneasiness in Colonial Pennsylvania

The first tremors of unease seized the Scotch-Irish frontiersmen when, in 1763, the Crown forbade colonial settlement of lands west of the mountains and placed the Indian trade under royal control. Pennsylvania had purchased part of the transmontane region from the Iroquois Confederation in 1754 (although some Indians never accepted the sale). Moreover, Pennsylvanians had helped the British defeat the French and their Indian allies at Fort Duquesne in 1758. Now a royal edict evicted the western settlers in favor of their late enemies, the Indians. To the westerners, the Proclamation of 1763 damaged relations with the mother country more seriously than any subsequent regulation.

Many aspects of the British "New Colonial Policy" affected Pennsylvania less than they affected other colonies. Benjamin Franklin, colonial agent in London in 1765, initially supported the Stamp Act, and his Philadelphia newspaper urged compliance. Not the artisans and common laborers, but the rich and well-born merchants enforced the boycott of English goods and aroused the anti-Stamp Act mobs. Pennsylvania had no complaint about the Declaratory Act because its own charter said the same thing: Parliament could tax Englishmen, including Pennsylvania Englishmen. The Townshend Acts of 1767, which imposed new import taxes, irritated New York and Massachusetts more than they did Pennsylvania by requiring that these colonies use colonial funds to provide barracks and living necessities for British troops stationed there. But Pennsylvania did enter its lively protest against a provision of the Townshend laws that assigned all customs duties collected in the colonies to pay the salaries of Crown officers serving in the provinces—governors, judges, customs agents, and others. Formerly the provincial assemblies had voted these salaries, and this practice had given the colonial legislators a powerful political weapon in dealing with the home government. Furthermore, the 1767 acts created a new customs service, which rigorously enforced collection of the import taxes to stop the smuggling that had become almost routine practice under the old colony-managed customs system. These new rules put

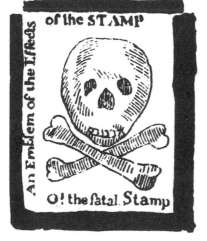

From The Pennsylvania Journal, *1765*

the administrative establishment of the colonies beyond local control. Resistance began immediately in the form of agitation, non-importation agreements, and attacks on revenue agents and their patrol vessels. Boston, center of violence, was placed under military rule for nine months. Massachusetts, in another circular letter, called for a renewal of the boycott, but the Pennsylvania Assembly refused to endorse this move.

John Dickinson: The Penman of the Revolution

As outrage mounted, John Dickinson set to work preparing a series of *Letters from a Farmer in Pennsylvania*, which were serialized in newspapers and later were reprinted as a collection. His letters circulated widely and became the polemical ammunition of the radicals until the appearance of Thomas Paine's *Common Sense* in 1776. Dickinson would have been more surprised than anyone to learn that he had become "The Penman of the Revolution," for he was essentially a conservative, and his letters tried to make a point in British constitutional law which might have staved off the Revolution had London paid any attention. Parliament, he wrote, had unquestioned power to regulate imperial trade as it saw fit, but it did not possess the power to legislate for the colonies where revenue was the primary objective. His argument was legalistic and dispassionate, but it gave the radicals a handle by which they could easily twist Dickinson's argument into the assertion that Parliament had no constitutional basis for legislating for the colonies at all.

Let these *truths* be indelibly impressed on our minds—*that we cannot be* HAPPY, *without being* FREE—that we cannot be free, *without being secure in our property*—that *we* cannot be secure in our property, *if, without our consent, others may, as by right, take it away*—that *taxes imposed on us by parliament*, do thus take it away—that *duties laid for the sole purpose of raising money*, are taxes—that *attempts* to lay such duties *should be instantly and firmly opposed*—that this opposition can never be effectual, *unless it is the united effort of these provinces.* . . .

John Dickinson

"Where Complaining is a Crime"

Uproar over the Townshend Acts had begun to die down in Pennsylvania when a harsh, dictatorial British response to the Massachusetts Circular Letter sent a new shockwave through the province. Even the leading local conservatives were roused to anger by the British presumption that a formal statement of colonial grievances bordered on treason. They could agree with Benjamin Franklin's remark upon his dismissal as colonial postmaster general by the ministry in January: "Where complaining is a crime, hope becomes despair." Town meetings in Philadelphia brought pressure on the Assembly until it forwarded a Pennsylvania petition of grievances to the Privy Council. Public demand forced the Philadelphia merchants to join belatedly in the nonimportation movement in 1769. The colonial tumult and the decrease of commerce induced Parliament to repeal all the import duties except that on tea in 1770. But serious damage had been done, mainly from the arrogant and contemptuous treatment of the colonists by the home ministry.

The TIMES are Dreadful, Dismal Doleful Dolorous, and DOLLAR-LESS.

Sentiment of the day as expressed in The Pennsylvania Journal *in 1765*

Pennsylvania and the Boston Massacre

The Boston Massacre, a direct outgrowth of this attitude, had little impact on Pennsylvania. The Quakers had suffered severely from Puritan intolerance a century before. Massachusetts had banished the sect, and had hanged four Quakers on Boston Common; Connecticut had ordered that any Friend, returning after expulsion, should have his tongue bored through with a hot iron. These events of earlier times had not been forgotten. Nor did the Germans have any love for the sharp Yankee traders who traveled the Dutch country. Finally, in 1769, the very year of the Boston Massacre, New England Yankees had moved into the Wyoming Valley—where Connecticut's sea-to-sea claim conflicted with the royal grant to William Penn—provoking a six-year series of skirmishes called the Pennamite Wars. Unruly mobs might suit Boston, but not Philadelphia, and few Pennsylvanians sympathized with the victims of New England mob violence.

Pennsylvania and the Boston Tea Party

Tax collector being tarred and feathered

The Tea Act of 1773 was another matter, for this strange law, while reducing the price of tea, retained the import tax on it and thus challenged directly John Dickinson's main article of faith, that Parliament had no power to impose duties "for the sole purpose of raising a revenue." Some Bostonians responded actively on December 16, 1773, when a cadre of vigilantes disguised as Indians broke into a British tea ship and destroyed its cargo. Pennsylvanians responded with threats but more restrained action. For several months before the expected arrival of their tea ship, handbills appeared on Philadelphia tavern bulletin boards threatening death to the ship's captain and to any "damned traitorous pilot who brought up the tea ship" from Chester. These printed notices bore the signature: "The Committee for Tarring and Feathering." When the ship, *Polly*, arrived at Chester on Christmas day, a committee brought the captain to Philadelphia, and on December 27 the largest public meeting in the city's history was held in State House yard to adopt a series of resolutions, the main theme being that Captain Ayres should promptly sail his ship back to England without unloading the tea.

The felonies committed on the tea ship at Boston precipitated punitive action against Massachusetts so patently vindictive that the whole colonial seaboard awoke to a sense of need for some kind of self-protective action. It was this message that Paul Revere brought to Philadelphia on May 19 of the following year, 1774, just after word arrived from England of the Parliamentary response to the Boston Tea Party. And the Philadelphia town meeting of May 20, where the local radicals thought John Dickinson's presence so indispensable, was the Pennsylvania response.

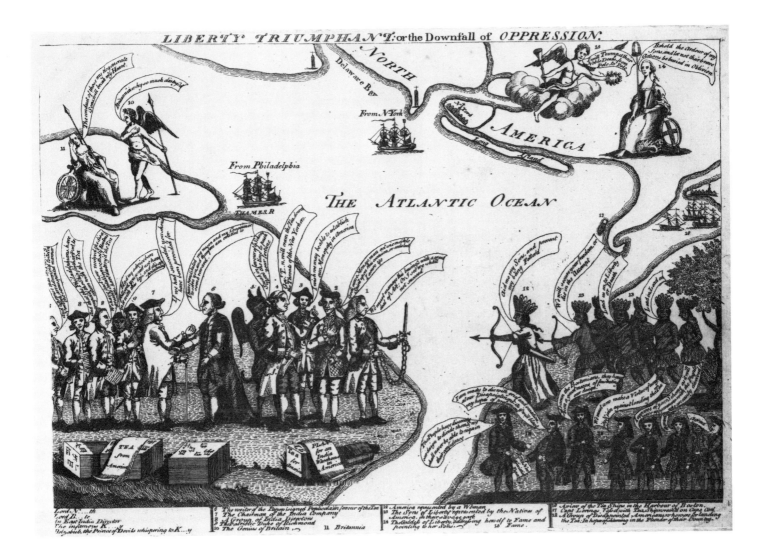

The Continental Congress Comes to Philadelphia

The resolutions of the Philadelphia town meeting of May 20 fell short of the hopes of the radicals, but they represented a wide concurrence in the need for an intercolonial congress to consider a continental course of action. Dickinson, Thomson, Reed, Mifflin, and George Clymer promptly called on Governor John Penn to ask him to convene the Assembly, but he refused. In the meantime letters began to arrive from inland town meetings endorsing the call for a continental congress. The Philadelphia leaders then called another town meeting for June 18 to consider further action. This meeting brought out nearly as large a crowd as had assembled to turn back the tea ship. It appointed a committee to correspond with action-minded leaders in all the counties, who would be instructed to appoint local delegates to a provincial conference that, in the absence of Assembly action, would proceed to name Pennsylvania's delegates to a continental congress. This seizure of the initiative led Governor

This 1778 cartoon depicts the triumphant forces of liberty (right) taking aim at the British leaders of government and industry. America is represented by a woman supported by the Sons of Liberty dressed in savage garb. At the top left Britannia laments the conduct of her degenerate sons, while the top right shows the Goddess of Liberty proudly observing the brave actions of hers. The bottom left shows tea the Americans returned. Disgruntled Tories are at the bottom right.

319

Penn to reverse himself and summon the Assembly to meet on July 18, 1774. Meanwhile, local committees of correspondence organized meetings to choose delegates to the provincial conference, which went into session a day before the Assembly was to meet. Since it was clear that if the Assembly did not name Pennsylvania delegates to a continental congress, the unofficial conference would do so, the Assemblymen approved the idea of a congress and named as delegates to it Joseph Galloway, Charles Humphreys, and Samuel Rhoads, all moderates, and Thomas Mifflin, Edward Biddle, John Morton, and George Ross, all radicals. As other colonies took action, plans emerged for a First Continental Congress to convene in Philadelphia on September 5, 1774, to frame unified answers to mounting colonial grievances.

The political situation in Pennsylvania had become highly unstable by the fall of 1774. In a province where most free men could vote—provided they met a relatively modest property qualification—and where the practice of religious toleration and the existence of a flourishing economy had attracted a more heterogeneous population than any other colony, political fragmentation might be expected. Yet, for nearly a century, the voters had maintained a fairly clear division between the Proprietary faction, whose primary loyalties were to the Penn family, and those who favored the elected lower house of the provincial legislature, the Assembly. The Proprietary faction, since William Penn's death in 1718 and the return of his sons to the Anglican fold, had attracted the support of the wealthier people, landowners, administrative servants, many Anglicans, and the Scotch-Irish Presbyterians of the frontier. They held to generally conservative policies, wishing to maintain adequate defenses against French and Indian threats, to dispossess the Indians of their land as rapidly as possible, to uphold sound fiscal practices, and to cooperate with the British government. The locus of power for this group was the governor, or chief Proprietor. An Anti-Proprietary faction, composed largely of Quakers and Germans and later joined by many Philadelphia merchants and workingmen, held firm control of the Assembly most of the time. The Assembly kept a tight rein on finances, refused to supply funds for frontier defense or military aid in the wars against France, sided with the Indians in land controversies, wanted inflationary money, and hoped to rid themselves of the Penns and their friends as an administrative establishment.

Men like John Dickinson, Justice William Allen, Robert Morris, and John Penn led the Proprietary group, while Benjamin Franklin, Joseph Galloway, the Norrises, and the Pembertons had traditionally managed the Anti-Proprietary policies. In 1755, Franklin and Galloway welded the Anti-Proprietary elements into an Assembly party, drawing support from associations of small merchants and tradesmen, called White Oaks and Hearts of Oak, until these clubs

Franklin's famous cartoon first appeared in 1754 in his Pennsylvania Gazette.

broke with the "Old Ticket" in 1770 for being too conciliatory toward the British government. Meanwhile, in 1764, the Proprietary elements, under Presbyterian leadership, had formed a Proprietary party or "New Ticket."

As late as 1774, the three original counties—Philadelphia, Bucks, and Chester—elected twice as many assemblymen as the other eight counties combined. This centralization of eastern power kept the Quaker-German combination in firm control of the Assembly, despite the defection of some of the western German farmers and Philadelphia tradesmen from the Assembly party. But these divisions had been based upon Pennsylvania issues, and when the imperial difficulties began to overshadow the provincial troubles, the lines of traditional loyalty broke. Judge Allen took the lead in attacking the Stamp Act, whereas Benjamin Franklin at first supported it. Mild and cautious John Dickinson produced the clarion call for resistance to usurpation of power by Parliament, but was horrified at the thought of independence. Many new names appeared on the scene as the struggle developed: Charles Thomson, Timothy Matlack, James Cannon, Robert Whitehill, George Bryan, and Benjamin Rush—men whose animosity toward the proprietary government of Pennsylvania equaled their hostility to the British ministry. By September 1774, the positions of these people had not yet solidified. Many would face heart-rending anguish in the choice between sustaining traditional loyalties or trampling them underfoot to ally themselves with old political rivals and new political objectives.

Into this bewildering political atmosphere came the delegations to the First Continental Congress, drifting into Philadelphia from north and south at the end of August. Philadelphia leaders had been

Timothy Matlack

This handsome Georgian structure, a carpenters' guild hall, stands near Independence Hall in Philadelphia. It was chosen as the site of the first Continental Congress specifically because it was not a government building.

warned to caution the Massachusetts delegation of four, including "the brace of Adamses," Samuel and John, to restrain themselves, for many believed that they were agitators for independence. Mifflin, Dr. Rush, and some others met the New Englanders at Frankford to tell them that Pennsylvanians suspected they might be too headstrong and rash, perhaps even wishing separation from England. Said the Philadelphians, "You must not utter the word independence, or give the least hint or insinuation of the idea. No one dares to speak of it here."

No meeting place had been agreed on for the Congress, but Joseph Galloway, Speaker of the Pennsylvania Assembly, invited the delegates to use its quarters in the main hall of the State House, while the Assembly would use the second floor. The Carpenters Company of Philadelphia also offered its newly constructed hall just off Chestnut Street. On September 5 the delegates met at the City Tavern and paraded as a body to inspect Carpenters' Hall. Impressed by its roominess, its privacy, its library, and the wide hallway where one could hold private discussions, the delegation voted on the spot to accept the Carpenters' invitation. Galloway frowned in disbelief, for the decision was a slap not only at him but also at the conservative Pennsylvania Assembly, which had so recently suggested that Boston might well pay for the tea dumped into her harbor. The two Adamses had kept discreetly quiet, but there seemed to be unmistakable evidence of some clever advance planning. The delegates chose Peyton Randolph of Virginia as their chairman, and then proposed Charles Thomson, "a gentleman of family, fortune and character in this city" as secretary. Galloway could not believe his ears, for Thomson, "the Sam Adams of Philadelphia," was not even a delegate—thanks to Galloway's influence. A preconcerted action against the conservatives showed clearly in these moves, and just as clearly the radicals had won.

The fifty-six delegates, mostly strangers to each other, constituted a remarkable body, and Philadelphia gave them a warm reception, as befitted both the distinction of the guests and the pride of the "Athens of America." From Virginia came Patrick Henry, George Washington, and Richard Henry Lee. Roger Sherman came from Connecticut, Thomas McKean from Delaware, and John Jay from New York. They all professed amazement at the conviviality and high living of a city reputed to reflect Quaker frugality and simplicity. But many could have testified to the accuracy of John Adams' diary: "a most sinful feast again. Curds and creams, sweetmeats, twenty sort of tarts, fools, trifles, floating island, whipped sillibubs. Parmesan cheese, punch, wine, porter, beer."

Though the First Continental Congress was mainly a body of moderates, its initial decisions favoring the radical viewpoint correctly forecast the tenor of its proceedings. During the first week a loud knock at the door interrupted the session and a post-rider entered carrying an urgent message from Massachusetts. President Randolph broke the seals and read to the stunned delegates that British troops had killed a number of Bostonians while seizing the colonists' powder stores, and that British cannon had fired on Boston all that night. Congress immediately adjourned and the news spread wildly through Philadelphia. Soon the State House bell began to toll. It was evident that war had started, and that the time for taking sides had arrived. No place for moderates now, no room for compromise! British arms had levied war on Massachusetts.

Congress could do nothing until further details of the frightful occurrence arrived. In two days the awaited news came. The report had been a hoax. The committees of Congress again began to formulate statements on colonial rights and grievances—the main objective of the meeting. Within a week, while some preliminary drafts were under consideration, Paul Revere again rode in from Massachusetts, this time with another alarm. The people of Boston's Suffolk County had drawn resolutions which they asked Congress to endorse. These Suffolk Resolves, full of lurid prose calling the royal government military executioners, villains, murderers, and enemies, proposed the formation of a colonial army, disobedience to acts of Parliament, and the channeling of all taxes into an independent provincial government. The language, carefully framed, roused the Congress by stages from surprise, to excitement, to passion, and to wild and thunderous applause at the peroration. A motion to endorse passed with a vociferous shout which Thomson's minutes recorded as a unanimous vote, although Galloway and some of his conservative friends had sat in dumfounded silence, believing this vote "tantamount to a complete declaration of war." It soon became apparent that Samuel Adams was deeply involved in the substance and the timing of the arrival of the Suffolk Resolves; and by implication Galloway thought him also the author of the earlier Boston Powder Alarm hoax. That device certainly had enabled the Boston firebrand to test the state of mind of many who, until faced with the apparent reality of war, had preferred the moderate, noncommittal stance.

The radical's preliminary tactics had undermined the major proposal of the moderates before Congress ever heard it. Joseph Galloway, after wide consultation, had developed a "Plan of Union" not unlike Franklin's Albany plan of 1754. Submitted on September 28, 1774, Galloway's plan proposed a colonial Council, chosen by the provincial legislatures, which would become a branch of the British Parliament. The Council would be charged with authority over intercolonial commercial, civil, and criminal issues, needing only the assent of Parliament to validate its acts. But the Pennsylvanian had been outmaneuvered. Voting by colonies, the delegates rejected this precursor of the British commonwealth system by a majority of six to five, a result which might easily have been different had

Galloway presented his plan before the Suffolk Resolves arrived.

The approval of the Suffolk Resolves and the defeat of Galloway's plan ended serious contest in the First Continental Congress. The Declaration of Rights and Grievances, despite much wrangling over phrasing, included no surprises. The Congress approved the formation of the "Continental Association," charged with the enforcement of a mercantile boycott of British goods; it urged all the colonies to organize central and local committees of Associators; and it called for a Second Continental Congress, to meet in the spring of 1775, by which time the delegates expected that Britain would reply to their petition. On October 26, the Congress dissolved itself; the delegates, after a convivial last night at the City Tavern, began drifting home. They would return to Philadelphia for a second session, if necessary, on May 10, 1775.

Pennsylvania Politics: Elections and a Constitutional Convention

While Congress deliberated, Pennsylvania had held its annual election for assemblymen, returning a moderate majority. The legislators promptly endorsed the actions of the Continental Congress—becoming the first colonial legislature to do so. The Congress had made a dignified, albeit strongly worded, appeal to the home government and had provided through the Association the economic pressure to emphasize the colonies' seriousness of purpose.

By the beginning of 1775, the old party lines in Pennsylvania had nearly disappeared. In the late 1760s colonists had begun adopting English party labels: "Whig" if their loyalty was primarily to Parliament, "Tory" if it was primarily to the King. George III (reigned 1760–1820) played on Whig divisions and complacency to control Parliament, building a strong executive branch that won many adherents on both sides of the Atlantic. By the 1770s, in the American colonies, many former Whigs moved toward independence, whereas those who remained loyal to King *and* Parliament became known as Tories, even though some of them, like William Allen, had led the first protests against British tax policies. Events of 1774 divided the Pennsylvania Whigs into moderate and radical factions, which differed in both objectives and methods. The moderates readily supported the Continental Association, for they hoped that economic pressure would hasten the achievement of their main purpose—some agreement which would keep the British connection intact and preserve the proprietary government of the province—and they favored the use of legal, nonviolent methods. The radicals supported the Association because they found in it an administrative device to destroy the proprietary government of Pennsylvania and at the same time to promote separation from Britain, and they were ready to use any means, including war, to achieve these ends.

George III

The Assembly elections of October 1774 disappointed the radicals, and to keep their organization sound, they called another Pennsylvania Provincial Conference for January 1775 in Philadelphia, not so much to take any action as to organize and exhort their partisans. They urged the collection of military supplies; established additional county committees of safety, vigilance, and correspondence; and encouraged local Associators (members of Military Associations) to take upon themselves such quasi-official functions as enforcing the boycott on merchants, checking prices to stop profiteering, inspecting ships and cargoes, and reporting on people they thought suspicious— that is, not basically in agreement with themselves. In short, voluntary groups, guided by the Philadelphia committee of correspondence, became a kind of "shadow government" dedicated to gaining its objectives either by controlling the legal government or else by supplanting it.

Tensions began to relax as the House of Commons agreed to Lord North's Conciliatory Resolution in February 1775, even though the Assembly rejected its terms as less than "just and reasonable." But the atmosphere swiftly changed with the clashes at Lexington and Concord on April 19. The day when the Second Continental Congress convened in Philadelphia, Ethan Allen captured Fort Ticonderoga from the British. The Second Congress would not concern itself with discussing peaceful solutions. It had to conduct a war.

Pennsylvania's delegation had changed. Rhoads and Galloway left Congress, and the Assembly named John Dickinson, Robert Morris, Thomas Willing, James Wilson, and Benjamin Franklin, recently returned from England. Within a month Congress had commissioned George Washington as commander-in-chief of colonial forces, called for eight companies of Pennsylvania riflemen to proceed to Boston, and started to build defenses on the Delaware. (The first Pennsylvania company to reach the new Continental Army was a largely German one from York County.)

From the summer of 1775 until the formal separation from England a year later, Pennsylvania lived in a state of governmental disarray. The proprietary government, the Associators, committees of various kinds, and the Continental Congress all issued commands, often conflicting, but there were no generally recognized agencies of enforcement. The Associators proved most effective; their local committees rapidly mobilized fifty-three battalions of militia, as well as four battalions of horse dragoons to serve in Washington's Flying Camp.

Even with war a reality, the Pennsylvania electorate in the October elections of 1775 returned to the Assembly essentially the same moderate majority it had chosen in 1774—but with Galloway gone and Franklin back. Since the Pennsylvania Constitution of 1701 provided for fairly broad male suffrage, this strong grassroots preference for the moderate view was impressive. (The growing middle

Robert Morris

and working classes of Philadelphia were most likely to be disenfranchised by property requirements for voters.) Most Pennsylvanians would fight for their rights, but they did not want to separate from the mother country. The Assembly lost no time in placing its view on public record. It instructed the Pennsylvania delegates to the Second Continental Congress to "dissent from and utterly reject, any Propositions . . . that may cause, or lead to, a Separation from our Mother Country."

The enraged radicals protested that the Assembly did not adequately represent the populace, and was rigged to prevent fair representation of the more revolutionary districts. To counter this charge, the Assembly created four additional seats from Philadelphia and thirteen more from the western counties, then ordered a special election on May 1, 1776, as a referendum on the question of independence. The moderates won again, gloating that only one Philadelphia radical had won election and the western counties had returned a majority of moderates.

During May, the radicals in the Continental Congress had proceeded far along the path to independence, and were awaiting only the certainty of a respectable majority to make the proclamation. Pennsylvania was proving a stumbling block. Its support would be essential to success not only because of its central geographical location but also because of its vast resources of manpower, money, munitions, and foodstuffs. Thomas Paine, who had recently come to Philadelphia with letters of introduction from Benjamin Franklin, in January 1776 published his *Common Sense,* a powerful brief in favor of independence, but it took time for its arguments to permeate the back country. In Philadelphia the leading moderates denounced Paine's pamphlet as mischievous and dastardly.

The most fiery radicals in Congress, notably the New Englanders, saw no way to solve the Pennsylvania impasse except to overthrow its proprietary government and to install the local radicals in its place. For this reason, Congress on May 15 resolved that wherever the old provincial governments seemed incapable of providing for the public welfare, new governments should be created. With this semblance of authorization, the radicals called another Pennsylvania Provincial Conference to meet in Philadelphia on June 18. This meeting declared that the old government was not providing for the public welfare and called for a provincial constitutional convention. The strongest support for this action came from the Associators.

How closely the activities of the Pennsylvania radicals were tied to the actions of the Congress may be seen from their timetables. The Conference met on June 18, 1776. On the twenty-fourth it approved Congress's preliminary draft of the Declaration of Independence and instructed the Pennsylvania delegates to support it. Congress called for approval of independence on July 2. The Pennsylvania delegates, now having conflicting instructions from the

Assembly and the radical Conference, voted their private convictions. Franklin, Morton, and Wilson endorsed the Declaration; Willing and Humphreys voted against it; and Dickinson and Robert Morris absented themselves. The Declaration of Independence was publicly read at a great open celebration in State House Square on July 8. That day had also been set as election day for delegates to the Pennsylvania constitutional convention. Only those willing to take oaths repudiating allegiance to King George III could be candidates, and only persons approved by local Associator committees could vote. These precautions, limiting the franchise and representation to those of the radical party, showed that the Pennsylvania radicals recognized themselves as a minority.

When the Pennsylvania Constitutional Convention opened on July 15, it assumed the powers of government, then delegated them to a Council of Safety with full power to act in the name of Pennsylvania until a formal governmental structure should be devised and approved. This action occurred on September 28, 1776, when the Convention proclaimed a new constitution of Pennsylvania, without providing for popular ratification. After elections, this new government, the first of the independent Commonwealth of Pennsylvania, assumed its duties on November 28. The old Assembly met in September, but, lacking a quorum, adjourned for the last time. These events consummated the revolution in Pennsylvania. A radical minority, by aggressive militance and superior organization and commitment, had succeeded in overthrowing the proprietary government and seizing power. The War for American Independence had a very different purpose. It sought not to subvert a government but to sever all connections with it. Strangely, the revolution in Pennsylvania was bloodless, but the will of the child to be free of its parent cost a decade of savage warfare.

Silver desk set, used in signing the Declaration of Independence, was made by Philadelphia silversmith Philip Syng. The famous "Rising Sun Chair" was used by the presiding officer during the Constitutional Convention.

"Committee of Safety" musket

The Pennsylvania Battleground

With the slogan "I refuse to be subjugated," this battle flag inspired Pennsylvania's First Regiment (Thompson's Pennsylvania Rifle Battalion). This flag led the regiment in action from Boston, in 1775, to Yorktown, in 1781.

The American War of Independence and the American Revolution were not identical struggles, though simultaneously conducted. For more than a year after Lexington and Concord, many Pennsylvanians looked on the remote, small-scale military contest as an unhappy crisis which conciliatory Whigs on both sides of the Atlantic would resolve. But the British Ministry, in a series of hostile and obdurate responses, destroyed that hope. In a curt reply to the Declaration of Rights and Grievances of the First Continental Congress, King George announced that New England was "in a state of rebellion," and that blows would have to decide "whether they are to be subject to this country or independent."

The Second Continental Congress, after war had begun, agreed that a number of moderate members acting as private individuals should send another dignified statement of grievances to the king as an "Olive Branch Petition," affirming loyalty and begging the cessation of hostilities pending a compromise of differences. John Dickinson drew up the petition, and forty-six members of Congress signed it on July 8, 1775. It was entrusted for delivery to Richard Penn, the brother of Pennsylvania's governor. He presented it in London to Lord Dartmouth, Secretary of State for the Colonies, on September 1, but the king refused to see it. Edmund Burke called it "a manly petition." Instead of conciliating, Parliament passed an act in December removing the colonies from British protection and calling for the seizure of all American ships at sea. This news reached Philadelphia in late February 1776. On March 1, the king proclaimed all the colonies to be in open rebellion and forbade further commerce with them. These British actions during the year following Lexington made even the Pennsylvania moderates recognize that there was no escaping war with Britain. Once committed, the moderates aided the war effort with as much energy, and—in the areas of management and finance—with more effect, than the radicals.

But the American Revolution in Pennsylvania had wider ramifications than the war against England. The radicals were just as eager to conduct war against the Redcoats as were the moderates,

Francis Hopkinson, Probable Designer of the Nation's Flag

The Continental Congress did not specify until June 1777 the form the flag should have. Unfortunately, Congress did not record who had submitted the pattern that was accepted, and eventually several people, including the flagmaker Betsy Ross, were given credit for designing the Stars and Stripes. However, one of Philadelphia's "Renaissance men," Francis Hopkinson, seems the most probable candidate for that honor. (There is evidence, however, that Betsy Ross did contribute to her country as a flagmaker. The minutes of the Pennsylvania State Navy Board for May 29, 1777, show that payment was ordered to Mistress Ross for "making ships' colours, etc.")

The evidence on Hopkinson's behalf does seem convincing. On May 25, 1780, Hopkinson, then Treasurer of Loans, sent a letter to the Board of Admiralty, whose seal he had just designed, claiming credit and a "Quarter Cask of the public Wine" for that and other "Labours of Fancy" including "The Flag of the United States of America." Several weeks later he submitted a revised bill for these designs, which the Commissioners of the Chamber of Accounts examined, finding that "the Charge [was] reasonable and ought to be paid." But the Board of Treasury repeatedly refused his claim, ostensibly because he had not furnished the proper vouchers to support his account.

Angered by such high-handedness, Hopkinson sent to Congress a list of general charges against the Treasury Board, which at first refused to come before the committee appointed to investigate the quarrel. Only under pressure did the Board heed a second call to appear, but not before refusing to pay Hopkinson's bill, giving several reasons for their action, the most important of which was that "the said Francis Hopkinson was not the only person consulted on those exhibitions of Fancy, and therefore cannot claim sole merit of them." However, when the Board finally came before Congress' committee, they did not deny that Hopkinson had made the various designs but defended their action on the grounds that he had not submitted the proper vouchers. The committee's report to Congress on November 24, 1780, makes no recommendation on Hopkinson's account but does point out that the matter would have been easily settled had not the "Demon of Discord pervaded the whole [Treasury] Department." The case was finally and unjustly decided

This detail from a 1790 French textile design is one of the earliest images of the "thirteen stars and stripes."

Francis Hopkinson

on August 23, 1781, when Congress passed a resolution "That the report relative to the fancy-work of F. Hopkinson ought not to be acted on." Hopkinson had resigned as Treasurer of Loans one month earlier, citing differences between him and the Board of Treasury.

Thus it seems probable that Hopkinson designed the Stars and Stripes and that only pettiness and the "Demon of Discord" denied him the honor he so believably claimed.

In CONVENTION for the State of *Pennsylvania*.

FRIDAY, August 9, 1776.

On Motion, *Ordered*,

THAT Two thousand Copies of the Particulars of the Rations allowed for the FLYING CAMP, be printed and distributed among the Men.

Extract from the Minutes,

JOHN MORRIS, Jun. *Secretary*.

The RATION *for each Man, as copied from the Minutes of the Honourable the Continental* CONGRESS, *is as follows*:

One Pound of Beef, or Three Quarters of a Pound of Pork, or One Pound of Salt Fish, *per* Day.
One Pound of Bread or Flour *per* Day.
Three Pints of Peas or Beans *per* Week, or Vegetables equivalent at One Dollar *per* Bushel for Peas or Beans.
One Pint of Milk *per* Man *per* Day, or at the Rate of $\frac{1}{72}$ of a Dollar.
One Half-pint of Rice, or One Pint of Indian Meal, *per* Man *per* Week.
One Quart of Spruce Beer, or Cyder, *per* Man *per* Day, or Nine Gallons of Molasses *per* Company of 100 Men *per* Week.
Three Pounds of Candles to 100 Men *per* Week, for Guards.
Twenty-four Pounds of Soft or Eight Pounds of Hard Soap for 100 Men *per* Week.

Description of rations distributed to fighting men by order of the Continental Congress

but they also waged a continuing political war against the moderates, who represented the traditional political elite of Pennsylvania. The radicals supplanted the old elite in power under the new State Constitution of 1776, assuring their own election by excluding from franchise or office anyone who would not take an oath never to seek any change in the Pennsylvania government. The radicals also tried to exclude moderates from serving in the Continental Congress, but were unsuccessful because Congress badly needed the financial and administrative capabilities of these Pennsylvanians. The radicals soon became suspicious of the centralized authority represented by Congress and emphasized the recruitment of short-term state militia, rather than the enrollment of Pennsylvanians in the Continental forces governed by Congressional authority. In part this was to keep the soldiers close at hand, since they formed a major part of the voting force of the radical party, and in part it was merely an unwillingness to commit the state to an enterprise it did not control. The radicals had little experience in government and proved almost totally unfit for financial or administrative responsibility. They taxed those excluded from the franchise and exempted themselves. They had very little control over the state militia units, which were governed by the whim of their unit commanders. They could not mobilize supplies and spent more time carping than acting. Washington's soldiers were freezing and starving at Valley Forge while eastern Pennsylvania had ample food, yet the radical Assembly could do no more than censure Washington for not attacking the well-fed British in Philadelphia. The radicals had performed invaluable service in bringing Pennsylvania to the point of independence, but once the war had begun in earnest the most capable radical leaders had left for military service and the remaining politicos showed little grasp of management. Their object, even beyond defeating the British, was to prevent the moderates from returning to power in Pennsylvania. These intertwined but different objectives had a bearing upon the military situation.

War did not come quickly to Pennsylvania, even though some of the more enthusiastic Pennsylvanians went quickly to war. The first troops from south of the Hudson to fight in the siege of Boston were the eight Pennsylvania rifle companies, which Washington in early 1776 dubbed the First Regiment of the Army of the United Colonies. Other Pennsylvania volunteers entered the Continental service as the Pennsylvania Line or as part of the Flying Camp. A Pennsylvania Navy, under Captains Henry Dougherty and John Rice, was organized in July 1775, three months before the Continental Congress ordered formation of a naval force. On the night of May 6, 1776, acting on orders from the Philadelphia Committee of Safety, thirteen armed boats and a fire-vessel from the Pennsylvania fleet drove two British warships out of Delaware Bay. Although the militia was established primarily for local defense, battalions sometimes were sent outside Pennsylvania. For instance, a Chester County unit under Anthony Wayne moved north with the ill-fated army of General Richard Montgomery, which invaded Canada in the fall of 1775, came to a standstill before Quebec at year's end, and would have fared even worse if it had not been for Wayne's covering of the retreat to Ticonderoga. The first Pennsylvania militia units, however, were chiefly Associator groups, which blossomed in every community during the spring of 1775 in emulation of the Minute Men of Lexington and Concord. Despite efforts of the Pennsylvania Assembly to regularize the Associators and to tax pacifistic non-Associators in the summer and fall of 1775, most of the Pennsylvania militia was plagued by short-term enlistments, desertions, insubordination, and poor equipment until the war eventually became a serious business.

Crossing the Delaware, Christmas 1776

After the British evacuated Boston in the spring of 1776, they regrouped under the command of General William Howe and his brother, Admiral Richard Howe, and—greatly reinforced—prepared to attack seaboard cities where Loyalists were concentrated. The British quickly captured New York after defeating Washington's army at Long Island and Harlem Heights, where the Pennsylvania

"The Passage of the Delaware," by Thomas Sully, 1819

"The Congress Voting Independence, July 4, 1776," by Pine and Savage, 1785. Left unfinished at the time of Robert Pine's death, and marred by the clumsy aftertouches of Edward Savage, this painting is, nevertheless, the most authentic representation of this historic event.

Key to chart for "Congress Voting Independence, July 4, 1776": (1) Richard Stockton, New Jersey; (2) Josiah Bartlett, New Hampshire; (3) Thomas Nelson, Jr., Virginia; (4) George Clymer, Pennsylvania; (5) Francis Lightfoot Lee, Virginia; (6) John Penn, North Carolina; (7) Abraham Clark, New Jersey; (8) John Morton, Pennsylvania; (9) George Ross, Pennsylvania; (10) James Smith, Pennsylvania; (11) Samuel Adams, Massachusetts; (12) Robert Treat Paine, Massachusetts; (13) Button Gwinnett, Georgia; (14) Robert Morris, Pennsylvania; (15) Benjamin Harrison, Virginia; (16) Carter Braxton, Virginia; (17) John Hart, New Jersey; (18) John Adams, Massachusetts; (19) Roger Sherman, Connecticut; (20) James Wilson, Pennsylvania; (21) Thomas Jefferson, Virginia; (22) Charles Thompson, Secretary; (23) John Hancock, Massachusetts; (24) Francis Hopkinson, New Jersey; (25) William Ellery, Rhode Island; (26) Edward Rutledge, South Carolina; (27) Benjamin Franklin, Pennsylvania; (28) Charles Carroll, Maryland; (29) Richard Henry Lee, Virginia; (30) George Read, Delaware; (31) George Taylor, Pennsylvania; (32) Stephen Hopkins, Rhode Island.

Voting for Independence

Ironically, Pennsylvania's John Dickinson—the leading spokesman for colonial rights since 1765—was among the strongest opponents of a resolution recognizing the colonies' independence from Britain, presented to the Second Continental Congress by Richard Henry Lee of Virginia on June 7, 1776. Dickinson was one of a dwindling yet substantial number who felt separation was premature and who still hoped for some compromise within the framework of the British Empire. Two days after Lee introduced his resolution, a vote on the issue found all of New England, as well as Virginia, North Carolina, and Georgia, supporting independence, while the Middle Colonies and South Carolina stood opposed. Those calling for separation were clever enough to realize that a partisan victory was no victory at all. What they needed was a unified American stand. Any move for permanent separation from England had to include the still hesitant Middle Colonies.

Of particular importance was Pennsylvania—the keystone for successful colonial resistance and for independence. Though the colony was more generous than any other in its contribution of men and supplies to the colonial resistance, its leaders held back from any rash move for independence. The party favoring a break with England had failed in its efforts to gain a greater voice in the Pennsylvania Assembly and had taken its cause to the people in the streets. The result was a stand-off between the separatist forces and the moderate-dominated legislature. Throughout the months of May and June the Pennsylvania Assembly sat on the second floor of the State House debating the issue of independence and the Continental Congress met below on the first floor waiting for a resolution of Pennsylvania's position.

Finally, on June 10, the Congress agreed to a three-week recess—the proponents of independence hoping for new instructions from moderate colonial legislatures, the moderates hoping that the delay would bring some conciliatory gesture from the Crown's representatives. Before recessing Congress appointed a committee to draft a declaration of independence. At the time there was no indication of sufficient sentiment among the delegates to approve any such statement. But the argument was that the committee should have something ready for discussion when the Congress reassembled. The committee selected Jefferson to write a first draft. One practical purpose of his draft declaration was to justify to the world the colonial break with England. A second and probably more important goal was to rally support at home for the cause of independence. However, the June recess had not yet brought unanimity to the colonies. The debate in Congress on July 1 lasted for nine long hours—with John Dickinson still calling for reconciliation and John Adams urging independence.

During the recess Pennsylvania's radical separatists had called a Provincial Conference which endorsed independence. This forced the Assembly to authorize its Congressional delegates to vote by their consciences. Several moderate Whigs, notably John Morton and James Wilson, conceded that the majority of Pennsylvanians were probably now for independence. Charles Thomson, an early separatist although otherwise a moderate, later revealed his motivation in a letter to Dickinson: ". . . by a perseverance which you were fully convinced was fruitless, you have thrown the affairs of this state into the hands of men totally unequal to them. . . ."

On July 2 all delegations except New York's voted to approve Lee's resolution. They then turned to Jefferson's draft declaration, which they accepted on the evening of July 4. Signing the Declaration of Independence from Pennsylvania were George Clymer, Benjamin Franklin, Robert Morris, John Morton, George Ross, Benjamin Rush, James Smith, George Taylor, and James Wilson. No other state had as many signers.

Battle flag of John Proctor's First Brigade (Independent Battalion, Westmoreland County, Pennsylvania), made in 1775, and carried at Trenton, Princeton, and many other engagements.

Line and three militia battalions suffered heavy losses. Howe pursued the Americans to White Plains, then headed for Philadelphia across New Jersey. But with winter approaching he returned to New York, leaving his mercenary Hessian troops in winter quarters at Trenton. Washington moved his army ahead of the British, at a distance of one or two days' march, and halted in Pennsylvania across the Delaware River from Trenton. The Continental Congress, fearing a sudden movement on Philadelphia, prudently retreated to Baltimore.

The American cause had become desperate. The British forays in New York and New Jersey had netted large stores of colonial military supplies. Desertions and the end of enlistment periods had cut Washington's army in half, and appeals for new recruits from New Jersey and Pennsylvania had brought in a scant 2,000 militia. The same day that Washington crossed over into Pennsylvania, hotly pursued by the troops of Lord Cornwallis, news arrived that the British had captured Newport, Rhode Island, and again threatened Boston. Unless he received more troops, Washington wrote, "I think the game will be pretty well up."

Morale had dropped so low after the succession of colonial defeats that Washington felt the urgent need for some kind of decisive action. New Jersey patriots and Pennsylvania Germans who had fraternized with the Hessians in Trenton to gain information reported that the enemy force in Trenton had settled into winter pleasures and had relaxed defenses. By December 20, the continental force had risen to around 6,000 effectives, and Washington planned a surprise attack on Trenton on the night of December 25–26. He had cleaned the river of boats when he brought his army across to Pennsylvania on December 7–8, and had an armada of some seventy small craft and a few heavy Durham boats at his disposal. Washington's troops had been stretched along the river for twenty miles, from New Hope to Bristol. He now concentrated 2,400 under his personal command at McConkey's Ferry (Washington's Crossing), about nine miles north of Trenton. Pennsylvania's General James Ewing would make his crossing from directly opposite Trenton and stay south of the city to cut off the British escape route. Further south, Colonel John Cadwalader of Philadelphia would cross from Bristol and draw off a nearby Hessian detachment, to keep them out of the action. The troop movement would start at nightfall of Christmas Day, and the attack would start at daybreak, led by columns headed by Washington and Sullivan converging on Trenton from the north and east. The password: "Victory or Death."

A wild gale, heavy snow and sleet, and the swollen river filled with ice made the crossing a superhuman feat, but Washington accomplished it without casualties except for two soldiers who froze to death on the Jersey shore waiting for the artillery to arrive. At eight in the morning, the Continentals entered Trenton and within an hour and a half had completed its capture, along with nearly a thousand Hessian prisoners—with American casualties of only four wounded. The Hessian commander, Colonel Johann Rall, was killed. Ewing, discouraged by the ice, had not crossed the river at all, and Cadwalader, after moving several hundred men over, could not load his cannon and called the infantry back. Before he learned of the battle, he sent a note to Washington: "I imagine the badness of the night must have prevented your crossing, as you intended." The British returned to New York, and Washington's army wintered at Morristown, New Jersey. The British overland attack on Philadelphia would not occur until the autumn of 1777.

Fanciful German version of American soldiers with the famous Pennsylvania long rifle. Europeans were greatly impressed by the range and accuracy of this innovative American weapon.

The Battle of Brandywine, September 1777

The British planned a new campaign for 1777. General John Burgoyne would move south from Canada into the Hudson Valley. General Howe would, if time permitted, take Philadelphia and then send his main army north from New York to meet Burgoyne. This movement would isolate New England and neutralize the two main colonial ports.

Howe planned a naval approach to Philadelphia, but did not embark his 15,000 troops at New York until July, far too late. He encountered foul weather, decided at the last minute not to risk the defenses in Delaware Bay, and in August sailed his eighty ships up the Chesapeake Bay to the Head of Elk. Storms had injured most of the horses, and the long, hot sail had ruined the water and sickened many of the troops. Washington, uncertain where the fleet was heading, moved his army now north, now south, as reports of presumed sightings came to hand. Reluctantly he sent 3,000 of his command north to reinforce General Horatio Gates, who was to hold the Hudson against Burgoyne. But by August it had become certain that Philadelphia would be Howe's target, and that he would attack overland.

"*The Battle of Paoli,*" *by Xavier della Gatta, 1782*

Washington hurried the army south and lined it along Brandy-wine Creek at Chadd's Ford, with Philadelphia at his back and Howe in front of him. The battle began on September 11, with a frontal attack by what Washington believed to be the main force of Howe's army. But this was a feint. The main force under Howe and General Cornwallis, guided by Joseph Galloway—thoroughly acquainted with the countryside and now turned Tory—was moving to a ford a dozen miles to the north, where it crossed unobserved and came down the east bank of the Brandywine to hit Washington's right flank under General Sullivan. Except for a remarkable rear-guard performance by Sullivan's men, under Nathanael Greene and Peter Muhlenberg, the Continental Army would have been demolished. But it escaped the trap, hurried to Chester, then to Philadelphia to pick up stores in the locality, and then moved west toward Paoli. Among the wounded at Brandywine was Lafayette, who was taken to Bethlehem to be cared for by the Moravians; other American wounded were taken to the Ephrata Cloister. Philadelphia now lay open, and patriots and the Continental Congress fled, the latter to Lancaster for a day and then across the Susquehanna River to York, where it stayed nine months.

The Paoli Massacre

Washington marched his army toward Whitemarsh to regroup, and Howe selected Germantown as quarters for most of the British army. Howe's baggage train and part of the army still was encamped near Paoli and would shortly move eastward. General Anthony Wayne, who lived nearby, persuaded Washington that his knowledge of the countryside would enable him, with 1,500 Rangers, to launch a surprise attack and destroy the British supply train. Washington reluctantly assented and the trap was set. Unhappily for Wayne, local Loyalists discovered his camp in the wooded hills and informed the British, who devised their own surprise. Coming into the camp in the dead of night, the British, after removing flints from their guns so that no alarm would accidentally be given, fell on Wayne's men. The attack has been called the "Paoli Massacre," but it was not quite that, since Wayne and his officers managed to bring their men rapidly into an orderly retreat; several companies, however, exposed themselves by running between the campfires and the enemy, becoming easy targets. The Rangers suffered nearly 400 casualties, mostly wounded, and Wayne himself was nearly captured.

The Battle of the Clouds—Howe Enters Philadelphia

Howe followed Washington's army, more intent upon capturing it

Romanticized painting of the Liberty Bell being taken to Allentown for safekeeping

By the nineteenth century the bell had become a national symbol. Publication of this sketch, July 10, 1869, in Harper's Weekly, marks the first use of the term "Liberty Bell."

The Liberty Bell as it was displayed in Independence Hall during the Centennial of 1876

The Two Liberty Bells

In 1751 Isaac Norris, speaker of the Pennsylvania Assembly, proposed the installation of a bell in the newly erected steeple of Philadelphia's State House (now Independence Hall) in commemoration of the fiftieth anniversary of William Penn's Charter of Privileges. Shortly thereafter an order was placed in London for a bell bearing the Biblical inscription "Proclaim Liberty thro' all the Land to all the Inhabitants thereof." The inscription, meant to underscore the liberties granted earlier, was to prove prophetic of the most momentous event in the history of the American colonies.

The bell arrived in 1752 and was readied for testing. But upon the inaugural stroke, a crack appeared. As a consequence, the quality of the sound was impaired and replacement of the bell was mandated. A new bell was ordered cast in London. While the colonists were waiting out the long process, impatience prompted the recasting of the original bell. The work was done in Philadelphia, and the mended bell was hung in early 1753 amidst great celebration. However, the recast bell proved inferior in tonal quality because of the excessive use of copper during repairs. The criticism leveled at Messrs. Stow and Pass, the foundrymen, was so sharp that they felt impelled to regain their professional reputations through yet another modification of the bell. This time they used tin to improve the tone. In June of 1753 the bell was ordered hung "temporarily" pending the arrival from London of its replacement. When the second bell, somewhat smaller than its predecessor, arrived later that same year, it was decided to use both bells together. The newer bell was attached to a clock. On July 8, 1776, the Liberty Bells tolled together during the public proclamation of the Declaration of Independence.

The next year, when British troops entered Philadelphia, the Liberty Bells and other city bells were sent to the town of Northampton (now Allentown) for safekeeping; the fear was that the redcoats would melt them down and use the metal for musketballs. The bells and other metal objects were transported by night in a caravan of seven hundred wagons, and arrived safely in Northampton eight days later. Patriots quickly spread word that the Liberty Bell (or Bells) had been sunk in the Delaware River—a report now known to have been a ruse to fool the British. Rumor put the bells' hiding place in Quakertown—a plausible notion since that Bucks County village was a popular stopping place on the sixty-mile trip from Philadelphia to Northampton. A debate still continues over the identity of the wagonmaster who transported the original Liberty Bell. One side favors Frederick Leaser of Lynn township, while the other makes a case for Jacob Mickley, who became Northampton's Commissary of Issues for the war. Leaser's partisans say that his wagon was commandeered for the assignment after he delivered a load of farm produce at the Philadelphia market, that his wagon broke down in Bethlehem, and that an unidentified teamster hauled the precious cargo on the last leg of its trip. Advocates of Mickley have him and his son carting the bell all the way, under a load of manure, with a stop in Bethlehem to repair a wheel. A compromise version, found on the historical marker at the Liberty Bell Shrine in Allentown, credits each driver with a part of the journey. This version has been enlivened by a reported wager between Leaser and Mickley, before they left Philadelphia, as to which of them would reach home first. According to this version, Leaser departed with the bell and was winning the bet until his wagon broke down, whereupon Mickley won both bet and bell. No one disputes the fact that the Liberty Bells remained hidden in the cellar of the Zion Reformed Church until the British left Philadelphia, when the bells were returned to the State House by persons unknown.

The first bell continued in service there through July 8, 1835, when, while tolling the death knell for Chief Justice John Marshall, it suffered a large crack. The bell was not ordered recast this time; instead, the sides of the fissure were enlarged by drilling in an attempt to correct the sound. Fear that greater damage would occur if it were rung again silenced the bell until 1846. When it pealed again in that year for Washington's birthday celebration, the crack worsened into the long cleft which has become the bell's hallmark. The big bell has not been rung since. The second Liberty Bell remained in the State House belfry until 1830, when it was sold with its clock to the Church of Saint Augustine in Philadelphia. It served there until 1844, when a fire destroyed the clock and damaged the bell. In the tradition of its predecessor, the second bell was ordered recast to hang on the campus of the new Villanova College. Villanova's Liberty Bell, a little-known item of Americana, today stands quietly on a pedestal; Philadelphia's Liberty Bell is also mute. Both bells bear silent testimony to a unique moment in the annals of the United States.

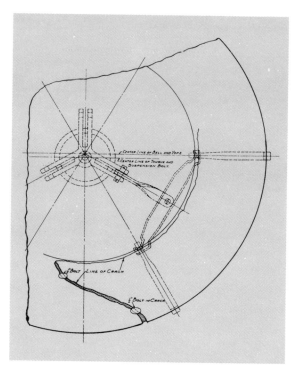

Engineer's drawing analyzing the famous crack

than Philadelphia, which he could enter at any time. At Warren's Tavern, west of Paoli, the two armies met again in what would have developed into a full-scale action, but a driving rainstorm on that September 16 made flintlocks and cannon useless, whereupon the engagement ended after the opening skirmish. It was so doubtful that the American army could have survived an all-out battle at this point that one historian has judged that this "was perhaps the best storm in American history, for it saved an American Army." With more certainty, the storm gave the encounter its name: "The Battle of the Clouds." Howe abandoned the chase and on September 26 entered Philadelphia, where he was received with warmth and ceremony by a large part of the inhabitants, who held firm to their loyalty to the mother country. Except for Continental Army spies, most of the patriots had fled, taking the Liberty Bell on a perilous journey to Allentown and the government files to Easton.

The Battle of Germantown, Early October 1777

As in the latter days of 1776, so a year later the Continentals desperately needed a military victory to counteract the growing despair. In part to bolster morale, and in part because it appeared strategically feasible, Washington planned the battle of Germantown. The colonials still controlled the Delaware River by means of several *chevaux de frise* and Forts Mifflin and Mercer, all south of Philadelphia and preventing naval access to it. If Howe's army could be defeated at Germantown, the remainder of his force in Philadelphia could be pushed to surrender because it would lack means of either supply or escape. Washington and his staff prepared one of the most complex and daring operations of the war, incorporating such sophisticated tactics as surprise, diversion, multiple column strikes, precisely synchronized troop movements, and recognition signals—all requiring detailed map work and rigid discipline. Four columns, moving into position at night over roads leading to Germantown, would strike simultaneously in the morning. Troops under Generals McDougall, Greene, and Stephens would bring in two columns from the north. Generals Wayne, Conway, and Sullivan would guide another two columns forming from the northwest. Maryland and New Jersey militia would guard the right flank, and General John Armstrong would bring his Pennsylvania militia into action to divert British attention by skirmishing on the left flank. The night before the attack, other militia units would set up campfires and raise commotion just outside Philadelphia to increase British anxiety about an attack there and draw some troops out of Germantown back to defend Philadelphia.

The plan was intricate, and required one ingredient that Washington lacked—a little luck. The diversionary force did its work on October 5, but Howe had good intelligence and recognized the action for what it was. He kept his eye on Germantown. A dense ground fog hampered colonial movement and prevented all the columns from arriving at Germantown simultaneously. Greene's troops lost their way and had to backtrack. Nonetheless, the Continentals drove the British back and were at the point of routing the enemy, who were as hampered and confused by the dense fog—rendered doubly thick by powder smoke—as were the colonials. Then a series of bad breaks turned the tide. Several hundred British holed up in Cliveden, the fortress-strong stone mansion of Benjamin Chew, and rather than passing it by, Washington's staff voted to follow the book-rule of not leaving an entrenched enemy in the rear. Instead of pursuing the retreating British in the open, they stopped to capture the Chew house, losing several hours. On another part of the field, General Adam Stephens proved to be too drunk to command, giving conflicting and unintelligible orders. Some of his subordinates tried to take charge. In the midst of this uncertainty, Stephens' men heard firing in front of them and returned it. They were shooting at the backs of Wayne's troops, who were pursuing the retreating British. Wayne's men, unable, because of the fog, to see who was assailing them from the rear, assumed that they had been outflanked and turned in retreat. The British now ran toward Wayne, seeking to surrender, but the colonial troops thought it a counterattack and

"The Battle of Germantown," by Xavier della Gatta, 1782. Although painted from an eyewitness account, the painting fails to demonstrate the dense fog which caused two American divisions to fire upon each other. It also fails to do justice to the fortress-like Chew House of which Colonel Pickering, who was with Washington, wrote: "This house of Chew's was a strong stone building. . . . Several of our pieces, six pounders, were brought up within musket shot of it, and fired round balls at it, but in vain."

Haym Salomon, Financier of the Revolution

Haym Salomon was born in Poland in 1740 but left the country when thirty-two after witnessing its dismemberment at the hands of Russia, Austria, and Prussia. As his friends Kosciusko and Pulaski had done, Salomon came to the British colonies in America. He established himself in New York as a broker with important business contacts in Holland and France.

Salomon's sympathies had always been with those who fought for freedom. The plight of the colonists in the context of British hegemony recalled his own countrymen's unsuccessful struggle for independence, and he soon allied himself with the subversive Sons of Liberty. Although his activities were clandestine, he must have been a visible rebel since the British arrested him on September 26, 1776, after a fire which devastated a large part of New York. But his imprisonment was brief.

Again arrested in 1778, but this time sentenced to be hanged as a spy, Salomon fled to Philadelphia. He moved effortlessly into the mercantile and banking life of the city, rising into prominence as a result of his trustworthy dealings with foreign nations on behalf of the American Revolution. From Philadelphia he directed crucial financial undertakings, and it was largely through his efforts that the War of Independence could be carried on. As bank records and the diary of Robert Morris attest, Salomon raised almost a quarter of a million dollars for the cause. He also helped out of their financial distress many prominent Revolutionary leaders, among them three who were to become presidents of the United States: Jefferson, Madison, and Monroe.

Beyond the scope of his activities in support of the revolution, Salomon performed many other public-spirited works. He argued unceasingly for a petition which ultimately was instrumental in deleting from the Pennsylvania constitution a clause requiring officeholders to take an oath of belief in both the Old and New Testaments: in effect, the abolition permitted conscientious Jews to hold public office in Pennsylvania for the first time. Salomon was also the primary source of funds for the construction of a temple for the Jewish congregation of Philadelphia; Mikveh Israel, with Salomon as a trustee, became the first synagogue in Pennsylvania.

Haym Salomon died in Philadelphia in 1785. Despite a life truncated when he was forty-five by a chronic illness ascribed to his first imprisonment, *his active patriotism earned him the gratitude of the leaders of the new nation and the epithet "Financier of the American Revolution." Today there are monuments to him in Chicago (with Washington and Morris) and in Los Angeles, as well as a commemorative stamp.*

Figure of Haym Salomon from the commemorative monument in Chicago

hastened their retreat. Armstrong's militia corps, which was supposed to cross the Wissahickon Creek to harass the British flank and keep it out of action, never moved. Ultimately the Americans became so disorganized that nearly the whole army fled in disorder. Wayne said, bitterly, "We ran from victory." Washington's army suffered nearly a thousand casualties to about half that number for the British. After the psychological build-up that preceded the battle, the sickening result plunged the patriot cause into deep gloom. The main reason for the disaster seemed apparent: the battle plan was too complex for a short-term volunteer army to execute. But the fog also played a role in the American defeat.

Lydia Darragh Prevents a Battle

Washington removed his army to Whitemarsh after Germantown, and Howe began clearing out the defenses on the lower Delaware. General Wayne urged another assault on Philadelphia, but Washington decided that his army, after several months of hard marching and defeats in two major battles, ought to get some rest and resupply. During October and November, Howe attacked Forts Mercer and Mifflin by land while his brother, the Admiral, used the British Navy to strike from Delaware Bay. By the end of November the British had cleared the Delaware of all the defenses which had been so laboriously constructed over the previous two years.

With an escape route from Philadelphia assured, Howe on December 4 tried to surprise Washington at Whitemarsh and to capture his army, a feat which he presumed would end the American rebellion. But the battle never took place, thanks in part to a quick-witted patriot, Lydia Darragh. Overhearing some British officers quartered in her Philadelphia home discussing the attack, she obtained a British pass to go to Frankford for flour. She passed her information to an American beyond the city, and then walked back to her home carrying a heavy sack of flour to complete her performance. When Howe's army arrived, it found the Continentals ready to meet it. After skirmishing briefly at Edgehill on December 5, the British broke off the action and returned to Philadelphia.

Winter at Valley Forge, 1777–1778

For several months after the capture of Philadelphia, Washington had been besieged by advice about where he should establish winter quarters. Lancaster and Reading, major supply depots, wished the army nearby for their protection, as did Wilmington and towns in New Jersey. Washington ultimately decided on Valley Forge, about twenty miles northwest of Philadelphia, which promised security

Carlisle's Molly Pitcher

"Molly Pitcher" is a name given since the Revolutionary days to a number of women who served as water carriers for soldier husbands manning artillery batteries. Of these perhaps the best known is Mary Ludwig Hays McCauley of Carlisle. Born on October 13, 1744, Mary Ludwig was a servant in the family of William Irvine at the time the Revolution began. She married John Hays, a young barber who in 1775 enlisted for a year in the Continental Army in Colonel Proctor's artillery. Returning to Carlisle, he reenlisted as an infantryman in the regiment then being formed by Colonel Irvine. Some historians of the Revolution place Hays and his wife at Fort Clinton, along the Hudson River just north of New York City, at the time of its capture in October 1777. They state that, upon the American withdrawal, this Molly Pitcher took charge of an abandoned fieldpiece and touched off the last shot at the British before they stormed into the fort.

More reliable evidence places Hays and Molly with Colonel Irvine's regiment when it wintered at Valley Forge (1777–1778) and then marched off to pursue the British retreating from Philadelphia across New Jersey. On a stifling June day during the Battle of Monmouth, Hays was assigned to a field battery; as the battle raged, Molly carried water for the gun and its thirsty crew. When her husband was struck down and carried from the field, Molly continued to fire the gun, located at a critical spot, until the battle ceased.

A number of sources state that her courageous behavior came to General Washington's attention, probably through General Greene, and that on the day after the battle Washington commissioned her by her husband's side. According to another story, Molly sought her wounded husband after the battle and found him among those left as dead. He was badly wounded, but she summoned aid and nursed him back to health. She and her husband served in the war for more than seven years.

John Hays died shortly after the war ended, and his widow then married a man named McCauley, who died a few years later. Molly remained a widow, residing in Carlisle and doing nursing and menial work until her death in January 1832, aged nearly ninety. She received a pension of $50 a year as the widow of a Revolutionary War veteran. In the last month of her life Pennsylvania recognized her as a veteran in her own right, and the legislature gave her an additional pension, which she did not live to enjoy.

The State of New Jersey honored Molly Pitcher by including her name on one of five tablets at the base of a monument at Freehold, the site of her famous exploit. The citizens of Cumberland County, Pennsylvania, on July 4, 1876, erected a monument at her grave in Carlisle. Here "the oaklike Molly" stands in bronze, grasping a ramrod before a Revolutionary cannon.

The image of "Molly Pitcher" has become part of American folklore

but was sufficiently close to the British that any move they made might be intercepted. The location also promised proximity to food and supplies, which eastern Pennsylvania had in abundance. The country had been cheered by news of General Burgoyne's surrender to General Gates at Saratoga on October 17, and the prospects of dislodging Howe in the spring looked much brighter now that Gates could return the troops Washington had given him earlier.

From the beginning, Washington's strategy rested on the principle that he could afford to lose a battle, but that the whole American cause would fail if he lost his army. He had, at times almost miraculously, saved the army, but the succession of defeats and the loss of Philadelphia and New York led a few high-ranking officers to disparage his abilities. An intrigue developed involving even some members of Congress. With the resounding American victory over Burgoyne's army by General Gates' forces at Saratoga, pressure built up to give Gates the supreme command. This affair, known as the Conway Cabal, came to Washington's attention and he confronted the principals with his knowledge of it. The leader of the conspiracy was a French-Irish soldier-of-fortune named Thomas Conway, who had been commissioned a major-general in the Continental Army against Washington's advice; upon being discovered he returned to France. The movement died instantly, but it poisoned the relations between Washington and some of his subordinates, including Quartermaster-General Thomas Mifflin.

Surveyors had examined the Valley Forge site and marked off the plots which each company should occupy. The army began to move from Whitemarsh in early December in miserable weather; an early winter storm which began as rain turned to sleet and snow, and then froze hard. The troop columns filled the road during the storm and tramped it into muddy slush, which soon froze into sharp ridges. Too late the men discovered that logistic planning had gone awry. The tents, which should have moved first, occupied the end of the column in wagons that could not pass the marching troops. Hence many had to sleep without cover in the ice-crusted snow. An epidemic of dysentery called the "black vomit" had weakened many of the men, and scores died along the road. Even those who survived the march found no shelter at Valley Forge; tents did not arrive for several days.

For two weeks, everyone fell to building shelters. Each company set up details to dig latrines, carry water from the creek, chop and trim trees, haul them to the campsite, and build log cabins of them. By Christmas, most of the camp was under roof. At that moment, the food began to run short. The reasons soon became apparent in ways most calculated to exasperate the troops. Profiteering and mismanagement, rather than actual scarcity, caused the trouble. The British paid gold for supplies; the Americans offered depreciating Continental notes or promises to pay later, and many farmers and

Mary Dickinson, wife of John Dickinson

Mary White Morris

Women of Pennsylvania in the Revolution

Few Pennsylvania women of the Revolutionary period were sufficiently famous—or infamous—to have earned recognition, for a climate conducive to women's achievement did not yet exist. A woman's place was in the home, even in her contributions to the war effort. Although individual enterprise by women was unusual, the names and achievements of some have come down to us.

Margaret Cochran Corbin, now buried at West Point, assumed command at Fort Washington in New York after her husband had been killed in battle, and fought until she too was wounded. Both Congress and Pennsylvania recognized her efforts and awarded her pensions until her death in 1800 from her wounds.

Another woman of note was Rachel Marx Graydon. After her son Alexander was captured at the Battle of Fort Washington, Mrs. Graydon ignored the opposition of Continental Congress President Hancock, and succeeded in traveling by horseback and boat to New York, although she was intercepted

and arrested several times en route. In New York she personally interceded with General Howe to effect the release of her son from imprisonment in Flatbush. Alexander was paroled to her custody.

Charlotte Este was only sixteen in 1777, when she accompanied her father, a surgeon with one of King George's Hessian regiments. Learning of a plot to capture General Washington, she worked her way through the British lines and succeeded in warning Washington of the planned attack.

Most women, however, were left behind to maintain the family properties, to oversee the harvest of the crops, to send supplies on to the troops, and to knit stockings or sew uniforms. One affluent Philadelphia matron of patriotic bent was Sarah Morris Mifflin, wife of Thomas Mifflin, quartermaster general and then adjutant general of the Continental Army (later president of the Continental Congress and first governor of Pennsylvania under the new Constitution). Mrs. Mifflin wrote to a friend in Boston, at the beginning of the war, "I have re-

346

Sarah Morris Mifflin

Julia Stockton Rush, wife of Dr. Benjamin Rush

trenched every superfluous expense in my table and family. Tea I have not drank since last Christmas, nor bought a new cap or gown since the affair at Lexington, and what I never did before, I have learned to knit, and am now making stockings of wool for my servants; and this way do I throw in my mite to the public good. I know this, that as free I can die but once; but as a slave I shall not be worthy of life. I have the pleasure to assure you that these are the sentiments of my sister Americans. They have sacrificed assemblies, parties of pleasure, tea-drinkings and finery, to that great spirit of patriotism which actuates all degrees of people throughout this extensive country." When the British occupied Philadelphia, Sarah Mifflin moved to the provincial German town of Reading and cared for the sick and wounded evacuated to the area. Always in delicate health, she died in 1790, just before she would have become Pennsylvania's first First Lady.

A little-known book published by physician Wil-

liam Henry Egle in Harrisburg in 1898, Pennsylvania Women during the War of the Revolution, *collects brief histories of sixty-nine "Matrons of the Declaration" without whom "the saviours of our country at Valley Forge . . . would have starved." Most of these ladies—like Mary Penrose Wayne, mother of General "Mad Anthony," Mary White Morris, wife of patriot financier Robert Morris, whose fortunes and misfortunes she shared, and Mary Carson O'Hara, daughter of the proprietor of the Harp and Crown public house in Philadelphia and wife of James O'Hara, quartermaster of the Western Army at Fort Pitt—are remarkable only for the fame of their fathers, spouses, or sons. Not mentioned in Egle's book are those who followed the troops to do the washing, mending, and cooking, nor those who provided even more intimate services. All of Egle's women were beautiful, noble, and dedicated. In retrospect it is perhaps reasonable that we think so of all of the women who participated in the first American cause.*

Washington's headquarters at Valley Forge

*Major General von Steuben,
by Ralph Earl, 1786*

businessmen preferred the gold. Ill-conceived political efforts to prevent inflation by placing price ceilings on food hurt the army most, as farmers would not sell at the designated price. Moreover, bottlenecks developed in the supply system as wagons became scarce, their drivers preferring to move from the interior into Philadelphia and New York, where they made undreamed of profits on each trip. In the meantime available food as near as New Jersey rotted for lack of transport. Company officers pleaded for authorization to forage the countryside and take what was needed, but Washington forbade pillage, and apparently little took place. For days at a time the camp had no meat and subsisted on Johnny cake. When flour was unobtainable for a while, some companies boiled leaves and shoe-leather. Once, when a shipment of flour arrived, those who opened the casks discovered them filled with wood, covered by a layer of flour. The arrival of a shipment of salt fish raised spirits until the men opened the casks. Careless handling had sprung the barrels, and too long storage in the rain and sun had transformed the contents into a stinking brown mush that even starving men could not stomach.

The winter at Valley Forge worked many changes in the American army. The severe hardships of the first month in some ways strengthened morale. Many malcontents and half-hearted patriots deserted and proved a good riddance. Those who stayed constituted a fully committed body of troops on whom officers could depend. The adoption of the Articles of Confederation by Congress on November 15 made them think seriously, for the first time, about their future as citizens of a new nation, rather than as state volunteers temporarily cooperating. After its first bitter onslaught, the winter grew milder in the early months of 1778. A reorganization of the commissary and quartermaster departments improved the flow of supplies, so that the camp could settle down to a tolerable routine. The men talked a great deal among themselves about the meaning of the war and about the ideas of equality, of self-government, and of the inalienable rights of man. In short, they developed into a crusading army, convinced of the important part they played in an unprecedented movement which might alter the world as people then knew it. They became convinced that they could conquer mercenary troops. Even the local antagonisms between militia of different states began to decline when each observed how well its rivals faced the ordeal of the first three weeks.

Baron von Steuben Comes to Valley Forge

These changes in attitude and purpose underlay the major accomplishment of Valley Forge. They laid the groundwork for the training and drill program begun in March by Baron Friedrich von Steuben.

Frontispiece from A Treatise of Artillery
used in training troops

Once impatient of drill and military discipline, the troops at last had begun to discover how largely the issue of victory or defeat rested upon their ability to respond correctly to standard orders. The battle of Germantown had hammered home this lesson. Steuben, who had served as aide-de-camp to King Frederick of Prussia, came to Paris in 1777 and there was recruited for the American cause by an envoy of the Continental Congress, Benjamin Franklin. Appointed inspector general of the Continental Army in February 1778, Steuben wrote a complete manual for a step-by-step training program which clerks translated and copied in English for distribution to company commanders. Steuben discovered that every state unit had its own drill procedures. He acquainted himself with the camp, visited with men in the ranks, and instituted a uniform program by personally drilling squads containing one capable man from each of a dozen different units. These then acted as drillmasters for their own men. Steuben worked the army hard, but gained its respect, for he could be found on the drill field every morning at daybreak with his wolfhound, and did not hesitate to move into a squad himself to show some awkward recruit exactly how a command should be executed.

The Pulaski weathervane honored the Polish hero of the Revolution, Count Casimir Pulaski, one of Washington's generals. It was originally installed on top of the York Courthouse.

York Courthouse, by nineteenth-century folk artist Lewis Miller, records its appearance in 1776.

Interior view of the Courthouse

York and the "Conway Cabal"

"To the town of York, seat of our American government in our most gloomy time." This toast, proposed by the Marquis de Lafayette during a visit to York in 1825, recalled those dismal months of the winter of 1777–1778 with a dispirited army under Washington at Valley Forge and a disgruntled and factious Continental Congress in session at York. The seat of government for nine months—September 30, 1777, to June 27, 1778—York was chosen so that "the Susquehanna should flow between Congress and the enemy." Here the Congress adopted a provisional plan of government which first formalized the thirteen states as the United States of America.

But the situation was not as unified as formal declarations might indicate. A bitter controversy arose in the wake of the American victory at Saratoga, and the relative merits of the military leadership of Gates and Washington became the primary topic of verbal and written innuendo in both Congress and the army. John Jay complained of the sessions held in the York Court House that "there is as much intrigue in this State-House as in the Vatican." Letters of informed leaders suggest many had concluded that Washington's army badly lacked training and discipline, that serious mistakes of leadership had been made, and that the tendency of aides close to the commander-in-chief to dismiss any criticism of Washington as lese majesté *was a dangerous form of aristocratic pride. The halo which later generations visualize above Washington's head was not yet in place for his contemporaries; a critical and questioning attitude could be expected from men committed to the risky venture of revolution.*

Although this affair has been called the "Conway Cabal," Washington's critics prepared no coordinated moves to replace him, and after learning of some indiscreet remarks by General Conway in a letter to Gates, Washington effectively turned aside the criticism of his leadership in a series of scathing letters to the principals involved. Conway was later seriously wounded in a duel with one of Washington's staunchest supporters, General John Cadwalader. Legend credits the symbolic defeat of the "Conway Cabal" to another toast given by Lafayette, at a banquet in Gates' residence in York. Here, in a room filled with Washington's severest critics, the French general proposed a toast—to the health of the beleaguered commander-in-chief.

The Gates House parlor, the scene for Lafayette's famous toast to Washington.

Rear view of the Gates House (left) and the Golden Plough Tavern. The buildings are rare survivals in York.

General von Steuben used step-by-step drilling diagrams to instill discipline.

By the time spring came, he had transformed the motley regiments of farm boys into soldiers, and the inexperienced officers into some semblance of a responsible and unified command. The crushed and discouraged state regiments that had straggled into Valley Forge in December marched out in June 1778 as an American army, more certain of what it fought for, and far more confident of its ability to meet the British regulars. Valley Forge did not merely symbolize, but visibly demonstrated the beginning of a national spirit that would soon replace the former uncertain association among jealous rival provinces.

Steuben was one of a number of young European idealists who came to the aid of the new nation. The Marquis de Lafayette had joined Washington in the summer of 1777, quickly becoming one of his chief field commanders with the rank of major general. Lafayette was only the most famous of a group of young French officers in the Continental Army. Volunteers came also from eastern Europe. Thaddeus Kosciusko, born in Lithuania and educated in Warsaw, was commissioned colonel of engineers in October 1776 and supervised construction of the fortifications at West Point. Casimir Pulaski, a Polish nobleman who arrived from Paris with a letter of introduction from Franklin in time for the Battle of Brandywine, was appointed brigadier general in command of a cavalry corps in 1778 and died of wounds a year later at the siege of Savannah, Georgia.

The British in Philadelphia

While the Continental Army worked during the winter of 1777–1778 at Valley Forge, the British spent a leisurely and sociable season in Philadelphia. Most of the officers quartered themselves in homes of the civilian population; the troops occupied barracks and camp grounds south of town. Many Philadelphians genuinely welcomed the troops as their own, and expressed relief at being rescued from "the rabble." Active patriots generally fled, but a considerable part of the population which sympathized with the revolutionary cause remained. At first Howe kept the army in restraint and appointed Joseph Galloway as superintendent of civilian activity in the city. But harsh military rule soon began. Although goods became scarce and costly, shipments up the Delaware and a steady inflow of farm produce from the surrounding countryside kept the city fairly well fed. The State House and a number of churches became hospitals, and captured provincials suffered through the winter in the miserable Walnut Street Prison.

Within a few weeks, the frightened Philadelphians had learned to live with an army in their midst; by November, when Howe attacked the river forts, they ran to the roof tops to watch the cannonading rather than to the cellar to hide. Two Tory newspapers began publication, parties and plays provided almost nightly entertainment, and tensions relaxed. An alarm on January 7 caused great excitement and, later, amusement. Americans up the Delaware, directed by David Bushnell, constructed dozens of mines made of powder kegs fitted with spring triggers to explode them on contact. These mines floated under water except for a spoke protruding above the surface. The plan was to sink warships anchored in the harbor, but it failed in this objective, for the ships had been drawn to shore to escape ice. The kegs did blow up, causing a rush of the whole city to the waterfront, and generated every kind of wild rumor until the facts became known. Francis Hopkinson's poem "The Battle of the Kegs" provided the patriots with some comic relief in an otherwise gloomy winter.

The British Withdraw from Pennsylvania

News arrived in early spring that the French had signed a treaty of alliance with the United States on February 6, 1778. Benjamin Franklin had persuaded Vergennes to seize the chance for revenge against England—a diplomatic stroke aided by the American victory at Saratoga and the rumors of peace feelers from Britain. The Earl of Carlisle reached Philadelphia in early May, just after Congress ratified the French treaty, with a proposal from Lord North that the Americans could have complete home rule with the single proviso that they acknowledge continuing allegiance to the British Crown. Under the new conditions North's proposal became useless, although it might have had a chance earlier because it appealed to the moderates.

General Howe had asked to be relieved of duty, and Sir Henry Clinton replaced him in command at Philadelphia. As soon as Clinton learned of the French treaty, he prepared to leave the city for

The Battle of the Kegs

Gallants attend, and hear a friend,
    Trill forth harmonious ditty,
Strange things I'll tell which late befell
    In Philadelphia city.

'Twas early day, as poets say,
    Just when the sun was rising,
A soldier stood on a log of wood,
    And saw a thing surprising.

As in amaze he stood to gaze,
    The truth can't be denied, sir,
He spied a score of kegs or more
    Come floating down the tide, sir.

    . . . . .

"Arise, arise," Sir Erskine cries,
    "The rebels—more's the pity,
Without a boat are all afloat,
    And ranged before the city.

"The motley crew, in vessels new,
    With Satan for their guide, sir.
Pack'd up in bags, or wooden kegs,
    Come driving down the tide, sir.

"Therefore prepare for bloody war,
    These kegs must all be routed,
Or surely we despised shall be,
    And British courage doubted."

    . . . . .

The cannons roar from shore to shore,
    The small arms make a rattle:
Since wars began I'm sure no man
    E'er saw so strange a battle.

    . . . . .

Such feats did they perform that day,
    Against these wicked kegs, sir,
That years to come, if they get home,
    They'll make their boasts
        and brags, sir.

    selected stanzas
    from Hopkinson's ballad

Mount Pleasant, now a museum in Philadelphia's Fairmount Park, was a gift from Benedict Arnold to his wife, Peggy. Arnold's need to raise money for the house was a factor in his later treason.

Elaborately engraved ticket for the Mischianza

Cartoon depicting Benedict Arnold as a traitor

354

Miss Margaret Shippen
daughter of Chief Justice Shippen

Peggy Shippen, Benedict Arnold, and John André

At the end of the festive British occupation of Philadelphia, the grateful officers of General William Howe staged a celebration of his glorious victories over the colonists. Called the Mischianza, meaning a mixture of entertainments, it was much the biggest bash the New World had ever seen: regatta, procession, triumphal arches, fireworks, mock-jousting, gambling, drinking, dining, and dancing into the dawn. The extravaganza was largely designed by the glamorous Major John André, who also drew a picture of Margaret (Peggy) Shippen, a socially prominent girl of the city. Prettier in life, she was expected to look something like André's drawing on the great occasion.

In spite of this great event, back in England skeptics doubted that Howe had any victories to celebrate. And Peggy was not the belle of the ball but the girl who missed it: her father said no when he saw her costume. Less than two years later John André was

dead, hanged by the neck as a spy. By then Miss Shippen was Mrs. Benedict Arnold, wife of the American general who had been dealing with André for the delivery of West Point to the enemy. Her hysterics at the time of her husband's exposure convinced George Washington and others that she was an innocent young woman caught up in a sordid affair. But she was not allowed to stay in Philadelphia, and she stuck with Arnold, "the best of husbands," through his long exile in England. A noted beauty with a pension from the King, she died at forty-four of cancer of the womb. We now know that she was deeply involved in her husband's treason, and may have urged him to it. But he never corrected the picture people still see here—unless they look closely at it—a guileless girl who married a monster. And she never showed him the lock of André's hair that she cherished till the end.

355

fear of being caught between a French fleet in Delaware Bay and General Washington at his rear. On June 18 he began moving his army into New Jersey for a march back to New York. Washington's army followed, crossed the Delaware above Trenton at Coryell's Ferry, and on June 28 engaged the British at the Battle of Monmouth in New Jersey. Here the work at Valley Forge proved itself. After a hard fight, the British withdrew from the field in the dead of night. Except for isolated Indian attacks on frontier settlements and the retaliatory expedition under General Sullivan in 1779, the evacuation of Philadelphia brought military activity in Pennsylvania to a close in June 1778.

Placed in command of Philadelphia by George Washington—in order to "prevent disorders which were expected upon . . . the return of the Whigs"—was the high-living Major General Benedict Arnold, hero of Saratoga, who two years later sold plans of the defenses of West Point to the British. The Continental Congress returned to Philadelphia from York, and established Departments of Foreign Affairs, War, and Finance—the last under Philadelphia's Robert Morris. On March 1, 1780, Pennsylvania became the first state to abolish slavery. In October 1781 the British general Cornwallis surrendered at Yorktown, and in November 1782 the Peace of Paris—negotiated by Franklin and four other American commissioners—recognized the United States as "free, sovereign, and independent." In 1785 and 1787 the Continental Congress passed ordinances providing for the territories between the thirteen original states and the Mississippi River. And on July 4, 1788, Philadelphia—the birthplace of independence and the nation's first capital—celebrated the ratification of a new Federal Constitution ordained to "secure the Blessings of Liberty to ourselves and our Posterity."

A N.W. VIEW OF THE STATE HOUSE IN PHILADELPHIA taken 1778

View of the State House as it appeared shortly after the signing of the Declaration of Independence.

"*Conference of the Treaty of Peace With England,*" *by Benjamin West, 1783. This painting immortalized the Treaty of Paris, signed in September of 1783, after two years of negotiations following the surrender of Cornwallis. It is incomplete because the British refused to sit for the artist. American negotiators, from left to right, are: John Jay, John Adams, Benjamin Franklin, Henry Laurens, and William Temple Franklin, who served as his grandfather's secretary.*

Epilogue

If Paul Revere found the Pennsylvanians he met more cautious and hesitant toward the idea of revolution than the people of Boston, he would soon find a Pennsylvania committed to the revolutionary cause, its people giving freely of its resources, perhaps because no colony had more to give. From its prosperous German farms came the food to feed the Patriot soldiers; from its iron plantations, the cannon and shot for their guns; and from the craftsmen in Lancaster, Lebanon, and Reading, the guns themselves—the "Pennsylvania rifles" known for their range and accuracy. To carry these weapons and materials, Pennsylvania supplied the Conestoga wagons, and the Conestoga horses to pull them. The commonwealth itself became a battlefield. Reading, Lebanon, Downingtown, and Lancaster served as major supply depots, and Yellow Spring and the Moravian towns of Bethlehem and Lititz provided important hospital facilities to care for the wounded. Pennsylvania also supplied its share of soldiers and officers, including Generals John Armstrong, Philip Benner, John Cadwalader, James Ewing, Edward Hand, William Irvine, Peter Muhlenberg, James Potter, Arthur St. Clair, Anthony Wayne, and Gerhard Weedon (born von der Wieden). Pennsylvanians in the naval service included Commodores Andrew Caldwell and Thomas Read; Captains Charles Alexander, Nicholas Biddle, Henry Dougherty, and John Rice; and there was Captain of Marines William Brown.

Individual Pennsylvanians contributed in other ways as well. General Thomas Mifflin for a time had charge of the Quartermaster Department, assisted by the Philadelphia merchant John Cox. Christopher Ludwig of Philadelphia became superintendent of bakers for the army. Dr. Bodo Otto of Reading served as the chief surgeon. Robert Morris, superintendent of finance for the Continental Congress, acted also as a purchasing agent of Pennsylvania to provide the state quota of army supplies. As the Congress gave him little and the state no money to perform these duties, he employed his private credit and sought the cooperation of other wealthy men like Haym Salomon, who used their fortunes to underwrite the war effort. Colonel Ephraim Blaine, whose careful planning prevented a complete breakdown of supplies at Valley Forge, became commissary general in 1779. In the diplomatic field, Franklin played a crucial role in negotiating the French alliance of 1778. The list could be extended, but this will suffice to show that Congress relied heavily upon Pennsylvania for troops, ordnance, transport, supplies, medical service, financial backing, and administrative talent. And through it all, Philadelphia served as the seat of government (except when Congress took refuge in Lancaster and York); it was there that the Declaration of Independence was signed and the Liberty Bell sounded.

Crèvecoeur had said that when the war ended the guilt would be with those who failed of success. In that sense he himself became one of the guilty, for despite his sympathy with the colonists and their plight, he could not endorse their revolution. As a French humanist, he hated the idea of war and could not see how these fortunate people had been so misused that they must take up arms. Moreover, he had been born an aristocrat, and most of his aristocratic friends among the New York gentry were loyalists. (It has been suggested that many of the patriots who emerged from the poorer colonists were as interested in throwing over the power of the American country squires as that of the British legislature.) Under suspicion by both sides, Crèvecoeur decided to return to France and take care of some family business. After the war he returned to America, only to find his home burned, his wife dead, and his children missing as a result of an Indian raid. He was able to recover his children in a Boston household, however, and before returning to France in 1790 he served as French consul to New York, New Jersey, and Connecticut. "There's nobody who understands more perfectly [than Crèvecoeur] the interests of the two countries as they relate to each other," said William Short, Jefferson's secretary, "and none more zealous to promote them mutually."

Joseph Galloway and Justice Allen did not fare so well. Galloway never returned from England after 1778, and his estates were confiscated by Pennsylvania. Allen died in England in 1780 after revisiting Philadelphia once in 1779, when he added to his will a codicil freeing his slaves.

To those who succeeded it was the best of times—although sometimes the worst of times were to follow. Thomas Mifflin was elected for three terms as Governor of Pennsylvania during the 1790s, but in 1799 he was forced to leave Philadelphia by an action brought against him by a creditor, and he died penniless soon after, buried at state expense. Financier Robert Morris was elected a senator from Pennsylvania from 1789 to 1795, with strong support from the Federalists. But disastrous speculation in western land cost him a position in Washington's cabinet as Secretary of the Treasury and landed him in debtors' prison from 1798 to 1801. He spent his last years in obscurity.

Tom Paine's story after the war was even more tragic. At the end of the war he was still a poor man because he had refused royalties for his pamphlets, giving his copyrights to the United States. He used what money he had to promote his invention of a steel bridge, for which purpose he went to England in 1787. However, revolution called again, as this time the French solicited his help and made him a member of their National Assembly. Paine accepted the new challenge, claiming "My Country is the world; to do good, my religion." Opposition to Paine's internationalism began a series of reactions in America which greatly diminished his prestige. For his efforts in France he was imprisoned during the Reign of Terror. In jail he wrote *The Age of Reason* (1794, 1795), which further outraged American opinion by its wholly rational approach to Scripture. After returning to America in 1802, he was maligned and humiliated until he died in poverty in 1809.

Other Pennsylvanians of 1776 settled more naturally and successfully into political life after the war. Peter Muhlenberg found himself a hero among the Pennsylvania Germans second only to Washington. He settled his affairs in Virginia and returned to his home state, where he became President of the German Society of Pennsylvania and was three times elected to Congress as a Democratic Republican. Robert Whitehill continued as a political figure representing frontier Pennsylvania. Never was his regional loyalty more evident than at the Pennsylvania Convention to ratify the Federal Constitution in 1787, where he tried to delay the election of delegates until the remoter regions of the state had more time to understand the new frame of government. John Dickinson became a delegate to the Constitutional Convention from Delaware, speaking vigorously for the rights of small states. For seventeen years thereafter he held no public office, but worked on his writings. Charles Thomson, the "perpetual secretary" of the Continental Congress, was chosen to inform General Washington of his election as President. Thomson retired from politics in 1789 to his estate at Harriton near Philadelphia, and during the next twenty years made scholarly translations of the Septuagint and the New Testament.

Anthony Wayne was also elected to office after the war, both in Chester County and in Georgia, where he was rewarded with a large grant of land for his achievements as a general in the South. But his most important activity in the postwar period was again military, for Washington called upon him to subdue the Indians of the Wabash and Maumee rivers. His victory at Fallen Timbers opened up the Northwest Territory.

Others went back to their previous lives and concerns. Benjamin Rush returned to his medical studies and teaching. In 1812 he published his famous *Medical Inquiries and Observations upon Diseases of the Mind*. At the University of Pennsylvania he helped create the best medical school in the United States, and more than any other man he was responsible for making Philadelphia the most important center for medical training in America during the first half of the nineteenth century.

Timothy Matlack returned to the problem of his relations with the Quakers. In 1781 he helped to form the Society of Free Quakers, composed of those who had been disowned by the Society of Friends or who had resigned because of their activities in the war. He was a member of the organization for the rest of his life and is buried in the Free Quaker burying ground in Philadelphia.

In May of 1787, Benjamin Franklin was eighty-one. But when concerned delegates met once again in Philadelphia, he was there, and when the Constitutional Convention was in danger of breaking up in disagreement over the nature of representation, it was Franklin who guided a conference committee toward the "Great Compromise" which resulted in our Senate and House of Representatives. (James Wilson of Pennsylvania led the fight to insure that a vote of the entire population undergirded the office of President, and another Pennsylvanian, Gouverneur Morris, wrote the final draft of the document which became the Constitution of the United States.) Four years earlier, in 1783, Franklin had been one of the peace commissioners, along with John Jay and John Adams, who signed the Treaty of Paris, ending the war; at the time of the Constitutional Convention he was serving his second term as President of Pennsylvania.

Franklin lived his last five years with his daughter on Market Street in Philadelphia, enjoying correspondence with his friends abroad and tinkering with inventions designed for the needs of an old man, like a specially constructed easy chair and a stick with moving parts to reach the highest books in his library (now called a "grocer's helper" when used for the top cans of tomato soup). In these years he also worked on his *Autobiography*, which he had begun in 1771.

In many ways Franklin was both the most famous and the most representative of the Pennsylvanians of 1776. His *Autobiography* reveals the spirit of the man and the values of his countrymen: industry, prudence, common sense, thrift, ambition, practical morality, worldly success, inventiveness, and humanitarian service. Surely he spoke for all of Pennsylvania and the new republic when he wrote with pride: "From the poverty and obscurity in which I was born and in which I passed my earliest years, I have raised myself to a state of affluence and some celebrity in the world."

The Development of Pennsylvania Counties

County	County Seat	Current Population (est.) Followed by Revolutionary Period (if available)	Decade of Earliest Significant European Settlement	Year Established	County or Counties from which Formed
Adams	Gettysburg	60,100	1730	1800	York
Allegheny	Pittsburgh	1,559,800	1760	1788	Washington, Westmoreland
Armstrong	Kittanning	77,200	1780	1800	Allegheny, Lycoming, Westmoreland
Beaver	Beaver	212,600	1760	1800	Allegheny, Washington
BEDFORD	Bedford	43,300 7,905	1750	1771	Cumberland
BERKS	Reading	304,800 22,900	1690	1752	Chester, Lancaster, Philadelphia
Blair	Hollidaysburg	137,400	1760	1846	Bedford, Huntingdon
Bradford	Towanda	59,200	1770	1810	Luzerne, Lycoming
BUCKS	Doylestown	442,200 18,463	1680	1682	Original Penn County
Butler	Butler	135,700	1780	1800	Allegheny
Cambria	Ebensburg	190,700	1770	1804	Huntingdon, Somerset
Cameron	Emporium	7,200	1810	1860	Clinton, Elk, McKean, Potter
Carbon	Mauch Chunk (Jim Thorpe)	51,700	1740	1843	Monroe, Northampton
Centre	Bellefonte	103,800	1760	1800	Huntingdon, Lycoming, Mifflin, Northampton

Note: Counties indicated by capital letters are the counties of Pennsylvania in 1776.

County	County Seat	Current Population (est.) Followed by Revolutionary Period (if available)	Decade of Earliest Significant European Settlement	Year Established	County or Counties from which Formed
CHESTER	West Chester	286,600 21,016	1640	1682	Original Penn County
Clarion	Clarion	40,800	1800	1839	Armstrong, Venango
Clearfield	Clearfield	76,900	1800	1804	Huntingdon, Lycoming
Clinton	Lock Haven	38,400	1760	1839	Centre, Lycoming
Columbia	Bloomsburg	57,400	1770	1813	Northumberland
Crawford	Meadville	84,900	1780	1800	Allegheny
CUMBERLAND	Carlisle	166,800 24,279	1720	1750	Lancaster
Dauphin	Harrisburg	226,700	1720	1785	Lancaster
Delaware	Media	601,600	1640	1789	Chester
Elk	Ridgway	38,800	1810	1843	Clearfield, Jefferson, McKean
Erie	Erie	273,400	1790	1800	Allegheny
Fayette	Uniontown	157,000	1750	1783	Westmoreland
Forest	Tionesta	5,000	1800	1848	Jefferson, Venango
Franklin	Chambersburg	102,000	1730	1784	Cumberland
Fulton	McConnellsburg	11,200	1750	1850	Bedford
Greene	Waynesburg	38,300	1750	1796	Washington
Huntingdon	Huntingdon	40,800	1750	1787	Bedford
Indiana	Indiana	83,900	1770	1803	Lycoming, Westmoreland

County	County Seat	Current Population (est.) Followed by Revolutionary Period (if available)	Decade of Earliest Significant European Settlement	Year Established	County or Counties from which Formed
Jefferson	Brookville	45,100	1800	1804	Lycoming
Juniata	Mifflintown	17,800	1750	1831	Mifflin
Lackawanna	Scranton	237,000	1760	1878	Luzerne
LANCASTER	Lancaster	334,400 35,493	1700	1729	Chester
Lawrence	New Castle	108,600	1790	1849	Beaver, Mercer
Lebanon	Lebanon	103,500	1700	1813	Dauphin, Lancaster
Lehigh	Allentown	259,700	1720	1812	Northampton
Luzerne	Wilkes-Barre	346,800	1760	1786	Northumberland
Lycoming	Williamsport	115,700	1760	1795	Northumberland
McKean	Smethport	52,500	1800	1804	Lycoming
Mercer	Mercer	129,000	1790	1800	Allegheny
Mifflin	Lewistown	46,100	1760	1789	Cumberland, Northampton
Monroe	Stroudsburg	49,300	1720	1836	Northampton, Pike
Montgomery	Norristown	628,500	1680	1784	Philadelphia
Montour	Danville	17,800	1770	1850	Columbia
NORTHAMPTON	Easton	221,300 15,495	1720	1752	Bucks
NORTHUMBER-LAND	Sunbury	100,100 6,895	1760	1772	Bedford, Berks, Cumberland, Lancaster, Northampton

County	County Seat	Current Population (est.) Followed by Revolutionary Period (if available)	Decade of Earliest Significant European Settlement	Year Established	County or Counties from which Formed
Perry	New Bloomfield	32,200	1750	1820	Cumberland
PHILADELPHIA	Philadelphia	1,881,300 63,060	1650	1682	Original Penn County
Pike	Milford	12,900	1680	1814	Wayne
Potter	Coudersport	17,500	1800	1804	Lycoming
Schuykill	Pottsville	161,900	1740	1811	Berks, Northampton
Snyder	Middleburg	31,100	1750	1855	Union
Somerset	Somerset	78,400	1760	1795	Bedford
Sullivan	Laporte	6,000	1790	1847	Lycoming
Susquehanna	Montrose	36,900	1780	1810	Luzerne
Tioga	Wellsboro	41,800	1790	1804	Lycoming
Union	Lewisburg	29,500	1760	1813	Northumberland
Venango	Franklin	63,200	1790	1800	Allegheny, Lycoming
Warren	Warren	49,200	1790	1800	Allegheny, Lycoming
Washington	Washington	215,000 13,938	1760	1781	Westmoreland
Wayne	Honesdale	32,600	1750	1798	Northampton
WESTMORELAND	Greensburg	379,300 17,841	1760	1773	Bedford
Wyoming	Tunkhannock	21,000	1770	1842	Luzerne
York	York	282,000 30,748	1720	1749	Lancaster

Suggestions for Further Reading

Bibliographies, Guides, and Primary Source Materials

The most comprehensive bibliography on all aspects of Pennsylvania life is Norman B. Wilkinson's *Bibliography of Pennsylvania History* (Harrisburg, 1957). This important work is supplemented by *Year's Work in Pennsylvania Studies* (Harrisburg, 1965–), *Writings on American History* (Washington, D.C., 1902–), and *America: History and Life* (Santa Barbara, 1964–). Good bibliographies can also be found in Philip Klein and Ari Hoogenboom's *A History of Pennsylvania* (New York, 1973) and in S.K. Stevens' *Pennsylvania, Birthplace of a Nation* (New York, 1964). Of utmost importance to any serious study of Pennsylvania history is the *Pennsylvania Archives* (Harrisburg, 1835–1935), which includes information for the period 1664–1902. Details on this archive are provided in Henry Eddy's *Guide to the Published Archives of Pennsylvania* (Harrisburg, 1949). Some of the documents in the archive are reprinted in Asa Martin's *Pennsylvania History Told by Contemporaries* (New York, 1925). A detailed description of the works listed in this bibliography and other Pennsylvania studies in the context of the political, social, and cultural climate of Colonial and Revolutionary America can be found in Allen Cohen's bibliographical essay (University Park, 1976).

General Histories, Guides, and Periodicals

Standard histories of Pennsylvania are Philip Klein and Ari Hoogenboom's *A History of Pennsylvania* (New York, 1973) and S.K. Stevens' *Pennsylvania, Birthplace of a Nation* (New York, 1964). The WPA Writers Program's *Pennsylvania: A Guide to the Keystone State* (New York, 1940) is still very valuable, but S.K. Stevens' *Pennsylvania, a Student's Guide to Localized History* (New York, 1965) is a more recent work offering suggestions of places to visit in the Commonwealth.

Important work on the early history of Philadelphia includes Carl Bridenbaugh and Jessica Bridenbaugh's *Rebels and Gentlemen: Philadelphia in the Age of Franklin* (New York, 1942). A more recent work is *Life and Times in Colonial Philadelphia* by Joseph J. Kelley, Jr. (Harrisburg, 1973). And the WPA Writers Program's *Philadelphia, A Guide to the Nation's Birthplace* (Philadelphia, 1937) remains a very useful guide to the city.

Information on Pittsburgh and Western Pennsylvania can be found in Solon J. Buck and Elizabeth Hawthorn's *The Planting of Civilization in Western Pennsylvania* (Pittsburgh, 1969) and Leland D. Baldwin's *Pittsburgh: The Story of a City, 1750–1865* (Pittsburgh, 1937; rev. ed. 1970). A guide to the area is provided by the Western Pennsylvania Historical Survey's *Guidebook to Historic Places in Western Pennsylvania* (Pittsburgh, 1938). For this area the WPA Writers Program produced *Tales of Pioneer Pittsburgh* (Philadelphia, 1937).

The best magazine articles on Pennsylvania history and life are in *Pennsylvania Magazine of History and Biography* (Philadelphia, 1877–), *Western Pennsylvania Historical Magazine* (Pittsburgh, 1918–), and *Pennsylvania History* (University Park, 1934–). Information on the many regional Pennsylvania journals published by local historical societies can be found in *The Pennsylvania Directory of Historical Organizations*, compiled by Gail Gibson (Harrisburg, 1971).

Geography, Early Exploration, Maps, and Place Names

Raymond Murphy and Marion Murphy's *Pennsylvania, a Regional Geography* (State College, 1937) is the best general geographic survey of the Commonwealth. Ralph H. Brown's *Mirror for Americans: Likeness of the Eastern Seaboard* (New York, 1943) shows how a fictitious Philadelphia geographer in 1810 might have conceived the Eastern seaboard. A discussion of Colonial Chester and Lancaster counties is provided in James T. Lemon's *Best Poor Man's Country: A Geographical Study of Early Southeastern Pennsylvania*

(Baltimore, 1972), and John Losensky discusses the prairies and plains of central Pennsylvania and other areas of the state in his master's thesis, *The Great Plains of Central Pennsylvania* (University Park, 1961). *The Rivers of America Series* (New York, n.d.) includes books on the Allegheny, Brandywine, Delaware, Monongahela, Ohio, and Susquehanna. For the Schuylkill River, there is James Nolan's *Schuylkill* (New Brunswick, N.J., 1951). Flora and fauna are considered by E.L. Braun in *Deciduous Forests of Eastern North America* (Philadelphia, 1950) and by Samuel Rhoads in *Mammals of Pennsylvania and New Jersey* (Philadelphia, 1903). John Bartram's *Journey from Pennsylvania to Onondaga in 1743* (Barre, Mass., 1973) is an account of his early explorations. This reprint of a book originally published in 1751 as *Observations on the Inhabitants, Climate, Soil, Rivers, Productions, Animals, and other matters worthy of notice* (London) also includes "Extract from the Journal of Lewis Evans" and "Report of a Journey to Onondaga by Conrad Weiser." Also of interest is Peter Kalm's *Travels into North America* (London, 1770–1771).

Early mapmaking is discussed and illustrated by Walter Klinefelter in *Lewis Evans and his Maps* (Philadelphia, 1971) and Lloyd A. Brown in *Early Maps of the Ohio Valley* (Pittsburgh, 1959). A comprehensive guide to maps is Ruby Miller's *Pennsylvania Maps and Atlases in the Pennsylvania State University Libraries* (University Park, 1972).

The origin of Pennsylvania place names is treated by Abraham H. Espenshade in *Pennsylvania Place Names* (State College, 1925).

Agriculture

Lyman Carrier's *The Beginning of Agriculture in America* (New York, 1923) discusses Indian agriculture as well as Colonial developments. Percy W. Bidwell's *History of Agriculture in the Northern United States, 1620–1860* (Washington, D.C., 1925) is the standard work for this large region, and the standard work for Pennsylvania is Stevenson W. Fletcher's *Pennsylvania Agriculture and Country Life, 1640–1840* (Harrisburg, 1950).

Indians

The Pennsylvania Historical and Museum Commission has published important studies of the Indians of Pennsylvania. The best general survey is Paul A. Wallace's *Indians in Pennsylvania* (Harrisburg, 1961). Two works on archeological history published by the Commission are *Foundations of Pennsylvania Prehistory*, edited by Barry C. Kent et al. (Harrisburg, 1971), and W. Fred Kinsey's *Archaeology in the Upper Delaware Valley* (Harrisburg, 1972). For particular tribes see C.A.

Weslager's *The Delaware Indians: A History* (New Brunswick, N.J., 1972), Merle Deardorff's essay "The Cornplanter Indians" in *Pennsylvania Songs and Legends*, edited by George Korson (Philadelphia, 1949), and Lewis H. Morgan's *League of the Iroquois* (New York, 1904). Early contact with Indians in Pennsylvania is related by Paul A. Wallace in *Conrad Weiser, 1696–1760, Friend of Colonist and Mohawk* (Philadelphia, 1945).

Ethnic, Religious, and Racial Groups

John Bodnar's *Ethnic History in Pennsylvania: A Selected Bibliography* (Harrisburg, 1974) and a collection of essays, *The Ethnic Experience in Pennsylvania*, edited by Bodnar (Lewisburg, 1973), are guides to the twenty-three ethnic groups that settled in Pennsylvania. Important works dealing with European conditions that led to the first migrations are Marcus L. Hansen's *The Atlantic Migration 1607–1860* (Cambridge, Mass., 1940), and Carl Bridenbaugh's *Vexed and Troubled Englishmen, 1590–1642* (New York, 1968).

William Penn and the Society of Friends

Of all the biographies written about William Penn, some of the best are Thomas Clarkson's *Memoirs of the Private and Public Life of William Penn* (London, 1849), William I. Hull's *William Penn* (New York, 1937), Colwyn Vulliamy's *William Penn* (New York, 1934), Catherine O. Peare's *William Penn: A Biography* (Ann Arbor, Mich., 1957), Sidney Fisher's *The True William Penn* (Philadelphia, 1900), and William Comfort's *William Penn, 1644–1718, a Tercentenary Estimate* (Philadelphia, 1944).

The best one-volume work on the Society of Friends is Elbert Russell's *History of Quakerism* (New York, 1942). The standard work on the Colonial period is Rufus Jones' *The Quakers in the American Colonies* (New York, 1911). Pennsylvania is considered in William Comfort's *The Quakers: A brief account of their influence on Pennsylvania* (Gettysburg, 1948), Edwin Bonner's *William Penn's Holy Experiment, The Founding of Pennsylvania, 1681–1701* (New York, 1962), and Gary B. Nash's *Quakers and Politics: Pennsylvania, Sixteen Eighty-One to Seventeen Twenty-Six* (Princeton, 1968). Nash also discusses Quaker attitudes and relations with Indians and blacks in *Red, White, and Black: The Peoples of Early America* (Englewood Cliffs, N.J., 1974), and the same topic is considered in Robert Davidson's *War Comes to Quaker Pennsylvania, 1682–1756* (New York, 1957), a work dealing with Indian relations, and Thomas Drake's *Quakers and Slavery in America* (New Haven, 1950).

Germans

The standard work is Albert B. Faust's *German Element in the United States* (New York, 1909). Other works of importance are Russell Gilbert's *Pictures of the Pennsylvania Germans* (Gettysburg, 1962), James Knauss' *Social Conditions among Pennsylvania Germans in the Eighteenth Century* (Lancaster, 1922), Ralph Wood's *Pennsylvania Germans* (Princeton, 1942), and Fredric Klees' *Pennsylvania Dutch* (New York, 1950).

The first scholarly account of the Amish, which remains the best introduction, is Calvin Bachman's *Old Order Amish of Lancaster County* (Norristown, 1942). Charles Rice's photographs of many aspects of Amish life appear in *The Amish Year* (New Brunswick, N.J., 1956), and John A. Hostetler deals effectively with *Amish Society* (Baltimore, 1968; rev. ed. 1970). Other German groups in Pennsylvania are discussed in Gillian L. Gollin's *Moravians in Two Worlds: A Study of Changing Communities* (New York, 1967), Howard W. Kriebel's *The Schwenkfelders in Pennsylvania* (Lancaster, 1904), John Wenger's *History of the Mennonites of the Franconia Conference* (Telford, 1937), Donald F. Durnbaugh's *The Brethren in Colonial America* (Elgin, Ill., 1967), William Hinke's *Ministers of the German Reformed Congregations in Pennsylvania and other Colonies in the Eighteenth Century* (Lancaster, 1951), and James Ernst's *Ephrata* (Allentown, 1963)

Other Ethnic, Religious, and Racial Groups

Two important books on the Scotch-Irish are Wayland Dunaway's *The Scotch-Irish of Colonial Pennsylvania* (Chapel Hill, N.C., 1915) and Guy Klett's *The Scotch-Irish in Pennsylvania* (Gettysburg, 1948). The standard work on the Welsh is Charles Browning's *Welsh Settlements of Pennsylvania* (Philadelphia, 1912). Leo Fink discusses the Catholic experience in *Old Jesuit Trails in Penn's Forest* (New York, 1933), and Edwin Wolf deals with the *History of the Jews of Philadelphia from Colonial Times to the Age of Jackson* (Philadelphia, 1957). Ira Brown's *The Negro in Pennsylvania History* (University Park, 1970) and Edward Turner's *The Negro in Pennsylvania* (Washington, D.C., 1911) are important for an understanding of the black experience in the Commonwealth. The role of blacks in the Revolution is explored in Benjamin Quarles' *The Negro in the American Revolution* (New York, 1973).

The Colonial Experience

The importance of the New York, New Jersey, Delaware, and Pennsylvania region on the development of the colonies is dealt with in Daniel Thompson's *Gateway to a Nation* (Rindge, N.H., 1956). The most important book on Pennsylvania's situation is Theodore Thayer's *Pennsylvania Politics and the Growth of Democracy, 1740–1776* (Harrisburg, 1953). Also of importance are Dietmar Rothermund's *Layman's Progress: Denominations and Political Behavior in Colonial Pennsylvania* (Philadelphia, 1966), Winfred T. Root's *The Relations of Pennsylvania with the British Government, 1696–1765* (Philadelphia, 1912), William R. Shepherd's *History of Proprietary Government in Pennsylvania* (New York, 1896), and Mabel Wolff's thesis *The Colonial Agency of Pennsylvania, 1712–1757* (Philadelphia, 1933). For the various Colonial wars, there is Randolph C. Downes' *Council Fires on the Upper Ohio* (Pittsburgh, 1940), Donald Kent's *The French Invasion of Western Pennsylvania, 1753* (Harrisburg, 1954), and William Hunter's *Forts on the Pennsylvania Frontier, 1753–1758* (Harrisburg, 1960).

Cultural and Intellectual Development

Carl Bridenbaugh's *Cities in the Wilderness* (New York, 1955) and *Cities in Revolt* (New York, 1955) are excellent treatments of urban life during the Colonial period and the social history manifested in some of the cities, including Philadelphia. The best general survey on the development of intellectual thought is Merle Curti's *The Growth of American Thought* (New York, 1964). Also of importance is Max Savelle's *Seeds of Liberty; The Genesis of the American Mind* (New York, 1948). Thomas Wertenbaker deals with the cultural growth of the Quakers and Germans of Pennsylvania in *The Middle Colonies* (New York, 1938).

Benjamin Franklin

Still considered to be the best biography of America's Renaissance man is Carl Van Doren's *Benjamin Franklin* (New York, 1938). An earlier work considered in the same rank is James Parton's *Life and Times of Benjamin Franklin* (Boston, 1864). Max Farrand's edition of Franklin's *Autobiography* (Berkeley, 1949) is considered definitive. The best book on Franklin as a literary man is Bruce I. Granger's *Benjamin Franklin: An American Man of Letters* (Ithaca, N.Y., 1964), and the best collection of his writings is Chester Jorgenson and Frank Luther Mott's edition of *Representative Selection* (New York, 1962). His scientific and technological contributions are considered in two books by I. Bernard Cohen, *Benjamin Franklin* (Indianapolis, 1953), and *Franklin and Newton* (Philadelphia, 1956). Other aspects of Franklin's life are covered in William S. Hanna's *Benjamin Franklin and Pennsylvania Politics* (Stanford, 1964), Gerald Stourzh's *Benjamin Franklin and American Foreign Policy* (Chicago, 1969), and Melvin H. Buxbaum's *Benjamin Franklin and the Zealous Presbyterians* (University Park, 1975).

Education

A recent general work is Lawrence A. Cremin's *American Education: The Colonial Experience, 1607–1786* (New York, 1970). A valuable study of education in Pennsylvania is J.P. Wickersham's *History of Education in Pennsylvania* (Lancaster, 1885). Close ties between religion and education are noted in Thomas Woody's *Early Quaker Education in Pennsylvania* (New York, 1920), Charles Maurer's *Early Lutheran Education in Pennsylvania* (Philadelphia, 1932), and Mabel Haller's *Early Moravian Education in Pennsylvania* (Nazareth, 1953).

Printing, Publishing, and Library Activity

The classic guide to early publishing activity is Charles S. Hildeburn's *A Century of Printing: The Issues of the Press in Pennsylvania, 1685–1784* (Philadelphia, 1885). German publishing activity is covered in O. Seidensticker's *The First Century of German Printing in America, 1728–1830* (Philadelphia, 1893). The standard text on early publishing activity is Isaiah Thomas' *The History of Printing in America* (Worcester, Mass., 1810). More recent is Lawrence C. Wroth's *The Colonial Printer* (Charlottesville, Va., 1938). Important for its coverage of Colonial newspapers is Clarence Brigham's *History and Bibliography of American Newspapers, 1690–1820* (Worcester, Mass., 1947). Also of importance are two works of Frank Luther Mott, *American Journalism: A History, 1690–1960* (New York, 1962) and *A History of American Magazines* (Cambridge, Mass., 1930–1968). The book-collecting activities of the early Quaker leader James Logan is related in Edwin Wolf's *James Logan, 1674–1751, Bookman Extraordinary* (Philadelphia, 1971). The founding of the Library Company of Philadelphia by Benjamin Franklin and the story of the Junto Club are told in Austin Gray's *Benjamin Franklin's Library* (New York, 1937).

Literature

The definitive general history is *Literary History of the United States*, edited by Robert Spiller et al. (New York, 1974). A seminal work is Vernon Parrington's *Main Currents in American Thought* (New York, 1927–1930). Still considered one of the best works for the period is Moses Tyler's *History of American Literature during the Colonial Period, 1607–1765* (New York, 1897). Pennsylvanian literature is discussed in M. Katherine Jackson's *Outlines of the Literary History of Colonial Pennsylvania* (Lancaster, 1907), Ellis P. Oberholtzer's *Literary History of Philadelphia* (Philadelphia, 1906), and Earl Robacker's *Pennsylvania German Literature* (Philadelphia, 1943). A good anthology which includes selections of important Pennsylvania writers is *American Literature: Tradition and Innovation*, edited by Harrison T. Meserole et al. (Lexington, Mass., 1969).

Music

The best general history is Gilbert Chase's *America's Music: From the Pilgrims to the Present* (New York, 1966). *Pennsylvania Songs and Legends*, edited by George Korson (Philadelphia, 1949), examines the songs and folklore of various groups that lived in Pennsylvania. Religious music is discussed in *Church Music and Musical Life in Pennsylvania in the Eighteenth Century*, collected by the National Society of Colonial Dames of America (Philadelphia, 1926) and Robert Drummond's *Early German Music in Philadelphia* (New York, 1910). Moravian music is considered in William Armstrong's *Organs for America: The Life and Works of David Tannenberg* (Philadelphia, 1967). Some examples of the music can be heard on the following records: *Organ in America* (Columbia MS-6161), *Music of the American Moravians* (Odyssey 32160340), *Songs of Early Americans* (Golden Crest 7020), *Early String Quartets in the U.S.A.* (Vox SVBX 5301), and the series *Folk Music of the United States* (Library of Congress, Archive of American Folk Song).

Art

General works of note are Edgar P. Richardson's *Painting in America: From 1502 to the Present* (New York, 1965) and Oliver W. Larkin's *Art and Life in America* (New York, 1960) and *Arts in America: The Colonial Period* (New York, 1966). James T. Flexner has written a two-volume study of the social history of American art, *First Flowers of our Wilderness* (Boston, 1947) and *The Light of Distant Skies* (New York, 1954). Biographical essays on important Pennsylvania artists are included in Flexner's *America's Old Masters* (New York, 1939). The definitive work on Peale is Charles C. Sellers' *Charles Willson Peale* (New York, 1969). A special issue of *American Art Journal*: "1776—How America Really Looked" (New York, May 1975) covers various aspects of the arts.

Folk Art

In the 1930s the Federal Art Project produced the monumental *Index of American Design*. American folk and decorative arts are studied in detail in Clarence P. Hornung's *Treasury of American Design* (New York, 1972). A major exhibition catalog, Jean Lipman and Alice Winchester's *The Flowering of American Folk Art, 1776–1876* (New York, 1974), presents a good selection of Pennsylvania folk art, and Frances Lichten's *Folk*

Art of Rural Pennsylvania (New York, 1946) is considered the best work on this subject. Other important books are Henry J. Kauffman's *Pennsylvania Dutch American Folk Art* (New York, 1964), John Stoudt's *Pennsylvania Folk Art* (Allentown, 1948), and Donald Shelley's *Fraktur-Writings, or Illuminated Manuscripts of the Pennsylvania Germans* (Allentown, 1961).

Folklore and Folklife

The best collection on all aspects of folklore and folklife is *Pennsylvania Songs and Legends*, edited by George Korson (Philadelphia, 1949). Important publications have been issued by the Pennsylvania German Society, The Pennsylvania German Folklore Society, and the Pennsylvania Folklore Society. The WPA Federal Writers Project produced *Tales of Pioneer Pittsburgh* (Philadelphia, 1937), and the American Folkways Series issued George Swetnam's *Pittsylvania* (New York, 1951). An attempt to look at folklore as folk culture that includes material elements is presented in Henry Glassie's *Pattern in the Material Folk Culture of the Eastern United States* (Philadelphia, 1968; rev. ed. 1971). A periodical in this field is *Pennsylvania Folklife* (Lancaster, 1949–).

Architecture

Fiske Kimball's *Domestic Architecture of the American Colonies and of the Early Republic* (New York, 1922) is a classic. The best one-volume treatment is Hugh Morrison's *Early American Architecture* (New York, 1952). Philadelphia architecture is the subject of Frank Cousin's *Colonial Architecture of Philadelphia* (Boston, 1920) and George Tatum's *Penn's Great Town* (Philadelphia, 1961). For the western part of the state there is Charles Stotz's *Early Architecture of Western Pennsylvania* (New York, 1936). Harold Dickson covers the whole state in *A Hundred Pennsylvania Buildings* (State College, 1954). The barn is dealt with in Charles Dornbusch's *Pennsylvania German Barns* (Allentown, 1958).

Business and Commerce

Joseph Dorfman's *Economic Mind in American Civilization 1606–1903* (New York, 1946–1959) and Davis Dewey's *Financial History of the United States* (New York, 1934) are the most important books on this subject. A recent history is Thomas Cochran's *Business in American Life* (New York, 1972). The Colonial period is considered in Arthur Schlesinger's *Colonial Merchants and the American Revolution, 1763–1776* (New York, 1968), Louis Hartz's *Economic Policy and Democratic Thought: Pennsylvania 1776–1860* (Cambridge, Mass., 1948), Arthur Jensen's *The Maritime Commerce of Colonial Philadelphia* (Madison, Wisc., 1963), and Frederick Tolles' *Meeting House and Counting House: The Quaker Merchants of Colonial Pennsylvania, 1682–1763* (Chapel Hill, N.C., 1963).

Transportation

The best early work, with much material about Pennsylvania, is Balthaser H. Meyer's *History of Transportation in the United States before 1860* (Washington, D.C., 1917). Also important is Seymour Dunbar's *A History of Travel in America* (New York, 1915). There is also George Swetnam's *Pennsylvania Transportation* (Gettysburg, 1964), and a unique means of early transport developed in Pennsylvania is dealt with by George Shumway in *Conestoga Wagon* (York, 1968).

Technology, Industry, and Labor

Important works are Victor Clark's *History of Manufactures in the United States, 1607–1860* (New York, 1929). *History of American Manufactures from 1608 to 1860* (Phila., 1868) by J. Leander Bishop et al., and John Oliver's *History of American Technology* (New York, 1956). The development of early material culture is considered in William C. Langdon's *Everyday Things in American Life* (New York, 1937–1941). Industrialization is discussed in Arthur C. Bining's *Pennsylvania Iron Manufacture in the Eighteenth Century* (Harrisburg, 1973) and Paul H. Gidden's *Pennsylvania Petroleum, 1750–1872: A Documentary History* (Harrisburg, 1947). Carl Bridenbaugh studies Philadelphia craftsmen as urban manufacturers in *Colonial Craftsman* (New York, 1950). Important studies on the working and laboring classes are Richard B. Morris' *Government and Labor in Early America* (New York, 1946), Cheesman A. Herrick's *White Servitude in Pennsylvania* (Philadelphia, 1926), and Abbot E. Smith's *Colonists in Bondage: White Servitude and Convict Labor in America, 1607–1776* (Chapel Hill, N.C., 1947).

Science and Medicine

Brooke Hindle's *The Pursuit of Science in Revolutionary America, 1735–1789* (New York, 1974) is important, as are George H. Daniels' *Science in American Society: A Social History* (New York, 1971) and Raymond P. Stearns' *Science in the British Colonies of America* (Urbana, Ill., 1970). Some works on Franklin as a scientist are indicated in the section on him. Another important scientist is discussed in Brooke Hindle's *David Rittenhouse* (Princeton, 1964) and Edward Ford's *David Rittenhouse, Astronomer-Patriot, 1732–1796* (Philadelphia, 1946). Early interest in botany and natural history is exemplified by John and William Bartram. Some of their writings are collected by Helen C. Cruickshank in *John and William Bartram's America* (New York, 1957). William Bartram's contributions are detailed in Nathan Fagin's *William Bartram, Interpreter of the American Landscape* (Baltimore, 1933). General works about Pennsylvanians important in the development of medical science are Richard H. Shryock's *Medicine and Society in America, 1660–1860* (New York, 1960), Henry E. Sigerist's *American Medicine* (New York, 1934), and James T. Flexner's *Doctors on Horseback: Pioneers of American Medicine* (New York, 1930). Two works on a famous physician-politician who was a member of the Continental Congress and signer of the Declaration of Independence are Nathan Goodman's *Benjamin Rush* (Philadelphia, 1934) and Carl Binger's *Revolutionary Doctor: Benjamin Rush, 1746–1813* (New York, 1966).

The Revolution

The Middle Colonies are discussed in John Neuenschwander's *The Middle Colonies and the Coming of the American Revolution* (Port Washington, N.Y., 1973). Two important works on Pennsylvania are David Hawke's *In the Midst of a Revolution* (Philadelphia, 1961) and Robert L. Brunhouse's *Counter-Revolution in Pennsylvania, 1776–1790* (Harrisburg, 1942). Works concerned with various aspects of internal struggle in the Commonwealth are Charles Lincoln's *The Revolutionary Movement in Pennsylvania, 1760–1776* (Philadelphia, 1901) and J.P. Selsam's *Pennsylvania Constitution of 1776* (Philadelphia, 1936). Robert M. Calhoon's *The Loyalists in Revolutionary America, 1760–1781* (New York, 1973) includes a discussion of Joseph Galloway, and a detailed study of Dickinson can be found in David Jacobson's *John Dickinson and the Revolution in Pennsylvania, 1764–1776* (Berkeley, 1965).

Recently published as a guide to Revolutionary War sites is Sol Stember's *The Bicentennial Guide to the American Revolution* (New York, 1974). Important general works on campaigns and battles are Willard M.

Wallace's *Appeal to Arms: A Military History of the American Revolution* (New York, 1951), Christopher Ward's *War of the Revolution* (New York, 1952), and Ann Hutton's *The Year and the Spirit of 1776* (Philadelphia, 1972). The story of Valley Forge is related in Arthur Bill's *Valley Forge, the Making of an Army* (N.Y., 1952) Lynn Montross tells what it was like to be a soldier in *Rag, Tag and Bobtail; The Story of the Continental Army 1775–1783* (New York, 1952). Naval activities are discussed by Charles Paullin in *Navy of the American Revolution* (Chicago, 1906) and John W. Jackson in *The Pennsylvania Navy, 1775–1781: The Defense of the Delaware* (New Brunswick, N.J., 1974). Books about Anthony Wayne include Harry Wildes' *Anthony Wayne, Trouble Shooter of the American Revolution* (New York, 1941) and Glenn Tucker's *Mad Anthony Wayne and the New Nation: The Story of Washington's Front-Line General* (Harrisburg, 1973).

The Centennial Celebration (*1876*) and The Bicentennial (*1976*)

Accounts of the celebration of 1876 held at Fairmount Park in Philadelphia are John Maass' *The Glorious Enterprise* (Watkins Glen, N.Y., 1973) and Dee Brown's *The Year of the Century: 1876* (New York, 1966). A contemporaneous account is James McCabe's *The Illustrated History of the Centennial Exhibition* (Philadelphia, 1876). Also of interest is the U.S. Centennial Commission's *Official Catalog* (Philadelphia, 1876).

The idea of a Bicentennial celebration as another International Exposition in Philadelphia is presented in *Toward A Meaningful Bicentennial* (Philadelphia, 1969). Background information is provided by Robert Hartje in *Bicentennial U.S.A.* (Nashville, 1973). Two periodicals with current information on activities in Pennsylvania and the rest of the country are *Colonial Heritage* (Bound Brook, N.J., 1970–) and *Pennsylvania Heritage* (Harrisburg, 1974–). Bicentennial celebrations for children in Pennsylvania are suggested in *Project 1776: A Manual for the Bicentennial*, edited by Anne H. Cook and Jane T. Breinholt (Harrisburg, 1974).

Illustration Credits

Page numbers are in boldface type. On a page with more than one credit, illustrations are identified by small letters arranged alphabetically according to each image's position on the page, running from left to right and from top to bottom.

The following abbreviations are used for sources frequently cited:

APS American Philosophical Society

FLP The Free Library of Philadelphia

HSP The Historical Society of Pennsylvania

Landis Valley The Pennsylvania Farm Museum at Landis Valley, PHMC

LCP The Library Company of Philadelphia

PHMC Pennsylvania Historical and Museum Commission

PMA Philadelphia Museum of Art

Trussler John Trussler, *The Progress of Man in Society*, Bath, 1790

Winterthur The Henry Francis du Pont Winterthur Museum, Winterthur, Delaware

York The Historical Society of York County, York, Pennsylvania

Prologue

11 Detail from 186 **12** Detail from 107 **13** *a* Detail from 163 *b* Detail from 321*b*. **14** *a* Detail from 276 *b* Detail from 200 *c* Detail from 275 **15** *a* Engraving by A.H. Ritchie, drawing by C.N. Cochin, 1777; collection of George H. Beatty *b* Detail from 344

The Land and the People

16 Photo by Michael A. Ondik **18** Photos by Peirce F. Lewis **20** Designed by Peirce F. Lewis, drafted by Robert J. Texter **21** Map by Erwin Raisz in his *Landforms of the United States*, 6th revised edition, Boston, 1957 **23** Designed by Peirce F. Lewis, drafted by Robert J. Texter **25** Photo courtesy Western Pennsylvania Conservancy **28** Photo by Irwin Richman **29** Photo by Dick Brown **30–32** Photos by Robert S. Beese **33** Engravings from drawings by Alexander Wilson **35** Photos by Donald S. Heintzelman (fox & elk), Heinz K. Henisch (chipmunk), and Michael A. Ondik (all others) **36** Photos by George H. Beatty **37** *a* Old woodcut *b* Photo by Robert S. Beese **39** *a–c* Courtesy Trustees of the British Museum (Natural History) *d* Collection of George H. Beatty **40** Engraving by T.B. Welch from a painting by C.W. Peale **41–42** Courtesy Trustees of the British Museum (Natural History) **43** 19th century photo in *Popular Science Monthly* **44** Woodcut in Gerard's *Herball*, 1636 **45–46** Photos by Robert S. Beese **47–52** Drawings of trees by Rae D. Chambers, drawings of leaves, fruits, and flowers by Charles E. Faxon & Mary W. Gill, in *Manual of the Trees of North America*, Boston, 1905 **53** *a–b* Drawings by Rae D. Chambers *c* Drawing in Trussler, 1790; courtesy LCP **54–55** Woodcuts in Gerard's *Herball*, 1636 **56** *a* See 53*a–b*. *b* Drawing by C. Burton, engraving by W.E. Tucker, in Godman's *Natural History*, 1826 **57** *a* Drawing by N. Brown, in Tenney's *Natural History*, 1865 *b* Old woodcut *c* Drawing by L. Beckmann, in Wood's *Natural History* **58** Drawing by M.E.D. Brown, in Doughty's *Cabinet of Natural History*, 1832 **59** *a* Old woodcut *b* Drawing by F.S. Morse, in Tenney's *Natural History c* Drawing by N. Brown in Tenney's *Natural History* **60** *a* Drawing by J. Ryder, engraving by F. Kearny, in Godman's *Natural History*, 1826 *b* Old woodcut *c–d* Drawings by G. Mutzel, in Wood's *Natural History* **61–63** Drawings by Dorothy L. Bordner **64** *a* Drawing in *Das Heller-Magazin*, 1842 *b* Drawing by Mrs. J.W. Dickinson, engraving by N. Brown, in Tenney's *Natural History* **65** *a–b* See 64*b*. *c–d* Drawings by Lawrence A. Krezo **66** *a* Old woodcut *b* Drawing by Lawrence A. Krezo *c* Drawing in James Barbut, *The Genera Insectorum of Linnaeus*, London, 1780 *d* Drawing in R.A.F. de Reamur, *Memoires pour servir a l'histoire des insectes*, 6 vols., Amsterdam, 1737–1748 *e* Drawing from information supplied by John Bartram to Peter Collinson *f* See 66*c*. **67** *a* See 66*d*. *b–e* See 66*c*. *f* Drawing from Mouffet's *Theater of Insects*, 1634 **69** Old woodcut **70** Photo by Charles E. Douts, Jr. of PHMC site **71** Drawing for the engraved frontispiece in *William Bartram's Travels*, Philadelphia, 1791; collection of George H. Beatty **72** Courtesy PHMC **73** *a* Detail of map in William Smith, An Historical *Account of the Expedition against the Ohio Indians in 1764*; courtesy LCP *b–e* Photos by Fred Prouser of eighteenth century artifacts in William Penn Memorial Museum, PHMC **74** Frontispiece in a book published in Philadelphia in 1794; courtesy LCP **75** Photos—see 73*b–e*. **76** Courtesy HSP **78** Courtesy New-York Historical Society **82–83** Map by Robert Sayer and John Bennett, 1775; Library of Congress **84** Photo courtesy PHMC **86** Designed by Peirce F. Lewis, drafted by Robert J. Texter **87** Courtesy LCP **89** Maps by Herman R. Friis for the American Geographical Society, in his *A Series of Population Maps of the Colonies and the United States, 1625–1790*, New York, 1968 **90** Print by William Birch; courtesy HSP **91** Map in John Florin, *Advance of Frontier Settlement in Pennsylvania*, unpublished master's thesis,

University Park, Pa., 1966 **92** Courtesy PHMC **93** Photo by Karl G. Rath; courtesy PHMC **94** Courtesy Historical Society of Berks County **95** Designed by Peirce F. Lewis, drafted by Robert J. Texter **96** Courtesy PHMC **97** Drawing by J.R. Chapin, engraving by T.B. Smith **98** Courtesy PHMC **99** *a* Model at Fort Pitt Museum; photo by Holiday Displays *b* Courtesy PHMC

How They Lived

100 Trussler; courtesy LCP **101** Courtesy HSP **102** *a* Photo by Terry Musgrave, from collection of PHMC *b* Photo by Fred Prouser, from a private collection **103** *a* Courtesy HSP *b–c* See 100. **104** Photo by Fred Prouser at Landis Valley, PHMC **105** Photo by Dick Brown **106** *a* Courtesy LCP *b* See 104. **107** From H. & B. Cirker and Dover editorial staff, *Dictionary of American Portraits*, New York, 1967 **108** *a* Courtesy PHMC *b* Photo by Fred Prouser, from collection of William Penn Memorial Museum, PHMC **109** *a* Photo by Irwin Richman *b* Photo by Kenneth A. Thigpen *c* Photo by Irwin Richman **110–111** Photos by Fred Prouser, from Landis Valley collection PHMC **112** Courtesy Pennsylvania Department of Highways **113** Trussler; courtesy LCP **114** Photo by Fred Prouser, from collection of Mr. & Mrs. Edward F. LaFond, Jr. **115** *a* From *Lewis Miller Sketches & Chronicles*, York, in cooperation with PHMC, 1966 *b* Photo by Fred Prouser at Landis Valley, PHMC *c* Trussler, courtesy LCP *d* Courtesy LCP *e* Courtesy PHMC **116** *a* Photo by Dick Brown *b* Photo by Fred Prouser, from Landis Valley collection, PHMC **117** Collection of William Penn Memorial Museum, PHMC **118–119** Photos by Fred Prouser, from Landis Valley collection PHMC **120** *a–b* Trussler, courtesy LCP **121** *a* Courtesy FLP *b* See 120. *c* Engraving by Diderot in the *Encyclopedia*, 1765 **122–123** 18th century newspaper ads, LCP **124** Courtesy Quaker Collection, Haverford College Library **125** From Clarence Hornung, ed., *Handbook of Early Advertising Art*, New York, 1956 **126** Drawing by William Kneass; courtesy HSP **127** Photo by Ira V. Brown, from collection of HSP **128** *a* From an engraving published by J. Dainty, 1813; courtesy LCP *b* Courtesy National Trust for Historic Preservation **129** Portrait by Raphaelle Peale, National Portrait Gallery, Smithsonian Institution; on loan from The Wilmington Society of the Fine Arts **130** *a* Trussler; courtesy LCP *b* Old woodcut **131** Prepared by Raymond Bureau; courtesy Hopewell Village National Historic Site **132–133** Engravings by Diderot in the *Encyclopedia*, 1765 **135** Courtesy LCP **136–137** 18th century print; courtesy APS **136** *b* Courtesy LCP **138–140** 18th century newspaper ads; courtesy LCP **142** *a* Photo courtesy York *b* Photo by Fred Prouser, from Landis Valley collection, PHMC **143** Photos by Fred Prouser at Landis Valley, PHMC **144** Photo by Dick Brown **145** Photo by Fred Prouser, from collection of Hans Herr House Association **146** *a* Courtesy PHMC *b* Photo by Fred Prouser, from Landis Valley collection, PHMC **147** *a* See 146*b*. *b* See 145. *c* From Franklin's *Account of the New-Invented Pennsylvania Fire-Places*, 1775; courtesy LCP *d* See 145. **148** *a* Photo by Fred Prouser, from collection of Mr. & Mrs. Edward F. LaFond, Jr. *b* Photo by Fred Prouser, from Landis Valley collection, PHMC **149** From *Lewis Miller Sketches & Chronicles*, York, in cooperation with PHMC, 1966 **150** *a* Trussler, courtesy LCP *b* 18th century newspaper ad, courtesy LCP *c* Photo by Fred Prouser at Ephrata Cloister, PHMC **151** *a* Courtesy PMA, given by Mrs. J. Bunford Samuel *b* Engraving by Diderot, in the *Encyclopedia*, 1765 **152** See 151*b*. **153** *a* Drawings by Andrea Olson in Anne H. Cooke & Jane T.

Breinholt, eds., *Project 1776: A Manual for the Bicentennial*, The Bicentennial Commission of Pennsylvania, in cooperation with Chester County Commissioners, Historical Society Bicentennial Committee, and Intermediate Unit No. 24 *b* See 151*b*. **154** 18th century prints, courtesy LCP **155** *a* Drawing from *The Juvenile Biographer*, courtesy FLP *b* See 149. **156** From William Colwell, *The Child's Picture Book*, courtesy Rosenbach Collection, FLP **157** *a* Courtesy The New-York Historical Society *b* From *Little Pretty Pocket-Book*, courtesy Rosenbach Collection, FLP **158** See 157*b*. **159** *a* Photo by Fred Prouser, from collection of Mr. & Mrs. Edward F. LaFond, Jr. *b* Photo courtesy PMA, from museum collection **160** *a* Old print, courtesy HSP *b* Courtesy William Penn Charter School **163** Courtesy HSP **164** Courtesy LCP **165** 18th century cartoon; courtesy LCP **166** Courtesy Insurance Company of North America **167** *Pennsylvania Magazine*, 1775; courtesy LCP **168** Photo by Fred Prouser, from Landis Valley collection, PHMC **169** *a* Courtesy Insurance Company of North America *b* Courtesy Rosenbach Collection, FLP **170** *a* Print by William Birch; courtesy HSP *b–c* Courtesy Trustees of the British Museum **171** *a* Courtesy Harvard University Library *b* See 168. **172** Tobacco ad, 1775; courtesy LCP **173** Courtesy LCP **174** *a* Courtesy Rosenbach Collection, FLP *b* 18th century newspaper ad; courtesy LCP **175** From *Lewis Miller Sketches & Chronicles*, York, in cooperation with PHMC, 1966 **176** Courtesy Harvard University Theater Collection **177** *a* See 176. *b* See 175. **178** Courtesy St. Louis Art Museum **179** *a* Old print, courtesy PHMC *b* Photo by Fred Prouser, from Landis Valley collection, PHMC *c* Courtesy York **180** *a* Courtesy Winterthur *b* See 176. **181–182** Courtesy LCP **183** From Dover editorial staff, *Catchpenny Prints*, New York, 1970 **184** National Gallery of Art, gift of Edgar William and Bernice Chrysler Garbisch **185** *a* Courtesy HSP *b* Courtesy LCP

Ideas and Beliefs

186 Courtesy the Pennsylvania Academy of Fine Arts **188** *a* Courtesy LCP *b–c* Courtesy PHMC **189** *a* From *Lewis Miller Sketches & Chronicles*, York, in cooperation with PHMC, 1966 *b* From *Materials towards a History of Baptists in Pennsylvania*, 1770; courtesy HSP **190** *a* Courtesy PHMC *b* Courtesy Moravian Museum of Bethlehem and PHMC **191** Courtesy PHMC **192** *a* Ephrata Cloister, PHMC *b* Photo by Fred Prouser at Ephrata Cloister, PHMC **193** *a* See 192*b*. *b* Courtesy FLP **194** *a* See 192*a*. *b–c* See 192*b*. **195** *a* Photo courtesy PHMC *b* Ephrata Cloister, PHMC **196** Courtesy FLP **198** From Theodore Bean, editor, *History of Montgomery County*, 1884 **199** Photo courtesy PMA **200** Courtesy Independence National Historical Park Collection **203** From *Lewis Miller Sketches & Chronicles*, York, in cooperation with PHMC, 1966 **204** *a* Courtesy FLP *b* From George Fisher, *The American Instructor* or *the Young Man's Best Companion*, Philadelphia, 1770; courtesy LCP **205** See 203. **206–207** Courtesy FLP **208** *a* Courtesy HSP *b* Courtesy Rosenbach Collection, FLP **209** Courtesy HSP **210** Courtesy APS **211** Courtesy LCP **212** Photo courtesy PMA, from collection of The Pennsylvania Hospital **213** Courtesy New York Public Library **214** *a* Courtesy APS *b* See 213. **215** *a* Courtesy APS *b* See 213. *c* Courtesy APS **216** Courtesy PMA, The Mr. & Mrs. Wharton Sinkler Collection **217** Courtesy APS **218** Title page of *William Bartram's Travels*, Philadelphia, 1791; collection of George H. Beatty **219** Frontispiece of William Darlington, *Memorial of John Bartram and Humphry Marshall*, 1849; collection of George H. Beatty **220** Courtesy APS

221 Engraved by J.B. Longacre from a painting by C.W. Peale; collection of George H. Beatty 222 *a* Courtesy University of Pennsylvania *b–c* Courtesy APS 223 Courtesy Drexel University 224 *a* From *Lewis Miller Sketches & Chronicles*, York, in cooperation with PHMC, 1966 *b* Courtesy Dr. Alexander Rush; photo by PMA 225 *a* Courtesy Winterthur: gift of Mrs. T. Charlton Henry *b* Medical Museum of Armed Forces, Institute of Pathology; photo by PMA 226 Photos by Fred Prouser, from collection of William Penn Memorial Museum, PHMC 227 *a* See 226. *b* From "Three Hundred Years of Pennsylvania Medicine" by Irwin Richman 228 See 226. 229 Drawing by William Strickland; courtesy HSP 230 *a* Courtesy University of Pennsylvania *b* Portrait by Jacob Duche; courtesy HSP *c* See 229. 231 Courtesy The Pennsylvania Hospital 232 See 224*a*. 233 Old newspaper ad 234 Courtesy PHMC 235 Courtesy LCP 236 *a* After a painting by Benjamin West; collection of George H. Beatty *b* Courtesy APS 237 *a* Courtesy APS *b–c* Courtesy HSP 238 *a* Trussler; courtesy LCP *b* Courtesy Winterthur 239 *a* Engraving by Diderot in the *Encyclopedia*, 1765 *b* Photo by Dick Brown 240 Photo by PHMC from its collection

The Arts

242 Photo by Fred Prouser at Landis Valley, PHMC 243 *a* See 239*a*. *b–c* See 242. 244 See 242. 245–246–248 Photo by PHMC at William Penn Memorial Museum 249 Courtesy Abby Aldrich Rockefeller Folk Art Collection; photo by Colonial Williamsburg Foundation 250 Courtesy LCP 251 *a* Courtesy LCP *b* Courtesy Lancaster County Historical Society 252 *a* See 249. *b* Courtesy William Penn Memorial Museum, PHMC 253 See 224. 254 Detail from "The Invasion," engraved by William Hogarth, 1756 255 Courtesy Samuel P. Bayard, drawn by Arabelle Carlson 256 See 224. 257 Photo by John Snyder 258 See 239*a*. 259 Print from Milan, 1776; courtesy LCP 260 Courtesy HSP 261 From Hopkinson's *Seven Songs for the Harpsichord*, Philadelphia, 1788 262 From *The Art of Dancing*, 1735; courtesy LCP 264–265 See 239*a*. 266 From *Book of Trades*, 1806; courtesy LCP 267 Courtesy HSP 268 See 239*a*. 269 Courtesy LCP 270 Title page from Cicero's *Cato Major*, Philadelphia, 1744 271 Courtesy LCP 272 Ephrata Cloister, PHMC; photo by Fred Prouser 275 Engraving by James Smither; courtesy LCP 276 From H. & B. Cirker and Dover editorial staff, *Dictionary of American Portraits*, New York, 1967 277 Courtesy LCP 280 From the original 284 Collection of George H. Beatty 285 Courtesy HSP 286 Courtesy Archives of the Moravian Church, Bethlehem, Pa. 288 Courtesy The Pennsylvania Academy of the Fine Arts 291 Courtesy The Metropolitan Museum of Art: gift of Samuel P. Avery, 1897 292 After a painting by Rembrandt Peale; courtesy George H. Beatty 293 Photo by Fred Prouser at Ephrata Cloister, PHMC 294 *a* Photo by Fred Prouser at Landis Valley, PHMC *b* Photo by Fred Prouser at William Penn

Memorial Museum, PHMC 295 Courtesy LCP 296 From Irwin Richman, *Pennsylvania's Architecture*, Pennsylvania Historical Association, 1967 297 *a* Photo by Fred Prouser; courtesy Hans Herr House Association *b* See 293. 298 Courtesy PHMC 299 Print by William Birch; courtesy HSP 300 Courtesy PHMC 301 From J. Gibbs, *A Book of Architecture*, 1728 302 See 299. 303 Courtesy LCP 305 *a* Courtesy Museum of Art, The Pennsylvania State University: gift of Mr. and Mrs. Roger Downing *b* On loan to William Penn Memorial Museum; photo by Karl G. Rath for PHMC *c* Courtesy LCP 306 *a* Courtesy Winterthur *b* Courtesy LCP 307 Courtesy Winterthur 308 *a* Photo by Karl G. Rath for PHMC *b* Courtesy Moravian Museum of Bethlehem; photo by Karl G. Rath for PHMC 309 Photos by PHMC, from collection of William Penn Memorial Museum 310–311 Courtesy Winterthur

Politics and War

313 Courtesy LCP 315 Courtesy LCP 316–317 Courtesy Emmet Collection, New York Public Library 318–320 Courtesy LCP 321 *a* Photo by Terry Musgrave from collection of PHMC *b* Courtesy Stauffer Collection, HSP 322 Courtesy HSP 324 Collection of George H. Beatty 325 Courtesy Pattee Library, The Pennsylvania State University: gift of George H. Beatty 326 *a* Courtesy PHMC *b* Courtesy LCP 327 *a* Photo by Karl G. Rath for PHMC *b* Courtesy York 328 See 321*a*. 329 *a* Courtesy Division of Textiles, Smithsonian Institution *b* After painting by C.W. Peale; courtesy HSP 330 Courtesy LCP 331 Courtesy Boston Museum of Fine Arts 332 Courtesy HSP 334 Photo by Terry Musgrave, from collection of PHMC 335 Courtesy Anne S.K. Brown Military Collection, Brown University Library 336 Courtesy Valley Forge Historical Society 338–340 Courtesy Independence National Historical Park Collection 341 See 336. 342 Courtesy Chicago Historical Society; from photo taken in 1952 by J. Sherwin Murphy 344 Courtesy The Radio Times Hulton Picture Library 346–347 *a* Courtesy HSP 347 *b* Courtesy Winterthur 348 *a* Photo courtesy PHMC *b* Courtesy Yale University Art Gallery 349 Frontispiece from John Miller book, Philadelphia, 1779; courtesy LCP 350 *a* Courtesy York *b–c* From *Lewis Miller Sketches & Chronicles*, York, in cooperation with PHMC, 1966 351 Courtesy York 352 From a recruiting poster; courtesy HSP 354 *a* Photo by A.J. Wyatt; courtesy PMA *b* Courtesy LCP *c* Courtesy HSP 355 Courtesy Yale University Art Gallery 357 By C.W. Peale; courtesy Stauffer Collection, HSP

Epilogue

358 Courtesy Winterthur: gift of Mrs. T. Charlton Henry

Index

A Note on the Type

The text and display type used in this book is monotype Caslon Old Style, No. 337E. Based on the great English eighteenth-century face designed by William Caslon, this version is the best modern rendering of this classic type design. Caslon's first specimen sheet was issued in 1734 and his designs, derived from Dutch models, brought English typography to the forefront of European developments. Among the first to appreciate the quality of Caslon's work was the American printer Benjamin Franklin, who had worked as a journeyman compositor for Caslon's sponsors in London and later imported Caslon types for his print shop in Philadelphia. Franklin championed the use of Caslon types in America and caused the authenticated copies of the Declaration of Independence to be printed in this face.

Composition by Bi-Comp, Inc. Printing and binding by Kingsport Press, Inc. Printed on Warren's Patina.